OVER AND OVER

THE STORY OF SEVILLE

edited by
Anna Smith and
Simon Houston

OVER AND OVER

THE STORY OF SEVILLE

Published by the Daily Record, One Central Quay,
Glasgow, G3 8DA.
Copyright: The Daily Record.

Pictures taken by Gordon Jack, Tony Nicoletti
and Mark Runnacles.

ISBN 0-9544202-2-5

Printed and bound in Scotland   -

Contents

Foreword

by Jim Kerr

I DIDN'T think it was possible, but I believe I came back from Seville with a new level of love and pride in Glasgow Celtic.

The team, of course, performed heroically in a thrilling final which could befit any tournament, but for me, it was as much to do with the remarkable number of fans who had amassed there as anything else.

Sure it was a great performance on the park, but being able to feel part of that tribe that had amassed in record numbers made the whole adventure so special.

It was a pleasure to be part of it.

Looking back, there was so much poetry involved in the whole Seville experience.

It was more than football. In my case, to be there with my dad, who took me to my first game, and my pals, watching a great Celtic team in the final of a great competition was truly wonderful.

To be in Seville with people who meant so much to me and realising what it meant to all of them, individually, made it just right.

We didn't see a great Celtic team in the same way the Lisbon Lions were, but great in the sense that it never knows when it's beaten.

It would have been a travesty if that tremendous, colourful and vocal support left the stadium that night without showing the world how to celebrate a goal, and thanks to Henrik, we had two chances.

In retrospect, we were very lucky the final was in Seville. Without trying to be disrespectful to other cities perhaps in northern Europe, it wouldn't have been the same in, say, Frankfurt or Brussels.

In Seville we were blessed with a beautiful city, beautiful weather and there was magic in the air.

I think it was Brian Dempsey who once said that while Man Utd might be massive, they are a mere football club, while Glasgow Celtic is a cultural phenomenon. He summed it up perfectly.

Myself and Charlie Burchill missed Lisbon but as young boys we stood at Hampden for the Leeds semi-final in 1970 and ever since have wondered whether we would witness anything like that again and feel the same way about a match.

We got our answer on May 21, 2003.

"FAITHFUL THROUGH AND THROUGH"

by Simon Houston & Anna Smith

THEIR hearts were breaking but oh how they sang.

The stadium clock said the journey was nearly at an end. Any moment now Referee Lubos Michel would blow the final whistle on a wonderful dream.

Twenty seconds, left, perhaps ten. Who had the ball? No one cared. Was there time for one last gutsy push to squeeze just a little more life out of the remarkable adventure? It didn't matter.

On the field before them, the men in green and white had given every last drop for Glasgow Celtic and now it was their turn to pick up the baton and carry them over the finishing line.

It was their chance to thank them for the time of their lives.

Thank them for their style in Suduva, their brilliance in Blackburn, their vigour in Vigo, their strength in Stuttgart, their aggression at Anfield and their belief in Boavista.

At that very second they all knew what song to sing. No prompting required. The song that above all typifies the spirit of the Parkhead masses, arguably the most unique travelling football support in the world.

With tears of pride streaming down sunburned faces and with breaking voices they sang: 'Over and over, we will follow you. Over and over, we will see you through. We are Celtic supporters, faithful through and through. And over and over, we will follow you.'

How can you explain what happened inside the magnificent Estadio Olimpico in Seville shortly before 11.30 p.m. on the night of May 21, 2003?

It was as though Big Jock himself had come down from the Heavens and slipped unnoticed into the hearts of every Celtic supporter, to conduct the choir one last time.

It was a moment which summed up the entire Seville phenomenon, when the largest single movement of sports fans in history descended on the Andalucian capital in their thousands to watch the Bhoys compete in their first European final for 33 years.

From the moment the final whistle blew in Oporto that balmy night in April when Henrik Larsson's goal secured the semi-final victory against Boavista, the only thing that mattered was to get to Spain.

So tickets were like gold dust, hotel rooms were disappearing by the second and the price of flights seemed to increase with every frantic inquiry. None of it mattered.

Celtic were back on the world stage and, by God, they'd be right there with them.

It was a stirring end to the longest day for Celtic fans who dared to dream of European glory.

But even though they were going home empty handed, for the rest of their lives they can say they were there on a night that will go down in the history of football.

And as they filed out of the stadium into the humid night air, it was with heads held high.

For Celtic fans who had travelled to Seville truly had their day in the sun.

All day long they had baked in temperatures of over 110 degrees, a sea of sun scorched shoulders and beer bellies striding through the historic town.

No one in the city knew what to make of these cheerful, colourful souls from the cold north.

They too love their football with a passion. But not like this.

To stand shoulder to shoulder with the Celtic fans inside the Olympic stadium was to witness a story that told more, much more than just a game of football.

Amid the blaze of giant green and white flags from across the world, they had come from Ballymahon, from Switzerland, Stornoway, Texas, Drumchapel, Blantyre and, of course, Heraghty's Bar, in Glasgow.

For it is not just football, but history that unites the very heart and soul of these people.

And the scattered masses of Scots and Irish from New York to Singapore become one big family, bound together wherever people gather in the name of Celtic.

That is why these legions of fans made Seville their mecca.

This was their pilgrimage, with or without tickets. This was their moment - the biggest movement in history of sport, of football fans ever to travel to a foreign land.

By plane, train, car and hitching, they came to be in a Celtc wonderland with kindred spirits who for a lifetime had longed for this day.

From midday the fans had trekked to the stadium in droves as though to make sure it wasn't all a dream.

Then, by early evening, a green and white snake of tens of thousands made their way across the city.

For hours before the match they were seated, and as thousands more arrived, the sound of 'It's a Grand Old Team to Play For' drifted into the evening sky.

As the clock ticked towards kick-off they waited for the men who have become giants in Scottish football history.

Any minute now they would come out of that tunnel on to the field of dreams, the heroes that could make it happen.

Then to a deafening roar, on they came. And all around the stadium, the cameras flashed for the famous Celtic huddle on the pitch. If they had to, these fans - as the song goes - would walk a million miles for one of their goals.

Exhausted and drenched in sweat from the searing heat, they suddenly found the energy from somewhere to carry on singing like they had never done before.

But on the stroke of 45 minutes - the worst possible time to lose a goal - 30,000 Celtic hearts stopped as Porto scored. There was a kind of disbelief in the towering green and white slopes which seemed to reach to the dark night sky.

Surely that couldn't be it? After all the fighting and scratching of the previous rounds, surely they weren't going to let it all slip away without one final battle.

Of course they weren't. Not this gallant team.

And two minutes into the second half the dream was on again, when Henrik rose at the back post to score the kind of goal that would be beyond mere mortals.

The eruption of noise and colour could have been heard back in Glasgow as fans in the stadium, and all round the city of Seville, went truly ballistic.

Not only had we reached a European final, we had scored in one!

For the next few minutes we were on a heart-stopping rollercoaster as first, Porto took the lead again, and then Henrik responded straight away, sending us once again into raptures.

The 90 minutes came and went and as extra-time commenced there was wide-spread optimism that, yes, we could do it. We were on top and the body language among the Porto players almost seemed to admit defeat. However the dismissal of Bobo Balde five minutes into the first period changed all that and suddenly Celtic were on the back foot.

By the end of the first period there was a sense of foreboding around the stadium.

And, alas, six minutes from the end as the players battled on even though they looked out on their feet, the dream died when the Portuguese netted the winner.

But the singing went on.

And when the referee blew the final whistle, a moment that every Celtic fan will take to their grave.

With scarves outstretched they began the anthem, 'Over and Over'. It was a tear jerking, haunting image of so many people torn with grief yet still singing as they cheered their heroes when they walked with drooping shoulders to collect their losers medals.

To the hordes of Celtic fans who will tell of this night when they are old and grey, every single man was a winner.

And the biggest cheer of all was for Martin O'Neill as he bowed his head to allow the UEFA official to put his medal on. He turned and applauded the fans then stood alone on the pitch, a boyhood dream in tatters, as his broken hearted players sat devastated waiting for the Porto team to collect the cup. They had been so near and yet so far.

But still the fans sang on. And so moved were the Porto team that they stood and applauded the Hoops, for this was a sight they had surely never witnessed.

Some fans were inconsolable. Big, burly men hugging each other and sobbing. Don't tell them this is just a game.

But when they dried their eyes, they took a deep breath and headed for the city they had made their own and for a celebration that will live in their hearts forever.

To see Celtic huddles all over Seville singing and dancing at daybreak it was hard to believe they didn't actually win the cup.

Perhaps they left with no silverware. But in Seville, every Celt was a winner as the whole of Europe watched a sleeping giant come back to life in the most magnificent fashion.

Chapter One

THE BUILD UP, TICKET TOUTS, THE TEARS

by Anna Smith

EVERY so often in life, it can take just one word to conjure up a million memories.

For Celtic fans the world over, it is SEVILLE.

The very mention of it can bring tears to the eyes of the tens of thousands who came, who saw, and who won the hearts of the people in this ancient Spanish city.

If truth be told, the bulk of the Celtic fans who travelled to the breathtakingly beautiful city in the heart of Andalucia knew little or nothing about Seville. Like me, they would be more acquainted with Spanish hotspots of the Costa sort where sun, sea and sangria are the main attractions.

So, nearly a month before the Cup Final, when the editor sent me on a fact finding mission to one of the most stunning cities in the world, I was careful not do my celebratory back flip until I was in the privacy of my living room.

Twenty-four hours later, began one of the most spectacular journeys I have ever had the privilege to be on.

More than three weeks in the sun, and every day that passed was a heartbeat away from the ultimate fiesta on May 21.

So seductive is the city it would have been easy to be swept away in a tide of vino rosso and euphoria. But there was work to be done. There was flesh to be pressed at the town hall, in the hope Seville's Mayor would be talked into wearing a Celtic kilt. There were police chiefs to meet and apartments to be found for the team of Record hacks and promo people who would eventually get here.

With barely a word of Spanish, I was at a loss in a city where few people speak English. So help was brought up from Malaga in the shape of freelance journalist Franco Rey, the fixer and translator who opened all the doors, and, as it turned out, was the procurer of many gold dust tickets for me from touts in the run up to the match.

From early on what was most surprising was that if you mentioned the UEFA Cup Final or Celtic to the average Sevillan, they shrugged their shoulders. There was no Spanish team in it so no big deal.

Even in the town hall, they laughed when we told them they were about to be invaded by upwards of 60,000 fans. No way, they said.

The police chief had done his homework and liased with the Scottish police. There would be only 30,000 at the very most.

How wrong they were.

Within days, Celtic shirts began to turn up outside Flaherty's Irish bar next to the Cathedral. Each had their story to tell.

Red haired Gerry Rooney, 39, from Denny, his face jumping with angry mosquito bites, had got up one Saturday morning and announced he was off to Seville to hunt for tickets.

He trekked the streets, carrying his rucksack, like a green and white tortoise, his peely wally Scottish legs scorched from the sun. He was on a crusade.

Nothing would stop him. He even got his hair dyed green and white by the Barber of Seville who had already set up in business.

He told me: "I don't care what it takes or how much it costs, I'm not going home without a ticket."

By the time he left us, eight hours later, we hugged like old amigos and I felt sorry for him as he headed for the bus station to take the 10 hour journey to the Portuguese town of Oporto to continue his quest.

Never underestimate the gritty determination of a Scot with a mission. I was delighted the next night when my mobile rang and an ecstatic Gerry announced, just before his last few cents ran out: "I've got a ticket. I've got one." The fact that it cost him 700 Euros didn't even enter his head. He was going to be there.

More fans followed. They came pushing babies in buggies, and with understanding wives on tow, having broken into their holiday on the Costa Del Sol to come to Seville in search of tickets. Most left empty handed, but determined to return with or without one.

As the big day drew closer, the ticket touts began to slip into town. Loud mouth London East End barrow boys wearing Celtic shirts for effect, talking into mobile phones in pavement cafes. Buying. Selling. Promising.

And every hour for the rest of my trip, my own mobile rang with pleas from friends and colleagues assuming that since I was in Seville there would be people stuffing tickets into my pockets.

"Can you get me a ticket? Can you get me four? I'd rather die than not be at the game." These were grown men, rational men, close to tears, so desperate were they that they might miss the historic night.

Ticket touting was not on my agenda, but I knew how much it meant to them. Franco got to work, schmoozing with the Spanish touts who stood outside the stadium buying tickets for ten times the price from locals minutes after they picked up their allocations.

Suddenly we were in business. One minute I was filing a story from an interview with the police boss, the next I was on a street corner dealing with touts.

I'm not being flash, but at 600 Euros a brief, my offshore account was taking a battering. I did not have time for this, but what could I do? Tickets were bought and stored away at my apartment waiting for the friends to arrive in Seville with the cash.

As the days drifted into nights, I often wondered how I have got through life in Glasgow without a siesta in the afternoon. (Some people at the Record would say I haven't.) What a civilised way to live. Nothing moves in Seville between the pulsating heat of three in the afternoon until six. So when people come out at night, they are bright eyed and ready to party until the bells in the Giralda peal in the dawn. More modest bon viveurs like myself, when I wasn't having to entertain, simply enjoyed quiet meals along the riverside with my companions Franco and Malaga based photographer John Snowdon.

Every day another plane load of Celts headed for the city.

Just as the atmosphere built up, so did the stupefying heat. In temperatures of over 100 degrees, unfazed Celtic fans, their faces crimson with the sun, claimed the steps of the Cathedral across from

Flaherty's bar and sang day and night.

They drank the pub dry on at least two occasions. They mobbed the Porto fans who stumbled onto their territory, and smothered them with hugs and kisses. When they drank too much they lay down and slept where they were, and people simply stepped over them as though it was one big house party that just went on and on.

In every drink laden table, on every corner, someone had a tale to tell. One guy who was wearing the Celtic scarf his dad wore to Lisbon, hitchhiked from Glasgow to be there.

Another man originally from Bo'ness had come from New York with his 18-year-old son as part of his education, to show him how much it meant to be a Celt.

Two old men in their 70s travelled from Canada to live the dream. They sat misty-eyed in the sunshine outside Flaherty's recalling how it was when they were just boys in Glasgow and Parkhead was their paradise. And as ever the Celts displayed their own off-the-wall humour. Catholic priest Father Steve Gilhooley from Our Lady's RC Church in Currie, Edinburgh in Celtic jersey emblazoned with Father Ted on the back, and wearing green and white Doc Marten boots, singing in the sunshine.

He told me: "I don't get to many games because of the vigil mass and matches on Sunday. But I would never have missed this for the world. I even got Archbishop Keith O'Brien to stand in for me at my parish."

A guy in a wheelchair being pushed through the crowds, singing at the top of his voice. Later, much later in the night, we would see him minus his mates, totally alone and fast asleep in his wheelchair, oblivous as the town council's refuse men hosed down the deserted streets around him.

Standing watching the masses with one united hope brought a lump to my throat. All those years since Lisbon. All those dreams dashed in the barren years at Celtic park. Now their time had come and they were knocking on Heaven's door. These were proud days they would tell of for generations to come. And they could be proud of themselves too, for there were none of the sick sideshows that have become part of other soccer fans' European tours. Yes, there was craziness. Yes there was off your head drunkenness. But it was all good humoured as the Celtic fans policed themselves.

It's just as well they did. For the backdrop for the Celtic fans' party was a splendidly cultured city full of decent people who welcomed them with open arms.

For me, long before the fans arrived, there were sights that will always live in the memory.

Like the way the sky turns the most amazing torquoise colour just before dark. Sitting at the fountain dwarfed by the awesome Giralda tower where the swallows soared as a lone violionist busker played Ave Maria sent shivers down my spine.

The almost nightly ritual of schoolchildren carrying a religious statue through the narrow, cobblestone streets, accompanied by a brass band was a picture of a byegone era, a fantastic sense of community in the midst of a big city.

And all night long, the sound of church bells across the city counting down the hours until match day.

I even went to the bullfight, at the insistence of Franco for my education, and was mesmerised by the ritual that is as compelling as it is brutal and cruel. I was beginning to feel like Ernest Hemmingway, if only I could write.

It was into this movie, for that's what it was beginning to feel like, that my two nephews, 19-year-old Matthew Costello and his brother Christopher, 14, arrived with their two mates Sean Stevenson and Henry Harper, both 19.

By the time they unfolded themselves from the tiny car that brought them and two others from Malaga, they had been on the road for 15 hours. But they were so dazzled by the tide of singing Celtic fans now descending on Seville that they never got any further than Flaherty's for the next four hours.

I allowed them to stay in my apartment for the first night. But wakening up in the morning to the debris and smells four teenage boys can leave in one small room compelled me to immediately find them an alternative gaff.

As far as they were concerned Seville was paradise found. The beautiful Spanish senoritas smiled as the wide eyed boys, clutching their hoops tops, tried out their Scottish charm with a hint of schoolboy Spanish.

'Verdiblanco Amigos.' Loosely translated it means green and white friends. They seemed to be welcomed with open arms. I didn't pursue the details.

The beer was flowing. There was no such a thing as tomorrow. Mañana doesn't matter when you're in heaven.

And still my mobile rang. 'Can you get me just one ticket?' Another deal was done, and by now I was on first name terms with the swarthy touts.

Cup Final day dawned with the energy sapping temperature racing towards 100 degrees. A five minute walk through town left you drenched in sweat.

By midday you could hardly move in the city. Every side street, every square, every cafe was bursting at the seams.

And yet in the middle of this mayhem I kept bumping into people I hadn't seen for years, and some, like Eleanor Grant and Joe Travers, I had seen just last week. Nonetheless we all threw our arms around each other like long lost friends. Emotions were spilling over and not a ball had been kicked.

Then in the late afternoon came the call to Franco's mobile. The ticket touts had done so much business with him they were giving him a free ticket to the match. He already had a press pass, and this was a chance for him to make a fast buck. But in a gesture of overwhelming generosity he immediately gifted it to my nephew Matthew. If only I could find him. I managed to get him on his mobile.

"I don't care where you are, I'll find you. Just tell me the name of the square. I'm on my way. Don't go without me." He sounded as though his entire life would have been in vain, if he had missed this chance.

For the rest of my life I will remember the moment where amid a thousand green and white shirts, the desperate face of Matthew emerged, racing through the crowds. No movie director could have scripted it. He had been running for 15 minutes in the sweltering heat and by the time he saw me, waving frantically, there was no skin left on the soles of his feet and he was at the point of collapse.

I was praying the ticket touts would come through when we arrived at the stadium.

For nearly two hours before kick-off we waited outside in the heat as fans arrived singing and waving flags.

Then one fan in tears with his head in his hands, came and planked himself down beside us. He was clutching what looked like a soggy, half-chewed Cup Final ticket and staring at it in disbelief.

And no wonder. For his story was unbelievable. To keep his ticket safe, he had shoved it down his sock - then proceeded to walk around all day in the blistering, sweaty heat. He had another 10 mates nearby who had done the same, and they all wore the look of condemned men.

"They won't let me in," he groaned. "But nobody can possibly be in my seat. This is my ticket. I brought it from Scotland with me. I never miss a match."

Franco took him back to the turnstile. I don't know what was said, but he got inside the stadium, and hopefully his seat.

Another group of lads had come up from Malaga and had been enjoying large amounts of beer, when one of their party disappeared. He was nowhere to be found and they were panicking because he was about to miss the game. They had to go inside without him. And when they did, they found him under their seats, sound asleep. He may have been drunk, but there was nothing wrong with his homing device.

The clock was ticking, but the touts hadn't arrived with the ticket for Matthew. He was trying to be brave. Franco was edgy, smoking furiously. I was praying. Then Franco's phone rang, and I swear there were angels singing overhead. We met the touts and they handed over the ticket. The joy in Matthew's eyes. Faces were kissed and the bemused touts smiled to themselves as they walked away. They had made their fortune over the last two weeks, and they could have made more by selling that ticket. But they didn't. And one ecstatic 19-year-old young man will be telling that story to his grandchildren.

Like everyone else who was there, I could talk all day about the game. The blood vessel bursting highs, the plumetting lows that brought tears streaming down my face as the dream faded into the balmy Seville night. When the final whistle blew, all three of us left the stadium with tears in our eyes.

But by the time we reached a nearby hotel to drown our sorrows, the fans were already dancing in the foyer as though they had won. And so it went on, right into the night.

In three weeks I had witnessed history unfolding to the echo of thousands of joyous voices and I had shed a few tears with the best football fans in the world.

Like so many others, I will keep Seville tucked inside my heart. A cherished memory to be relished, but not to be recalled too much - just in case the image disappears.

Chapter Two

FROM IRAQ TO SEVILLE - AND BETWEEN

by Simon Houston

ONE BY ONE they crept through the gauntlet, ashen faced. Hardened football stars that thought they had seen it all before were suddenly coming to terms with the magnitude of what lay ahead.

The opulent surroundings of the Barcelo Gran Hotel had never witnessed anything like it either, as the Porto players streamed hurriedly across the foyer to board their team bus three hours before kick-off to make the short mile-long journey to the stadium.

I was among the throng who had managed to breach security and chance our way into the building late on that blisteringly hot afternoon. Word had spread quickly that this was not only the base for the Porto squad, but it was also where Rod Stewart, Billy Connolly, Roy Keane and goodness know how many other members of Celtic's exclusive celebrity fan club could be found.

Led by captain Jorge Costa, the sharply-dressed superstars resplendent in their grey, made-to-measure, Italian suits, hoped they could shuffle past anonymously without attracting the attention of the merry band of sunburned revellers in the hotel bar. It was a forlorn hope.

Within seconds a crowd of up to 200 had lined their exit from the hotel intent on giving the Portuguese a little pre-taster of what was awaiting them when they eventually took the field that night. It was an ear bashing they won't forget in a hurry.

Hotel security staff simply shrugged their shoulders in defeat as fans, most in hoops and white shorts, pressed right up to within touching distance of the bewildered players. It was surprising the stench of the chanting, beery breaths didn't knock them off their feet.

First they were treated to a rousing chorus of 'It's a Grand Old Team to Play For', before the pièce de résistance: 'Bobo's Gonnae Get You!'

The look of fear in goalkeeper Vitor Baia's eyes will stay with me for as long as I live. The colour seemed to drain from his face as he nervously glanced from side to side at the finger-pointing, arm-waving maniacs, in a vein attempt to work out what in the hell was going on.

'Who is this Bobo?' he must have been wondering, as he scurried out the main door and past yet another screaming unit of the green and white brigade and on to the coach.

Later that evening, as the keeper performed some outrageous theatrics to deceive the referee and waste crucial time towards the end of the final, I shuddered to think what would happen to him if he had to walk the same gauntlet on the way back into the hotel – or if Bobo kept our promise.

Every second Celtic fan in Seville had arrived there without a match ticket.

Some were content to watch the game on the big screens or in one the many bars around town, while others refused to rest until they had blown hundreds of Euros on a single, treasured brief. Porto weren't the only winners. The touts who travelled from all corners of Europe to prey on desperate Hoops fans didn't do too badly themselves.

But of those who did manage to land a ticket on the day of the match, few can have enjoyed the same stroke of luck as Davie Jenkinson, from Dumbarton.

Big Davie, a 6'5" gentle giant was in the right place at the right time when a smartly dressed man wandered into the bar of the Barcelo Gran early in the afternoon clutching a spare.

However this wasn't just any ticket and the man, a journalist called Franco, explained that the person using it would have to be responsible, well behaved and certainly not the worse for wear with the drink.

Davie, a 38-year-old psychiatric nurse, fitted the bill – well almost. He had resigned himself to watching the game on the telly and had spent most of the day drowning his sorrows at the prospect of missing the match of a lifetime.

Fortunately, some of his more sober mates were around to do the negotiating with Franco. They assured him that their big pal wasn't there at the moment but not only was he the perfect gentleman he was also teetotal!

They neglected to tell him that Davie's nickname is 'Big Dangerous'.

Anyway, they must have been convincing because Franco parted with the ticket and told the lads to give it to their friend on his return, adding that Davie did indeed sound like the refined and cultivated thoroughbred he was looking for.

Then came the sucker punch.

Franco explained: 'You see this is a VIP ticket and your friend will be the guest of the President of the Estadio Olimpico. The invitation was given to a contact of mine but none of his friends are able to use it because most of them will be working at the game.

'Tell him to be on his best behaviour. He will be permitted to applaud if Celtic score, but nothing too crazy.'

Once they had stopped laughing, the boys of the Smiddy Bar in Partick launched Operation Sober Up Big Dave.

After a few glasses of mineral water – some down the throat and some over the face – the big man was back to his best.

He recalled: 'When I got to the stadium I showed my ticket to a policeman and asked for directions. He was very impressed and looked at me as though I was the King of Spain himself!

'I didn't even have to go through a turnstile and instead was shown through this very posh entrance where there was a lovely Spanish lady waiting for me. I don't know what she was expecting, but I'm sure it wasn't a bloke my size wearing a Celtic top and a pair of shorts.'

After explaining that the other guests had already arrived, she escorted Davie through a network of exquisite corridors to his glass-fronted executive box, where a handful of smartly dressed Spanish businessmen were seated.

He was handed a glass of Champagne and introduced to the somewhat bewildered looking gathering.

Davie added: 'I'm not sure what they made of me at first but I got some strange looks, I can tell you.

'When the game kicked off most of them spent more time looking at me than the action on the park.

'But after about 20 minutes or so they began to realise just how important this match was to me and they all began to cheer for Celtic.

'They even began bringing me drink after drink, and told me to sit where I was because they didn't want me to have to take my eye off the match for a split second! They were lovely and when Henrik hit the net we were all dancing and cheering together.

'The outcome was obviously a big disappointment but I'll never forget the night I was made to feel like royalty at a European final.

'And there are also a dozen or so new Celtic supporters in Seville!"

There were of course others who took a less conventional route into the stadium that night.

You may have heard about the mysterious pair who sneaked into the ground the previous night, duping security guards with some cock and bull story about being Scottish reporters keen to have a look around.

Unbeknown to the hapless Spaniards, they had grappling hooks secreted on their person and were able to climb into the ventilation system above one of the toilets.

John Houston and pal Michael McGurk, both from Glasgow, were among a group of disbelieving supporters who witnessed their dramatic reappearance shortly before kick off.

John said: "We were all standing in this packed toilet when all of a sudden there was a strange sound coming from above our heads.

'Then they proceeded to rip the vent cover away and drop down to the floor with their grappling hooks before pulling a couple of Celtic shirts out of a bag, slipping them on and disappearing into the stadium.

'They told us they had been up there since the night before.

'You have to give them ten out of ten for initiative – especially as they got in for free when so many other people were forking out hundreds for one ticket.

'There'll probably be a song written about these guys one day!'

On the subject of songs, the Celtic fans could give Tim Rice a run for his money with their ability to churn out hilarious lyrics with consummate ease.

Just ask BSkyB presenter and resident Rangers fan, Jim White, who picked the wrong day to fly from Glasgow to London to catch an onward flight to Senegal to film a feature with Arsenal star Patrick Viera.

It was the day before the final and delays were playing havoc with just about every plane heading out of Glasgow. Jim therefore had time on his hands and decided to take it on the chin, by strolling proudly into the bar to enjoy a drink with the Seville-bound Hoops fans.

At first he was met with roars of disapproval, given that his loyalty to the light blue side of Glasgow is legendary, but it didn't take him long to win over the doubters – by sticking a green curly wig on his head and throwing a Celtic scarf round his neck.

In unison about 300 cheering souls began to chant: 'He used to be a Hun, but he's all right now, Jimmy, Jimmy!' before mobbing the startled presenter.

Gerry Wright, from Glasgow, was among the first to shake his hand.

Gerry said: 'It was great moment, and you have to hand it to Jim for being such a sport.

'He could easily have turned the other way and sat in relative peace in a quiet corner of the airport but he decided to brave it out and good luck to him.

'He sat and chatted to the fans for ages and bought some drinks and then wished us all the very best for Seville.'

Everyone lucky enough to have made it to Spain, kept room for a bagful of memories in their luggage.

Roy Keane playing football with all six of Paul McStay's children on the grass outside their hotel. What a sport.

My brother-in-law Liam swapping his new Celtic strip for a girl's Real Betis top in a bar before the match – and being abused all the way to the stadium by angry Seville supporters outraged that he had the audacity to sport the outfit of their sworn enemy.

Great times, fanatstic memories.

NONE of the 37,000 present the night we beat Lithuanian minnows Suduva 8-1 at Celtic Park could have predicted what was in store for Celtic over the next eight months.

For me, it was an unforgettable journey, which took me to Blackburn, Stuttgart, Boavista and ultimately Seville.

Work commitments prevented me from being in Vigo, having already been assigned to report from Geneva on the outcome of the ill-fated Scotland-Ireland bid to host the 2008 European Championships.

Being something of an explorer, however, I managed to stumble across an Irish bar that was showing the game on Setanta Sports.

The entire hierarchy of the Football Association of Ireland had the same idea, so it's safe to say the black stuff was flowing in copious amounts – especially when Big Bad John hit the rigging for the crucial away goal that sent us through.

A memorable evening ended with FAI president Milo Corcoran, leading the assembled gathering in a rousing chorus of The Fields of Athenry.

Blackburn was a trip of mixed emotions. Delight at the outcome, and heartbreak at being one of the many unfortunates locked out of the

Darwin End, despite being in possession of a genuine ticket.

So when Stuttgart came round, I promised myself I would be in the stadium in plenty of time.

Mind you, when I learned that I'd spend the morning of the match in a lecture theatre in Chelsea Barracks in London, preparing to be sent to the Gulf as a war correspondent, I feared that once again the fates would conspire against me.

Thankfully the British Airways service from Heathrow to Stuttgart was running on time and I managed to catch the 2 p.m. flight in the nick of time. A special thanks at this stage should go to the Hoops fan that sat next to me on the plane and was kind enough to share some of his very suspicious lemonade.

Then, having made use of the lightning quick rail link into the centre of the city, I arrived at my hotel at the same time as my mates who had set off by car from London at the crack of dawn.

Apart from the electrifying start by the Celts which put the tie beyond doubt before the Germans had pulled their boots on, my outstanding memory from that round is the fantastic way in which the local supporters accepted defeat so gracefully and partied with us until the wee small hours.

Oh, and who could forget Bonnie Tyler on the pitch before kick-off? Wondered where the old girl had got to.

Nursing sore heads but happy hearts, five of us squeezed into a car for the long ten-hour drive home the next morning.

The chat, which was largely designed to keep my friend Hector awake at the wheel centred, not surprisingly, around plans for Anfield. A trip I knew I wouldn't be making, having been told I'd be heading to the Gulf two days later for an indefinite period.

Thanks to my little short-wave radio, I was able to listen to the first leg on the World Service. There I was, cowering under a tent during a sand storm in the northern Kuwaiti desert, straining to make sense of the crackled commentary.

But what came through loud and clear was the wonder in the bloke's voice at having just experienced what he described as the most remarkable and emotional rendition of Walk On he had ever had the privilege to witness.

I closed my eyes and for a few precious moments I was in my seat in row S, section 105 of the North Stand, with my mates.

Anfield was a different story. The game fell the night the ground invasion into Iraq began and because we'd be moving before sunrise we were ordered to get our heads down before the game even kicked off. Making matters worse, I couldn't even make a sneaky call home under my sleeping bag because of a communications blackout. Just imagine trying to get to sleep that night without knowing the score.

I did, however receive the best alarm call imaginable from my colleague Tony Nicoletti, the Record photographer and fellow Celtic fan.

He had heard the score through the Army radio network and frantically pushed at my shoulder to wake me up from my slumber.

His first few words told me all I needed to know.

He beamed: 'Well big man, what do you think the score was?'

I replied: 'How many?'

He yelled: 'Two! Thompson and Hartson!"

What a sight we must have made. As nervous squaddies prepared their tanks and armoured vehicles for the dreaded journey into the unknown, there were two daft eejits prancing around like school kids who've just been given a year's pocket money.

The first leg of the semi final fell a couple of days before we left Iraq. The war itself was largely over and to toast our imminent departure – and the fact that the game was live on British Forces radio – one of the officers broke open a bottle of Famous Grouse. It was our first drink in five weeks and it showed. After the game finished it took me about an hour to find my camouflaged tent as I bounced around a Basra airfield, slightly the worse for wear, if the truth were told.

Well, if they will make them same colour as the desert.

Soon we were on our way home and one of the first calls I took after landing back at Heathrow was from my brother-in-law Lloyd telling me I had a ticket for the return leg. What a return to civilisation!

The last time I'd been in the city of Oporto was for that horror story Champions League defeat in 2001, but something told me this would be a far happier occasion – and thanks to the King of Kings, it most certainly was.

Two moments stand out above the rest.

Turning to hug Lloyd at the final whistle and seeing the tears streaming down his face and then the scenes of jubilation at Oporto airport as the team received a hero's welcome in the departure lounge. One by one the players were hugged by adoring fans as they walked through to the gate.

Last through was Big Bobo, who took one look at the cheering masses in green and white and couldn't help himself – he charged right in, arms punching the air in triumph, and must have hugged about ten people at once!

We were going to Seville and no one was happier at the prospect than this whopping giant of a man.

Looking back, we might not have won the Uefa Cup, but there's not a Celtic fan alive that would have swapped the Seville sojourn for any amount of silverware. It was a one-off.

To be surrounded by all your mates, in one of Europe's most beautiful cities, under a sun-kissed sky, watching the 'tic dine at the very top table of European football, was indeed a dream come true.

Chapter Three

A CELTIC KILT FOR THE MAYOR

by Bob Shields

I'VE been involved in a few daft stunts in this business. But asking one of Seville's leading politicians to drop his trousers in the back of a darkened bus has to be up there in my crazy situation top ten.

This story begins where most of my adventures begin - in the boozer.

I'd been asked by the boss to come up with some ideas for feature stories we could run in the build up to the big game.

Over a pint, Sunday Mail reporter Charles Lavery, no stranger to Celtic Park by the way, asked if I had a spare kilt he could take to Seville.

Kilt? Seville? The words rattled around my head for a few slurps of Guinness. Then the idea was born.

Why not get the most important man in Seville in a kilt. They must have a Mayor or something. A Celtic tartan kilt would be even better. In fact, full Highland dress would be better still.

It would be a gesture of goodwill from Scotland to Seville. And Hoops fans would appreciate the Mayor himself decked out in their colours.

Next morning, I ran the idea past the boss. Operation Kilt was now my personal responsibility.

Great ideas in the pub are one thing . . . the reality is usually another.

Walking back to my desk, I began to ponder a few key elements to making Operation Kilt work.

For a start, did Seville actually have a "Mayor"? Well, a city that size must have some kind of administrative leader, I reckoned.

How wide would he be? How tall was he? Would he even agree to wear a kilt in the first place?

Then another thought struck me. What if the Mayor of Seville was a woman? A Celtic tartan ladies kilt? But that wouldn't have the same impact.

I put this scenario to the back of my mind. The Mayor of Seville being a burd was too dreadful to even contemplate.

I called our chief reporter, Anna Smith, who was already in Seville. Anna is used to bizarre requests.

My call to determine the gender, girth and height of the Mayor of Seville - and if he was publicity minded - was just another one.

At the Scottish end, I called Howie Nicholsby of kiltmakers Geoffrey (Tailor).

Howie had designed my lightweight kilt for the New York marathon last year. He was a sound bloke. And by a fluke, his company had the license to manufacture kilts in the official Celtic FC tartan.

"A week to ten days - once you get me his size," said Howie.

The Scottish end was sorted in a 60 second call. I couldn't imagine how Anna would even begin getting the Seville side tied up.

Thankfully, Anna's Spanish "fixer" - an incredible character called Franco Rey - seemed to know all the right doors on all the right floors down at the Seville town hall.

Just a few hours later, Anna was back on from Seville to tell me Seville indeed did have a male Mayor - he was about six feet tall with a 42 inch waist.

"But will he wear it for us . . . ?" I asked her.

"No idea yet. But we hear he's a fun bloke who will probably be up for a bit of laugh," said Anna.

Time was now against us. I decided to go ahead and order the kilt in his size and hope for the best.

If push came to shove, I would give the Mayor's office a bit of el patter. I'd tell them our national dress was of supreme historical and social significance. I'd tell them is was a huge honour to be presented with one. And what a grave insult it would be to refuse to put it on.

Was the Mayor aware that in 1664, the Clan McPudden went to war with the McTumshies of Inversnooky for simply spurning the gift of a kilt?

Operation Kilt went on the back burner while Howie's people got to work. There were other Seville features to be organised.

But everything possible that could be done, had been done. It was now all up to the Mayor.

I was due to fly out the Friday before the game and the days couldn't count down quick enough.

I'd been at World Cups, Olympic Games and even The Oscars. The bigger the event - the more I liked it.

But Seville had a buzz surrounding it that I'd never experienced before. Every cab driver or barman in Glasgow was going . . . or knew someone who was.

Tickets, or the lack of them, dominated every conversation.

And every morning, I'd come to work to find a screenful of red, unopened e-mails waiting on my computer.

Some started with "Bob, you might remember me from . . ." Others began "Bob, you don't know me but . . . "

I got stories of dying uncles, handicapped children and all sorts of tear-jerking tales. Most, I'm sure, would be quite genuine.

But the final line of every e-mail was the same. "Can you get me a ticket . . ?"

To be honest, all this time, there was only one name on my list for tickets. And it was mine.

The Daily Record's meagre UEFA allocation had gone, rightly, to the sportswriters who needed to be in the stadium.

I was going to Seville to write about the fans, the fun and the hoop-la of the Celtic circus. Getting to the match wasn't part of the deal.

Not that it wasn't tempting though. I got a call from a friend who had connections at Carlsberg, one of the main sponsors of the match, promising me a precious brief.

And as more and more touts began to appear in Seville's shadowy doorways, the more I thought about going to the game.

After all, here I was in Seville, with the chance to personally witness a piece of Scottish football history. Win or lose.

But, then I thought of all the true Hoops fans who deserved to see the match much more than I did.

How could I, a well known Ayr United fan, look these ticketless fans in the eye as I walked past their inevitable desperate pleas outside the ground?

Of course, there were a few supporters who just wouldn't believe me when I answered their requests with "Sorry pal, I haven't even got a ticket myself".

"Aye, that'll be f***** right! It's a disgrace people like you will see the game and real supporters won't . . ", I was told by fans, usually with a drink in them.

But I didn't have one. Never did.

So let me end any argument over this with a wee bet.

There must have been 35,000 Hoops fans at the Estadio Olympico. And at least 25,000 of them would have a camera.

I'll buy a Celtic Park season ticket, for life, for anyone who's got a picture that shows me at the match!

Meanwhile, back at Operation Kilt, the now infamous garment had arrived from Howie's kiltmakers. Complete with sporran and a pair of green socks.

As I packed my bags on the Thursday night, I put my own kilt in my main bag and the Mayor's kilt in my hand luggage. I wasn't going to this effort to see the kilt become the proud property of a dodgy baggage handler.

Photographer Mark Runnacles and I had a fairly routine hop to Gatwick. But as soon a we hit the airport bar, we were engulfed by the first wave of travelling fans.

I spotted a father and his young son, dressed immaculately in Celtic tartan kilts and white shirts.

We marked them down as a potential picture when we landed - hopefully with some kind of "Welcome to Seville" sign in the background. But we lost them as we waited for our bags.

I reckoned that of 180 people on the plane - just over half of them were Celtic supporters. And this was SIX days before kick-off.

"This is going to be huge . . ." I thought to myself as our taxi swept us into the city centre.

Seville reputedly has more bars per head of population that any other city in Spain. It broke my heart to be driving past dozens of them in the sweltering, early evening heat.

It was on the same journey that I first noticed the huge "Vota" billboards on every street corner. An hour later, Spain's forthcoming elections were to throw a spanner into the works of "Operation Kilt".

After checking into a swank marble-floored city centre flat which Anna and Franco had somehow procured - we met them for drinks at Flaherty's, the Irish pub Anna had commandeered as the official "Hoops HQ".

She'd done her homework well. Flaherty's was opposite the Cathedral, right in the heart of Seville's tourist haunts.

And the Cathedral's giant stone step surrounding would be ideal for fans to sit in the sun and have their beers.

And it was here I first met Franco the fixer. He was a story all by himself. There was no job he hadn't done - from cowboy stunt rider to playing the handsome doctor on the ill-fated BBC Costa-based soap, "El Dorado".

He also had a short career as a restaurant owner and a club singer.

Not bad for a highly qualified opthalmist and optician who spoke English, German and French fluently.

Best of all, he picked all the wines from the restaurant wine list that I would have chosen. Me and the Franco boy were going to get on just fine.

But then again, maybe he was just using the chilled Gran Feudo to prepare me for the bad news.

"Have we got a time for the Mayor fixed yet?" I asked.

"Sorry, man, the Mayor says no f***** chance, man," said Franco dolefully.

The Spaniard went on to explain that the elections - due four days after the match - had put all the major politicians very much on edge.

Getting the Mayor to pose in a kilt was the equivalent of getting Jack McConnell to swan around in a sari four days before Scotland went to the polls.

"He can't be talked around, then?" I asked, recalling my Battle of Inversnooky strategy.

"Bob, the Mayor says that as long as he's got a pair of b***s, he ain't wearing no f***** skirt, man", said Franco, bluntly.

But it wasn't all bad news. Franco had spoken to the depute-Mayor. And he would be delighted to wear our kilt.

It turned out that Pablo de los Santos was a rising star in Spanish politics and had been tipped for the very top. That's top, as in, Prime Minister kind of top.

A huge sports fan and the Minister for Sport, he'd been campaigning for twelve years for Seville to improve its facilities and bid for major events. The UEFA Cup Final coming to Seville had been largely down to Pablo, and his team. And later in the week, we learned that Pablo had also landed the 'big one' - The Champions League Final - for Seville in 2005. So maybe he was the right man to get our kilt after all.

"This Pablo - I hope he's about six feet tall and has a 42 inch waist," I asked Franco.

"Hey, no problem man. We'll sort it all out tomorrow," grinned Franco, pouring me another generous glass of Gran Fuedo.

The next morning, Franco rang to confirm that everything had been fixed for 2.00pm that day.

"This guy is very busy. He'll only have a few minutes. And his wife just gave birth to a baby boy about four hours ago - so don't forget to congratulate him," said Franco.

The meeting place was the "Toro D'Oro" - down by the riverside.

This ancient landmark used to be covered in gold tiles - hence it's name, the 'Tower of Gold' - but it was still an impressive monument and a popular tourist attraction.

Photographer Mark, myself, Franco and the kilt were all there at 2.00pm prompt. But no sign of Pablo.

By 2.20pm I was starting to sweat - and it wasn't because of the 95 degree heat.

"If I was an important government figure, it was days before an election and my wife had just given birth to a son, I wouldn't be fannying about dressed as a bullfighter for a Spanish newspaper," I told Franco.

"No problem, man, He gave me his word. Relax . . " said Franco, lighting up his ninth consecutive Fortuna cigarette.

"Oh . . and I brought the safety pins," he added.

"What safety pins . . . ?

"Hey, just in case the kilt is a little bit big, man," said Franco.

Suddenly, there was a shouted greeting in Spanish and Franco ran over to greet our arriving VIP.

If Pablo de los Santos was even close to six feet tall with a 42 inch waist - then I was Henrik Larsson.

Swift greetings - and congratulations on the birth of his son duly completed - we then had to find a place for Pablo to get changed.

"Let's try the Toro D'Oro," the depute-Mayor suggested.

Franco did his best to explain the bizarre situation to the security guard but was getting nowhere.

Then Pablo produced his Government identity card. Surely that would do the trick?

No chance. The guard was having no dropping of trousers in his golden tower. Not on his shift.

We looked around for a pub or a public toilet. There was nothing.

I looked at a couple of thick shrubs on the riverbank, then looked at Franco. I could see from his eyes that he wasn't even going to ask this very senior government member to get his kit off behind a bush in a public park.

A giant bus pulled up and about thirty elderly tourists trooped off, blinking in the sunshine.

As soon as the last person came off, Franco leapt on and grabbed the driver. There was an exchange of Spanish . . . and I believe there may be been a little exchange of Euros as well.

We clambered on with Pablo and the kilt. Thanks to the dark glass windows, we couldn't really see what we were doing. Which was maybe just as well.

I fumbled with the leather buckles at the side as Franco stabbed the depute-Mayor with safety pins from behind.

Pablo kept looking at his watch. We only had a few minutes left.

Finally, we got him outside where Mark had set up his cameras for a picture.

It was then I noticed we'd put the kilt on backwards. The pleats were on the front instead of the rear.

"It looks great," said a beaming Franco.

"Fantastic!" said photographer Mark, who is a Geordie and has never worn a kilt in his life.

"It's very beautiful," said the depute-Mayor.

"It's . . . great," I eventually nodded. It was too late to ask him to put it on again.

We got a great set of pictures and good interview.

Finally, Pablo said his farewells, still wearing his back to front kilt.

"I must go to the hospital and let my wife see me in this beautiful kilt," he smiled as he climbed into a taxi.

Franco, Mark and I trooped back to Flaherty's for a pint.

"Operation Kilt" had started with a pint of Guinness. I wanted it to finish with one as well.

Chapter Four

WE WEREN'T EVEN GOING TO SEVILLE

by Frances Traynor

WE WEREN'T going to Seville. No, we'd somehow convinced ourselves that we had no chance of getting a ticket in the ballot and that no way would we be forking out to journey to southern Spain to watch the match on a big screen in blazing sunshine drinking hot beer and queuing up for overflowing Portaloos.

No, we wouldn't cough up 20 times its face value to buy a ticket from a tout and worry that it was a dud. No, we'd stay here in Glasgow and watch it at home, or go to Celtic Park to be with like-minded fans.

Secretly, each of us – Mary and I have had season tickets beside each other for six years – was praying, hoping against all hope that some miracle would get us tickets. It was an unspoken prayer, almost as if we were afraid to jinx ourselves by saying out loud what each of us had spent every single waking moment obsessing over from about 9.35pm (approximately) on Thursday, April 24 – from the very moment Henrik

Larsson's shot hit the back of the Boavista net and we knew that Celtic would be playing Porto in the final of the UEFA Cup.

As we heard of an increasing number of friends and acquaintances who hadn't been inside Celtic Park in years but who were heading to Seville regardless, we started to smart a little. Would we have to stay at home while these glory-hunting gits soaked up the atmosphere in Seville, or should we just go anyway without tickets?

But then a miracle did happen. Incredibly, we got tickets in the ballot, two season ticket holders who had been on the infamous European away registration scheme for four seasons and had never been offered so much as a Thursday night jaunt to Lithuania.

When they arrived, I did Martin O'Neill star jumps Zebedee-like around the house, no mean feat when you're an overweight short arse. Mary told me later she did the same at work when she'd managed to decipher my screams of "we got them!".

The tricky matter of last-minute holidays was negotiated and we'd got ourselves booked on a two-day trip with 67 Travel. Now we just had to count down the days until the trip of this or any other lifetime.

Bizarre as it may seem, in the most exciting climax to a domestic season since 1986, I was able to put the league to the back of my mind. I'd conceded the title to Rangers back on April 19 when we lost to Hearts. If we could just get a result in Portugal, went my reasoning, I won't care what happens in Seville and I certainly won't care if we don't win the league. Reaching a European final is the ultimate dream for every football fan and I was about to live that dream.

For me and for most Celtic fans, European glory is the stuff of bygone days, of glorious times that my parents and older cousins can recall in perfect clarity but are only real to me on video. My greatest Celtic-supporting moment – until the Blessed Martin arrived – was winning the double in our centenary year, though 1998's last-day win under Wim Jansen was sweet, too.

The week or so before the game had a certain air of unreality to it. We're more used to early exits from Europe, not getting to stay until the very end to play with the big boys. Every conversation was about Seville, but it felt distant and unreal to me. I kept telling myself that it would sink in later. You could tell the Celtic fans around the office and in the streets and pubs – we were the ones who couldn't stop smiling, who couldn't quite believe this big adventure we were embarking on.

My brothers Martin and Tony – in a rare burst of optimism and forward planning – bought final tickets on the UEFA website after Celtic beat Liverpool. Their trip was a re-run of Planes, Trains And Automobiles (without the laughs). In an exhausting 24 hours, they flew to Luton, then on to Gerona and took the train to Barcelona before finally hopping on another flight to Seville.

Our journey was a lot more civilised. We were flying straight from Glasgow to Jerez, an hour south of Seville and also the place where the team were making their base in a palatial five-star hotel so the potential for stalking was high (only kidding). The gang at our slightly less luxurious surroundings were in high spirits from the off. Half of them didn't have tickets, knew they had no chance of getting them and could have cared less.

One guy had brought his mum because she had just turned 67 and he thought it would be a good omen. He was going to the game and his old dear was going to the square to watch the game along with Jeanette and Nan, from Coatbridge. Parkhead regular Jeanette (some chanter that she was) couldn't bear not to be with the Celtic family on our most momentous day in 33 years. Nan, with no interest in football, came along to keep her company and found herself swept along with the euphoria. The 66-year-old gran told me: "My daughter works in Marks & Spencer and she's mortified that I'm here. She said she's going to disown me and told me not to mention Seville ever again to her. But she doesn't know what she's missing. This is fantastic."

Nan also provided us with most of the laughs, all unintentional. In the hotel bar (officially the world's smallest but still lavishly stocked), she told us she was buying a drink for John Lennon. She was, in fact, buying a beer for John, from Dalmellington, who had Lennon 18 on the back of his hoops.

John's strip was covered in signatures. He and his pal had bumped into John Hartson, Tom Boyd and a pride of Lisbon Lions in Jerez's main square. Hail Hails were exchanged and a beaming John got everyone's autograph and a fantastic tale to tell. Hey, who's kidding who? Everyone in the bar that night felt as if we too had shaken Big Bad John's hand and asked Boydy where his Zimmer frame was.

My own minor brush with celebrity came as Mary and I walked back to our hotel in the afternoon's baking heat. Strolling towards us, without a care in the world, was Billy Connolly. I couldn't resist a "how you doing, big man?" at him and he smiled and waved. He passed us again a few hours later as a gang of us stood outside our hotel and gave a big Hail Hail across the street to the delight of everyone.

Dennis, from Glasgow, was fielding fraught calls from his nephew who was trying to get a ticket from someone in Italy. Dennis, whose T-shirt proudly proclaimed that he had been in Lisbon and Milan, was more worried about squeezing into the younger man's strip the next day. Like a Henrik Larsson goal, it was inevitable that Dennis would be wearing the hoops like a second skin by breakfast time. It was just as inevitable that his nephew would be gutted when his ticket didn't appear.

Bob, from Livingston, sensibly paced himself in the bar. Wise man. We, on the other hand, drank too much Spanish brandy and exhausted our repertoire of Celtic songs in a competitive sing-song until the wee hours. On the day of the game, we gave thanks for Bob's good sense because he not only didn't have a hangover, he had also had the presence of mind to pack two bottles of juice in his bag and was kind enough to share.

To say that Seville was awash in green and white is undoubtedly the understatement of the year. Outside of a sell-out home game, I have never seen that many Celtic fans in one place at one time. It was truly awesome and the excitement and nerves were threatening to overwhelm me as we walked into the city centre from the stadium. I felt close to tears all day and could barely keep a lid on a rising tidal wave of emotion.

Sweltering in the heat, we decided to stop for some water and, naturally, we met someone we know in the first bar we went into – actually, it's someone Mary knows. I'd clocked the guy with the dyed green and white hair and thought to myself 'he's a bit old for that' just as he came over and threw his arms round Mary. This was her cousin, Benny, who actually sits eight rows in front us at Celtic Park.

It was the first in a series of meetings that day that proved to us that it's a small world after all and the best of them came in the wonderful chaos of the main square where we waited in vain for friends to turn up – like everyone else, our plans to use mobile phones to make arrangements were scuppered when 70,000 other Celtic fans decided to text all at the same time.

Trying to find shade under the world's smallest tree, we spotted a striking figure in full Highland regalia – Phil Boswell, originally from Coatbridge and now living in the Middle East. It was the first time we had seen him in more than three years. Phil had no intention of missing an occasion like this. The day before he'd flown from Qatar to Morocco, then took a boat to Spain and a train to Seville. And as the mercury nudged 40 degrees, he confirmed that he was indeed officially roasting under his heavy plaid. But he had a ticket, he was going to see the Celtic in a European final and what was a little chafing of the thighs on such a magnificent day?

That was a little too much information for us so we took refuge in the wonderful air-conditioned restaurant of swanky department store El Corte Ingles. The staff are more used to serving ladies who lunch and looked utterly bemused at the scarf-laden, hoops-wearing hordes scoffing bocadillos and chips.

Talk of forgeries had everyone wary about their tickets. We knew ours were kosher, but the worry was that there would be a repeat of the debacle at Blackburn when genuine ticket holders were locked out while the dodgy ones watched the game in comfort inside. We weren't the only ones to decide to get to the stadium early, but we all had to stand outside the locked gates without any shade or protection from that relentless sun. Fortunately, the police took pity on us and ordered the stadium staff to open the turnstiles. We were there, we were really there and although the place was virtually empty – this was only 6.00pm – our hearts beat a little faster as we looked down at the pitch and imagined what was to come.

As the stadium began to fill up, we saw yet more familiar faces – there was Michael Clark, from Glasgow, who had worked with Mary for years sitting across from us. Up the steps laughing his head off at the sight of us came Kenny Burns, originally from Ardrossan and now working in Ireland. We'd met Kenny and his wife Shirley in a bar in Lanzarote during an Old Firm game last year where I discovered I knew her cousins and auntie in Irvine – didn't I tell you it's a small, small world? Our final coincidental meeting came minutes later when, scanning the crowd behind us, Mary spotted her niece's husband. Kevin McKeown, from Ayr, was another of those supremely confident and organised chaps. On the night of the return leg at Anfield, he took his laptop to a mate's house and as John Hartson's goal hit the back of the net, Kevin was buying his tickets and sorting out his flights. Don't you just hate guys like that? Only kidding, Kevin.

I had sung myself hoarse before kick-off and with queues the length of Argyle Street at the bar, my voice had gone completely by the time Celtic went into the huddle. The game itself passed in a blur, but I can still remember those agonising seconds when Henrik's header looped over Vitor Baia – the Laurence Olivier of Portuguese football – and seemed to take an eternity to reach the net. When your team scores a goal like that in a European final, you make a lot of new friends during the celebrations because you always end up miles away from your seat. I haven't had that many kisses since I played postman's knock at a pal's 10th birthday party. The celebrations for the King of Kings' second goal minutes later were even wilder. And we made a new friend for life when the guy next to Mary shared his can of Coke with us before two middle-aged women pegged out for good.

In the end, as we all know, our victorious night was not to be. The whistle for full-time was barely heard because we – 35,000 Celtic fans – were singing for our team. Singing because they had done us proud, because they had run themselves into the ground in stifling heat that we could hardly bare to sit in and because they had got us here, they had played magnificently in 12 matches from Lithuania to Lancashire to reach this place. All around me, grown men and women were crying, tears pouring down their faces. I couldn't cry. I'd been close to blubbing all day, but by 11.20pm on that boiling hot May night, I was so drained by my emotions that I could barely mouth the words to You'll Never Walk Alone.

Since Martin O'Neill came to Celtic, I've chalked up an awful lot of firsts as a Celtic supporter, every one more incredible than the previous one. I'd never seen my team win a treble (I'm too young to remember 1967 or 1969), I'd never seen us beat Rangers so many times in one season and I'd never seen us outplay teams from England, Germany and Spain in European competition with such style and panache.

As I write this, it's exactly two weeks since Celtic lost to Porto in Seville's Estadio Olimpico but I still feel like a winner. We travelled to Seville more in hope than expectation. What we got was the biggest family day out in world football. I have never felt prouder to be a Celt, never felt prouder of my fellow fans, who made the day such a fabulous fiesta, and never felt such pride in my team who gave us everything. If it's a grand old team to play for, it's an even grander team to support.

Chapter Five

A MONTH'S RENT FOR A FOOTIE MATCH

by Brian McIver

IT'S 6.30pm on Wednesday May 21st and there are just over two hours before the most important moment in the life of any Celtic fan under the age of 40.

I'm standing outside my hotel on the Avenida Menendez Playo and I've just spent a month's rent on two hours of football, and have just sixty minutes to travel five miles across the busiest city in Spain.

It's possibly the most stressful moment of my life and I am loving every minute of it.

The last four days of green and white parties, late night drinking and desperate inquiries for holy grail tickets to every single person we have met on our travels in Glasgow, London and Seville have led up to the deal we just entered into with a Luton based tout.

My friend had just received an unbelievable offer from an old friend of a face-value ticket if we can make it to the stadium within the hour, and my mate has volunteered to half in for the £400 the tout in our hotel was charging for his ticket of unknown, but apparently sound, origin.

So six weeks after we booked our hotel and flights to the football capital of the world, an astonishingly brilliant piece of luck and wheeler dealing with an old school friend, our hotel clerk and his English pal, have brought us to within touching distance of becoming part of the select group of football fans who will live to see their team compete in a European final.

Even if that touching distance does happen to be five miles away and on the other side of what is currently the busiest metropolitan area in western Europe.

If one percent of world flight traffic is supposed to have been taken over by thousands of Celtic fans today, then at least half of them are currently clogging up the city streets and highways between me and the Estadio.

As Glasgow based football fans, we are used to nipping on the quick train out to the east end, grabbing a taxi or even trundling along the Gallowgate on a bus to make it in time for the kick-off.

But we had spent our four days in Seville so preoccupied with our ticket quest that no one had remembered to check where the train stations were, if in fact there were any, and we soon found out that any form of road transportation just wasn't going to happen.

The city had been gradually busying up since the Sunday we arrived and every day it was taking longer and longer to get served in Flaherty's Bar. And every night the city cleaners were having to cope with more and more cans of Tennents Super and bottles of Buckfast on the 600-year-old streets.

When we woke up on Wednesday, it seemed like every Celtic fan in the world had descended upon the city, which is not much bigger than Glasgow or Edinburgh, and bemused tourists from Arizona and the home counties had no idea what was going on around them.

To be honest, the volume of hooped pilgrims was increasing so rapidly that none of us could really believe it either.

By the afternoon of the game, the 100,000 Celtic fans had divided off into three camps.

There were the lucky ones who had tickets and were already waiting for the stadium doors to open, the steamers who were heading for the pubs and parks to watch the game on big screens, and the two white skinned and wide eyed guys who had just used up their share of good fortune for their entire adult lives by scoring tickets, albeit of questionable origin, two hours before kick off.

The city itself was absolutely mad - huge crowds were heading in every direction. The picturesque old Mediterranean city had turned into Turin on the day of The Italian Job robbery - traffic lights meant nothing, no cars were moving anywhere and even all the horse and carts were fully booked.

We decided that the clotted arteries of the Sevillano road network were a waste of time and headed on foot for what we thought was the best path to the stadium which lay on the other side of the river and several miles along the left bank.

We started pounding along the streets, crossing from one side to the next at every junction trying to work out the most direct route to the river and avoid the speeding horses and drunken Scots charging down the streets. After two minutes, the initial high of knowing we were actually on the way to the game wore off and the 120 degree heat started to kick in, melting my green hair dye and sweating up my lucky Celtic socks which had been worn to every leg on the way to Seville and weren't about to quit now.

We were walking as fast as we could and it seemed like we weren't getting anywhere - our hearts and our adrenal glands were pumping as hard as the Spanish sun would allow but the city appeared to have become glued to the overheated tarmac and wasn't moving at all.

In frustration, we started running in brief energy-wasting bursts and finished our first litre of water before we even reached the riverside.

In a bar next to the road, some drunken Celtic fans were getting friendly with a bunch of drunken Portuguese fans and while most supporters were exchanging shirts or scarves, they started swapping booze.

In some of the most bizarre photos ever to be taken in Seville, the Porto fans were crowding round to taste their first drop of Buckfast and were happily posing for pictures holding the specially imported vino with their new pals from Coatbridge.

Which was only slightly more sane than the lobster tanned Glasgow boys who were braving the blistering heat in trainers and Celtic shorts and were relaxing in the late afternoon by swigging straight vodka - ice or water is for girls' blouses - from the bottle and washing down their dehydration with a Kensitas Club Light.

As for us, we were struggling to keep going, even with litres of bottled water flowing, and we clung to every bit of shade by the riverbanks.

Only the memory of the Porto fan who had died earlier in the week when he fell into the Guadalquiver stopped either of us joking about the idea of jumping in and taking our chances swimming to the Olimpico.

But we also couldn't stop for a breather. Every moment to say hello to an old pal or catch some air was another minute we might miss the ticket master at the stadium, and another minute we might miss the kick off.

All along the riverside roads, open top bus tours were starting to fill up with desperate Celtic fans tying to get to the Isla de la Cartuja by any means necessary.

The open top bus sales rep interrupted our left, right, left with a quick sales pitch offering to swap our hike - 90 minutes by her reckoning - for a cheap bus ride through the city and out to the ground within half an hour.

The sweat pouring down through our new 'Sevilla 03' emblazoned hoops made us consider it for a second but adrenaline-fuelled paranoia conjured up images of the bus getting caught in the traffic logjam, leaving us stranded even further away from the stadium than we already were.

We started to quicken our pace.

Another bottle of water down and we figured we must have made the halfway mark as we decided to follow a swelling crowd across the river and through the Triana district, which we hoped someone, somewhere, had discovered was a shortcut.

Becoming increasingly unsure of our route as we marched through the cobbled streets, we asked every driver with his window open and every man or woman on a street corner "donde esta el Estadio Olimpico?" and followed the drifting fans who all seemed to be heading the right way.

As we started through the windy streets, every corner became like a trek up some rolling hill or mountain - you're sure that just over the next peak or round the next bend you're going to see the summit, but there always seems to be just another incline or street corner, and then another one, ahead of you.

And as the Sevillian dales kept rolling on in front of us, the kick off time kept creeping up on top of us.

It was already 7pm, and we started to fear that we had gone in the wrong direction or weren't going fast enough and were going to miss the ticket that was going to be waiting for us outside the Celtic End at 7.30 sharp.

It was only when we crossed a street and found ourselves among another huge throng of green and white drones heading for the mother ship that we started to relax and soak up some of the atmosphere of the moment.

We started to look for friends and familiar faces among the thousands walking nearby - the pre Seville joke of 'look out for me, I'll be the one wearing green and white' started to ring true as we tried to pick out faces from the flowing tide.

I thought I recognised my mate Andy, who I'd seen last night for the first time in six years and who paid £2,000 to fly 26 hours on a plane from Perth, Australia, via Bangkok, Los Angeles, Paris and Madrid only to get a ticket at Seville airport for £450 within five minutes of landing on the day of the game.

I was also looking to see if the girl I stayed next door to when I was five years old had left Flaherty's bar yet to make her way to the game, or if the old friends I'd met from primary school, two high schools and university had managed to get tickets and were walking along like us.

The relief at finding the right road quickly changed back into paranoid flapping when we ended up at one of the big screen parks showing the game.

To a fan without a ticket, it must have looked like heaven on earth - thousands of partying, hooped up maniacs dancing along to Celtic songs and getting ready to watch the big game on the even bigger screen - kind of like Glastonbury with Henrik Larsson playing lead guitar.

But to us, it was just another set of grey hairs added to our growing collection as we were terrified we had spent all that time heading in the wrong direction.

The policeman I frantically asked for directions has probably seen less distressed and fraught expressions from armed robbers or young mothers looking for a lost child, but he must have met enough deranged Celtic fans by this point not to let it bother him and calmly pointed us to the right road, assuring us "five minutes" to Estadio.

When we rounded onto the main boulevard which stretched out ahead of us to what we hoped was the stadium, we realised he had meant five minutes by car, as we still had at least two miles in front of us.

But at least we were heading the right way, and then I started to worry about the authenticity of the ticket in my pocket.

The stories and rumours doing the rounds in the Seville bars suggested that the inevitable forgeries were good but still easily detectable by a system of barcodes, and that under Spanish law, the local police were happily jailing anyone with a fake.

Not getting into the ground was one thing, but as we started picking up the pace and the stadium got inches closer every second, I started going into worst case scenario mode and imagined spending the night of the game in a police van or cell and explaining to my boss why I couldn't turn up for work on Monday because I was in the Andalucian equivalent of El Bar-L.

Now at just past 7.20pm, we were still a way to go and becoming genuinely worried about our chances - the mobile phone networks had started to seize up and the occasional signal that could get through from our ticket source was telling us to hurry up.

By now I was convinced my trainers were beginning to melt like marshmallows and stick to the road, my hair dye was dribbling down the back of my neck like tear stained mascara, and we had just about had enough as we entered the final lap.

The horses and carts we had seen earlier in the city centre were now cantering merrily up to the stadium and the few taxis left operating in the streets had already dropped off for the evening and were returning home.

I optimistically waved a hand out at one of the passing cabs heading away from the mayhem, and we didn't even have the energy to smile or whoop when the driver decided to cash in on our fatigue and stopped in front of us.

One minute and 20 Euros later, the entire journey had been worth it as we jumped out of the cab, met the ticket seller at the gate and realised we were actually there.

The last hour disappeared and all the fretting, worry and angst started to subside as the echoes of You'll Never Walk Alone resonated out of the ground (to us it sounded more like You'll Never Walk Again) and we decided to go for our moment of truth at the turnstiles.

Six weeks before the game, two faithful fans optimistically booked flights and accommodation the day after the Liverpool quarter final win, and two hours before the match, we managed to secure the tickets no one thought we would get.

In the departure gate at Glasgow Airport four days previously, a sleazy little Portuguese called Luis offered us and some other waiting fans 11 tickets at 1,000 Euros each and he was booed in that Lounge just like his team was rightly booed in Seville.

We had spent the entire trip determined we wouldn't be fleeced by people like him and as we walked up to the stadium, we were just hoping we had spent £200 for two hours of football rather than a night in the cells.

At the first perimeter barrier, the steward passed us through without a hitch.

Climbing up the stairs to the main stadium entry gates, we felt like we were stepping up to take a penalty kick as the armed guard took people's tickets and passed them through the barcode reader.

A red light meant forgery, a very appropriate green light meant everything. He took my piece of decorated and valuable embossed paper, scanned it and gave me the happiest moment of my life when he passed it green and wished me good luck for the game.

And then, an hour and two minutes later, and right in front of our seats, Henrik Larsson leapt up higher than the sun to score the best goal I've ever seen, and nothing after that mattered.

In the two hours leading up to the game, I thought we had made a stressful and arduous journey to see our heroes.

But on Thursday afternoon, as I was staring blankly out of our taxi heading for Seville airport, the funniest sight of the trip pulled up alongside our cab.

A scabby little Ford Fiesta with Glasgow number plates and filled up with Ma, Pa and two kids in the back - all in Celtic tops - stopped next to our car, and the bright red faced driver leaned out his window to ask our driver, "haw pal, where's the road to Madrid."

He had just dragged a family of four on a 2,000 mile pilgrimage in a Ford Fiesta and was heading north to the Santander-Plymouth ferry, via the main motorway to Madrid.

They had arrived on Tuesday, slept in their car, were returning another 2,000 miles the next day and none of them had tickets.

No other club in the world could inspire that - which is maybe just as well.

Chapter Six

INSIDE FLAHERTY'S BAR FOR THE MATCH

by Jack Mathieson

TO those who were there it was almost as good as having a ticket for the match.

Flaherty's Irish pub, in the shadow of the ancient cathedral, had become a home from home to thousands of Celtic fans who made the pilgrimage to Seville.

They ate and drank there as they gathered to belt out raucous tributes to the generations of legends who had worn the green and white hoops. With time running out and the prices demanded by the touts still out of reach, it became for many THE place to watch the final.

And the breathless excitement, the colour and the passion generated in that noisy bar will live in the memory when details of the match have long been forgotten.

The sense of anticipation began to build early in the day. Fans arrived on the train from Barcelona to swell the numbers of the Flaherty's-based green and white army.

As the hours ticked by, those enjoying a beer in the sun among the crowds outside made their way indoors to try to 'reserve' a decent position.

Two hours before kick-off, the place was crammed to capacity and the busy bar had taken on the look of the old Celtic Park jungle.

Flags flew, banners were unfurled and the club anthems were being roared out at eardrum-bursting volume.

Only the lack of room to manoeuvre prevented a repeat of the night before when fans had drank the pub dry.

Bar manager Keith Todd, an Irishman who had been in Seville for nine years, watched the big match countdown unfold and chose the appropriate soundtrack.

Fans' favourites Charlie and the Bhoys went down a storm, and Sinatra's version of New York, New York instantly became Seville, Seville to the appreciative choir.

By the time the big screen descended, the supporters had made Flaherty's their very own Olympic Stadium and nothing could dent the growing mood of optimism.

Even the first sight of TV match presenter Gary Lineker drew roars of approval, and a glimpse of the UEFA Cup itself was greeted with hysterical applause.

Celtic took the pitch like Gladiators entering the amphitheatre - and 400 tickless fans knew the moment had arrived.

Late arrivals who had missed out on the best vantage points were forced to squeeze into nooks and crannies and peer through doorways at the big-match action.

In contrast with the excitement which accompanied the build-up, the opening exchanges were nervy ones for the bar-bound punters.

Rab Douglas gathered a long-range shot in the opening minutes and the exaggerated applause reflected the tense mood which had replaced the pre-match bravado.

It wasn't until Henrik Larsson replied with a dead ball effort which forced a save from Baia that the supporters settled.

"It's a reasonable start - it could have been far worse," said John Paul Clarke, 30, of Tollcross, Glasgow, from his perch almost underneath the screen.

Minutes later, an inviting cross from Agathe just failed to find Sutton and 400 pairs of hands reached for heads in one-long squeal of frustration.

Then disaster struck on the stroke of half-time. Derlei gave Porto the lead and Celtic's already difficult quest looked like mission impossible.

Tommy Higgins, 38, of Paisley, lamented: "They had more possession than us and the one good chance they had they put it away.

"They're a class side and it's difficult to get the ball off them but we're not out of it yet."

However, the subdued mood at the interval suggested that, in the minds of many, the task had become too great.

The half-time chat found some Celts mentally preparing themselves to accept Scottish football's customary role of good-natured loser.

It took only two minutes of second half football to restore their faith.

Agathe swung in a cross to the back post and Larsson met it perfectly. The ball looped back across the goalmouth and time almost stood still. Even when the ball crossed the line via the far post it seemed to take an age for the hushed faithful to grasp what had happened.

Hundreds, watching the screen through a forest of arms and heads, stood in mute disbelief as the match was squared at one apiece.

When the roar eventually came it was deafening. Beer flew, tables crashed over and for seven full minutes Flaherty's took on the appearance of a giant, seething green and white tidal wave. The Celtic songs of praise rang out again in a prolonged outpouring of jubilation that seemed to pierce the flesh and grip the nervous systems of all who were there.

Then Alenichev scored Porto's second and the song died instantly in 400 throats. You could touch the silence.

James Johnson, 30, of Cumbernauld, had struggled to enjoy the finer points of the match.

Hundreds of agitated bodies, some clad in hooped shirts which had seen several day's service, stood between him and the TV pictures.

His specs kept steaming up and he had to endure regular beer shampoos courtesy of the inebriated fan standing on a stool behind him.

But his spirit remained unshakeable. "We'll win 3-2," he asserted. "With Larsson getting the winner."

Three minutes later the Super Swede squared the match, the party started all over again and James was ecstatic.

"Told you so.' he said. "Just call me Mystic Meg."

A roar of Celtic, Celtic went up as the patrons of Flaherty's exhorted the Hoops heroes to make one last push for a winner in normal time but it was not to be.

History will record that the game ran away from Celtic in extra time. Balde was dismissed - to howls of disapproval - and Derlei's late winner for the Portuguese sent heads bowing, knees sagging and a giant collective groan rolling round the pub.

But still the songs rang out and in the end the mood was one of defiance rather than despair. The final whistle was drowned out by a feisty chorus of Hail, Hail the Celts are Here - though those doing the singing were almost blinded by tears.

Fans who had journeyed from Scotland said that watching the game in a swaying, heaving bar had done nothing to detract from their Seville experience.

Flaherty's had become so popular that managers had difficulty in getting in drink supplies or even Euros for change.

It had become an unofficial information centre where the local tourist trade kept staff posted about any accommodation which became available.

The bar had even become a tourist attraction in its own right with Spanish parents bringing in their children to enjoy the spectacle of the odd Caledonian invaders.

To supporters who had failed to get tickets, it was the perfect venue to watch the biggest game of their lives.

Kevin McLoughlin, 21, of Chapelhall, Lanarkshire, said: "I thought Celtic did Scotland proud. They were unlucky but we will be back again.

"The whole experience of being here was brilliant and the atmosphere in the pub was electric. Hail, Hail."

Angela Johnston, 28, of East Kilbride, said: "I was never, ever going to get to the match but watching it here was nearly as good."

But for those who travelled to Andalucia in May, it was about far more than 90, or even 120, minutes of football.

It was a pilgrimage which drew them in their tens of thousands from all points on the globe.

Strolling round the plazas and bars in the build-up to the match, you could meet fans who had made meticulously planned round-the-world journeys from Australia.

Other Celts living it up in the city had caught a last-minute flight from Glasgow or driven across Europe in a rickety old minibus.

Well-heeled businessmen had splashed out a fortune in Euros to pack out Seville's plushest hotels. The more budget-conscious roughed it under the walls of the cathedral or in a children's playpark.

Big names from the international jetset like Billy Connolly and TV regulars like Jackie Bird and Elaine C Smith rubbed shoulders with jobless Scots.

And figures from the Glasgow underworld mingled with priests.

Long-parted relatives who had allowed several years to pass without a visit found themselves catching up over tapas in the balmy heat of an

Andalucian evening.

Hogmanay street parties are one night wonders. Film TV and music awards are dominated by celebs and their hangers-on.

Celtic's expedition to Seville, on the other hand, truly earned the right to be called the biggest party in the world.

For sheer fun, excitement and a sense of unity that demolished all social boundaries it was a week-long feast of fun that could not be beaten.

And the fact that it all sprang from heartfelt devotion to a Glasgow football team gave the lie to the notion that it is only a game.

A generation of Celts reared on tales of exploits in Lisbon 36 years ago wanted to be part of history in their own right.

And older fans who had been in Portugal were motivated by a desire to repeat that glorious experience.

The lure of Seville was almost magnetic as fans began looking out their passports before the headline writers had even finished capturing the semi-final triumph against Boavista.

Andy Ferguson, 23, and Paul Noras, 26, looked just like any other fans as they sauntered down a side street the day before the match.

Only a small logo on a T-shirt betrayed the fact that they were two of the farthest travelled Celts - from Western Australia.

The pair had followed the fortunes of the Hoops from afar since their families emigrated Down Under almost 15 years ago.

Paul, originally from Falkirk, said: "We have tried to get tickets but we were not prepared to pay over the odds. At the end of the day we came here just to be here."

Andy, who hails from Govan, admitted: "It's the first time I have been out of Australia since I emigrated."

Also in Seville was Tom Bole, 65, a founder member of a supporters club in Los Angeles, and his wife Margaret.

He decided to make the journey from his current home in South Carolina after being impressed by Celtic league matches on cable TV.

A veteran of the European Cup final defeat in Milan in 1970, he said simply: "I'm here to party."

During the build-up to the game, Celtic fans took over hotels, bars and plazas. The more cultured could be spotted on open-topped tour buses or seeing the city in more sedate fashion by horse-drawn carriage.

It was impossible to go anywhere without hearing 'Hail, Hail' or the simple but joyous chant of 'We're in Seville, We're in Seville'.

Like any massive gathering of people the influx brought with it one or two roguish elements.

Talc' McAlpine, 33, headed a group of fans from the Manchester area.

They boasted about how they had blagged their way into the stadium for a look round by pretending to be a TV crew.

They intended to return there for the final using photocopies of genuine match tickets. The fate of their mission is unknown.

There were also stories of outrageous good luck and heartbreaking bad luck.

Steve Carlin, of Tranent, East Lothian, got a ticket for the match after his girlfriend Pamela wrote a cheeky letter to Martin O'Neill offering to name the baby she was expecting after him.

The Celtic manager phoned her to say Steve could have a brief - leaving her the problem of getting it out to him to Spain.

A friend duly obliged and Steve was able to get to the final.

Pamela said: 'I still can't believe that Martin O'Neill took the time to phone and arrange for us to have a ticket.

'When I called Steven with the news, he told me to get lost. He wouldn't believe me.'

But spare a thought for devoted Celtic fan Colin Veldon, of Airdrie, Lanarkshire.

The 35-year flew out to the Costa del Sol on the Friday before the game, delighted to have secured a match ticket.

Two days later he broke his leg in a kickabout on the streets of Malaga. He had to undergo surgery and he was still laid up in hospital as the Hoops took the field at the Estadio Olimpico.

He said: 'To go through this and to miss the biggest game of my life is just totally sickening.'

It was the magnificent eve of final Party in the Park which truly illustrated the deep-seated passions which link Celtic Football Club to its supporters.

The dusty Prado de San Sebastion, set among towering trees and ornate fountains, shook to a medley of Celtic songs and pop classics as the countdown to the match began.

Ten thousand hoarse voices belted out Irish folk numbers and rude ditties about Gazza, and the spectacle was truly awesome.

Supporters, already high on adrenaline, met up with estranged relatives and others hugged neighbours from back home.

Old school pals whose lives had taken different directions recognised each other with whoops of delight and exchanged family news.

Lisbon Lions captain Billy McNeill took to the stage to urge fans to roar the team to new European glory and the mood of breathless anticipation was almost complete.

There was hardly a dry eye in the park as McNeill told them: 'You've got to get behind the team. Give them your backing and let them see you want the cup.'

The 1967 skipper was mobbed as he left the stage, almost disappearing in the tidal wave of green and white which engulfed him.

It could not get any better but it did. Thousands more Hoops devotees arrived on match day to expand the parties from the jam-packed central plazas into the winding side streets.

Accommodation was by now a forlorn hope but the late arrivals just did not care. They partied until they were exhausted then slept where they fell.

For some that meant a kiddies' play park in the city centre.

Katrina Young, 38, of Grangemouth, said: 'There were about 25 of us sleeping in this park. There were people on the chute and inside the kiddies' boat.'

Porto fans too arrived in numbers at last, and to a relentless drum beat accompaniment, shirts and scarves were swapped and photographs were taken. Some were kept as souvenirs, others were offered as gifts to charm the sultry local lovelies.

Rival fans exchanged good-natured banter at top volume across busy streets as the big kick-off loomed.

The aftermath of the match, with all hopes dashed and all passion spent, could only ever be an anti-climax.

One American journalist described the scene at the airport the next day as being like Braveheart after one of the big battles, with shattered fans laid out as far as the eye could see.

It was a spectacle which was replicated at all of the major gathering points. The Cathedral walls, Flaherty's and the side streets around the Placa Espana were eerily quiet after what had gone before.

There were plenty of bodies - but the Sombrero-clad army had momentarily lost its gallous edge as the fans who remained contemplated their disappointment.

However, the Scottish football fan is not easily crushed.

More than 24 hours after the final whistle, groups of tourists were sitting dining at an open air restaurant more than a mile from the Cathedral area which Celtic fans had made their own.

It looked for all the world as if the match had never happened. Courting couples walked hand-in-hand, businessmen exchanged anecdotes over a glass of beer, and the sounds of a pop concert on the opposite river bank drifted over.

There was hardly a scarf, flag or football top in sight. Then somebody stood up and broke the late-night tranquility with a raucous roar of

'C'mon the Hoops.'

The cry was taken up at the next table, then repeated by somebody who had just popped their head out of waterfront bar.

A minute later, dozens were chanting the mantra in unison and the sound was rolling down the street like a powerful tidal wave.

The locals, far from resenting the intrusion to their evening, laughed and applauded.

Like the rest of the world they could only salute the Green and White army and its indomitable spirit - and hope that these superb fans will one day follow their team to new European glory.

Chapter Seven

CELEBRITY TALES

by Jim Kerr, Elaine C. Smith, Tony Roper

IN HIS Hoops shirt, comedy writer Tony Roper, a Celtic shareholder, sweated it out with the throngs of Celtic fans for the most moving night of his life.

This is his story of tears and laughter.

"It was after the Liverpool game I decided to go and got booked up. A few of us went on the trip and we were staying four or five days in Albufeira.

"Even the plane over was like a Celtic flight. And from the moment we arrived in Portugal it was just one long party. There was an Irish bar up the road from our hotel and that's where we spent the nights singing all night long.

"We drove up to Seville on the day of the match and booked into a hotel six miles out of the city, so we spent the whole day in town. It was absolutely amazing. It is an event that will never be equalled. There were something like 140,000 football fans in that city, counting the Porto fans, and yet there was not one arrest. The pubs ran out of beer and the heat was phenomenal yet there everyone was so well behaved.

"You would have to have been there to experience just how awesome the entire occasion was. There were loads of my cousins there who I hadn't seen for ages and we made the trip a reunion, so there was that kind of thing happening as well.

"The match itself is something I will never forget as long as I live. Seville is known as the frying pan and I have never experienced temperatures like that during the day and the run-up to the match. You were standing there in the heat, deyhdrated, yet with the adrenalin pumping because you had got this far.

"The game was absolutely fantastic. Since I came home I have watched it on video twice and even though I was there and know the result, I'm still half expecting us to score when it gets to 2-2. It's had that kind of effect on me.

"All of the players must have been ready to drop but they just kept on going and the fans were so moved by that we all sang through our tears. I was standing there with tears streaming down my face but I was singing because it was such an incredible moment.

"After the match, I didn't see anybody with their head in their hands thinking, 'Oh God, we got beat'. People were disappointed because we wanted to win and we came so close. But every single fan I met coming out all had the same message - What a performance. This was a great team playing in 100 odd degrees with 10 men and it was unbelievable.

"At the end of the game I was crying as we stood up and applauded. I just felt so proud of what they did and how they did it. If I felt sad it was for them because they had put so much into it and come away with nothing. They had given it everything. Neil Lennon was still chasing balls at full tilt until the last second. They were magnificent, and their handling of themselves throughout the season has been magnificent.

"When we left the match we had to walk for three and a half hours because we couldn't get a taxi. We weren't even sure if we were walking in the right direction, we just kept walking. There were blisters on our feet and blood oozing from them. Eventually a Spanish couple stopped in their car and offered us a lift for a few Euros. It's just as well because our hotel was across a motorway and God knows how we would have got there.

"We got into the hotel absolutely knackered and could hardly walk for blisters. All of us were the same. There were four of us sharing a room and I had a cot bed. I was so exhausted I just collapsed on the cot bed and it collapsed underneath me. I lay there with my nose tucked in between my knees and we all fell about laughing. I couldn't get up and couldn't move. I was so tired I decided just to lie like that and slept.

"The next day we drove back to Albufeira because we still had two or three days. The singing was still going on all the way back and when we got there it was still party time.

"When I look back now I will never forget the feeling of pride I had at the end of that game. Look how far we've come. If you think that three years ago we were a laughing stock. We had no credibility, but three years later we were contesting the second biggest club football trophy in the world and just narrowly missed it.

"I felt pride, astonishment and glad to be a Celtic fan. I looked around me and the tears were flowing out of people's eyes, not because we were being beaten. Everyone was thinking the same thing. They were remembering their fathers, their grandfathers, somebody taking them to the game as a wee boy. It was the most emotional moment, and that is what I will take to my grave."

ACTRESS and comedienne Elaine C. Smith, a Celtic season ticket holder, travelled to Seville with her husband Bob to pursue the Celtic dream. This is her story:

"Seville 2003 was all about dreams. And what a joy that was.

To be Scottish and to allow yourself to dream about what could be - about what could be possible - now there's a thing eh?

As a nation we tend towards the pessimistic, the naval gazing, the insecurity and lack of self belief. Yet here in May 2003 in the beautiful Spanish city of Seville , Scottish Celtic fans were allowed to dream! Not only that, most of the nation were sharing the dream. Fair enough, if you were a 'Gers fan you could be excused for believing that a terrible nightmare was unfolding in front of your very eyes! The only consolation for the bluenoses would be that if the Celts won then they would be saved from watching the 67 Lisbon Lions footage again!

But the atmosphere for the majority of the country was one of hope and anticipation. After a long winter, a very boring and disappointing election campaign and the terrible war in Iraq, we certainly needed something to cheer ourselves up. Our national team weren't doing anything for our self esteem and neither were the tales of the parliament building so we needed something!

It hadn't fully dawned on me that I would be travelling on a charter plane with the Celtic support! Don't ask me why that passed me by but it did, I was just desperate to be there. We were lucky enough as we have investors seats to get a ticket each (that's part of the deal for buying the "dear" seats) but that also explains my naivety about the fans. I tend to come and go from Celtic park and the mass of the fans don't know I am there. I don't like all the Rod Stewart celebrity fan stuff , but I am quite protected where I sit and the fans around us are used to us being there!! So the full impact of boarding the top deck of a jumbo jet to full applause and several cuddles and kisses was a bit of a shock. But the banter and the patter was worth it - though I didn't go to the lavvy for the entire flight, that heady combination of beer and pee was a bit much for me! The guys were hilarious, kind, generous and full of hope. All knew the importance of the journey win or lose. All knew that Porto were a very good side and the favourites , but all knew what this team were capable of.

I have fantastic memories - the beautiful cathedral, one of the nicest I have ever seen, though many fans will know it as the wall they slept against next to Flaherty's bar! The pipers in the street, the Porto fans and the Celtic fans taking turn about singing their songs in a Tapas restaurant much to the bewilderment of the Spanish diners! The hundreds of photographs I am in because the fans couldn't get a footballer or Billy Connolly so as the nearest available celebrity I was in them! The boys from Kilsyth (Lodge 39 they know who they are!) that we had breakfast with every morning. The feeling of fear and anticipation on the day of the match and on the way to the ground, the fact that you could taste the atmosphere in the stadium on that boiling hot, sticky night. The applause of the Celtic fans as Porto unveiled their beautiful banner in the crowd (slight embarrassment that Celtic FC seemed to have organised bugger all for their fans to do!).

And wonderment that this team and the wonderful Martin O'Neill, who had come so far were able to walk never mind run in the heat!! I'll never forget the feeling of having a heart attack for all of extra time.

But above all, the majesty that is Henrik Larsson. He was the one player who knew exactly what was at stake - the enormity of it all - the fulfilment of the dream, so many dreams. His second goal will stay with me forever. I could not and cannot believe that a human being could jump so high. I have thought he had wings in the past but he certainly won them that night. My heart broke for him more than anyone. How can you score two goals in a European Final and go home with a runner up medal. No justice.

The four mile walk back to the city from the stadium, like a defeated army after a battle. No histrionics. Thousands of us just walking and still dreaming of how close we had come. Yes we were gutted but unbowed and proud, distressed not at losing but at the manner in which Porto won. And the Real Betis fan who took pity on us as we walked the final mile to our hotel who said."Very sad. Your team should win," and gave us a lift at 3am, and refused to take money!

So thank you Celtic for letting us dream, for allowing us to lift our eyes and our hearts and look at the bigger picture and not at our naval. To allow us to celebrate who we are as Scots and football fans without the hatred of bigotry to sour it all. For a moment we glimpsed at who we could become. What a gift!"

Massive Celtic fan, JIM KERR also enjoyed the experiences' of Seville.

"WHAT was to be a relatively painless jaunt from Sicily to Seville hit a snag in the departure lounge at Barcelona, when we were told our final leg would be delayed for five hours.

Like everyone else, we just wanted to get to the party and this unexpected hitch was not on the agenda.

There was myself, my dad, my best friend and partner in the band Charlie Burchill and some of my Italian friends from Taormina, in Sicily. Annoyed by the hold-up I have to confess I began to let my frustration get the better of me and started to curse about the inconvenience of it all.

It was then that my old man brought me back down to earth with a few carefully chosen words of wisdom, which perhaps best sum up what the whole experience meant to the people of Celtic.

'Look just read a book,' he snapped. 'I've waited more than 30 years for this and you can't wait another five hours? Give us peace.'

For me, it was important to take my dad there, to repay him for taking me as a young boy to Celtic Park in 1967 to see the Lisbon Lions come back with the European Cup.

When the team flew out for Lisbon from Glasgow Airport all those years ago, I don't know how many times my dad shook his head because he was skint and we would have to miss it.

There was no way he was going to miss it this time.

It was also fantastic to be there with Charlie.

We grew up together in Toryglen, close to Hampden Park, and I remember fondly the night we stood on the slopes to watch Celtic beat Leeds in the 1970 European Cup semi final, a match which to this day holds the record for the largest attendance at a European tie when 135,826 of us squeezed into the old stadium.

We were only ten or eleven at the time, but we still talk about that match as though it was yesterday because it was such an enormous occasion.

To be honest, we've said on more than one occasion that we never thought we would feel the same way again about a game of football.

Then along came May 21st, 2003.

I've been in Sicily for a while now and since arriving, I've made a point of taking some of the local guys to Celtic Park - a particular pleasure since Martin O'Neill arrived on the scene.

In a strange way, they've become more impassioned than me. I took one of the them to the Juventus thriller which we won 4-3 and also the famous 6-2 win over Rangers. So whenever there's a big game when we might need a lucky charm, he gets wheeled out!

The lads compete in a local league in Sicily under the name AS Celtic Taormina and even wear the Hoops and the away strip, having really bought into the whole Celtic thing.

I think it's because they have never felt anything like the passion they experience while being among Celtic people. When they travel up to Turin to watch Juve, they find the stadium often just a quarter full and it's just not the same.

We finally arrived in Seville on the Tuesday evening and made for the centre of the city to soak up some of the atmosphere.

The scene outside the Irish bar Flaherty's next to the Cathedral was incredible.

The best way to describe it for me is to compare it to the Islamic haj, when hundreds of thousands make the pilgrimage to Mecca, the central pillar of Muslim devotion.

This was Celtic's haj! All those people in green and white crawling around outside, it was a sight to behold.

On the day of the game itself, I woke up early and sensed it was going to be a long, long day and a long, long match. I was right on both counts.

I've never been one for carrying a camera, even back in the days when Simple Minds were at their peak. I've just never bothered with one and have probably missed some great pictures as a result.

But that night I remember thinking, for the first time, how I wished I had one with me.

I found myself staring at the faces around me, faces from every age group and generation, faces of hope, faces of despair. Even if I didn't know them personally, I felt I knew them. People I grew up with, people who showed me how to grow up.

During the build-up to the game I would have been lying if I said I thought we were going to win. We were always going to need some luck.

Having said that, if there's a team that throws away the rule book, it's Celtic. There's no script, that's what makes them so thrilling.

When the game began and Porto began to press there was a certain fatality about it. It was only a matter of time, especially in the first half when I hoped we were just playing it cool on purpose, before hitting them hard in the second half.

Then they scored on the stroke of half time and that seemed to be it. The match was just going to peter out.

But that's when the rule book was chucked away, the script torn up, and we came roaring back.

At one stage during the game I nipped out to the toilet and was struck by how deserted the place was.

Here I am, so many people, so much noise, yet alone with my thoughts while a European final rages just yards from me. It was a strange feeling.

When I went back again during extra-time, the place was heaving with Celtic fans who couldn't bring themselves to watch.

The tension was that unbearable and we just didn't know what was likely to happen.

Then Balde went off and suddenly we knew what was going to happen after all.

There were so many great things that will live with me forever.

Like meeting big Billy McNeill at our hotel and watching him walk humbly to the back of the taxi queue, only for a chorus of voices to tell him: 'You've got to be joking! Get to the front.'

We stayed there for a couple of days after the match and met so many wonderful characters, from cotton workers, to philosophers, to second hand car salesmen, to dodgy cousins, you name it.

Great memories and let's hope it won't be long before we're all making a similar pilgrimage to another beautiful European city to watch Celtic compete with the best - and next time we'll come home with the trophy."

Chapter Eight

GOADED INTO GOING BY AN OLD RANGERS PAL

by Paul English

HALF an hour before kick-off, a giant, glitter-loaded party popper fired a shimmering stream of green and white high into the stifling Spanish air.

Klaxons blared, the crowd roared, rolling and billowing like a massive green and white quilt.

On stage at Puerto de Triana, a tall, skinny Scotsman wearing a kilt, baseball cap and a 1967 European Cup Winners commemorative Celtic t-shirt had just finished leading a charged crowd through another rendition of You'll Never Walk Alone.

"Good singing Seville," he congratulated them, punching beachballs back into the sea of scarves and flags. "Beautiful voices."

AT 9am on May 19 2003, I was the first customer through the door of Gentry barber's shop in the west end of Glasgow.

There was no-one else around, save for me, two barbers and a livewire Cocker Spaniel called Charlie.

I took my seat and sat, head bowed, launching into my barber's first inane chat of the day.

Property prices. Flat hunting. West end versus south side. Security firm turf wars. Parking tickets. Television. What did I think of Kelly Macdonald in State of Play last night? Football. Celtic. Larsson. Seville.

Did I have a ticket? No.

Where was I going to watch it? Port Glasgow.

Did I not fancy Seville? Not without a ticket.

Apparently, practically everyone who'd been in the shop in the last week, was going to Spain from Glasgow. According to my crimper, there was no contest. Seville was the only place to be.

Just then, as if to compound my discontent, a voice that had been teasing me for weeks came back to resume battle with my resolve.

"Is this you getting your hair cut for Seville then, mate?"

There was no escaping it. Not even in a deserted barber's shop, first thing on a Monday morning.

I didn't even turn to look at the guy who'd sat down in the next chair. Knew his voice right away.

I'd gone to primary school and grown up playing football with him.

Back then, as an impassioned 12-year-old, high on the euphoria of watching the Centenary Celts do the double, I knew this guy shouted for Rangers.

Now, 15 years later, and bizarrely high on the prospect of watching the Celts in Seville via a big screen in a social club managed by my dad in Port Glasgow, this former teenage team-mate was still torturing me.

"I'm flying out today at 4 o' clock," he said. "Enjoy the game mate. I'll text you the score..."

I sunk deeper into the chair, jealousy simmering.

Most folk, like him, get their hair cut before going off somewhere hot and sunny – Seville, for example.

Yet, here was me getting a crop before finalising my ticketless plans for a night with family and friends in a windowless hall in Inverclyde.

He'd been at it three days before as well. While buying an anniversary card in a shop at Braehead, my mobile phone vibrated with a new text message.

"You'll no' find a ticket in there, you know," it teased.

Walking out of the shop, I clocked his grinning mug, soon to deflate me with the news that he was odds-on to land a ticket for the game.

We chatted for 15 minutes or so, me voicing my disbelief that he was going to Seville, him voicing his that I wasn't.

Years ago, something had clicked in this guy. When he was old enough to think straight, he realised the error of his footballing ways.

Besides, I have since reasoned, it's natural for kids to be drawn to winners, and with Rangers dominating Scottish football in the late 80s and 90s, it was excusable for him to fall in line under peer pressure, finally being seduced by Celtic's charms during the entertaining – yet relatively fruitless – Burns/Stark era.

These days, he's a confirmed Hoops follower, and regularly texted me his half-time views on the Blackburn, Celta Vigo, Liverpool, Stuttgart and Boavista games as I sat in the stand.

Indeed, the day after we beat Boavista, he had booked his tickets and had called to ask me what flight I was on...

Yet here he was now, cruelly goading me about the turnaround in circumstances.

An ex-Rangers fan was going to text me the score from within the Estadio Olympico.

And that hurt like hell.

I headed into work that day with one aim - not to think about it.

But by 10.30am, the textual abuse had started. My pal Frannie was quaffing Cruzcampo on the continent. And so it went on. Gus was in Madrid, Ernest was en route to Heathrow, Neil was leaving Bearsden for a 17-hour journey, Kevin was by the pool in his Benidorm hotel, Brian had even clocked the UEFA Cup.

The hours dragged by. I overheard colleagues plan their late night trips that evening, and was asked several times when I was going, being met by muted surprise when I lamely explained I wasn't.

You'll Never Walk Alone? By this point, I was beginning to think I would. On Tuesday May 20, the day before the final, I would turn 27. Unbelievably, I half joked, no-one – not my sisters, parents, aunts, uncles, cousins, colleagues, anonymous benefactors, friends, or even enemies – had come up with a surprise ticket and travel package, having secretly organised time off with my boss.

Surely they were leaving it a bit late, I kidded them. After all, my dad had pulled a ticket for the 1989 Scottish Cup Final out the bag on the day of my 13th birthday... But this was to be too big an ask.

Resigned to watching the game from home shores, earlier that weekend I'd turned my attention towards pulling together a Seville-outfit involving a sombrero and a Celtic kilt. But this was fruitless too.

Sombreros in Glasgow were as elusive as tickets for the final itself.

Even at the Barras - where any other week you'd be able to find countless stuffed donkeys, sombreros and Espania '82 Panini World Cup sticker albums – there were none to be had. Bairds Bar had allegedly been selling them for £10 on Sunday. But they'd sold out by mid-day.

Acting on a trader's tip-off, I ended up standing on the road outside the market waiting for a man selling a batch from the back of his green Vauxhall Astra to come by and save the day.

I waited half an hour, accosting various motorists at the traffic lights in despration, before giving in and going home.

No ticket, no trip, no surprise birthday present, not even a sodding sombrero.

Monday continued to drag. More texts came from Spain, and people left work for the airport with good luck wishes and slaps on the back.

Then, at 5pm, my boss suddenly accused me of procrastinating.

Not on a professional level, thankfully, but a personal one. She couldn't believe I wasn't making the trip, and she couldn't give a toss about football.

"You can pay whatever it costs to get you to Seville on Wednesday and have the rest of your life to pay it off," she said.

"Or you can spend the rest of your life moaning that you never went. Make your own mind up."

Talk about motivating your staff. Putting it in those simple terms, and with the growing feeling that I was missing out on being part of the history that we sing about making our hearts go "whoah-oh-oh-oh", she'd flicked my spontaneity switch.

Forty-five minutes later, my name was on a plane ticket from Glasgow at 4.30am on Wednesday 21 May. My Andalucian adventure was about to begin. I was going to Seville.

Having got my hands on a kilt, and by now in posession of all sorts of green and white paraphernalia given to me as birthday presents from my sister (Tic Tacs, hats, chewing gum, bottles of water, beach balls) I arrived at Glasgow airport with thousands of other last-minute day trippers.

Dad, a veteran of the unsuccessful 1970 European Cup Final supporters brigade, dropped me at the airport.

All along he'd been overly-cautious, worrying that Sevillian authorities wouldn't be able to cope with the inlfux of fans.

But, as he drove off from the airport with my mother and sister in tow, tossing a chant-starting "C'mon the hoops" into the crowd collecting their tickets, I'm sure he wished he was coming with me.

After that night, Glasgow Airport will never seem the same again, having witnessed it heave with huge, snaking queues of green and white-clad men, women and children at the check-in hall.

From that early point in the journey, the whole world seemed to support Celtic.

From the fast-food bars and departure lounges of Glasgow Airport at 2.30am, to passport control at Malaga at 9am, you could count the number of people not wearing Celtic colours on your hands.

It was like a retro Celtic sportswear show, with strips from the '60s, '70s, '80s and '90s all being dusted down as if to give them their right to take part in this momentous occassion.

More striking still was the coach ride up the N340 from Malaga. Literally, every second car seemed to be racing north-east to Seville. Driving through the dusty planes in the bright sunshine it was a bizarre, yet truly heartening sight.

The man next to me on the bus commented that there were more cars with Celtic scarves and flags on the road than you would see on the M8 for a home game. True enough. As each flag-bearing car overtook our slowcoach, it felt as if a friend had just passed by.

A refreshment break at the equivalent of Harthill Services on the road "a Sevilla" drove home the enormity of the motorcade.

Everywhere were busses and cars, with thousands of thirsty fans queuing to stave off the dehydrating effects of searing 37 degree heat with, er, Cruzcampo beer.

Memorably, amid the mayhem stood an elderly Spanish couple, who'd stopped off to use the facilities.

Bewildered, they attempted to wind their way through the impenetrable singing throng, before stopping and simply staring at the scenes of green jubilation erupting around them.

Whether they made it to the loos or back to their cars is anyone's guess, although it's not beyond the limits of imagination to assume they were inadevertantly swept onto a coach, each given a curly green wig and flip flops and taken off to the biggest street party of their lives.

Who knows. Maybe they've since bought season tickets for Celtic Park. Arriving at midday, the initial sense of disorientation was numbed by the sight of so many Hoops on the streets.

Texts had been sent on arrival in Malaga, attempting to arrange meets with those already in Seville. But as the bus drew nearer our destination, mobile phone networks crashed under the weight of more than 80,000 visitors.

No matter. The last thing any lone Celtic fan in Seville felt on May 21 was alone.

Any ticketless day tripper need have known only three main locations –

Flaherty's bar, opposite the city's stunning Cathedral, the main square, and Puerto de Triana, where the game was being shown for Celtic fans on the big screen.

Wandering down the tree lined streets, amid the imposing Gothic architecture of the city, there was something eerie about the familiar echoing chants of CELTIC, CELTIC, CELTIC as they bounced off the ancient walls of the narrow streets. It's as if they came from one giant mouth, just around the next corner.

At Flaherty's came random meetings with old family friends, followed by more of the same with colleagues and relatives in the main square.

One day in Seville threw up more random meetings with familiar faces than any afternoon in Glasgow could. It was almost as though if you thought about someone hard enough, you'd suddenly see them waving a flag as they passed in the back of a horse and cart.

Celtic – the proud social institution, not just a club and its supporters – was everywhere.

Members of this all-inclusive society seemed to outnumber their Portuguese counterparts by 100-1.

That afternoon, this feeling alone was enough to inspire an incredible confidence. Surely we'd do it.

A calamitous succession of horse-drawn cart and taxi rides finally left myself and my mate John, who I'd met on the plane, at Puerto de Triana, the big screen venue.

We were early, but rumours had swept the main square that police had stopped letting fans in, so we arrived by six. And just as well.

You wouldn't believe it from some of the sights around the city, but, short of standing in a queue for an hour, beer wasn't so easy to come by that day in Seville.

And even then, if you did get to the front of the queue, the language barrier often proved insurmountable.

One punter, with a Glaswegian accent so thick you could build roads with it, found this to his disadvantage.

Omitting the "t" in water, he asked the cool Spanish barmaid at the tent in Puerto de Triana for "Two beer 'n' two waa'aaa."

He was, obviously, unsuccessful, and repeated the request twice more.

Finally, she understood, giving him two beers, but still not understanding the second part.

He tried again. "Two waa'aaa," he said.

Nothing.

"'Sake man. Waa'aaa. Waa'aaa! Waa'aaa! Waa'AAA!"

Finally, he reached over and lifted two bottles of water, gave the bemused girl her Euro vouchers, and made off muttering about how "they Spanish don't have a clue, man".

Meanwhile, at the food tent, Spanish hospitality broke new grounds. As several fans argued for their vouchers to be refunded having been given burgers that wurny cooked right, a defeated Spanish attendant started to throw bags of crisps and sandwiches out into the baying crowd, in a successful bid to beat them back. A good call.

With the park filling up, there was still space to be had at the side of the screen, so John and I made our way there to drink our beers.

A Beatles tribute band had left the mob a little nonplussed, and with kick-off approaching, the atmosphere needed geeing up.

This, at least, was the argument of a girl I'll only ever know as Ruth. I'd never seen her before, will probably never see her again, but I'll remember her for as long as I live.

As chance would have it, out of 25,000 fans, she approached me with the kind of request I'd only ever dreamt about.

"Can you sing Celtic songs?" she asked, which, considering I was dressed head to toe in green and white was a daft question.

"Then come up on stage and sing with me. The crowd need lifting."

Who she was, where she came from, and what she said to the Spanish security I'll never know.

But, seconds after meeting this girl, I was on stage, in front of 25,000 people all here to see Celtic.

My heart raced, I gasped for breath, took the microphone and let rip.

"Good evening Seville."

A cheer. Flags. Horns.

"We're going to sing some of your kind of songs now, okay?"

A louder cheer.

"Anyone with a scarf, a flag or anything green, I want to see it in the air for this one..."

As a set-opener for Celtic fans, they don't get much better than You'll Never Walk Alone

Starting in too high a note, my impromptu rock-God performance wasn't the best, so I turned the microphone on the crowd, pointed to them, and let them take their anthem's crescendo.

A huge plume of glitter exploded in the sky. Flags waved, scarves were held aloft. My heart bursting, I needed to let them know how good they were.

"Good singing Seville. Beautiful voices."

Roars. Green, white, gold, everywhere.

"Okay, let's see you jumping to this one....Hail! Hail! The Celts are here..."

As crowd-working goes, it wasn't a bad show. For the briefest of moments, as the massive sea of green and white bounced before me, I fantasised that I'd written The Celtic Song myself.

But then they pulled the plug on us, on the final line of the song, and the crowd carried it home.

Ruth and I walked offstage, totally charged, and took our places in the crowd for the kick-off.

Cloud nine is an unusual place to be at the start of a football match. But I was floating.

Henrik Larsson, and co kept me, and 25,000 others in Puerto de Triana up there for a while, before we finally climbed down.

But we did so with our pride and dignity intact, which is more than can be said for the brilliant, yet diving, time-wasting Portuguese winners.

As we walked away from the park after an incredible 120 minutes of emotion, I heard that voice again.

Only this time there was no teasing.

"I'm so glad you came for this," said my old hoop-clad chum from the barber's shop, tears welling in his eyes. "I'm so glad you made it."

I wouldn't have missed it for the world, mate.

Chapter Nine

A STRESSED OUT, HAPPY PROMO'S TALE

by Katrina Tasker

WHEN the final whistle blew to secure Celtic's place in the UEFA Cup final, my first emotion was one of sheer elation.

Then, after checking my husband Graham's blood pressure had dropped below the danger zone, reality kicked in.

As the longest serving member of the Daily Record's marketing team, I had been involved in some chaotic campaigns in my time, but something told me it had all been a practice run for what was to follow.

I was only eight years old when Celtic last reached a European final and I still remember my dad's early morning return from Milan - full of joy even in defeat.

Over the years I've marvelled at his memories from that trip – about the fantastic atmosphere and the characters he met along the way.

And we still have the photographs of him playing his bagpipes outside Milan Cathedral, amidst a sea of green and white hoops.

It had been a long time coming, but now Seville was about to provide more of those fantastic memories for the next generation of Celtic fans. On a professional level, a mild panic set in as I realised we had less than three weeks to arrange a Seville campaign.

The next morning the front page of the Daily Record screamed Here V Go above a fantastic picture of Henrik Larsson, arms outstretched, celebrating the fact that the V factor was taking Celtic all the way to Seville.

This strong image was to become the theme for the whole campaign.

After a brainstorm the next day where various crazy ideas were exchanged, I spent the weekend securing as many travel packages to Seville as I could for contest prizes.

As I was working on the Sunday, I took the opportunity to do some Seville research.

Thankfully the Sunday Mail printed a guide to the city for the thousands of Celtic fans who were planning their trip.

In it, was an interview with Gerry Enright, owner of Flaherty's Irish bar in the centre of Seville, about the forthcoming Celtic invasion.

As I glanced down at the picture of Gerry, resplendent in a See You Jimmy hat, little did I know that I had just encountered my very own Mr Fixit.

Together we would embark on a wonderful partnership which saw us fixing tickets for Rod Stewart, buying up the last green and white sombreros in Seville and making a few dreams come true along the way. I'm sure if Gerry had known what was in store for him – he'd never have taken my call.

Thankfully he did and as well as agreeing to Flaherty's becoming the Daily Record's Hoops HQ, he gave me contact names and numbers for all the people that became invaluable to me over the coming weeks.

One quick call to Gerry's friend Enrique who arranged the hire of his open top bus and all the permission required, and the Daily Record was most definitely on the road to Seville.

PRE-MATCH BUILD UP

Gerry very quickly became 'Our Man in Seville' and our daily phone calls ensured that the Daily Record didn't miss a trick out there.

It was at this point that our chief reporter Anna Smith, flew out to set up a Daily Record base over there.

Anna teamed up with Spanish journalist Franco Rey and photographer John Snowdon and quickly got cracking on some great stories as well as sussing out any available promotional opportunities.

Meanwhile the marketing team had gone into overdrive - sourcing and ordering all the giveaways and goodie bags which had to be designed, printed, packed and dispatched to Seville in time for the big match.

Two green and white Hoops HQ banners were sent out to Gerry who promptly hung them outside Flaherty's to welcome the very first Celtic fans arriving in search of tickets.

That Here V Go front page featuring Henrik Larsson was printed on the front of thousands of t-shirts with the victorious fixtures list on the back. Green banging balloons and green and white fans which looked like huge lollipops, were all ordered.

Souvenir posters and signs welcoming Celtic fans were printed up and goodie bags containing Coca-Cola, Walkers crisps and Tunnocks caramel wafers were hastily packed.

All had to be ready to leave on the Seville Express transit van the Friday before the match.

However, the jewel in our crown was the Henrikmobile.

A fantastic design featuring that huge Henrik photo and the Here V Go headline was created by our agency in Glasgow and dispatched to Jeronimo in Seville.

He arranged the printing of the image onto huge stickers which turned a very ordinary open-top bus into our spectacular Seville showpiece.

We even found time to make a few dreams come true as we gave away over 20 trips to Seville to lucky prizewinners.

Which brings me to Scotland's best brother, Raymond O'Donohue and his family from Coatbridge.

Raymond was the guy who won our Ultimate Trip to Seville contest with NTL. His prize was four trips to the match – two flying with the official Celtic party –a signed Celtic shirt and £500 spending money.

Much to our amazement, Raymond donated all the tickets to his delighted brothers and nephew, gave his money to charity and kept only the signed shirt for himself.

I had the pleasure of meeting Raymond, his mum, most of his seven brothers, sisters, nieces and nephews at their home, where I informed them of their good fortune.

This Celtic daft family were on their way to Seville, thanks to the Daily Record – and Raymond.

Meanwhile back in Seville, Anna and Gerry were making daily visits to the town hall informing officials that over 50,000 ticketless fans were planning to make the trip to Seville and that they really had to prepare for the invasion.

Eventually, with barely a week to go, the message got through and Gerry got permission to create a Celtic meeting point at the Puerta de Triana where fans could watch the match live on a giant screen. The Daily Record agreed to foot the cost of the screen to make this possible.

It was now the Friday before the big match and with everything loaded on to the Seville Express, it was time for me to head out and make it all happen. Although I was excited at the prospect, I dreaded being away from Jake, the three-year old light of my life. However with the promise of a sombrero and a big green balloon, I was granted leave.

I flew to Seville with big Bob Shields and photographer Mark Runnacles and our first stop was Flaherty's pub.

SQUAD MEETING

There we met up with Gerry who by now had become like a long lost friend, Anna, photographer John and a familiar looking man from my days as an El Dorado fan who turned out to be Franco Rey.

Franco played the doctor in El Dorado but his new role was as Anna's right hand man in Seville.

That night, we all went out for dinner where Anna and myself became aware that our male companions were otherwise distracted by the continual bevvy of pretty senoritas passing our table.

Now Anna and I scrub up quite well, but even we were beginning to feel like Maggie and Daphne Broon dropped onto a Baywatch set – thanks guys!!

Over the weekend I enlisted the help of American students, Erin and Kelly, and embarked on a whirlwind flyposting tour of Seville.

Before long, Henrik Larsson's jubilant smile was beaming from Daily Record posters on every street corner

During this time I had watched a trickle of green and white grow into a sea of hoops - and they all headed to Flaherty's.

The Hoops HQ was well and truly up and running.

On the Monday, there were meetings to attend regarding the giant screen, banners to put up, more fly posting to be done and green and white sombreros to stick Daily Record logos on to - all the sweltering Seville sunshine.

And in the midst of all the mayhem, I received a SOS from my boss Kirsten – could I get Rod Stewart two tickets for the match. A call to Gerry fixed that.

Then after another call from songwriter John McLaughlin, Gerry made it possible for John to take his dad Ignatius to the match.

This was the first time Ignatius had been abroad – he got his first- ever passport for the trip. I was delighted to be able to help.

I kept in daily contact with Michelle Mone who had an anxious Rod

Stewart checking that the tickets were sorted. I passed them onto to Michelle's hubby Michael when he arrived and he in turn gave them to Rod.

PRE-MATCH TRAINING

The best things are always worth waiting for and on Tuesday May 20, 2003 the Henrikmobile made its debut in Seville – and promptly broke down!

Thankfully a mechanic arrived and fixed the minor mechanical fault, which in turn kick -started my heart.

But that was only the beginning.

I will always remember this day as being the most stressful, hilarious and also amazing in my career.

Just imagine everything that could go wrong, going wrong, mix that with the language barrier and the sweltering heat, and it's welcome to the world of promotions.

Our team included myself, Bob, Mark, George Easton, our Deputy Circulation Director, Susannah – from the bus company, four young Spanish promotions girls, one highly excitable security man, a bus driver with a dreadful sense of direction and Jesus the driver of the people carrier.

Now Jesus had to be drafted in at the very last minute when Susannah informed me that although this was a bus – it couldn't actually carry passengers. It only had a license to drive around and look fantastic.

This is the minor detail that I would have appreciated knowing before we hit the road, so to speak, but hey, when in Spain.

Anyway once the bus was on the road again, we toured the usual tourists haunts of Seville looking for Celtic fans.

Susannah was confused – where were they all.

At Flaherty's of course – which just happened to be the most impossible place to park a Henrikmobile in Seville.

And this is where the fun began as we embarked on a comedy of errors which the Keystone Cops would have been proud of.

It went something like this – the bus stops, the girls stock up with Daily Records, free sombreros and t-shirts and set off to Flaherty's where they sell out in minutes.

Back they dash to refill and lo and behold the bus moves off without warning.

Now you would expect the local bus driver to know his way around Seville – wrong.

I'm sure this one learnt to drive on the Whirlies roundabout in East

Kilbride.

Eventually he arrives back, the girls stock up and we get the show on the road again - but not for long.

I instruct the driver (in pigeon Spanish and sign language of course) to make a quick detour to enable him to park on the opposite side of the road so Mark can get the picture he wants. Bob Shields decides to stay on board to keep the bus in his sights.

Mark and I breathe a sigh of relief and keep watch for the Henrikmobile after it's swift u-turn.

Unfortunately the driver decides to take Bob on an extended city tour before the bus breaks down again.

With the stressometer reaching breaking point, I call Jeronimo, we make a quick substitution for a driver who both knows his way around town and how to fix a bus, and the Henrikmobile duly returns with a frazzled looking Bob Shields on board.

At this point there are no words written, no pictures taken and the normally unflappable Bob Shields is looking very flapped. Even Jesus is clean out of miracles.

As if by magic, Jeronimo appears and arranges permission to park in the Plaza San de Francisco, behind Flaherty's.

In a matter of minutes with 'Hey Henrik' blasting from the sound system, the Henrikmobile has finally arrived in Seville.

Delighted Celtic fans hop on-board, snap up our sombreros and pose for the great pictures that contradict the trauma we had all ensued to get them.

A few snaps of fans cooling off in the fountain later, and Mark and Bob depart to file copy and pictures, leaving George, the girls and me to hand out the papers and the freebies.

Meanwhile on the top of the bus the Flamenco show is in full swing and quick as a wink, the Celtic fans try out the fancy footwork for themselves.

The dancers repay the compliment by shaking their castanets along to 'Hey Henrik' – just one of the many magical moments that was Seville.

I then received a call from STV who wanted to film Scotland Today live on match day from the top of the Henrikmobile – they had witnessed for themselves what a big attraction it had become.

That evening I was joined by my parents who travelled down from their holiday in the Algarve to join in the carnival atmosphere. My husband had also flown out that day with 10 friends to join the green and white invasion.

MATCH DAY

The big day had arrived and with it came the biggest number of day-trippers Seville had ever seen.

I met John McLaughlin and his dad Ignatius to hand over their tickets and as a thank you, John led the Celtic sing-song from the top of the Henrikmobile.

Our DJ kept the party going with a succession of Celtic classics, the piper played the Fields of Athenry and Scotland Today beamed the whole thing live to the stay at home fans in Scotland.

With temperatures soaring, the girls kept everyone cool by handing out our green and white fans, along with maps directing those without tickets to the Puerta De Triana where they could watch the match live on the Daily Record's giant screen.

A steady succession of fans boarded the bus – everyone wanted their photo taken on or beside the Henrikmobile. That was after I got them past our highly excitable security man who was trying to get them to form an orderly queue.

And as far as the eye could see, thousands of Celtic fans filled the Plaza de San Francisco to join in the Daily Record party.

Amidst all this chaos, I was delighted when my colleague John arrived to provide much needed back up and to buy gallons of water for the team.

When the fans started heading for the stadium, the Henrikmobile travelled on to the Puerta De Triana where thousands had gathered to watch the match.

My parents had planned to watch the match there, but as the heat got the better of them, decided to head back to either Flaherty's or the apartment instead.

Their taxi had just pulled off, when I bumped into Gerry and his son Darryl – a chance encounter for which I will be eternally grateful.

With all hands to the beer pumps, Gerry and Darryl had realised that there was no way they were going to get away to see the match - and gave me their three tickets to take my folks.

With my heart already racing, I ran to look for a taxi which by this stage were thin on the ground.

Just then one pulled up to drop off some Celtic fans.

I reached the taxi just as another Celtic fan was asking the driver to take him back to the city centre.

Now I'm a great believer in fate, and being in the right place at the right time   - and so that is how I came to meet Brian Murphy from Kirkintilloch.

Brian offered to share the taxi with me, and as we chatted about the whole wonderful experience, Brian told me that he hadn't got a ticket and that he was hoping to catch the match on a pub TV.

In that short taxi ride, I was touched by just how genuine a person Brian was and also how much Celtic meant to him.

And I also knew how much one of the three tickets I was clutching would mean to him.

In a special moment that I will remember all my life, I gave Brian one of the tickets Gerry had given me.

I will never forget the look on his face as his mind raced to cope with the fact that it wasn't a wind-up and then the sheer emotion when he realised he was going to the match.

All we had to do now was find my dad.

Brian stayed in the taxi as I fought my way through a packed Flaherty's with no success, before we sped off to my apartment.

Another magical moment took place when I told my dad we were going to the match and rushed him to the waiting taxi.

When the driver saw our tickets, he sped off on two wheels and got us to the Estadio Olimpico just as the half-time whistle blew.

As the three of us walked along, Brian laughed out loud and yelled with joy in between phoning his friends and family at home to tell them that 'this wee lassie from the Daily Record' had given him a ticket.

At this point we split up as Brian's ticket was for Section B and my dad and I were in Section C.

We settled in our seats in time for the second half, and the wonderful sight and sounds in the stadium were just awesome.

It was also really special for me to be sharing the experience with my delighted dad.

There was a real feeling that this was Celtic's night and with each of Henrik's two equalisers, I really thought we could do it.

As the minutes ticked away in the second half of silver goal time, I could take the pressure no longer and headed outside to say a few prayers.

And it was at this point that I bumped into Rod Stewart.

As I was concentrating on asking God for a few favours, a lift door opened and out popped Rod, only to be whisked back in sharpish when his people realised they were on the wrong floor.

Rod will never know how close he came to that 'wee lassie from the Daily Record' who arranged his tickets.

I got back to my seat, just as Porto scored their third goal and even after that, the Celtic fans refused to give up their dream as they sang their hearts out to the final whistle.

And then the crowd broke into 'Over and Over' to honour Martin O'Neil and his team and to remind us all what it means to be a Celtic supporter. Even now, it feels like Celtic won – such was the strength of feeling in Seville.

It was an honour to have been there.

From the Henrikmobile where we rallied the thousands of Celtic faithful, to that special moment when I gave Brian Murphy a ticket for the match, Seville was a truly magical experience.

Even in the midst of over 50,000 strangers you felt you had a friend on every corner.

And now with Seville playing host to the 2005 Champions League Final, there's always the chance that we can do it all over again to look forward to.

Chapter Ten

THE HENRIKMOBILE AND MEMORABLE FANS

by Bob Shields

HOOPS fans will one day talk about Seville in the same way Hippies talk about the Sixties. "If you can remember it - you weren't there . . ."

You couldn't blame a visitor from Mars for thinking the big sporting event in town that week wasn't a football final but some kind of Lager Olympics.

I recall one Celtic fan greeting his newly arrived friend on the Plaza Espana.

"What's Seville like?" asked the breathless newcomer.

"It's Swally Town!" slurred his mate.

Seville boasts more boozers per head than any other Spanish city. And the Celtic supporters somehow sniffed out every single one of them.

In the rare event there wasn't a pub within a hundred paces in any direction - they'd sit down in the sun with their carry-outs and open their own.

On the day before the game, one of these informal watering holes was set up . . . on the grass of a major roundabout.

It was a little island of Bhoys and bevvy in a noisy, fume-filled seething sea of cars, buses, trucks, taxis and scooters.

The Scottish equivalent would be throwing a barbie on the central reservation of the M8.

Kids being driven home from school hung out car windows and pointed at the largely topless group of lads, swilling and sunbathing in the heart of the traffic.

Then came a peeping of horns and the short blast of a police siren.

The police van, lights flashing, dodged through the car lanes and finally pulled up on the little grassy island.

Having some smattering of the local lingo - I decided to risk the six lanes of crawling cars and see if the lads need any help.

I could explain to the police - if needed - that these were harmless lads having a few drinks and would move on if requested.

I got trapped in a succession of lorries and buses and lost sight of the island for a few minutes. I had visions of some hapless Hoops being herded in handcuffs onto the meat wagon.

But as I made a dash to reach them, I saw the police van pull away . . . with the Celtics lads merrily drinking away as normal.

"Eh . . . any bother with the cops there, boys?" I asked.

"Nae bother pal," said one. "They were just saying there were no litter bins here and gave us some bin bags to take our empties away . . " he added, waving a sheaf of black plastic sacks.

I could think of a dozen European cities, including London, where they'd have been huckled on the spot. But this reaction from the police in Seville lifted my heart.

I was in a taxi about two hours later and, by chance, happened to pass to very same roundabout.

There wasn't a Celtic fan to be seen. Or an empty beer can. My heart was lifted again.

On arrival in Seville, I had wandered the streets near my flat and stumbled on a pub called "The Trinity", in the ground floor of the posh Hotel Inglitera.

It was a faked up Irish pub but they sold Guinness and Bacardi and had air conditioning - which instantly made in my Spanish 'Pub of the Year'.

There wasn't a hooped jersey to be seen and I was confident this cosy little cocktail bar could be my hideaway from the all madness I knew was about to ensue.

No chance. By Sunday night, every second accent was a Scottish one.

And by Monday, the joint was jumping with Hoops.

It was here I met Arthur and May from Glasgow. Taxi driver Arthur had got his seats from the Internet before Celtic had even qualified for the final. It was a gamble that paid off.

"We got our tickets and booked our flights and hotel as soon as we could. Of course, Celtic being here was the icing on the cake," Arthur told me.

"But we'd still have been here if it had been a Boavista v Porto final. We booked it as a holiday with a bit of football in the middle".

Arthur and his wife travel everywhere with Celtic. When Arthur went to the toilet, I asked May, with all due respect, how they could afford to follow the team around Europe on a cabbie's wages.

"He works all the hours God sends him," she told me. "And when he goes back from Seville, he'll be out driving all sorts of shifts to help pay for this trip - and start saving for the next one."

Photographer Mark Runnacles joined us and Arthur overheard us discussing a potential problem with telephone lines to "wire" pictures.

Our flat was a temporary let with no telephone link. We were talking about possible alternative locations around the city centre.

"So, what do you need?" asked Arthur.

"A room with a telephone jack-point," we explained.

"Then use mine, it's just upstairs," he said.

It was a generous offer. But we had to point out that several Daily Record photographers might need to send pictures. And well into the night.

"Och, we'll be out celebrating anyway. It's no bother if it helps you lads out," he smiled.

Mark and I were confident we'd get access to an office building nearby. We'd already checked it out and the owner seemed happy.

But in an emergency, Arthur's offer could be a lifesaver.

We thanked him and explained that if we did need his telephone line, we'd pay for all our calls and give him a payment for his inconvenience.

"Listen lads, you don't need to pay me anything. If there's a few quid going spare, I'd rather you gave it to charity. I'm not helping you out for any money," he insisted.

Outside the hotel, a couple of hundred quid was the difference between getting a ticket or not. Arthur's generosity of spirit was quite touching.

We met again several times and Arthur and his wife were great company. My only regret is that I didn't get their surnames. It hardly seemed important at the time.

If they read this, I'd be delighted to share a drink with them again. But

Arthur, I can't guarantee those Spanish measures!

If my week in Seville had one drawback - it's that I was there to work! If I'd gone for a beer with everyone who invited me, even a month in Seville wouldn't have been long enough.

But for some folk, like old friends, it would be rude not to make a wee exception.

There was Joe "The Goose" O'Donnell. He's propped up the 'podium' at the Daily Record's "Copy Cat" pub even longer than I have.

When we met at the Hotel Ingletera, the bar was heaving, so we sat in giant leather armchairs in the marble reception like a couple of Arab potentates on their thrones.

While the rest queued ten deep just to see the bar, Joe and I, the men who would be kings, were served cold beers and bowls of nuts by men with black ties and silver salvers.

I had a gargle or three with Ian and Alan Adie. They run a merchandising business in Glasgow and are champions league drinkers and storytellers. I enquired after the third musketeer, their brother William.

"In his bed, blootered," said Ian. But any meeting with the Adie mob has always been a bit like that Meat Loaf song. Two out of three ain't bad.

I ran into Don Lawson, mine host at the famous Johnny Foxes watering hole in Inverness. And Calum Fraser, better known to Madonna and the Tartan Army as "Spud the Piper".

Don is a sober, serious businessman . . . until you put him in a kilt. Then he's crazier than a bag of squirrels. In a tiny bar full of locals - he insists on buying everyone a drink. No-one turns down The Don.

Spud tours the world playing his pipes - from society weddings in Colorado to whisky tastings in Tokyo.

He can play drunk or sober, asleep or awake, vertical, horizontal or even upside down. And in any combination.

In one street, like a scene from Romeo and Juliet, young office girls thronged onto a wrought iron balcony to see the handsome piper in full highland dress serenading them from below.

From the giggling above, you could tell all the girls were wondering what he was wearing under his kilt.

And from Spud's skyward grin, you could tell he knew exactly what they were wearing under theirs.

I met fellow journalist and namesake Tom, who has travelled widely through Spain - or should that be through Spain widely?

He takes me to a wonderful local bar where the tables are old sherry casks and the barman counts your drinks with chalk marks on the counter.

It's just a few hundred yards from Hoops HQ, Flaherty's, and I wonder how they'll cope when the real Celtic hordes arrive.

But the next day, the bar is closed. And it doesn't open again until the Friday.

This was a pub that probably hadn't changed in over fifty years. And they wanted to keep it that way.

Probably the easiest part of my job in Seville was looking for "stories". You didn't have to look hard - there was a good tale to be told around every corner, in every street cafe and on every bar stool.

Three lads who gave me a real laugh were New Jersey boys Ian Gilmartin and Rob McCourt of Kearny Celtic Supporters Club and their mate from Manhattan Celtic Supporters Club, Frank McDonald.

Sadly, some American employers don't seem to appreciate the importance of Celtic playing in a Euro final.

So poor Frank had to tell a couple of pork pies to make sure he got the time off work.

"I told them a close relative had died," he explained, "And I had to return to Scotland for the funeral".

So why were Frank and his mates hiding in a quiet, darkened pub instead of larking with the lads in the Seville sunshine?

"Well, if I go home with a sun tan, the boss will know right away I haven't been to Scotland. So we hide in pubs until it's dark - then we really come out to play", he laughed.

The North American lads went on to tell me about the "Garage Boys" - who are a legendary supporters club based in Fresno, California.

"There's just the three of them - but they're Celtic daft," they said.

"Over there, the games are all in the middle of the night. So they all meet at 3.00 am or whenever in a garage at the foot of a garden.

"The garage is a shrine to Celtic with posters and pictures. And they've got a fridge full of cold beers. They just train their satellite dish on whichever channel in showing Celtic and they don't surface again until daylight!"

Just around the corner were three wonderful ladies - let's just say they were in their senior years - all in their hooped tops and having a ball.

It turns out Celtic daft Catherine Wightman, 58, from Alexandria, had got herself a ticket in the Parkhead ballot.

And there was no way she was going miss out. Even if she had to travel all by herself.

When her sisters Mary, 78, and Margaret,70, heard this - they decided they had to come along as well. To look after Catherine, of course.

"She might be 58 - but she's still our wee sister," said Margaret.

"We've looked after her since she was in her pram - and we decided she couldn't some to Seville on her own.

"So she's here - and her big sisters are here to keep a wee eye on her," she smiled.

There was Jimmy Grier from the "Top End Tims" - the Celtic fans from Darwin, at the "top end" of Australia.

The Celtic match had brought Jimmy and his brothers Johnny, Charles and Colin together for the first time in 22 years.

And there was Jim Kerr of Simple Minds fame. His dad had taken him to Celtic Park to see the European Cup when Jock Stein brought it home after Lisbon.

Thirty six years and a couple of million albums later, it was Jim's turn to treat his old dad to witness a little bit of Celtic history, Marvellous stuff. On the day before the match, I had to drag myself away from all these stories - to visit a top secret garage on the outskirts of town.

One of my original ideas had been to take the Daily Record's famous Tartan Bus to Seville. But doubts remained if the bus we used for our Tartan Army adventures would be truly appropriate for a game involving one half of the Old Firm.

And there was another thing. Some people thought the old tartan war-horse wouldn't make it as far as the south side of Glasgow . . . never mind Seville.

It was decided we'd hire a bus in Seville and have it specially decorated with Celtic in mind. My job was to get it out on the streets and write about the fans' reaction.

On the Monday, a rival newspaper arrived with their bus. But I was relieved to see it had no special reference to Celtic or Seville.

And from what I'd been told - the Daily Record bus would look spectacular and beat anything ours rivals could offer.

But by Monday afternoon, it has still not been completed. I travelled to the garage where a team of locals were applying a giant Henrik Larrson vinyl to the coach. Strips of Henrik was hanging everywhere - bits of his hands and feet were lying on the floor.

"How much longer?" I tried to ask in Spanish.

"Six hours - maybe more." they said.

Meanwhile, our marketing and promotion people, led by Katrina Tasker, had brought masses of goodie bags with sombreros, T-shirts and other give-aways.

After a chat with Katrina, it was decided there was no point in launching our "Henrikmobile" in the darkness of evening.

Tuesday would be H-Day.

We were waiting by the riverside near the Toro D'Oro when it finally arrived in all its glory. A 30 feet long Henrik adorned either side. The hours of work had paid off. The bus looked fantastic.

It got huge cheers from Celtic fans - many of whom adopted the "we're not worthy" pose and bent over to hail with outstretched arms this giant version of their hero.

We boarded the bus and headed for the city centre - getting huge cheers from fans all the way.

We were just passing a busy square when the bus lurched to a lifeless halt. The driver made several unsuccessful attempts to get it re-started. Finally, he threw up his hands and began rambling in Spanish down his mobile phone.

The local police came by and sped off again after the driver explained he's broken down but called for help.

It was embarrassing enough - but then I spotted our rival bus at the other end of the busy square.

There's no quarter shown as this level of the newspaper business. They would happily splash a photo of our broken down bus all over their pages.

I dashed out to shut the engine compartment. If no-one was fiddling with the engine, it might look as if we were stuck in traffic - or stopped deliberately just for effect.

Then I ran back upstairs to see if where the rival bus had gone. But keeping my head down of course, I didn't want to appear in a rival paper either!

It was like being stuck in a stricken submarine, waiting for an enemy frigate to come broadside and open fire.

And every few minutes I would "up telescope" with my head for a quick look - then disappear below decks again.

Thankfully, we got away with it. The bus was repaired about 40 minutes later and we were back on our way.

On match day, we took it to the Plaza Espana where some 25,000 fans had gathered.

Jim Delahunt did some TV stuff from the roof. "Spud the Piper" played a few tunes and Don Lawson, kilted and topless, belted out his own unique treatment of the "Fields of Athenry."

As a finale, the Celtic fans raised their scarves for a mighty rendition of "You'll Never Walk Alone".

The sight of all those Hoops in that magnificent and historic square in Seville will stay with me forever.

I had a fantastic seven days in Seville . . . but the Hoop madness had clearly got to me.

As we packed on the last morning, snapper Mark Runnacles asked me if I always sang while taking a shower.

"You were belting it out big time," he laughed, "the whole street could hear you".

"What was I singing, anyway?" I asked.

"Something about Henrik Larrson being the King of Kings", he said.

And he wasn't joking. It was time to leave town.

Chapter Eleven

THE PILGRIMAGE AND THE TEARS

by Thomas Smith

SEVILLE Airport was in tears.

As we waited by the conveyor belt, a Celtic fan produced her bagpipes from the cases and bags that were snaking their way through.

Within seconds, the entire building was filled with the sounds The Fields Of Athenry.

I've heard that song hundreds of times, in many places, but this was different.

Without exception, every fan had tears in their eyes, myself included.

No words were spoken. There was no need.

The wave of emotion that had descended upon us, in an instant, said it all.

Win or lose, we knew we were standing on the verge of something historic.

There's a danger we can over-dramatise our memories as we look back on our individaul journeys.

But those of us fortunate enough to be in Seville that Sunday evening before the final will know exactly what I mean.

Until then, Celtic had only ever reached two European finals in their history.

This was their third - and we had just arrived to witness it.

My pilgrimage began the moment John Hartson scored the second at Anfield.

While the Celtic players were still congratulating the goalscorer, my mobile phone rang.

My friend and colleague, Brian McIver, screamed down the phone: "Thomas, let's get to Seville! Let's just book up and go!"

Before the Celtic players had even got back into their own half for the game to restart, we had made up our minds to go to the UEFA Cup Final. From that moment, we were determined to be there.

Within a few days, we were booked up for a four-night stay in Seville.

Many people thought we were crazy spending our cash before Celtic had even played the semi-final.

But even if Celtic didn't make it, we would still enjoy one of the top matches on the footballing calendar.

And if they did, we had already booked our place at a game every Celtic fan in the world wanted to be at.

So when Henrik Larsson scored against Boavista, our faith was repaid.

We didn't even have tickets for the game.

But we would worry about that later. We were on our way to Seville.

I refer to the journey as a pilgrimage because it was like no ordinary trip.

We flew out to Spain on the Sunday morning, three days before the match.

On the way to Glasgow Aiport, there was car after car with Celtic flags and scarves hanging out of the windows and sunroofs - and this was 4am in the morning!

The terminal building was just as colourful.

Hundreds of fans waited at check-in desks, dressed in sombreros and Celtic shirts.

Arriving at Gatwick Airport to collect our connecting flight to Seville, we noticed another example of the phenomenon that is Celtic.

Seeing that no Celtic shirts were on sale at a sports shop in the terminal building, we asked staff why this was the case.

Their reply was simple: "We're sold out!"

As we waited at the departure gate to board our flight to Seville, an announcement was made over the public address system.

"Would passengers Smith and McIver please make themselves known to British Airways staff at the security desk."

Fearing the worst, myself and my colleague approached the desk.

Although neither of us said anything at the time, we were terrified something terrible had happened to halt our epic adventure.

But to our amazement, staff informed us that due to a fault with our seats, they had no other option but to upgrade us to Club Europe!

Now football fans are a very superstitious bunch.

The moment we heard this it was like a sign, an omen that only good things were destined to happen on this trip.

When we boarded the aircraft and spent the next two hours having our champagne glasses topped up on demand, we were certain Celtic were going to lift the trophy.

Arriving in Seville, the first thing I did was have my passport stamped. It read: 'Sevilla 03'.

This may not seem like the most important goal on a journey such as this.

But in years to come, that small ink stamp would be tangible proof that I had been there for one of Celtic's proudest moments - again, regardless of the final result.

The moment I laid eyes on the Estadio Olimpico, I wondered if this stadium was soon to be held in the same regard as the National stadium in Lisbon.

It wasn't the most striking football arena I had ever seen.

To be honest, from the outside it looked more like a giant tax office.

But none of that would matter at kick-off time on Wednesday evening.

During the drive into town, I was amazed to see hundreds of Celtic fans settling into the city as if they had been there for years.

We thought we had arrived early, but these guys looked so at home that they were almost like locals dressed in Celtic shirts.

All along the road fans were standing around in groups singing Celtic songs, next to the fountains, in many of the city's remarkable plazas, or sitting at the many pavement cafes, bars or restaurants.

Not for the first time, and certainly not for the last time in the coming days, I battled hard to hold back the tears.

Thousands of Celtic fans standing in the sunshine, preparing for a European final. Was it real?

But it wasn't a dream. There were pockets of Celtic fans everywhere.

Strangers greeted each other like long-lost brothers, happy to welcome more Hoops fans to the party.

I have to admit to feeling very privileged.

Celtic fans all over the world would have given their last penny to be where I was at this moment.

Many had done just that. That was the humbling part.

People who didn't have much, spent what little money they had getting here,

You could see it on their faces, in their eyes.

This meant so much to them.

There was an overwhelming sense of pride and achievement at finally returning to football's top table to dine with the big boys.

Every Celtic fan knew that the eyes of the world would be on us.

Fans of every European club would now sit up and take notice of Glasgow Celtic.

Even the top players would be forced to look at this mass exodus of Celtic fans from their native countries to the south of Spain.

We were representing the club every bit as much as the players were and we were determined to put on a show that would be revered for generations.

The Daily Record headquarters had been set up at Flaherty's Bar, next to Seville's magnificent cathedral.

When we arrived at around 6pm on Sunday evening, there were around 1,000 Celtic fans singing and dancing in the sunshine.

And they weren't sung like songs at Parkhead, where sections of the stadium burst into song at different points throughout the match.

Here in Seville, everyone joined in.

Even tourists who just happened to be in the city and got caught up in the surge of emotion.

The feeling and atmosphere was so intense that I felt compelled to call my family and friends to somehow let them share the experience, if only at the other end of a telephone line.

Just then, a sudden thought struck me - if this is what it's like three days before the final, what will it be like on match day?

The answer to that question would quickly be rammed home to me many times over the next few days.

Almost every hour brought another wave of Celtic fans into the city.

The stories of how they got here were even more remarkable than the fans themselves.

Many had flown via countless airports in different countries just to arrive in Seville.

Others had made the journey by car, over land and sea.

Despite the different modes of transport, everyone agreed with one principle. They just had to be here.

Monday and Tuesday saw tension build in anticipation of the match itself.

I met family and friends, many of whom I hadn't seen in years.

But no matter who I met, they all shared that same look of awe and amazement at the scale of what we were witnessing.

Despite the sweltering heat, the Celtic fans did their best to keep hydrated.

At 2pm on the Tuesday before the match, I watched three of Scotland's finest sitting on deck chairs outside Flaherty's Bar.

One of the guys handed out plastic cups, into which he poured straight vodka.

No ice, no cold drink to ease it down. Just neat vodka in the afternoon sun.

That image was to be repeated in various different forms over the next few days.

With just over 24 hours to go before the match, we stopped at a pavement cafe for a drink.

A Celtic fan then informed us that the UEFA Cup was on display just around the corner.

Moments later we were having our picture taken alongside the famous trophy.

Match day was like nothing I have ever experienced.

We arrived in the city centre at around lunchtime and the moment I saw the crowds around the cathedral and lining the streets, I immediately realised that there was no word in the English language to accurately describe the scene.

Thanks to the thousands who had jetted into Seville on day trips for the match, the already massive crowd had almost doubled overnight.

There has been much debate as to how many fans actually travelled.

Official UEFA and Spanish police estimates put the Celtic crowd at around 65,000.

But there were no less than 80,000 fans in Seville on the day of the final.

I have been to Celtic Park many times and know what a 60,000 crowd looks like.

This was much bigger than that.

The city was seething, teeming with fans.

They were dancing in the fountains and on top of statues in football's equivalent of Mardi Gras.

At this point, we had given up hope of getting a ticket for the match.

The cheapest price we had been quoted was 600 Euros each from the touts.

We had resigned ourselves to watching the match on one of the big screens around the city.

But as we walked back to our hotel three hours before kick-off, my mobile phone rang.

It was my friend Angela McCormack, who I went to school with.

Her words rooted me to the spot: "I've been trying to reach you all day - I've got you a ticket for the game."

I stood in silence for a few moments in the middle of the street, completely numb.

I was going to the match, I was actually going to the match!

Angela was in Seville with her husband Gerald and his aunt and uncle Lorraine and Colin Martin.

Colin had managed to get his hands on a spare ticket and asked Angela if she knew of any 'deserving causes'.

But due to a fault in the mobile phone network in the days leading up to the match, they couldn't contact me to see if I still needed a ticket.

I had come that close to missing out on the big game.

Thankfully, they waited more than 24 hours before finally reaching me.

I will be forever in their debt for giving me the chance to be at that match.

The next hour was played out in fast-forward.

Brian, my mate, didn't have a ticket and my delight was tempered by that reality.

But at no point did I think that he wouldn't be going to the match with me - even though it was now just a few hours before kick-off.

Now that we had a ticket at cost price, we could easily afford to split the cost of a ticket from the touts.

And that's exactly what we did.

We raced back to our hotel and made the necessary arrangements.

Ten minutes later we were on our way to the stadium.

It was the stuff of fairytales.

At 4pm we were all set to miss one of Celtic's greatest days.

An hour later we were getting ready to set off for the stadium.

I still didn't have my ticket and had agreed to collect it outside the stadium.

But because of the mobile phone networks being down, I still hadn't arranged a meeting place.

Despite this, we set off on foot for the stadium.

We couldn't get a taxi and the shuttle buses laid on for the fans were packed full.

That meant we had no other option but to embark on a five-mile speed march in 110-degree heat.

We eventually arrived at the Estadio Olimpico an hour before kick-off. Both of us were totally exhausted.

But thankfully, my contacts reached me on the mobile phone and we met up outside the stadium.

After a few emotional group hugs and pictures, we each went our separate ways, as our tickets were for different parts of the stadium. Mine was for the Porto end.

As I was making my way around to the entrance gate, a white truck pulled up and out jumped a group of Spaniards.

Moments later they were throwing cans of Irn Bru at the thirsty Celtic fans on their way into the stadium.

As I entered the turnstile, a member of the security staff took my ticket from me and held it under an ultra-violet light for authentication.

A moment later, a green light lit up on top of the barrier and I walked into the stadium.

The feeling of relief was overwhelming.

As I climbed the stairs and walked out into the Porto end of the stadium behind the goals, all I could see was two tiers of blue and white, from corner flag to corner flag.

I looked down onto the pitch and the Celtic players were out for their warm-up.

Just then, I raised my head and saw a sight that nearly took my legs from under me.

Three sides of the stadium, both top and lower tiers, were completely covered in green and white.

Celtic had taken over 75 per cent of the entire ground.

Just then, the Coldplay song 'Clocks' started playing on the stadium sound system.

I remember looking around the stadium thinking that life couldn't get much better than this.

As kick-off approached I spotted a barrier separating the Celtic and Porto fans.

Making sure, there were no security guards around, I jumped the barrier and climbed in among the Celtic fans.

I then made my way along to the half way line to take up a perfect seat at the rear of the lower tear.

Very few people were sitting in the exact seat number printed on their tickets and it was easy to sit where you wanted.

Just then, I noticed a mum and her three sons sitting next to me.

The boys all had full Celtic kits on with the name 'Sutton' on the back.

Next to them I noticed another youngster sitting with his mum with the name 'Larsson' on the back.

I then realised I was sitting in the section reserved for the Celtic players' wives and families.

As kick-off approached, I started chatting to fans sitting next to me.

One guy had travelled from Boston, in the United States, another from Rio, and another guy had made the journey from Perth, Australia.

That's how much this match meant to people.

When the teams walked out, the roof nearly lifted off of the stadium.

The noise was then even greater when Celtic went into their famous huddle.

Sounds of 'Walk On' were deafening and I hoped beyond hope that we could do it.

A few minutes before half-time, I left my seat to get a drink of water, as I was still dehydrated after my speed march in the blistering heat.

When I heard the roar of the Porto fans, my heart sank.

Normally I would have hated to miss a goal at a football match.

But this time I didn't care.

I still haven't seen it and probably never will.

Moments later, before the half-time whistle was blown, I saw Henrik Larsson's wife Magdalena and his son Jordan walking along the corridor.

I had heard that she didn't always watch her husband playing football and so the tension must have become too much for her.

But as she walked along holding her young son's hand, Larsson-junior was at her side kicking an empty water bottlet with his left foot.

I'm not joking when I say the boy showed remarkable skill for his age - and goodness knows what he might manage with an actual ball!

After the match was over, I stayed in the stadium until the last Celtic player had left the pitch.

As Martin O'Neill led the players around the pitch to salute the fans, I finally cracked.

Four days worth of emotion spilled over in an instant.

It wasn't supposed to end like this. But it had.

But at least we had reached this level and enjoyed the occasion.

No one could take that away from us.

That night, I realised even more just how big a sacrifice people had made to get to Seville.

Many were sleeping on the streets. Just happy to be here, whatever conditions they had to endure.

As I discussed the match with friends over a beer later that night, a group of Porto fans were applauded as they walked through a busy street.

In reply, the Porto fans started singing 'Henrik Larsson is the King of Kings'.

To hear a Celtic anthem sung in a Portuguese accent was both comical and moving.

It had been an epic adventure, an unforgettable pilgrimage.

But the Celtic fans ended their journey the way it began - in song.

Chapter Twelve

I SWAPPED MALAWI SAFARI FOR THIS

by Mark McGivern

IT WAS the best news I'd heard in years. That Al Qaeda had put Kenya at the top of its hit list.

Not that I've anything against the Kenyans.

The news, on May 16, meant that I was given the window of opportunity I'd been looking for.

Months earlier I had smugly congratulated myself on scoring a top freebie, a week on Safari in Malawi, with scuba diving thrown in.

All I had to do was turn up and sample the best living this impoverished African nation could muster, joining a raiding party of travel writers on the shores of Lake Malawi.

Celtic's wins against Liverpool and then Boavista, however, served to lop off my holiday head.

Come May 21 the only show around was going to be the UEFA Cup Final. Certainly, my own personal Rumble in the Jungle wasn't figuring too prominently on the holiday Richter scale.

Adding a poetic finality to my situation, a twist of fate meant my flight left London Heathrow at 8pm - 15 minutes after the kick-off.

My mood advanced through deepening shades of grey as the days and weeks passed. As the scores of stories flooded in to the Daily Record newsdesk from random Celtic fans, accounting for how they would get to Seville I found myself struggling to share in the cheer.

There were times when I felt like hanging up on them on the grounds that they sounded like smart arses from where I was sitting. I was even called a Hun on one occasion by a particularly enthusiastic 'Celtic-minded' reader.

At times I had to pinch myself to realise I was the only guy ever to have visited Celtic Park who wasn't packing their bags for Spain.

The dodgy dreamscape gave way to a final acceptance that I was going to Malawi, which isn't documented as a strong outpost for Jungle Jims. History was never my strong suit at school but such was my negative frame of mind I seemed to recall that the great explorer David Livingstone was a Rangers fan.

I'd rather have poked my eyes out with knitting needles than go to Malawi under the circumstances I found myself in.

It's not that I have anything against Malawi either. I just felt like a spare bongo in a jungle band under such circumstances, a bit like a contestant on I'm a Tim, Get Me out of Here.

Anyway, I was looking for a minor miracle - and then it came, courtesy of Osama bin Laden on the Friday, five days before the match.

The Al Qaeda head honcho apparently decided that aircraft coming in and out of Nairobi were fair game for bombs, casting a sufficient amount of doubt over my Heathrow-Nairobi-Malawi connections to allow me to justify pulling the plug on the trip.

All of a sudden it was Seville, not Llilongwe that was looming on the horizon.

For a Celtic fan like myself, who has followed the team to varying degrees for more than 20 years, I was aware I wasn't entirely among the fold.

I recall clearly attending games such as the 5-1 victory over Sporting Lisbon in 1983 and the crushing 5-4 defeat by Partisan Belgrade and the end of the eighties.

And obviously I was there to shout Celtic on as they whacked Liverpool, Blackburn, Celta Vigo, Stuttgart and Boavista.

That I missed most other games in between should be of minor consequence, I would have thought. I have over the years unfairly been treated like a pariah for my failure to maintain a season ticket. I've never felt prepared to give up my life for the Hoops, like many guys I know. But despite this, a 'part time supporter' like me could plainly understand that Seville represented history in the making. This was to be the new Lisbon and I wanted to be part of it.

In any case, given all the Seville hysteria, there were thousands of big game hunters heading to the match whose Celtic credentials were far more shaky and spurious than my own.

Many of the chancers had tickets for the match, a fact regarded by some, including me, as sacrilege.

Both my own brothers had their travel plans set out well in advance although my elder sibling, John, a High School teacher, had been told to cancel as his head reckoned the time off would be 'inappropriate'.

Other friends known to be heading to Spain ran into scores. I could easily name more than 100 acquaintances who would be lapping up the Spanish sunshine during the same week in May.

My own plans were hatched on Friday morning when my mate, dapper Dan, a journalist with another newspaper and a champion fixer, with the skin of a rhinoceros, got wind of a flight from Heathrow to Madrid, leaving on Monday, coming back on Friday.

He'd even arranged for us to stay initially in the Westin Palace - 'the best hotel in Madrid', he'd said and he was probably right. And among the businessmen residents and other guests - like Brian May from Queen, we stuck out like a sore thumb. Out in the city we were more at home. Despite the Spanish capital being some 200-odd miles from Seville, the Celtic presence could be felt, two days before the match.

Curiously, with the sparse pockets of green and white congregating in bars, it reminded me of the typical mark a travelling support would tend to make in Glasgow on the actual night of a European tie.

After a couple of phone calls I'd arranged to meet some guys I knew were sharing my travel route, teaming up with former inmates of Holy Cross, Hamilton, like Marcello Luisi, Raymond O'Neill and perennial Celtic daftie Martin McDonald.

A couple of Irish bars later and the scene was well and truly set, as our troupe joined hundreds of Celtic fans to blast out the same songs heard on match days back home. Finbar's pub managed to run out of beer on Monday night. The proprietors should have known better.

The next day's train journey to Madrid featured two and a half hours that would put Scotrail to shame. The trip was uneventful, other than meeting the Chewin' the Fat guys, the Canadian Greg Hemphill and that other guy, Paul something (Reilly, as it turned out).

To say these guys were sociable was an understatement. By the end of my trip it seemed that everyone in Seville had met them at some point and had a bit of a chinwag.

Normally I would feel a bit wary of approaching people from the telly from fear of being too uncool but everyone here had a common purpose. Supporting Celtic, or any other team, proves a natural leveller and I've never felt that more acutely than in Seville. Even after all the ballyhoo and great expectation I was set to be knocked out by what I was to behold in that city.

The Monday night Madrid blow-out was planned well in advance, way back on the previous Friday afternoon. A night on the batter on Tuesday had also been placed on the agenda at an early stage.

But first we had to get from the station to the city, a trip which was hampered by a 30 minute traffic jam on the main highway, which I attributed to the huge pilgrimage by Celtic fans.

As our taxi approached the bottleneck we became aware that the cause of the snarl-up was a bus breaking down in the middle lane, which surprised me given the quality of the transport system I'd witnessed up to that point. But, lo and behold, as we passed the offending vehicle and immediate flash of realisation hit as I recognised the red and white livery - it was the Daily Record bus, commissioned to follow Celtic to Seville, which brought a bit of a sardonic chuckle. All the same, I couldn't quite hear our circulation boss George Easton laughing as the mechanics set about their work.

As we drove past I thought to myself that would be the last I'd see of that particular vessel. After all, I was over for the party and such work paraphernalia wasn't part of the holiday picture.

The arrival in Seville, however, was not complete until reaching the city's famous cathedral, which in mid-afternoon on Tuesday appeared to be under siege from the green and white army.

It didn't take long to discover that it was, in fact, the Irish bars that were under siege and I was happy to lend my weight to the war effort.

One of the first sights to meet my gaze was a huge Celtic flag draped between orange trees in the street on the cathedral's left side, adjacent to Flaherty's Irish bar. The flag read 'The Plough' a patron of the Rowan Tree bar in Uddingston, a pub frequented by my father and brother David. From this point on I didn't spend an hour without encountering a new familiar face or sight as the sheer enormity of the joint odyssey became clear.

But first of all I had to get accommodation, which proved easier than I'd feared. Within one hour of embarking on a march around the city's dingier hotels (I figured anything decent was a no-hoper) I struck gold, hiring a room for two nights for a mere 40 Euros per night. Which meant a rickety bed for me and a scratchy old couch for Dan. Which translated to a palace for two guys who, up until then, were sleeping on the streets. More importabtly, it freed us to get kitted up in kilts before hitting Seville's bars. In the first hostelry we visited the man behind the bar would supply a glass of cold beer for a mere one Euro.

The following day his price had gone up to three Euros - which reminded me of some of the lesser attractive points of foreign travel.

I wasn't too dismayed at this sudden emergence of greed and opportunism. In fact it played into my game plan for match day, as today I was determined to savour the occasion by avoiding getting into a state of intoxication.

I didn't want to tell my grandchildren (in the future, I mean) that I went to Seville but unfortunately can't fill them in on what happened because I was too pissed to recall.

But the best laid plans often go awry, with me in any case, and this would be the case. eventually at least. Wednesday morning brought an early rise, in relation to the time I got to bed - around noon.

Left on my own as my travelling companion set to his work, filing a 'colour piece' on the behaviour of the Celtic crowds, I thought I'd take a wander through the streets of Seville, just to take my foot off the gas for a few hours and actually see the city in daylight hours.

I did manage to put in a good hike for half an hour or so before the inevitable happened. Given that half of Glasgow had emptied into this stunning city I was bound to meet a few familiar faces and sing a few familiar songs.

Given that it's 15 or 20 years since I regarded myself as a diehard Celtic fan, I've never identified myself as a major crooner - more an occasional part of the chorus. That was about to change as I wandered into the Plaza de San Francisco in Seville's centre at 2pm, smack into a sea of all-singing, all-dancing green and white nutters.

The hub of the action was the Daily Record open top bus, which had obviously been subject to a flying visit by the Spanish AA. It was by this time fully functional, with its huge sound system pumping out the music the fans wanted to hear.

I initially felt slightly divorced from the army of Hoops fans gathered there. Was I the only one not to have bought the new Celtic strip in the week prior to the match? In the heat I figured I'd get my t-shirt off anyway to join the throng.

As chance would have it, I walked straight into my brother David, who had travelled up on the day from Torremolinos with wife Nicola - another diehard fan stopped from attending every match only by the responsibility of two young daughters.

He was a brave man bringing the missus but he'd have been a braver one if he tried leaving her at home.

It was around about this moment that the penny dropped that something truly unique was happening. The kind of seething crowd that faced me seven hours before the match was something to behold. In each and every bar in the narrow streets around the square, Celtic fans filled each table. Seville was full up, fuller than I remember ever seeing Glasgow and fuller surely than than it has been in its history. I wouldn't have fancied the scenes if they'd tried running a few bulls through the Plaza de san Francisco at that particular point. Can't think the bulls would have been too keen either.

My original reticence over joining the Daily Record staff who were over for the graft was soon chucked out the window as the magnetic effect of the huge PA toook over, making the bus a focal point. It was the place to be, certainly as far as my brother was concerned and he soon persuaded me to use my influence to get us both on the top deck.

Bob Shields was happy to oblige in getting the stroppy security guards to let us on. And the sight that met us, standing there on the top deck, as the sun beat down on the square, was worth making the trip for alone.

Within 20 minutes of boarding, a strange phenomenon became apparent. A crowd of 20,000 excited Celtic fans, or any other fans, require a focal point for their fun, particularly in the absence of opponents. While the music was blaring, they would sing to their hearts content. Over and Overs 40-odd verses were reliably negotiated by this knowledgeable bunch.

When the music stopped, however, it was another matter. After a few minutes of silence, more mischievous elements would seek alternative and less wholesome anthems, which which can't be mentioned in a family book.

During one such lull my brother seized the initiative, grabbing the microphone and roaring: 'Hail hail, the Celts are here'. As if Seville hadn't already realised.

He was met in return with: 'What the hell do we care, what the hell do we care. Predictably, it went down a storm with the faithful. The look on his face could have belonged to a lottery winner.

I had started the day hoping to keep myself to myself and quietly savour the atmosphere. In the end, stripped down to kilt and bare chest I accidentally resuscitated my jungle theme going. I resembled some kind of tartan Tarzan, only not as well mannered.

With my top off, arms urging on the fans to sing as the sweat visibly glistened on my forehead, I sort of lost the place. I still confess to feeling slightly mortified about this gung-ho abandon but I maintain my defence.

This was unlike any other situation I've ever been in. The weight of the common cause was huge and marked also by a lesser degree of the anti-Rangers mentality than you'd be likely o witness at your average Celtic game. It was all about Celtic's achievement and the net effect was genuinely inspiring.

I was later presented with a video of the performance, which clearly showed nutters, myself, David and Record writer Paul English, conducting the singing, faces beaming brighter than the Spanish sun.

Grown men behaving like savages and loving it. We did our best to make the crowd rammed right up to the doors of the bus seem civilised, refined even.

I hope one day to watch it through without cringing.

And then came the match.

Watched it in a pub, in a far more inebriated state than I ever intended to be. I didn't even try to get a ticket, as I had decided in advance that I wasn't going to pay £500 to line some tout's pockets.

Whatever, I shared the same highs and lows as everyone in the stadium and elsewhere. I was left to cry into my beer by the final whistle.

Afterwards, I stumbled into a wide range of fellow Celts, each one with a different tale on how they fared during the match. John Brannan - nicknamed Brainy - and Tony McKay, for instance, told how they marched all the way to the Estadio Olimpico in the hope of buying a late brief.

The pair, among at least a score of fans I met with whom I'd attended Holy Cross High School in Hamilton, did better than they expected, actually paying less than the cover price for the tickets from a UEFA official one minute before kick-off. By this stage they risked missing the game entirely, as there were few TV screens within a mile of the stadium.

I wished I had taken a leaf from their book and taken the long walk to the stadium. It might have sobered me up a bit for starters.

The night witnessed many long slogs on the Seville pavements. I personally walked for two hours after the match, long faced and looking for a party to cheer myself up.

My brother, I later discovered, pounded the streets for six hours in an equally disheveled state, seeking a taxi in what was a seller's market. The last thing thousands of defeated green and white hooped fans wanted was a marathon walk but they had no choice. In the end David paid 250 Euros for a taxi to Torremolinos at 5am. He and Nicola hadn't been boozing in a pub or nightclub, he simply waited that long to get a cab. He resumed his Torremolinos holiday on Thursday, as I returned to Madrid, where I was meeting my girlfriend Julia and her parents, who flew over for a weekend break.

The trip was definitely set up to be a game of two halves and that's exactly how it turned out. Madrid's tapas restaurants and art galleries were a million miles from the football carnage I encountered in Andalucia.

It was also quite a bit removed from Malawi, a country which didn't enter my thoughts through all the Spanish experience.

Flying back from Madrid on Monday, a week after arriving, my thoughts returned to how splendid it would be to witness the beauty of Lake Malawi underwater.

I managed to get the trip postponed to September, terrorists permitting.

Chapter Thirteen

JETTISONED IN FOR 48 HOURS OF MAYHEM

by Cara Page

'Caesar Caesar Caesar!'

The deafening chant could be heard across the Costa del Sol as the Lisbon legend Billy McNeill clamoured on to a makeshift stage and punched his fist in the air.

It was the eve of the game and 10,000 fans had gathered at a massive open air concert to worship their hero.

I'd been in Seville just one day - jettisoned from an air conditioned office in Glasgow into the thick of this city heaving with Celtic fans.

I've never been much of a football supporter of any kind so why did this make the hairs stand up on the back of my neck?

It's because this was so much more than just football.

The legendary captain was at Seville's Prado de San Sebastian to rally his green army and roar Celtic to European victory.

"I see no reason why we shouldn't do it again," he bellowed into a

111

microphone, silencing the fans who were in full chant.

Then his rousing plea: "You've got to get behind the team. Give them the backing and let them see you want the cup!"

A bare-chested fan in a green wig turned to hug me and spin me around as I struggled for breath in the 120 degree heat.

Around me a sea of sombreros bobbed up and down. Women wrapped in scarves did jigs with young children, who squealed excitedly behind their green face paint.

In the ornate fountains that dotted the park others splashed around and everywhere people guzzled lager like a Club 18 to 30's holiday gone ballistic.

That night I wandered home with my new buddies listening enthusiastically to their passionate dreams of victory, hearts bursting with hope and optimism.

The peal of bells from Seville's landmark cathedral woke me on the morning Celtic's faithful had been waiting 36 years for.

I pulled back the dark shutters and leaned out across the black iron balcony on tip toes to catch sight of the spire just visible at the end of the the winding street.

Oh the bells, the bells! They'd seemed to ring on the hour every hour all night, resounding through the maze of streets.

God knows how those poor souls sleeping on the steps of the cathedral had got a wink of sleep.

The ever growing band of homeless Hoops had made the gothic cathedral their home.

Unable to find a room in the jam packed city, they simply slept where they dropped - snuggling up under the giant flags they had brought emblazoned with the logos of Celtic Supporter Clubs from all over the world. I giggled as I pictured the row of sunburned faces I'd seen the night before with a huge banner tucked under their chins and assorted trainers poking out from under.

"Good night the Hoops", I'd shouted cheekily as I walked past, and I could have sworn I heard one of them snipe to another: "Hey, you've got too much of that flag!"

But that was the spirit of Seville. Improvise, overcome, adapt, and most of all have a right good laugh doing it.

As I walked down past thronged cafes and bars towards the cathedral it was clear the party had been in full swing since early morning.

Sun-tanned groups of lads, couples and families sat in the shade of umbrellas - some with cooked breakfasts, others with bottles of water but most with 'dos cervezas.'

In the space of two steps I was promoted from a Glasgow Daily Record reporter to a Spanish ticket touting senorita.

As an olive skinned brunette, I was clearly a Spaniard through the beer goggled eyes of the Hoops hoards.

"Ola senorita" a young lad in a green and white top with pink legs called to me as I walked down the street in my shorts under a much-needed sunhat.

"Ola" I obliged him smiling over. It would be a shame to spoil it for him. "Do you have any tickets doll," he shouted back drawing a huge rectangle in the air: "TEE......CKETS!"

"Sorry pal, ah cannae get one masel," I told my stunned customer and left his pals ripping him to shreds.

Around the corner Celts from across the globe gathered outside Flaherty's bar - the adopted Irish bar used as an international meeting place opposite the cathedral.

They had long taken over the narrow cobbled street outside and were determinedly attempting to drink the bar dry. The Irish owners were well on top of things and had ordered 150 barrels containing 7,800 pints, to be exact, just for that day.

I watched as the crowd parted to let through a pick-up truck emblazoned with the words Cruzcampo and laden with shiny silver coloured barrels of the refreshment.

Several of the appreciative drinkers got down on their knees and worshipped the cargo as the bemused driver began rolling the barrels in a back door.

I leapt out of the way as I heard hoofs behind me and turned to see one of the open topped horse drawn carriages, normally used by tourists to take in the sights of this architectural and cultural city.

Two bare chested men wearing floppy hooped top hats were stretched back inside clasping plastic beer tumblers and waving royally to their fellow fans.

They directed their bemused driver through the mass of bodies outside Flahertys and proceeded to lap the cathedral to cheers and hoots of approval.

Before setting out on the road to Seville I'd exchanged a flurry of emails with globe trotting fans making the pilgrimage from Singapore, Canada, the US and Australia.

Celtic fanatic Jim McQuillan of Govanhill, Glasgow was by far the craziest travelling 30,000 miles to see his heroes without a ticket.

He'd bought a round the world ticket to get from his new home in Australia and back, involving a total of 10 flights and 62 hours in the air.

Joanne Stewart of Ayrshire, who works for an investment management company in Singapore, was one of many who chose Seville for a family reunion.

She flew to Dubai then on to Casablanca and caught a train to Tangiers, before jumping on a ferry to Algeciras in Spain to catch up with her loved ones.

Stephen McGinningle from Elderslie, Renfrewshire had abandoned his wife and kids on a caravanning holiday in Holland and flown in on a 24 hour pass via Malaga to see the game with his pals.

"We've got to get him on the 7 o'clock train back to Malaga in the morning or his wife will kill us,"his brother Kevin confided in me.

I had pledged to meet up with everyone I'd spoken to in Glasgow when we got to our Spanish destination although no one really believed in a crowd of 60,000 that we would.

But there was something magical about Seville. It was a bit like a New Years party in your home town, where you keep bumping into people you least expect to.

Martin Sweeney of the Sydney C.S.C was someone I'd spoken to back home, then found myself standing feet away from him and a banner with the words "We are the boys from Botany Bay, here to hope and pray."

Martin, 35, flew half way around the world to link up with three generations of his Glasgow family - dad Gerald, 70 his grandson Mark, 12 and a brother Derek who jetted in from the Virgin Isles.

I was on my way to meet a one in a million Hoops fan to hear his miracle story.

John Macdonald, 30, was walking ticketless through Seville when a simple gesture of friendship was rewarded with a dream brief.

It was the ticket of a 17-year-old Porto fan who had tragically drowned in Seville's Guadalquivir river the day before.

I found John from Balfron sitting deep in thought on a monument step on the opposite side of the cathedral away from the spirited throng.

He told me he had been wandering through Prado de San Sebastian Park after the monster open air party with Billy McNeill, when he spotted a forlorn Porto fan on a bench.

He stopped to give the young man dressed in blue and white a cigarette and asked him: "Are you having a good time. What do you think the score will be?"

John told me: "He said 'No. My friend had an accident today in the river and he's dead.'

"I started apologising but he just kept saying, 'Thank you, it's okay.'

"He asked if I had a ticket and said it was hard for Celtic fans to get them.

"Next minute he said , 'I've got something for you,' and nipped into the bushes and came out with some hand luggage.

"He pulled the ticket out of his bag and said , 'I want you to have this ticket and go for my friend.'

John bit his lip and pulled the treasured brief from his pocket turning it over and over in his hands. It was for the Porto end of the stadium with the ticket number Puerta G Sector 222B.

He whispered to me: "He put his hand on his heart and said 'I want you to go for my friend. Go and remember him'."

John said the chances of it happening were one in a million and that he had hardly slept a wink that night wondering how the poor guy must be feeling.

He was clearly cut up about the experience and as I left him and girlfriend Jo Field he still wasn't sure what to do with the golden piece of paper.

He kept telling Jo she had been to more away games than him and deserved the ticket more but she wouldn't take it.

I heard later that he returned the kind gesture by handing the brief to a ticketless Porto fan outside the stadium, just minutes before the kick-off. For the tens of thousands who didn't have tickets there was the Daily Record's giant TV screen.

By late afternoon the green army, many of whom had been with their heroes every step of the way in the campaign, set out on the the final leg of their journey. They extracted themselves from the crammed bars to form a green and white snake to the park Puerta de Triana on the opposite side of the river.

And they chanted their arrival from the tops of their voices along every step of the baking hot 40-minute route from the city centre.

Spanish residents hung over their balconies and peered through slatted wooden shutters in bewilderment as we marched along in an never ending singsong following the sound of a distant beating drum.

Of course, by now I knew all the words to every song, having already been in the bosom of the Celtic cult for 48 hours.

Cries of 'Can you hear Porto sing' carried back to us and with the rest of the gang, I answered 'No, no' as the tune rippled on behind me and out of earshot.

By then another anthem had reached my ears and I belted it out next to merry strangers who felt like friends as I crunched through plastic cups and kicked aside bottles.

Along the way quick thinking fans nipped into bars and ordered waiters to fill up empty plastic water bottles with litres of cool draft beer.

TV's Chewin' the Fat and Still Game star Greg Hemphill was outside one such bar chatting to fans on his way to the stadium.

I stopped to talk to him and was suddenly deluged with a mountain of cameras from my marching mates and asked to take their fotie.

"It's been total bedlam but the atmosphere is just electric," Gregg told me as I snapped away handing back cameras only to be handed more. "There were massive predictions about how many would be here but I didn't expect this. There's just something incredible in the air," he said.

I spotted an empty horse drawn carriage and a couple trying to decide if they wanted to hire it from a disinterested looking Sevillian puffing a smelly cigarette.

What the hell, I thought. Improvise, overcome adapt.

I ducked out of the slow moving marathon sized crowd over to the side of the road.

I hired the carriage and offered a lift to the couple.

My travelling companions Paul and Sarah Shields from Greenock told me they had left their three young sons aged three, five and seven home alone with a trusted baby sitter.

"We told them mum and dad were going away for a couple of days to the football," chuckled Sarah. "They understood we had to be here and we promised to bring them back presents."

We turned back onto the main boulevard skirting the river and into a sea of motorised traffic tooting horns and flying green and blue flags from every window.

A camper van with its side door wide open overtook us and the Celtic fans inside reached out and jeered us as we pulled up to our destination in style.

Inside the park thousands of supporters dressed in an assortment of green bikini tops, wigs, and trusted Celtic tops, took shelter under specially erected white plastic awnings or under leafy trees.

Families and women with children stood at the side of the huge 30 foot screen while a writhing mass of 20,000 bodies sweated it out at the front.

Next to me, sitting on a small wooden chair and leaning on a walking stick was 62-year-old Hughie Cassidy of Motherwell.

His sons Chris and Gerry and nephew Charlie Millar had brought the veteran fan, who had also travelled to Milan to see his team in the 70's.

Everyone respectfully gave him plenty of room as he sat transfixed to the screen dressed in a smart shirt and slacks.

"That shirt belongs to his son Anthony who died of a brain haemorrhage," said Charlie as he tucked into a vodka and coke carry out stashed under Hughie's seat.

"His son was 27 years old and a huge Celtic fan. He's here for him."

Huge speakers reverberated with the running commentary and some supporters bit their nails while others could not bear to watch.

A small group of uniformed policemen watched over us casually smoking cigarettes and posing for photos with fans.

Everyone clasped their hands to their heads and stood in stunned silence when the Seville dream ended in the final minutes.

We streamed home, quiet at first, across a huge road bridge back into town a sad exodus.

Many were hoarse after shouting, screaming and weeping at the drama packed finale to Celtic's fantastic season.

But it wasn't long before they picked themselves up and meandered home to a moving rendition of "You'll never walk alone."

Win or lose they swore they would party and they were true to their word that night as their singing could be heard until dawn.

But there's always a morning after, and as they woke up bleary eyed and nursing hangovers, fans wandered out of hotels and hostels with sombreros tied to their rucksacks. Others slumped against luggage in the shade waiting for taxis.

They began to leave hours after the match at the same time as a huge clear up operation began in the city.

Dozens of teams of cleaners appeared from nowhere to hose down the streets and rid them of the mountain of plastic cups, cans and bottles.

It was also the time to wave good bye to our new found friends the Sevillians.

Juan Robles, the president of the Association of Hoteliers and Restauranters of Seville had nothing but praise for his Scottish guests who had pumped £18.2 million into the local economy.

He told me how one drunken group who left his restaurant without paying their pay their bill, had returned the next day apologetic with their 78 Euros.

He said: "I found the Scots be very honest and polite. Not many people here speak English but the Celtic fans went out of their way to understand us and be understood."

The mayor of Seville, Alfredo Sanchez Monteseirin said the welcome mat would always be there.

"Like all finals there can only be one winner," he said sympathetically. "I hope that in your next visit to Seville you will remember with affection our city and leave it victorious."

That night, after I enjoying my last supper in Seville, I walked home through the silent streets reflecting on the history I had witnessed.

The cathedral steps were empty except for a sheet tied to the railings daubed in a marker pen with a message to the people of Seville.

It read: "Sevillanos, Muchas Gracias de la Celtic. Thanks Martin and the Bhoys."

As it fluttered in the Spanish breeze I could still hear singing in my ears.

Chapter Fourteen

MORE AMAZING CHARACTERS

by Janice Burns

THE match ticket said kick-off 8.45 p.m. but the spectacular Estadio Olimpico had become a green and white shrine almost as soon as the sun rose above Andalucian mountains on the morning of the 21st.

Some wanted to soak up the unique atmosphere, some wanted inside as soon as the ground opened – to touch their seats and make sure it wasn't a dream – and for some it was the last chance saloon in the hope of landing an elusive brief.

Those working at the stadium must have thought their watches were eight hours slow when, even as early 10 a.m. the surrounding streets were choked by the Hoops.

For those fans lucky enough to have a ticket, this was also their chance to snatch the souvenir programme which will one day provide the evidence when the grandchildren are told the story of Seville for the umpteenth time.

Bus loads of chanting supporters from all over Scotland, Ireland and beyond had poured onto the already roasting hot carparks on the outskirts of the grand stadium before many of their comrades had returned from the local nightclubs.

Many just stopped and stared for a while at the theatre of dreams, trying to picture the moment. The moment it would erupt if glorious Celtic triumph.

Many had paid a fortune to get to Seville, some had even taken out loans or sold their cars. Nothing was too extreme if it meant being there with Celtic for the club's special day in more than three decades.

Some told me of sleepless nights that preceded this historic day and how their wives and children were sick listening to their uncontrollable rants! Their sheer dedication and love for their team seemed to rise above all else and everyone I spoke to was just so grateful to be in Seville – even if they didn't have tickets for the game.

The frustration of massive delays at airports across the country and landing in Seville to find out their hotel had been double booked or cancelled didn't seem important any more.

The moment they arrived at the stadium all their troubles faded into insignificance and all that mattered was Celtic.

It was as though the sight of the ground triggered emotions many didn't even know they had, as they choked back tears and talked of their hopes and dreams for the night ahead.

Others stood speechless proudly sporting the green and white, their flags wrapped around their shoulders for protection against the blistering heat.

One by one they sought out reporters such as myself and were only too willing to share their stories of how they got to Seville.

Love knows no bounds for Marie Murphy, a fan since the age of six, who gave her husband Danny her treasured brief outside the park.

The couple, from Chapelhall, Lanarkshire, were staying near Jerez where their team were preparing for the match at a plush hotel.

Their friends and season ticket holders Maureen Eadie, Irene English and Joe McVittie were ticketless but it was enough just to be in Seville.

As it got hotter and closer to lunchtime, the fans got thirstier and hungrier and as no facilities were laid on outside the ground so early in the day, there was a sudden rush for taxis to the centre of Seville.

I shared a taxi with two charming fellows Michael Smith and his nephew Denis, from Paisley.

Decked out in their Celtic tops after a nightmare trip fraught with problems, they had finally reached their Mecca and were looking forward to letting their hair down in the sunshine.

So I took them to the Cathedral where it was already so mobbed you could hear the chants from miles away.

Minutes after leaving the stadium with my two new companions, another fan jumped in and begged a lift.

Mark Glennon introduced himself and explained that he was lucky to be in Seville at all because his wife was due to give birth any day!

Exasperated but delighted to be part of the whole scene, Mark told how the rest of his mates had flown out to Spain days earlier for a week-long party.

He admitted he was green with jealousy but didn't want to miss the birth of his second baby for anything.

After weeks of begging and promising to give up the fags, his wife Claire eventually agreed to give him a day pass for the match and he was eternally grateful.

When we arrived at the Cathedral, the lads couldn't believe the crowds that had gathered outside Flaherty's Bar – it was truly a scene to behold as thousands congregated outside in the shadow of the city's beautiful and historic Cathedral.

I spent the rest of the afternoon mingling with the world's best behaved fans and just enjoying the friendly banter and a sing song.

Later I was under strict instructions to return to the stadium to view the security and make sure no fans with tickets got a knock-back.

But the photographer and I couldn't get transport for love nor money.

We even offered to pay an old Spanish man with a horse and cart to take us but he insisted he didn't understand our pigeon Spanish.

So, we had no choice - we walked to the stadium and it took us over two hours through the mass of fans who were in the same boat.

When I arrived I barely recognised the stadium as the place I had been hours earlier. I thought it was busy at 10 o'clock, but this was quite sensational.

It was a sea of green and white, flags flying, hoarse fans chanting at the top of their voices as they queued up to hand over their briefs to waiting police and security guards.

Even the police couldn't resist a laugh at some of the hilarious antics of the desperate, ticketless fans.

One guy showed them a letter from his doctor saying that he had to get in to the game for medical reasons! It was, alas, to no avail.

In the main, the officers were pretty relaxed because they knew that there was no malice in the behaviour of these unique supporters.

Despite pre-match warnings, it seemed that even the most well-oiled wouldn't fall foul of the local constabulary who by now were learning to appreciate what it meant to be here, in Seville, on this famous day.

As long as their mates could hold them up they got into the match.

A fellow reporter who was off work and purely there for pleasure tells me he witnessed something quite unbelievable.

He said a fan turned up at the security gates wearing a Hawaiian shirt, green sombrero with flag around his neck and holding a surf board.

He handed over his ticket to the police but they insist that he leaves the board at security.

Then the lad produces another ticket (of questionable authenticity) for his board. The policeman laughs, shakes his head in disbelief and lets them both enter!

Ticket touts made a fortune on the night including Porto fans who were willing to flog their briefs to the highest bidder.

One made £1,000 in seconds after two desperate fans handed over bundles of cash for the chance to see Celtic - even if it was from the wrong end

Hundreds of fans who didn't get tickets or even entry into the Daily Record big screen park just stood outside the stadium waiting patiently for cheers of celebration.

Some of them were so overcome with emotion that they just sat down at the gates and cried with frustration at failing to get a last-minute brief.

After kick-off I headed back to the centre of Seville where the pubs were packed out to the street and the beer was flowing.

Some poor souls never even made it to the pub for the match and lay drunk and scorched on the steps of the Cathedral and in back streets.

I did a circuit of all the bars around the centre to get a feel for the passion flowing through the veins of those without tickets and it was rapturous.

After the final whistle Seville went deadly quiet while devastated fans came to terms with the result.

I was on the verge of tears as I watched the unbelievable distress and disappointment on previously joyous faces - it is an image that will never leave me.

My heart was in my mouth as fans from all over the world hugged each other and wept on their Hoops tops as they contemplated what could have been.

My thoughts instantly switched back to the day before when I stood among the masses at the open air concert in San Sebastian park.

More than 10,000 ecstatic Hoops fans gathered to celebrate the fact that they were in Seville to support their Bhoys.

The pride beamed from their faces as they awaited the guest appearance of Caesar himself, Billy McNeill.

I jumped on stage for a quick chat with him before he spoke to his followers and nearly got my head knocked off by angry fans.

Their unbridled passion for this man was such that I was warned within an inch of my life to let the "big man" speak first and I obeyed.

For such a quiet humble man, Billy held the audience of man, woman and child in a vice-like grip as they savoured his every word in total silence.

The legendary skipper spoke the words they all wanted hear - that Celtic would bring home the UEFA Cup - there was no doubt.

Billy was swamped with admirers begging for his autograph as he climbed down from the stage.

Then they rocked the night away to the sounds of Celtic band Charlie & the Bhoys belting out Irish favourites.

I never imagined for one minute that with all those hearts and minds behind them that Celtic would come home empty handed.

The blind admiration was evident from the start and, even when Celtic lost to Porto, songs of pride for their team still echoed through Seville into the early hours of May 22.

Some fans I remember better than others - take daft David Griffin who ripped up his ticket and threw it in the bin by mistake.

We told how David called Uefa and Celtic devastated that he had torn his Seville brief into eight pieces.

He was told he had no chance of a replacement ticket and had to go to Seville with his ripped ticket and a letter from Uefa.

To cut a long story short David got into the ground without even showing the letter to officials after he used blue-tac to stick the pieces together.

David, from Rosyth, Fife, couldn't believe it when the ticket scanning machine bleeped him through and he got the thumbs up from a smiling policeman.

Before flying out to Seville David was a hero for a day as he arrived to a round of applause at Glasgow Airport from fellow fans.

He said everyone was pointing at him and saying "that's the daft git in the Record who tore up his ticket."

Another fan Robert Caw was an inspiration to us all when he set out to raise £10,000 for a children's hospital by launching a special edition CD C'mon the Hoops to celebrate Seville.

He was joined by more than 20 fans calling themselves the Sombreros to make the CD before heading for the Cup Final.

They sold enough to have punters on the Costa Del Sol from Fuengirola to Puerto Banus dancing in the streets but still hadn't reached their target.

Robert recorded the CD to raise cash for the Princess Royal Maternity Hospital in Glasgow after his friends Linda and Paul Rooney lost their baby Orla at aged three weeks.

Tribute

THE FANS GO HOME TO BILLS, BUT THE PLAUDITS ARE WORLDWIDE

by Simon Houston

IN the end, the Celtic supporters conducted themselves as only they can – with dignity, honour and pride.

But more than that, we took defeat on the chin and kept smiling, kept singing.

More than 70,000 people and next to no arrests. Read it again. Quite remarkable.

It's a statistic that, even now, weeks later, seems hard to fathom.

It's also little wonder that the power brokers of European football were falling over themselves to heap praise on the wondrous Parkhead faithful in the hours that followed the historic Andalucian festival.

At a time when violence and dwindling attendances across the Continent are threatening to strangle the life out of the beautiful game, along comes the forgotten army of Paradise.

Like a happy drunk at a dreary house warming, we staggered in right on cue to save the party.

If the game was overcast before Seville, the sun came out on May 21st, in glorious rays of green, white and gold.

Every supporter who made the pilgrimage can be proud of themselves for not only keeping the good name of Glasgow Celtic intact, but also enhancing it on the grandest stage.

Those with tickets, those without.

Those from Glasgow, those from New York, those from London, those from Cork.

Those with top jobs and money to spend, those without jobs who had to beg and borrow.

Those who travelled first-class and stayed in five-star hotels, those who hitchhiked and slept on the Cathedral steps, beneath the stars.

Those who travel all over Europe in support of the Hoops, those for whom it was a first overseas adventure.

Each and every one played their part to make it a grand old dream.

Sit back and enjoy the plaudits. Enjoy the praise from the men in power, the men who have been sickened by the so-called British disease of hooliganism, who have become tired of passing only negative comment on the tribal warfare that so often wrecks the name of football.

MICHEL PLATINI, French legend and UEFA executive committee member:

"The Celtic public have been amazing and I was told that there are around 70,000 of them here, many without tickets. These fans have rejuvenated the UEFA Cup by the very presence of Celtic.

"It is quite amazing. If it was, say, Monaco from France against Porto in the Final in Seville, then there would maybe be 10,000 from France and 15,000 from Portugal. It shows again how the Scottish people love their clubs and the game."

GERHARD AIGNER, UEFA chief executive:

"I have not seen anything like it, especially with so many fans coming without tickets.

"We had a marvelous example in Seville, with about 60,000 Scotsmen, 30,000 not being able to go to the game. It doesn't mean that people who come and have no ticket must be automatically troublemakers."

LENNART JOHNASSON, President of UEFA and vice-president of FIFA:

"Why shouldn't Seville hold another European final – as long as we could guarantee a Scottish team in it! I pay tribute to the magnificent supporters of Celtic and thank them for what they have contributed."

DR JOHN REID, Cabinet Minister:

"Celtic did us proud by their performance. The behaviour of the fans has been a credit to Scotland and to us all."

MIKE LEE, Uefa communcations executive:

"All credit to the fans of both Celtic and Porto but particularly the Scottish fans. They had a drink or two and a party and their behaviour was magnificent. It is a message to the whole of the footballing world and every football fan that it is possible to travel, have a beer or two, enjoy yourself and have a good response to other fans from Europe. Celtic fans should be very proud of themselves."

ANTONIO BERTOMEU, Seville Police chief :

"In the name of all my officers, I would like to thank the fans. We saw nothing but good behaviour and a great sense of humour."

RARAEL CARMONA, president of the cup final stadium:

"The Celtic fans have set an example to follow. This is the way football should be and we wish all football fans were the same.

"The stadium authorities would like to thank every single one of the Celtic fans. In our opinion, they are the best in the world."

ALFREDO SANCHEZ MONTESEIRIN, the mayor of Seville:

"I would like to express, in the name of all Sevillians, my most sincere thanks for the extraordinary good behaviour of the Bhoys that came here to experience the final of the UEFA Cup.

"Like in all finals, there can only be one winner. I hope that in your next visit to Seville you will remember with affection our city and leave it victorious."

JUAN ROBLES, president of the Association of Hoteliers and Restaurateurs of Seville:

"I have been left with so many good memories.

"I had two Scottish men and a woman who left my restaurant at three-o'clock in the morning without paying the bill for 78 euros.

"I couldn't believe the next day when they came and apologised and gave me the money. They couldn't say sorry enough but I was just surprised and delighted."

MARTIN O'NEILL, manager of Glasgow Celtic:

"It was a fantastic effort by the players and the supporters.

"When we came out onto the pitch over an hour before kick-off, the scenes were amazing and they were even more amazing when the game started. They are a wonderful support and I think there was many outside the ground as in it."

The tributes went on and on.

In the hours and days that followed the final, when it might have been easy to let frustrations boil over, the behaviour remained impeccable.

Even amid the carnage of Seville Airport on the way home, supporters managed to keep their spirits up in the most trying of circumstances.

By then the hotels, travel agents and airlines had made their money and by the unceremonious way in which many of us were herded from gate to gate like cattle, as delay after delay appeared on the departure boards, it seemed that those who profited out of Celtic's appeal were only interested in counting the cash.

Reps were nowhere to be seen, the airport shops shut early and the bars said thank you and good night, as hundreds upon hundreds of jaded souls lay slumped against the concourse walls sharing what little water was available.

Now it was all about getting home, to face those massive credit card bills that seemed so unimportant a couple of weeks earlier when all that mattered was being there, in Seville. Home to fulfill all the promises made to spouses in return for letting then go in the first place.

The new replica strips, so pristine at the start of the week, now appeared as fatigued and punch-drunk as their crumpled owners.

And then there were the wallets, as empty as the tills of the Seville bars were full.

Patiently we waited for the tannoy announcements heralding the imminent departure of yet another charter flight home, but all that came were more delays.

As queues snaked out of the lounges and around the terminal building, it seemed some were too tired to speak. Nods and smiles replaced words as friends and acquaintances wandered passed each other during the long, slow hours.

This must be it, I thought to myself, late on the Thursday evening, as I huddled together with my mates at the entrance to Gate 5. The show's over and the Seville tank is finally empty.

But that was underestimating the greatest support in the world.

Just as we had carried the team over the finishing line during those final few emotional seconds in the Estadio Olimpico, it was time to dig deep again.

And with that, a few familiar words began slowly echoing their way up the concourse, a little louder with each new line, until the entire airport had joined in.

It was that song again. The song that says it all.

'Over and over, we will follow you,

'Over and over, we will follow you,

'We are Celtic supporters, faithful through and through

'And over and over, we will follow you.'

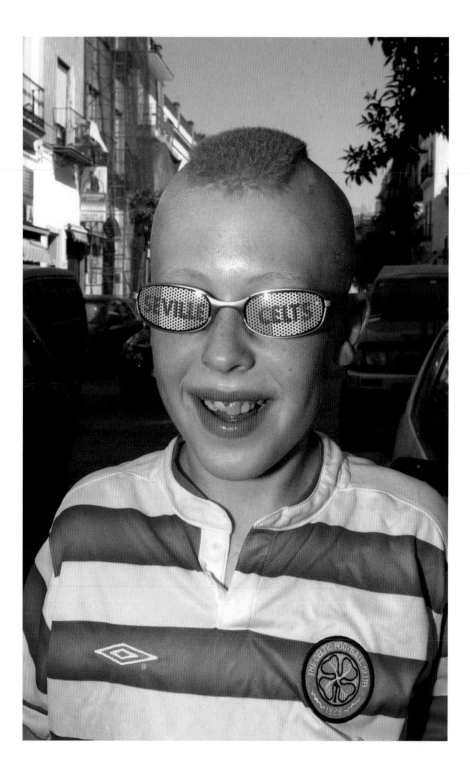

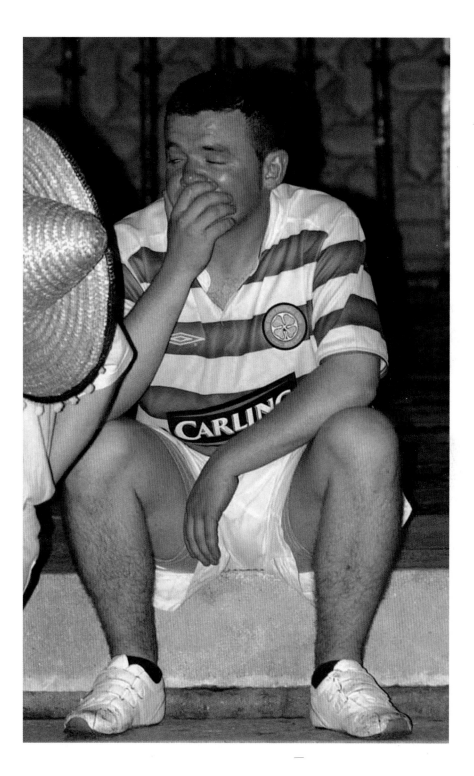

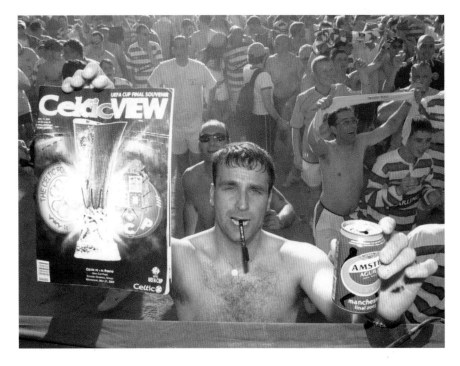

Chris Wilson from Uddingston and his Aussie friend Gerry O'Neill in front of the Sydney Harbour bridge after cheering the Hoops on to victory against Hearts in December.

Gerry's Tale

THE PUBLICAN

HIGH ON every Celtic fan's agenda was making sure there was enough drink to keep them going. And so Flaherty's Irish bar became the Daily Record Hoops HQ as hordes of fans invaded Seville. No matter how much pre-organising bar owner Gerry Enright did, nothing prepared him and his staff for the sheer numbers.

This is Gerry's story: "Celtic's win over Boavista in the 78th minute was like manna from heaven for us, because Celtic was coming to Seville. The thought of two Portuguese teams was not one to be relished, because the Portoguese fans simply come and go. They don't have the same cameraderie or craic about them, and of course they don't have much money. They don't have the same urge to drink and sing all day the way Celtic fans would.

"For days after they qualified, we had a steady stream of Celtic fans, who had been holidaying on the Costa, arriving to check out accommodation and ticket availability.

"Then I got a call from the Record and we agreed to make Flaherty's the Hoops HQ. The bar then became the main watering hole and meeting place for Celtic fans.

"Next to arrive on the scene was the touts and they were also in Portugal to buy tickets at lower prices.

"The early bird fans arrived on Friday before the game and there was a steady build up over the weekend and by Monday there were larger numbers. Lots of people didn't have accommodation and it was extraordinary to see how they operated. Some of them found some hidey-holes down in the car parks and other places, but a lot of them lay down at the cathedral. Unfortunately some of the thieves that come in from other places were having a field day. Some guys woke up with no shoes, nothing. One guy ended up in a police station after losing everything he had. He couldn't communicate with the cops, so they got onto the bar and they brought him back here. One of our managers gave him 20 Euros to get the bus back to Malaga and go home.

"Before the crowd arrived we made sure everything - all the beer pumps etc, were in good working order. We bought huge stocks, tons more than we would normally buy. Our best day was the equivalent to the amount of drink we would sell on three St. Patrick's Days put together

- and that is our biggest day of the year. Even the beer pumps couldn't keep up to the demand.

"But these guys would have drunk anything. As long as they could get a few cans they were happy. But the amazing thing was that the city was a sea of green and white, yet these people were so well behaved. The words 'hooligans' had been on the lips of local Sevillians before the Celtic fans arrived, because they associated football fans with trouble, due to everything they have seen in the past. But they had nothing but praise for the Celtic boys for the whole event. And everyone got a turn out of it - even the pharmacist. I was talking to the lady the other day and she said she has never sold so much Vaseline because guys had rashes from wearing the kilt in the heat. All the restaurants and bars did fantastic trade.

"We were all fascinated by the fans' dedication and committment to the game, and even their graciousness in defeat. They were fabulous, wonderful ambassadors for their club and country. Even now, some of our barmen are still whistling or humming some of the Celtic tunes.

"It was a memorable time. There was one story we found of about 30 guys who came in from Faro and hired motor scooters because there were no taxis or buses. But when they got over the border into Spain they discovered that you are not allowed on anything smaller than a 50cc. So the police intervened and escorted the whole lot of them in a convoy right into Seville. That was a great touch.

"The whole experience for us was fantastic. We met some fabulous people - some great, ordinary blokes who were just a great gas when you engaged them in conversation.

"More than anything I will never forget the sheer dedication and commitment of the Celtic fans. I have never seen anything like that before and they will be remembered in Seville for a very long time."

The Fans

EXCUSES for missing your lift home don't come much better than the one put forward by Glasgow brothers Charlie and Danny McGee.

Come lunch-time on the day after the game, the brothers from the city's Toryglen area were sitting forlornly in Seville Airport, desperately trying to hitch a flight home.

The pair had earlier missed their train to Madrid - because they asked assistants in a shoe shop to mind their luggage!

Like so many countless others, the McGee's had arrived in Seville without accommodation, so had to find somewhere in the city centre where they could deposit their bags before heading off to the stadium.

After all, who wants to trek the four miles to the ground with all your possessions in tow?

Explained Charlie, 37, an area manager for a communications firm.

"At first, the girls in the shoe shop were reluctant to take our bags. I suppose from their point of view, the bags could have contained anything.

"But eventually, they agreed and we headed off to the Celtic game. Unfortunately, we discovered the next morning the shop did not open until almost 10 am, and that was the time our train was due to leave.

"By early afternoon, we had picked up our bags and had travelled out to Seville Airport in the hope of finding a space on one of the dozens of charter flights due to fly back to Scotland."

Danny, 40 added: "The trip has been fantastic. If we got a victory, all the hassle would have been worthwhile."

Store manager David McMenamie, from Cumbernauld thought he was in real trouble when he became embroiled in the chaos that was the stadium coach park after the game.

For what seemed like hours, David searched in vain for the bus due to take him to Jerez Airport for his flight home.

But his transport could not be found at the agreed spot in the coach park outside the Estadio Olimpico.

David, 46, said: "You had all these supporters milling around, looking for their bus. When I couldn't find it, I decided to wait at the only exit to the coach park in the hope that it might come along.

"When it did come along, the Spanish driver would not let me board, even though I knew the password we had agreed earlier.

"I must have walked all night trying to find a taxi that would pick me up.

Eventually, at 5am I got one."

He wisely made his way out to Seville Airport, where he mingled with thousands of other fans already booked on to flights.

Travel agents Cambuslang Travel arranged for David and a number of similarly-affected fans to board a jumbo jet leaving Seville around 2pm.

Added David: "When the company found out what had happened, they did everything to get us on board this flight."

His reward? A seat in the VIP upper deck of the Air Atlanta 747, where David was waited on hand and foot by a blonde Icelandic stewardess.

The three amigos looked a sorry sight as they trudged the streets of Seville the morning after the game.

It transpired that the trio had missed their bus. Not usually a problem at home, as another one inevitably comes along.

But in this case, it was the bus taking them all the way back to Scotland - and it contained all their money, clothes and passports.

Charlie O'Donnell, Charles McCue and Gerald Coll had travelled the hard way to Spain with the Govan Emerald Supporters Club from Glasgow.

Charlie, 41, a caterer from Anniesland in Glasgow said:"We were in the town centre but our coach was parked near the stadium.

"It was impossible to get to the ground for the 2am departure time so it left without us.

"We had no money, some of us had no passports and we had no idea how we were going to get home.

"Having said that, we had a great night and it was all worth the three-day journey to Seville."

Fortunately, they teamed up with the British consul, who had sent a squad of officials to Seville from Malaga to help the stragglers get home.

And the three chums had the last laugh on the bus load of mates who were convinced they had seen the last of the three amigos.

As the coach sat in a traffic jam in Milton Keynes, on the final leg of the journey home, they got a mobile phone call from Glasgow.

It was from three guys in the pub in Govan. And they wanted to know how long the bus would be because they were getting tired of waiting! The consul had got them on a flight from Seville. And they had beaten the bus by two days!

See the Spanish? Take the shirt off your back, so they would!

Celtic fans Stephen Taylor and John Alexander discovered the truth of the phrase as they tried to battle their way out of the post-match chaos at Seville's Estadio Olimpico.

As thousands failed to find taxis to take them to their airport or hotel, the friends eventually found someone willing to pick them up at 5am - almost six hours after the game had finished.

But there was one condition.

Explained Stephen, 45, a director of an electronics company:"They pointed to our Celtic tops and insisted we hand them over or there was no lift.

"I was raging because it was the new £40 Carling shirt and this was its first time on.

"But we were desperate and we reluctantly took off our shirts and handed them over."

After watching the UEFA Cup Final at the ground, the friends had managed to return to Seville's city centre by 12.30am. They had a few beers before deciding to head back to their hotel.

Said John, 46, a financial adviser from Cumnock:"We seemed to walk for hours before we eventually had to stop for a breather.

"We asked a policeman where we were and when he pointed to the map, we discovered we were almost back to where we started. It appeared we had also crossed the main river through the city though neither of us can remember going over a bridge!"

Two Spanish strangers sitting in a car agreed to take them to their hotel on the other side of town, but at a price.

Laughed Stephen, from Strathaven:"Now I know the Spanish will take the shirt off your back."

And John added:"My shirt has gone. I had to swap it for a car!"

.......AND IN THEIR OWN WORDS

Richard Tranter & Des Healy, Didcot, Oxfordshire. .

"On the way to the game from the Costa del Sol we drove through Malaga. We got loads of waves from pedestrians and other drivers all giving us the thumbs up and hoping that we would win. We got distracted by all of this and lost our way. We ended up in a dead end in some industrial estate.

By this time panic was starting to creep in as time was getting on, then we saw a police car in front of us parked up in a layby. Out of desperation we asked him for help, and without a moments hesitation he said he would. I thought he would just point us in the right direction but to our surprise he gave us a police escort all the way to the motorway. At the end of our personal escort he gave us the full treatment with the lights and sirens before giving us his best wishes for the game. Viva Espagne"

Paul Carr.
"Would you really like to hear about 60,000 kilted fans walking through the streets of Seville at the end of the match with sweat rash between there legs. Just imagine John Wayne coming off his horse. We all looked like big tarts and I don't mean tartan army."

Andrew Fairlie, restaurateur and businessman David Douglas.
"Never has there been such an incredible high and incredible low in such a short period of time.
We cried as we stood surveying the stadium just before kick off.
After watching the Scotland versus Brazil opening of the World Cup in France it seemed impossible to imagine a more electrifying atmosphere. But boy were we wrong.
It was almost biblical to see so many people so united in one common hope."

Donald Macleod
"On the morning of the game myself, Robertto Chichetti and Carlo Citti, friends and business associates of mine, left for Seville from Glasgow Airport only to be told that we would be flying into Faro, in Portugal as Seville was overcrowded.
On arrival we decided to take a taxi and driver, Georgio, tried to kill us three times on the motorway by turning round to talk to us.
Phones were down, which was murder as I had two spare tickets and I had planned to give them to Becky Arnoot, my kids babysitter, and her boyfriend Gary. They had travelled over to Malaga earlier in the week and were coming up to Seville like so many thousands of fans just to say they were there and to savour the atmosphere. They did not know I had tix for them and were unaware that I was trying to phone them as their phones were off as well.
Arriving at a restuarant, and realising that I had a fat chance of now

meeting them in a city with 100,000 Celtic fans roaming about the place I decided to sell them, when a voice booms over the bar: "Hey Donald. Is that you? What are you doing here." It was Becky and Gary.
You should have seen their faces when I pulled out the tix - stunned, shocked mixed with a few tears."

Michelle Foy, Leon.
"While lying outside the cathedral in Seville with around 1000 other Celtic fans snoring around us my cousin's friend, who had travelled all the way from Donegal, piped up with "Hey, it's not fair I paid for a single room!". It kept us laughing for hours!"

Angie, Inverkeithing.
"I had headed out on my own to meet up with guys from work. I travelled Edinburgh-Gatwick-Zurich-Madrid where I stayed with the guys. As I couldn't get on their train to Seville I ended up hooking up with three guys from Fife - Mick the haun (as in big hands), Eddie and Eddie's laddie from Fife who took me under their wing.
We slept on the streets the night after the match and I was awoken in the early morning by an Australian back packer picking his way through the masses of bodies on the ground.
The guy had just arrived in town and greeted her with the words : 'G'Day what's been going on here then!"

Gerry Paterson
"We had seven brothers,three wives Five cousins and four pals all in Seville and we were ALL at the game. We bought tickets before we played Liverpool."

From diary of Allan and Avril Kilcullen, Brian, Mark and James McEwan:
"The sights that met us when we arrived in Seville is something I will remember for the rest of my life. A beautiful city centre with hordes of Celtic Supporters, some in horse drawn carriages being shown the sights of the city, everyone happy and with everything to look forward to. Finally head back to the campsite at about 3.30am.
The day of the match, we got up bright and early and queue for the 10.00 am bus from the campsite to the city centre, it finally arrives at

11.15am. Once in the city centre we have a tour on one of the horse drawn carriages and see some beautiful buildings and have some fun with the Celtic supporters and Porto supporters. Great time singing and dancing in the Temple bar where we stay until 6.30pm. Had to watch the match at the open air park but found out that it is now full. Returned to a pub which we knew had a big screen but were told to queue outside until 8.00pm, (to allow staff to clear up). We were happy to do so and when hundreds of fans start to join in we all clubbed together and got a carry out to keep us going until the pub opens, which it does at precisely 8.00pm. We all head in and grab a seat to wait for the match to begin, Watched the very emotional ups and downs of an excellent match and all left in tears and feeling very disappointed."

Tam O'Hare and Mary Collins, with 18-months-old Bari.
"We thought ahead and booked our holiday before Celtic got through - we just knew they would qualify.
On Wedensday morning we set off from Edinburgh to Malaga. We were sitting next to a guy called Mick who was travelling alone and had already hired a car to drive to Seville so we hitched a lift.
At the time I thought it was a wrong move because he bumped every kerb on the road he smashed his wing mirror off and nearly knocked a couple of people down after all that he was going about a hundred miles an hour down the motorway. We took the wrong road and ended up a big mountain. We were that high up the mountain it was freezing and so misty you could not see fifty yards in front of you, but we thought hey we are going to see Celtic! We were the only Celtic fans on that route that we could see. After around 12 hours travelling from Edinburgh we finally arrived at Seville. Luckily, Bari slept through the car journey from Malaga to Seville. When we got there we were greeted by the Celtic fans who gave us drinks and took pix of Bari because he looked so cute in his Celtic strip. We would like to thank all the celtic supporters we met and Mick and Neil Lennon north Staff celtic supporters bus from Stoke for getting us the tickets of a lifetime."

Shona Turbull.
"I would like to tell you what happened to my husband Owen Turbull when we were in Seville. We come from Kilmarnock and are members of Irvine No. 1 Celtic club. That is who we travelled with. My husband is a very shy person so he would not tell you his story himself. After

watching the game we made our way back to our bus on the way my husband found a wallet when he opened it he found out it belonged to a Porto fan his name was Jose Joaquim de Freitas. It had over a hundred pounds bank cards. We did not know what to do so we decided to wait until the next day, and when we got home we sent it all to the address that was in the wallet. Until yet we have not heard from Jose but we like to think that we will soon. This is not a funny story but its a story of an extremely honest Scot."

From diary of retired schoolteacher Edward Garland, from Ayrshire.
"The Planning: Post-Liverpool chat in Stevenston pub.
Colin: Ahm gaun tae Seville! Ony takers?
Me: Ahm yir man. How?
Colin: We fly. (I concur as this seems sensible.)
Me: Where dae we stay?
Colin: How about Big Al's?.
Me: That's Alicante.
Colin: Is that faur fae Seville?
Me: Need to check.(633 Km. as it transpires but too late to check momentum)
SEVILLE 6pm:
Stifling heat. Find Cathedral.
PARTY IN THE PARK
9pm. Long walk to San Sebastian park. Pass very plush Alphonso 13th hotel. Spy Dr. Jo Venglos, Jack McGinn and a scunner of other UEFA fat cats who will certainly not be kipping in the back of a Ford Focus tonight.
Party wonderful. Confidence high everywhere. Long trek back to underground car park. Some continued party there.
REVENGE-SEVILLIAN STYLE;
6am. Horrific night. Atonal Arabic music blasted through Tannoys at Concorde decibels. Numerous hit-squads failed to find the *******'s office. Toilets indescribable. On the street at 6.30 looking for decent ablutions. Success. Feeling human.
MATCH DAY CAMEOS;
Wee wifie berating husband for leaving windows open in Cumnock.
Wild-eyed giant in Hoops top, full highland gear, snare drum and Indian chief's war bonnet taking issue with Tapas bar owner over absence of mince and tatties from tapas menu.
Elderly, portly fan suffering from heat joins me on Cathedral steps. I

empathise. Response: "It still beats the **** out of Shettleston, son. Fair enough."

COLIN'S BROTHER

Travelling up from the Algarve for the game. Arranging meeting by text messages.

Examples: " I'm near a big fountain with a statue in it near the Cathedral." There must be a dozen fit the bill. " We're wearing Hoops tops". This narrows it down to about 40,000 - give me strength! Incredibly, we find them and head to Betis stadium for the big screens.

THE GAME

Agony, ecstasy, agony, ecstacy, despair. Game over. Numb. I fancied them on penalties.

AFTERMATH

Few tears in evidence as we re-crossed the river and headed for berths, doorsteps and parks.

A few young Hoops are still belting out the old ones but few have the appetite for any more. A sense of inevitability has descended. Heads in hands. Heads shaking slowly. Bodies curling up on doorsteps,facing inward. Sadness now. The lump in the throat wont go away. All around, tears are close. Let's get out tonight. Colin 100Km up the motorway and a services. Full of Hoops. Silence. Quite surreal. Then the last 500 Km.

RETRO

Feet and ankles like balloons (wife warned-too old for this nonsense.) Did I enjoy it? Can't decide but I was there!
Would I do it again? AYE!"

Tom Bailkoski

"I booked this trip for my son and myself as my wife and daughter aren't into football. Any excuse I suppose. Anyway, I had no tickets, and was being wound up in work by the guys with tickets, but I had my mind set on going to the party anyway, as well as showing my son what a real football support was. He wasn't to be disappointed.

We were due to leave Hamilton by bus on the Sunday, destined for Manchester, then fly to Malaga, taxi to Marbella, and finally onto Seville. On the Saturday night, my father phoned me, he had acquired two tickets for the Final from Didier Agathe, who had become a friend since giving him some golf lessons. Unbelievable. I was completely beside myself, jumping up and down like Martin O'Neill at trackside.

In the stadium, our seats were right at the front and behind the goals. On turning around, to look at the sight of the mass hoards of Celtic fans,

I was delighted to see Davie Hay two rows behind me (see photos), who was sat quite calmly throughout the first half. When Henrik scored our first in the second half it was complete elation, as you can imagine; and I completely forgot about the great Celt sitting close behind me.

Porto scored again to make it 2-1, and the atmosphere changed calmed, briefly. But when Celtic equalised to make it 2-2, we were absolutely ecstatic again, and this time I had the presence of mind to clock Davie Hay. He was a man possessed. I quickly grabbed the camera, and caught him as you would have any other Celtic fan in the land Euphoric!! Let's face it you can take the boy out of Celtic, but you can't take Celtic out of the Bhoy!

I had a fantastic time thanks to Celtic, Martin O'Neill, and the image of Davie Hay when Henrik scored to make it 2-2 will also stay with me."

Gerry O'Neill

"I left Sydney on Friday after work, flew to Bangkok and on to London, had a day in London then onto Gibraltar which is near where my parents were staying for the match, then train to Jerez and on to Seville.

Had 3 days in Seville, then back via Gibraltar, London, Glasgow, London and arrived back in Sydney 8am Wednesday morning to start work at 8.30. Skint and hungover, limping (stood on a broken bottle of cerveza) and smelling badly.

It was all worth it though as had the time of my life. dont think I've ever celebrated a defeat like I did this one.

The journey back was pretty tough. But my sombrero was still glowing when I landed in Sydney to pick up all the pieces, and I have converted a lot of Australians into Celtic fans by making sure they watched the game."

Lesley Ramage

"My Seville memories are when we qualified it was a must for me to go, I went home that evening and stated to my husband, a Rangers fan, that I was going. He agreed and also paid for my flight, which was even better. I am a member of a supporters bus and there was a number of us booked to go.

First things first on the Sunday before the before we left Glasgow I fell and sprained my ankle, so the day of the Final off I go with my leg strapped up and with a big BLUE Hospital Shoe on. Later that day we meet up with the other ten guys from our supporters club and had a ball.

As you can imagine my husband took a lot of stick about the fact I was going to Seville with 11 guys.

When I returned from Seville I was feeling really tired as you would, but on the Saturday morning it crossed my mind that I may be pregnant. Yes I had come back from Seville pregnant and yes it its my husband's. He is getting a lot of stick, but my trip to Seville will never be forgotten."

Mike McBride

"Well - it was the best of times - the worst of times - but mainly the best of times.

Two stories particularly spring to mind. The first was the scramble for tickets. We had managed to get a 'promise' of four tickets from a political party, and with a Spanish tour guide Miguel, we had to search for the offices. Unfortunately Miguel had never been to Seville before either - so it was like the blind leading the blind!

Eventually we got there only to find out that they had been given counterfeits. Imagine the dismay. So off to the pub, and joining in the singing along by the cathedral. Then Miguel got a phone call. They had got us tickets! Off we went on the dodgiest sounding scheme - over the bridge, outside the cinema (I think it was a cinema!) wait for the Blue BMW - receive a sealed envelope and pay the 240 Euros.... (you'd almost never believe it!) But it all worked out. What an adventure - not just the Seville trip, but the whole Euro run. Magical. I'm still elated by it - no silverware - but some brilliant memories. Has any team ever been booed lifting the cup before?"

Jim Flynn

"I'm a member of the Henrik Larrson Celtic Supporters Club Manchester branch. Most of our supporters club members made the trip to the final, although we had to go by many different routes. We had lots of problems with rooms, transport and keeping in touch with mates because phones were down. But it's all part of the European adventure of being a tim. After the match we had to make our way to Alicante to fly home on the Saturday, which was another nine hour trip by coach. But we'd do it all again for the Celtic."

Thomas McQuade, Blantyre

"I left Glasgow for Seville on Tuesday 20th May and flew to Faro in

Portugal, then onward by bus to a place called Porto Prento on the Border with Spain but still many miles from Seville. On the Tuesday evening our party of 14 Celtic fans went for a few beers as you do, hit the town, local beach bar and then off to bed. In the morning I was rudely awakened by loud thumping on the bedroom door and the balcony window, the lads were screaming at me that I had slept in for the bus to Seville and that I had five minutes to get ready and downstairs. In great haste I jumped into the shower, pulled on the Seville gear and then, shock horror where the hell had I put my SHOES. After tearing the room apart I decided that there was no more time to waste and so set off for Seville SHOELESS. On arrival in Seville the bus parked at the stadium many miles from the city centre, and so there I was faced with a 100 degrees shoeless trek to the city. As I made my way there I stopped a street trader who was selling bags of iced cold beer. I drunk one can and then opened a second which I proceeded to pour over my boiling hot feet,as I was doing so I heard a policeman shout momemto I looked round and saw he was shouting at me. Immediately thinking of the laws in and around Glasgow I tried to hide the bag of beer, he came over and said, "No. You have to drink it ees to warm." So, hey presto, out came the beer. The policeman then said, " Where ees your shoes?" So between lots of arm moving and various levels of non Spanish I tried to tell him that they were lost. He made some sort of gesture and then walked away. Thinking no more of it I tried to hobble after the rest of my group. As I caught up with them a police patrol car drew up along side us.

"Come. You get in back of car," the officer said to me.

I looked at him thinking, God what's this about. And then without thinking, myself and one of my friends complete with bags of beer, leapt in to the patrol car which sped off at a great rate. On stopping at the first set of traffic lights the patrol car was immediately surrounded by many of my friends anxious as to what we had done, and also trying to get our tickets for the game.

"Do not worry," says the policeman. "We take friend to SHOESHOP."

My friend and I then spent the next one and a half hours complete with bags of ice cold beer, Celtic scarves draped out of the car window touring the sights of Seville in the back of a police patrol car looking for a SHOE SHOP.

We`ve had the Lisbon Lions, The Nine in a Row and now we have the Shoe Shop Two."

Andy Fitzpatrick - Coatbridge

"Just a funny wee story, As we were about to take off I turned round to the wee 18 year old from Clelland near Wishaw and said "how do you open the window to put my scarf out", and the reply was"I don't know it's my first time on a plane"."

Neil Baillie, Glasgow.

"I bought one ticket for the game and gave it to my dad as a birthday present for his 70th. But I struggled to find another ticket and only managed to come across one an hour before the kick off. Imagine my surprise when I found out I was sitting right next to my dad."

Danny, Arbroath.

"I was at work in the middle of north sea when we got through, and I was on the phone next day to get fights sorted with my mates. I am a 33-year-old season ticket holder and this is something I dreamed all my life. Got flights for eight of us, then my girlfriend called me at sea to tell me she got me a ticket. I could have cried. So off we went. Got to Malaga early hours. My mates, Sean, Sticky and my mother got taxis to Seville and stopped at a garage in the middle of nowhere so we could get fags.

There was a high wind blowing and as I got my money out my ticket was among it and got blown away. I was shouting, "My ticket. My ticket." The taxi driver, the petrol attendant and everyone was on our knees looking for it. But no joy. I just dropped to my knees and cried. It was such a long journey to Seville. Even when we got there I just kept crying, saying "Why me?".

About 2pm we met this guy we know who had paid £425 for a ticket and my mate Sticky said sell it to me. I snapped at it. I was going to the game again and I didn't think about the money or what my girlfriend would say. (she wasn't happy when she found out.)

So we walked for two and a half hours to get there, but as they say we'd have walked a million miles. I wouldn't have missed the game for anything. I'd also like to thank the guys who got my mobile I left in a taxi in Seville. Thanks for the memories, Celtic, and the rest of the fans who did us proud."

Stevie Coyle, Glasgow

"After having had a few drinks in there comes a time when nature must be obeyed, now was that time for me. A visit to the gents loo in the Alfonso X111 hotel provided me with my most abiding memory of Seville '03. As I made my way I noticed 2 or 3 well tailored guys hanging around the area, unbeknown to me, these were friends of and the brother of the rock god that is Rod Stewart. I entered the lavatory and there he was, doing his ablutions as you do, on completion of his task he turned to wash his hands in the wash hand basin and almost simultaneously he started a chorus of "Hail, Hail". I couldn't believe it Rod Stewart, live and unplugged for me and a limited privileged audience in the acoustic friendly amphitheatre that was the gents toilet of this hotel - a not to be forgotten souvenir of this great trip."

Alan Burns, Glenboig, Coatbridge.

"I arrived in Seville on the Monday night, dropped my bags in the hotel, and went for a pub crawl beginning in Flaherty's, wearing my trusted Celtic tartan kilt. Standing outside some bar I heard some commotion behind me. Someone shouted: "Get the bhoys in!" Then this mad women dragged three of us into a photograph. It was Jackie Bird! After the photograph the young lady walked into the night like a million dollars. The picture was in the all the papers the next day and when I arrived home tin Glenboig I was a local celebrity.

On Wednesday morning around 3am I was sitting on the street with a friend chatting and laughing when I notice this bhoy who had walked past three of four times looking lost. We stopped him to see if we could help and got chatting. His name was Paul Callaghan, from Perth Australia. As a long shot I asked him if he knew my uncle Francis who lives in Perth, Australia and was a member of the Manchester United squad who won the European Cup in 1968. He replied: "Franny Burns! We go to the same Celtic club." Small world, indeed."

Ross Moran, Glasgow.

"Some may have seen a banner behind Rab Douglas in the first half, which read: "Paul Houston can't be here to raise a can, C'mon the bhoys."

This is in reference to a good friend and huge Celtic fan, who tragically lost his life on Christmas Eve 2002.

Paul was a pupil at St. Ninians High School, Glasgow, and was immensely popular amongst his friends.

He would have been in Seville, and I like to think that somewhere he was. Paul or "Housty" as everyone called him, was 24 and before working for the Prudential, studied financial services at Caledonian University. He was a popular member of St. Joseph's Parish in Clarkston, were the attendance for his funeral mass was unprecedented.

Paul lived in Clarkston, he loved a beer and followed the Celts all over the place."

Mark Tolland, Glasgow

"Imagine my surprise when I turned up at the airport to find out I was on the same flight as Billy McNeill. Well, imagine my elation when it transpires that the very man is staying at the same hotel as us for the duration of the Seville trip. Our initial approach was not to bother him, however after a few beers at the pool and realising he is a normal approachable person, we made the first move! "Mr. McNeill," I said sheepishly, "Do you mind getting your photograph taken with me and the boys?" He replied "No problem son," and we were in! We managed to keep a hold of the great man for some 10 minutes. His stories of old and views of what was ahead fascinated us all. You could tell he done it a hundred times before and would probably do it a hundred more over the course of the next few days, however he did it, with us, and we appreciated it. We soon noticed that our hotel seemed to house all of the major figures in Scottish media. They were all there. Graham Spiers, Hugh Keevins, Jim Traynor, Alan Rough, David Tanner to name only a few. There were also a few celebrities like Jim Kerr and Roy Keane. Chatting to these people gave us an insight to the person behind the image which was fascinating and made us realise that they are actually good people doing a job - well most of them...

The four-day trip was fantastic however my greatest memory was of match day. We all had tickets, but not together. I was sitting with my dad - brilliant, what a memory. We were bonding on the biggest thing to happen in Scottish football in years. It doesn't get much better. Only one thing superseded that event - being there with him when the teams walked out. I've never experienced anything like it and probably never will again."

Stewart McKernan, Dumbarton.

"Standing outside the Estadio Olimpico on that fateful day in May, I had absolutely no intention of buying a ticket for the game on the "black market" (honest Jacqueline). In fact I only had about 100 Euros on me. That was until I heard my son Gary in discussion with a young Spanish lad who had what seemed to be several match tickets in his hands. "Dad, he's only wanting 300 Euros for a ticket," said Gary. "Go on then son if you think it's a genuine ticket, just get it," I replied. Before I knew what was going on , one of the briefs was in my own hand for closer examination. It certainly looked okay with the hallmark and the water margin, it seemed genuine, not a fake. Gary then said that no way was he going to the game without me!! What was I to do ? What the hell - it was a one off, 600 Euros for two tickets, the deal was done! Thanks to my pals Kevin, Justine, Pat, Michael and my nephew Stephen, who had a whip round for me. I honestly believe that I was temporarily insane for those few minutes, as I had no intention of buying tickets for the game on the "black market" (honest Jacqueline.)

After the initial euphoria , an awful dread came over me, what if they were fakes? What would we do? A decade of the rosary seemed appropriate. Kevin and Justine also managed to get two tickets (I don't know what they paid, Kev just says X amount).

Time to go to the game. Up to the first gate and the tear off bit of the ticket, no probs, up to the turnstile, ticket in and back out, no probs, we were in, Ya Beauty!! Section 204 - I won't forget that in a hurry - up the 20 stairs and almost there when a young Spanish lad stopped us and said: "Passes." I proudly showed our tickets. "No, no, passes!" My heart sank, unbelievably we had bought stolen tickets for the press/media section of the ground. They were looking for laminated press passes. I felt sick. Gary was almost in tears and we could see Henrik and the Bhoys out on the park warming up. We were so near and yet so far. Maybe it was the thought of a 46 year old man crying uncontrollably or his 18 year old son impersonating a dying fly or maybe it was the amount of times we said: "Please don't throw us out", but they relented and let us sit down next to the people every self respecting Celtic fan loves to hate, the press and media. I didn't care - we were in and the rest as they say is history. I wouldn't have missed it for the world, and honest Jacqueline I had no intention of buying a ticket for the game on the "black market"."

John McGovern, from Gourock, who travelled with friends Martin McLaughlin (Hull), Paul McGarrity (Greenock) Stephen Queen (Gourock)

"Thankfully the game was not a blur. I enjoyed every minute of it. All credit to Porto for winning. Some people say they dived and cheated their way to victory but that's the way these team's play. Celtic realise that, in fact they knocked out Porto's neighbour shortly before and were well aware of what the Portuguese get up to. I stayed to the end as the support chanted we'll support you ever more. A lot of people were dejected at the result as you could imagine but it was still special. Had Celtic won Seville would have come alive; it would have been hectic in the city."

Andrew McArthur , Auchtermuchty , Fife
"We heard distant choirs of Celtic fans and decided to follow the noise. Into a large square surrounded by beautiful buildings. Past the riot police who were helping some fans put a flag up. They knew there was fun in the air.

In front of us was a large double decker bus. King Henrik on the side. Thousands of fans singing at the top of their voices. I mean really singing. You know when you sing a song with real feeling. Walk on. Walk on.

The scarves are up in the air and we are all singing a popular Irish song, you know the one about the Potato famine. God, I could have been in those fields. My imagination going into overdrive when I closed my eyes. I have to admit it. I cried. I tried to hide it. I struggled to sing.

I have never felt so overwhelmed. Emotion that seemed to emanate from everyone. We were here. We were in Seville. We were at home.

We didn't even try to get a ticket. Yes it would have been something else. In the end it didn't matter. We could spend the night with twenty thousand other fans watching the big screen.

A few things will stick with me for the rest of my life.

To a man, at the final whistle, the crowd raised their hand and clapped. We were beaten but not defeated. We were proud. We deserved to win, if only for the supporters. The best in the world.

This group of Irish lads stopped to chat with us when we were consoling ourselves.

"Will you have a drink?"

"Aye."

The tallest of the three lads uttered the following words: "It is difficult for us Dublin lads. We have Man Utd , Everton, Liverpool and Celtic. Thank God I support Celtic. Thank God."

This says it all. This is more than a football team. This was more than a football match. This was a pilgrimage.

Thank you Martin. Thank you Lads. Thank you Celtic. Thank you Seville. Thank you Porto."

Stuart McEwan, Kilwinning, Ayrshire

"My favourite memory is after the game we made our way up to the train station the worst for wear, to sleep rough. This was proving impossible, as they wouldn't let us inside the station, and the mono-block pavement wasn't exactly the best surface for a sleep. There must have been around 3000 of us, all unable to sleep, but lying around, when at around 3am, we heard some laughing and looked up to see two bhoys with mattresses shouting "1.5 Euros doon the wee shop doon the road mate!" These were not blow-up mattresses but real single-bed ones. Just goes to show us Celts will find a bed at anybody's door!"

Nicola Richardson (Port Glasgow) and Joanne Halliday (Bishopbriggs), currently of Leon, Spain.

"Being part of a group of students from Glasgow Caledonian University who are currently studying in Spain, myself and my friends decided to take the opportunity to go to Seville to be involved in the celebrations with all the other Celtic fans.

Studying here in Leon, Spain we have picked up our knowledge of the Spanish language and being in Seville we helped a few of the fans and we are sure a few of the Sevillians to understand each other, mostly in the bars - or in McDonalds!

On the day of the match whilst in a restaurant, quite a quiet establishment at that, we found it enjoyable listening to two groups of Celtic fans trying to order some food and drinks, the waiter taking the order was obviously Spanish, appeared to be quite offended and probably unable to understand what the fans were asking for.

One fan at a table asked: "Do you have Harry Ramsdens?". But it being a Spanish restaurant all they mainly appeared to have was Spanish Omelette! Another fan seated at another table thought the waiter would have a better chance of understanding him if he shouted his order at him, even though the waiter was standing right next to him!

We have learned that you have to speak Spanish to every Spaniard to get what you want and we found it particularly funny that the Celtic fans still got what they wanted even though they didn't know the local lingo. This made our trip to Seville even more enjoyable and memorable and we are grateful to the fans for keeping us amused and reminding us of how great Scottish people are, at home and abroad."

Carol Docherty, Coatbridge.

"My brother-in-law and son left almost a week before the game, but when they got to Glasgow's Buchanan Bus Station, the office was closed and they couldn't get their pre-booked tickets for the bus. They had to pay another £45 to get to Manchester where they were staying for the night.

There, they got stopped by two working girls who got my brother-in-law a little excited as he had never had it offered to him so easily. He refused and moved on to find a taxi but then realised she had stolen from his pocket the note I had written for him with the flight number and accommodation!

After some frantic calls, they found out the flight number but when they arrived in Spain, the accommodation was locked up and they had to stay in a hostel for the next two nights.

Myself, my husband and four friends flew out on the Saturday and went hunting for them on the Sunday - four days after they left! I pulled up in a taxi to find them just getting to there accommodation. What a slagging they got when we later realised you needed a ticket number to get in the side gate of the hotel and that's how it appeared to be closed whenever they turned up.

On the day of the game, none of us had a ticket and we slept in a park for the night - but what an experience I would do it all over again."

John Cadden, Dalmuir Emerald CSC

"I am a season ticket holder and a member of the Dalmuir Emerald CSC. I am in the Royal Navy and watched the Boavista game in RAF Brize Norton and when the final whistle went I had to fly down to the Falkland Islands for two weeks. I was so desperate to be in Seville my wife had to spend hours and hours on the phone and on the web to get me over to Seville. The Navy so kindly gave me a few days off to support the Bhoys. My wife eventually sorted my travel arrangements while I was down in the Falklands.

My brother and myself hired a horse and cart to take us to the park for the game and it was a great laugh.

It was great to see most of the members from the Dalmuir Emerald in Seville, some travelled by car, some by bus and some by air.

We are all still on a high in Dalmuir and imagine if we had won the cup?

My mates in the Navy thought I was crazy going to Seville and not even getting into the stadium. Memories are a wonderful thing and you just can't buy them.

Ally Farquhar, Stenhousemuir
Sitting outside a tapas bar the day after the game, some older gentlemen got up to leave. They came over and said we had been cheated and that they had applauded Celtic. We thanked them for their support. A few minutes later they came back and gave us all a key ring, which was a lovely gesture. We had so many Spanish people say the same thing to us and it made us feel a lot better."

Elaine McGill, Anniesland, Glasgow
"This is how my husband, George McGill earned his title of "The Flying Scotsman of Seville".

George went to Seville with some of his family and they then met up with his cousin Andrew Rock who flew with a few of his friends from Los Angeles. None of them had any accommodation for their two night stay in Seville, so Andrew came up with the bright idea of hiring a transit van. This was the night before the match and what else was there to do but soak up the atmosphere and the booze. After a few hours in a local Spanish pub, it was time to get a few hours kip in the van. As there were too many already in the van George and Andrew volunteered to spend the night on top of it. You guessed it - George required to visit the little boys room in the middle of the night and proceeded to vacate the van, not realising he was twelve feet up and still completely pissed. From a car parked behind the van his cousin Jim and his girlfriend Sharon had full view of the events. Instead of jumping out to his aid, Jim and Sharon fell about laughing at the sight of George dangling from the side of the van. At this point everyone jumped out of the van to find George on the ground surrounded by a couple of men who had been hosing down the street and witnessed the whole event. Apparently he hit a parked car on the way down smashing his wrist. When everyone had stopped laughing they picked George up who promptly started walking down the street. "Where are you going, George?" they shouted. "Home" said a very drunk George. "Well you've got a long walk."

Needless to say, his first port of call when he got back to Glasgow was the Western Infirmary to x-ray his injured wrist. Very badly bruised but, thankfully, not broken."

Stephen Reilly, Wishaw.

"Myself and five mates drove all the way to Seville in a 1975 Volkswagen camper van like the ones the hippies used to drive.

We had the windows painted with Celtic colours and a seat reserved for a life size cardboard cut out we had of Henrik Larsson.

Only one of us had a ticket to the game. We were all schoolmates and are now going to register ourselves as an official travelling Wishaw Celtic Supporters Club with our mobile headquarters being the trusty wee camper van. The travellers in question are myself, Jonathan Warner, John McClelland, Brian Costello, Kevin Higgins and David Costello.

My mate Jonathan's uncle Benny is the owner of the van. It was left to him in a will from a dear Celtic supporting friend. We saw it fit to take the van in his honour without actually thinking that it would make it. We met Benny just outside Seville by sheer chance when we entered our very first pub. He was delighted to see that we had made it intact and with only a few bump starts to speak of.

You cant beat a 1970's Volkswagen camper van, or Celtic fans, for sheer reliability."

James Brown, Barrhead.

"Trying all avenues and getting desperate for a ticket I text my friend Gary in Aberdeen who happens to be high up in a company who he frequently travels abroad for on business and half jokingly ask does he not have any contacts for a cup final ticket. He gets back saying he will see what he can do.

About a week later he contacts me with the news of a ticket he has secured through his contact in Bilbao who he sees now and then when over doing work through their two companies.

He gets back a couple of days later asking for the name of my hotel and when I will be arriving as his friend Nacho in Spain assures him a ticket will be delivered to the hotel reception on the morning of my arrival. Gary not as sceptical as me says there will be no problems as the ticket is coming straight from the president of F.C. Seville as a favour to the president of the Bilbao company. On arriving at my hotel I wasn't getting my hopes built up too much just in case, but low and behold waiting for me behind reception in a wax sealed envelope one top of the range ticket from the president of F.C. Seville. Not a bad contact to have."

Donald Finnigan, Glasgow

"My 15-year-old son Samuel and I booked our tickets from Uefa before the Liverpool game and decided to head to Spain for a week.

With my birthday falling the day after the match, all the omens were there for a good trip - or so I thought!

My brother Owen said he would take us to the Airport on the Saturday, but that morning he phoned to say he couldn't manage. I was about to arrange a taxi when he started to laugh and said he was only joking.

So cases packed, showered, shaved, fed, ready to go, I put on black shirt to travel in but Samuel told me I HAD to wear the Hoops for the flight. Owen then phoned and once again said he couldn't take us to Prestwick. I laughed and said I wasn't not falling for that one again.

But it turned out he had just had an accident, swerving to miss a car and hit the pavement, damaging both wheels on one side of the car.

I phoned a taxi and was told we'd have to wait between 30 minutes to an hour - which was cutting it too fine.

I phone around everyone I knew for a lift but to no avail.

Then I phoned my mum who said her friend would take us.

It was now 12:15pm and the flight to Stanstead was at 13:55.

Unfortunately mum's friend decided to drive at 10mph below the limit. It was nice of her to take us- but I wanted to ask if I could drive!

We made it in the nick of time, only to find the flight had been delayed. So instead of having two hours to make the connection for the Jerez flight, we only had one hour, 20 minutes.

By Stanstead we're sweating buckets. We got the luggage and ran from one end of airport to the other, to discover the queue for security was an hour long!

Luckily an official took pity and took us to the front of the queue. We now had 20 minutes to go and ran like hell to find gate 50.

Got there, sweating buckets, and the gate was closed and we could people boarding the plane on the tarmac.

I was banging on the doors demanding they open up when an air stewardess said the gate had been changed to 54.

We're off again! Got down stairs and it was still open even though we were the last two to board - but we were on our way to Seville!

And that's when the problems really began...

Good news when Samuel's case was first off the conveyor belt but we waited and waited and there was no sign of mine.

After lengthy debates at the information desk and lost luggage, a lady appeared who spoke English but struggled with the Scots accent.

I told her my case was blue and orange - and explained that no other

Celtic fans would have luggage that colour!

Eventually, to my delight, they told me they had found it - only to produce and old bin bag covered in tape!

Turns out it was still in Stanstead and I was assured it would arrive by 9 p.m. the next night.

So I borrowed some of Samuel's stuff - but I'm a size seven and his trainers were a 12 so I felt like Coco the Clown.

Fortunately my tickets weren't in the case, but everything else was - my kilt, camera, phone charger. Just as well Samuel nagged me to put on the Celtic top to travel in

So never mind we still saw the final. Samuel was nearly in tears at the result but I told him the best team lost. The more experienced team won and we were naive in some areas and they exploited this, as well as the inexperienced referee .

As if things couldn't get worse, we tried to check out on the Saturday and my credit card was inexplicably blocked.

Luckily I had my switch card and that was accepted.

So we got the airport and guess what was waiting for me in lost luggage - the only blue and orange case in Spain!

What a trip - but I would do the same every year for the Hoops!"

Neil Cremin, Menstrie

"I travelled with my friend, Douglas Carlin and my parents Jim and Dolina Cremin.

To cut a long - and very lucky - story short I'm the only one with a ticket, so on match day we head up to the stadium at 6.00pm to take some pictures. We step outside our hotel to get a taxi when a Dutch fellow asks us if anyone wants a ticket as he has one spare. My mate was prepared to pay 300 Euros and after a lot of haggiling - especially after he tells us it's a Porto end ticket - we persuade him to accept the offer. On entering the stadium, Douglas was delighted to discover he was actually in the main stand which was mostly celtic fans.

I then say good-bye to my parents, organise a meeting place for later and join the masses inside the stadium.

Unbeknown to me my dad starts talking to a Celt who is getting quite flustered because his friend hasn't turned up and is probably pissed in the city centre. Now, it isn't nice but he had to ask what he was going to do with the guys ticket.

He replied: "Well, if he isn't here in ten minutes it's getting sold."

Obviously my dad asks the angry Celt to keep him in mind if his mate fails to show.

Ten minutes comes and goes and the guy signals my dad over. My dad asks: "How much do you want for it mate?"

The guy didn't take this remark well. He angrily replied: "What do you f****g mean, how much do I want for it? I'm a Celtic supporter - I'll sell the ticket for what it says. I don't rip Celtic fans off."

In his defence, he was still still angry about his pal but my dad was only asking him a fair question as the ticket was still worth something, be it 30,40 or 60 Euros.

My dad couldn't thank the guy enough but now he has to tell my mother that she's the only one without a ticket. He was distraught. This was the situation he didn't want to be in. But mum was for him.

My dad entered the stadium with barely 15 minutes to go before kick-off, with my mother agreeing just to wait at the front of the main stand during the game.

This is the best bit. My mother will go to a few games a season if the season tickets aren't getting used. Now at half time milling around the outer cordon she spots a tunstile door open whilst all the rest are closed. So my wee mum then shuffles past the outer security, mingling with Uefa officials coming and going in and out of the stadium. She goes inside the door and up the steps inside but unfortunetly all the doors inside are locked. At this point you have to realise my little mum is shaking like a leaf and nervous as hell, but then two stewards chap on a window and signal her over.

They asked: "Can we help you?"

Mum replied (in a frantic western Hebridies accent with her eyes welling with tears) "My husband is in there, I've lost him and can't get back in etc, etc."

A Uefa security guard turned up and hears the same cry for help to which he replies, and this is unbeliveable: "Oh go on then, just go in."

No ticket, no idea where my father was, or me and there goes my wee mum. She has just blagged her way into the Uefa cup final without a ticket!

When we all met outside the ground we were shocked with disbelief to say the very least.

Unfortunately we had to walk all the way back to the hotel which must have been about eight miles.

But we met up with Greg Hemphill, of Chewin the Fat, and his brother. A truly remarkable trip with our luck just running out at the end result."

Paul Donnelly, Dunfermline

"Seville produced both funny and moving moments, the funniest being on our way back to the bus to take us to Seville airport.

We were trying to finish off the camera spool and since we did not have many photos of the three of us in the group, we decided to ask a passer by to take a snap of us.

A tall bronzed guy sporting an Espana shirt and designer shades came passing.

My best interpretation of 'You take photo of three of us' pointing to the camera.

The reply came back 'nae bother wee man, where do I press'.

Subsequently the guy was from Greenock, looks can certainly be deceptive.

Certainly the most poignant moment was in the early hours after the game. We were wandering the streets of Seville in the vain hope of trying to get a taxi back to our hotel in Huelva which was about 50 miles South of Seville. We were wandering aimlessly in the bowels of Seville, and in passing a barren play park containing a solitary bench, we were met with a cry of 'Come on the hoops' from a sole voice who had made this bench his resting place for the night.

It was obvious from his dress and appearance that this guy had drained every financial resource in order to get here.

My friends and I all looked to each other at the same time, with the same thought 'we deserved to win this', it sure can be both a beautiful and cruel game."

Stephen Henry, London

"The night before the match six of us went out in Seville to see the local delights. All was fine and dandy, had a great time and headed for a taxi - a feat that seems easy in theory, but was an absolute nightmare!

After 40 minutes, two of the party managed to get a lift. The idea was to meet up at the hotel for a few drinks when the remaining four returned. After about another 40 minutes of more walking, moaning and hopelessly flagging anything that was white and had four wheels, we managed to stop a local Police car to ask for help.

The two chaps got out the car and waited with us to try and flag a cab, but after about 10-15 minutes they mumbled something in their native tongue and pointed us into the back of the Police car.

Somehow, and I'm not quite sure how we actually managed it, the four of us crumpled into the back seats of the Police car, and sat giggling to the entirety of our journey back to the Hotel.

On arrival, it seemed appropriate to take a snap of the two lads with me, my girlfriend Yvonne and my brother's girlfriend Glynis. Poor Chris was left to take the photo!

When I got back home I sent the photo to one of the officers and this is the response I got:

Gracias a ti por enviar la fotografía (siempre es grato tener un recuerdo). El vehículo policial no era lo mas adecuado pero ya comprobasteis que los taxis estaban imposible Disculpa por no responder antes pero el trabajo me ha tenido muy ocupado. Un abrazo Fernando. Agente 206 Policía Local de Sevilla.

Translated: Thank you for sending the photograph, it's always pleasant to have a memento. The police vehicle is not the most adequate but I'm sure you understand that all the taxis were taken. I'm sorry for not replying earlier because work has kept us very busy. A hug to you, from Fernando.

Great ambassadors for Spain!"

Statistics

19/9/02	**Celtic 8-1 FK Suduva**	
	Larsson 3, Petrov, Sutton,	
	Lambert, Hartson, Valgaeren	Att: 36,824
03/10/02	**FK Suduva 0-2 Celtic**	
	Fernandez, Thompson	
	(agg: 10-1)	Att: 1,200

31/10/02	**Celtic 1-0 Blackburn Rovers**	
	Larsson Att: 59,553	
14/11/02	**Blackburn Rovers 0-2 Celtic**	
	Larsson, Sutton	
	(agg: 3-0)	Att: 29,698

28/11/02	**Celtic 1-0 Celta Vigo**	
	Larsson Att: 53,726	
12/12/02	**Celta Vigo 2-1 Celtic**	
	Hartson,	
	(agg: 2-2 Celtic win on away goals) Att:26,000	

20/02/03	**Celtic 3-1 Vfb Stuttgart**	
	Lambert, Maloney, Petrov	Att: 59,000
27/02/03	**Vfb Stuttgart 3-2 Celtic**	
	Thompson, Sutton	
	(agg 5-4)	Att: 50,600

13/03/03	**Celtic 1-1 Liverpool**	
	Larsson	Att: 59,759
20/03/03	**Liverpool 0-2 Celtic**	
	Thompson, Hartson	
	(agg: 3-1)	Att: 44,238

10/04/03	**Celtic 1-1 Boavista**	
	Larsson	Att: 60,000
24/04/03	**Boavista 0-1 Celtic**	
	Larsson	
	(agg 2-1)	Att: 11,000

| 21/05/03 | **Celtic 2-3 FC Porto** (aet) | |
| | Larsson 2 | Att: 52,972 |

Scorers:

Larsson	11
Sutton	3
Hartson	3
Thompson	3
Lambert	2
Petrov	2
Maloney	1
Fernandez	1
Valgaeren	1

Games Played	13
Goals Scored	27
Ave Goals per game	2.1
Total Shots	147
Ave shots per game	11.3
Shooting Accuracy	43%
Goals to Shots %	18%
Passes	5,365
Ave passes per game	412.7
Pass Completion %	75%
Tackles	405
Goals Conceded	12
Ave goals conceded per game	0.9
Fouls	216
Ave fouls conceded per game	16.6
Yellow Cards	22
Red Cards	1
Clean sheets:	6
Minutes played:	1200

Celtic played the first leg at home in every round right up until the final.
Celtic scored an average of 2.1 goals per game.
Celtic scored a goal every 44 minutes.
Celtic scored first in 10 out of 13 matches.
Every opponent up until the final had a 'V' in the name and the final was of course in SeVille.

Appearances in Uefa Cup.
Subs in brackets.

Balde	12
Douglas	12
Lennon	12
Petrov	12
Valgaeren	12
Thompson	10 (2)
Agathe	10
Larsson	10
Hartson	9 (2)
Sutton	9 (1)
Lambert	8 (3)
Laursen	6 (2)
Mjallby	5
Guppy	3
McNamara	2 (4)
Sylla	2 (4)
Maloney	2 (2)
Smith	1 (3)
Fernandez	1 (2)
Crainey	1 (1)
Gould	1
Healy	1
Kennedy	1
Petta	1
Lynch	(1)
Miller	(1)

With thanks to Opta for supplying some of the statistics.

Roll of Honour

Andrew McAllister, Greenock, Billy McAllister, Greenock, Danny McAllister, Greenock, Tony McAllister, Greenock, Bradley Abbott, Hyvots, Grant Abraham, Liverpool, Lindsay Annette Ackroyd, Bradford, West Yorkshire, Craig Adair, Motherwell, David Adair, Holytown, Jim Adair, Holytown, Kelly-Anne Adair, Clydebank, Kevin Adair, Motherwell, Kieron Adair, Motherwell, Stephen Adair, Motherwell, Billy Adams, Bellshill, Brian Adams, Livingston, Christina Adams, Bishopbriggs, Glasgow, Claire Adams, Bishopbriggs, Glasgow, Daniel Adams, Dundee, Ian Adams, Aberdeen, Jim Adams, Gowkthrapple, Wishaw, Jim Adams, Julie Adams, Glasgow, Lynsey Adams, Winchburgh, Mark Adams, Bishopbriggs, Paul Adams, Bishopbriggs, Stephen Adams, Houston, Renfrewshire, Allister Adamson, Canada, Tom Adamson, Saltcoats, Tyler Adamson, Alloa, Adamson, Canada, Del Adder, Coatbridge, William Addie, Westhill, Daniel Addison, Stirling, David Addison, Kippen, Greig Addison, Stirling, Maureen Addison, Stirling, Paul Addison, Stirling, Michael Adear, Austrialia, Stevie Aeron, Cumbernauld, Thomas af Geijerstam, Stockholm, Neil Agathey, Johnstone, Renfrewshire, Claire Agnew, Glasgow, Claire Agnew, Glasgow, Lisa Agnew, Glasgow, Michael Agnew, Oxford, Paul Agnew, Glasgow, Stevie Agnew, Glasgow, John Ahern, London, Anthony Ahmad, Lurgan, Nazir, Naveed and Nabeel Ahmad, Pollokshields, Glasgow, Paul Ainsworth, Bishopton, Renfrewshire, Alan Aird, Greenock, Jack Airlie, Hamilton, Barry Aitchison, Lochgelly, Fife, Raymond Aitchison, Vancouver, Canada, Brian Aitken, Balloch, Heather Aitken, Aberdeen, Kenneth Aitken, Bannockburn, Maureen Aitken, Balloch, Dunbartonshire, Richard Aitken, Springburn, William Aitkenhead, Grangemouth, John Aiton, Glasgow, Heather Ajagsfan, Michael Ajagsfan, Aleah Alexander, Stirling, Cathy Alexander, Barton, Newarthill, Greta Alexander, Luton, Beds, Kelly Alexander, Ayrshire, Kevin Alexander, Hamilton, Lynda Alexander, Raploch, Stirling, Paul Alexander, Hamilton, Richard Alexander, Bishopbriggs, Richard Alexander, Robert Alexander, Stirling, Roddy Alexander, Rutherglen, Glasgow, Stuart Alexander, Bridge of Allan, Stuart Alexander, Glasgow, Wullie Alexander, Egremont, Sybaris Ali, Eldergrove Glasgow, Zaiba Ali, Eldergrove, Glasgow, Frank Alingham, Motherwell, Alec Alison, Irvine, J Alison, Sarah Alison, Irvine, Steff Alison, Gallowgate, Andrena Allan, Glasgow, Bob Allan, Stonehaven, Clair Allan, Coatbridge, Dave Allan, Glasgow, Francis Allan, Glasgow, Gail Allan, Methil, Fife, George Allan, Knightswood, Glasgow, Jamie Allan, Florida, USA, Jessie Allan, Glasgow, Jillian Allan, Methil, Jim Allan, Coatbridge, Jim Allan, Coatbridge, Joanne Allan, Swinton, Joe Allan, Glasgow, John Allan, Glasgow, John Mark Allan, Scotland, Joyce Allan, Mosstodloch, Moray, Margaret Allan, Coatbridge, Mark Allan, Glasgow, Michael Allan, Murrayshire, Michael Allan, Stonehaven, Michelle Allan, Leamington Spa, Mick Allan, Glasgow, Robert Allan, Coatbridge, Scott Allan, Boness, Stuart Allan, Boness, Tommy Allan, Paisley, James Allen, Mary Hill, Jane Allen, Alexandria, Joanne Allen, Swinton, John Allen, Belfast, John Allen, Walney Island, Raymond Allingham, Glasgow, Declan Allison, Irvine, George Allison, Penicuik, Graeme Allison, Easterhouse, Glasgow, James Allison, Glasgow, Jim Allison, Lesmagow, Joe Allison, Moodiesburn, Joshua Allison, Pollok, Glasgow, Liam Allison, Airdrie, Martin Allison, Airdrie, Michael Allison, Glasgow, Paul Allison, Irvine, Robert Allison, Hunterhill, Paisley, William Allison, Airdrie, William Alliston, Springburn, Archie Amato, Bridgton, John Amato, Haghill, Lanarkshire, Sarah-Annette Amato, Haghill, Lanarkshire, Vera Amato, Bridgeton, Glasgow, Alexander Amos, Glasgow, Alan Anderson, Holy Town, Ann Anderson, Cowdenbeath, Ann Anderson, High Burnside, Billy Anderson, Cowdenbeath, Chantelle Anderson, Parkhead, Glasgow, Colin Anderson, Mansfield, Daniel Anderson, Cumbernauld, Daniel Anderson, Stirling, Daniel Anderson, Stirling, Danny Anderson, Rutherglen, Glasgow, Darren Anderson, Aberdeen, Darren Anderson, Fraserburgh, Aberdeenshire, Dave Anderson, Guernsey, David Anderson, Denny, Derek

Anderson, Brighton, Derek Anderson, Hamilton, Dermot Anderson, Glasgow, Eilidh Anderson, Hamilton, Frankie Anderson, Bishopbriggs, Glasgow, Gary Anderson, Kennishead, Glasgow, Gemma Anderson, Gordon Anderson, 'D' Shift, St Fergus, Graham Anderson, Geneva, Iain Anderson, Stirling, Iain Anderson, Stirling, Jackie Anderson, Stirling, Jackie Anderson, Stirling, James Anderson, Clydebank, Jamie Anderson, Falkirk, Jim Anderson, Glasgow, John Anderson, Ibiza, Lesley Anderson, Glasgow, Marty Anderson, Broomhill, Michael Anderson, Huxter, Shetland, Mick Anderson, Stirling, Patrick Anderson, Edinburgh, Paul Anderson, Foxbar, Paisley, Peter Anderson, Greenock, Ralph Anderson, Bishop's Stortford, Hertfordshire, Ray Anderson, Greenock, Richard Anderson, Dunoon, Richard (Spurs) Anderson, Oakley, Dunfermline, Robert Anderson, Parkhouse, Ryan Anderson, Falkirk, Sarah Anderson, Falkirk, Sophie Anderson, Brighton, Stephanie Anderson, Parkhouse, Glasgow, Stephen Anderson, Glasgow, Stevo Anderson, Cumbernauld, Stuart Anderson, West Wemyss, Susan Anderson, Glasgow, Tasha Anderson, Cumbernauld, Thomas HP Anderson, Gracemount, Edinburgh, Wilma Anderson, Wishaw, James Anderson O'Neil, Forres, James Anderson O'Neil, Forres, Yan Andrejak, Carntyne, Barry Andress, Ayr, Jason Andress, Ayr, Benny Andrew, Auchtermuchty, Fife, Ann-Marie Andrews, Glasgow, Danielle Andrews, Glasgow, Robbie Andrews, Glasgow, Robert Andrews, Glasgow, Shandan Andrews, Glasgow, Celtic Angus, Govan, Neil Angus, Inverness, Cliff Anyon, Aberdeen, Clare Appleyard, Rothwell, John Appleyard, Corby, Liam Appleyard, Market Harborough, Leicestershire, Mark Appleyard, Manchester, Dixie Apsley, Livingston, Kellyann Archibald, Barrhead, Glasgow, Rayo Archie, London, Kevin Arden, Glasgow, Ally Armadale, Eileen Armadale, Stovie Armadale, Stephen Armour, Bournemouth, Thomas Armour, Fairhill, Hamilton, Thomas Armour, Hamilton, Cameron Armstrong, Bonnyrigg, Midlothian, Darren Armstrong, Glasgow, Derek Armstrong, Bonhill, Dunbartonshire, Gary Armstrong, Bonnyrigg, Gary Armstrong, Bonnyrigg, Midlothian, Joe Armstrong, Cardonald, John Armstrong, South Nitshill, Renfrewshire, David Arnold, Arbroath, Fowzia Arshad, Gorbals, Glasgow, Andrew Arthur, Bishopbriggs, Glasgow, David Arthur, Edinburgh, Jonathan Arthur, Bishopbriggs, Glasgow, Linda Arthur, Port Glasgow, Stephen Arthur, Bishopbriggs, Glasgow, Wullie Arundel, Shettleston, Brian Ashe, Thornliebank, Glasgow, Dylan Ashe, Rutherglen, Glasgow, Tam Ashley, Irvine, Robert Aske, Inverness, David Askew, Bedfordshire, Lindsey Atkinson, London, Mark Atkinson, Coatbridge, Margaret Attley, Glasgow, James Auchincloss, Suffolk, Frank Auchterlonie, Glenrothes, Fife, Scott Auchterlonie, Glenrothes, Fife, Colin Auld, Bishopbriggs, Glasgow, Chris Austin, Oxford, Ryan Ayr, Linwood, Maria Azevedo, London,

Viny B Jnr, Bearsden, Jesper Backstrom, Stockholm, Louise Bacon, Saltcoats, Ayrshire, Luke Bacon, Coleraine, Gerry Bagstad, Greenock, Raymond Bagstad, Greenock, Theresa Bagstad, Greenock, Annie Bailey, Scarborough, Gillian Bailey, Largs, John Bailey, Dumbarton, Paul Bailey, Bellshill, Lanarkshire, Chris Baillie, Barrhead, Lyndsay Baillie, Barrhead, Glasgow, Stevie Baillie, Barrhead, Glasgow, David Bain, Thurso, Caithness, John Bain, Thurso, Caithness, Tam Bain, Paisley, Colin Bain, Lanarkshire, Justine Bainbridge, Stirling, David Baine, Denny, Dougie Baird, Barrhead, Kevin Baird, Rutherglen, Glasgow, Wilma Baird, Penilee, Glasgow, Averil Baker, Largs, Connor Baker, Glasgow, Lawrie Baker, Largs, Robert Baker, Dalry, Sean Baker, Glasgow, Simone Balata, Giffnock, Jim Balfour, Knightswood, Glasgow, Linda Ball, Kilmacolm, Renfrewshire, David Balloch, Greenock, Joanne Balloch, Kirkintilloch, Holly Balls, Glasgow, Stuart Balls, Glasgow, Des Balmer, Balloch, Francis Balmer, Skelmorlie, Ayrshire, Michael Balmer, Skelmorlie, Ayrshire, Patrick Balmer, Skelmorlie, Ayrshire, Jordan, Glasgow, Emma Banff, Aberdeenshire, Zander Banff, Aberdeenshire, Phillip Banister, Glasgow, John Banks, Wirrall, Brenda Bannerman, Glasgow, Raymond Bannerman, Glasgow, Raymond Bannigan, Bishopbriggs, Glasgow, Jim Bannon, East Kilbride, Bobby Banus, Erskine, Carousel Bar, Bellshill, McCormicks Bar, Bellshill, Peppes Bar FC, Stevie Barber, Glasgow, Claire Barbi, Isle Of Bute, Darren Barcik,

Dunfermline, Alex Barclay, Fresno, California, Bryan Barclay, Bellshill, Linda Barclay, Fresno, California, Martin Barclay, Townhead, Glasgow, Robert Barclay, Renfrew, Fiona Bardintulloch, Thurso, Caithness, Willie Bardintulloch, Thurso, Caithness, Jarek Barecki, Opole, Poland, Ellis Barilli, Bracknell, Hugh Barilli Snr, Port Glasgow, Bill Barker, Methil, Fife, Ian Barker, Methil, Fife, Martin Barkley, Larne, Northern Ireland, Scott Barlow, St Ninians, Stirling, Sean Barlow, St Ninians, Stirling, Jade Barnard, London, Jean Barnes, Dalkeith, John Barnes, Kirkcaldy, John Barnes, Newcastle, Ryan Barnes, Glasgow, Steve Barnes, Fulham, Paul Barnes Jnr, Tollcross, Stephen Barnett, Germiston, Roy Barney, Morayshire, Allan Barr, Toryglen, Allan F. Barr, Toryglen, Andrew Barr, Old Pollock, Carol-Anne Barr, Toryglen, Christopher Barr, Craigend, Debbie Barr, Irvine, Debbie Barr, Toryglen, Graham Barr, Pollok, Glasgow, Ian Barr, Irvine, Jackie Barr, Pollok, Glasgow, Jamie Barr, Bletchley, John Barr, Greenwich, Keiran Barr, Barrhead, Kieran Barr, Bletchley, England, Malky Barr, Pollok, Glasgow, Malky Barr, Pollok, Glasgow, Scott Barr, Sandyhills, Stephen Barr, Erskine, Tricia Barr, Montrose, Wullie Barr, Port Glasgow, Rab Barr, Nottingham, Mark Barras, Mid Calder, Adele Barratt, Dunfermline, Austin Barrett, Thornliebank, Glasgow, Des Barrett, Baillieston, Donnie Barrett, Thornliebank, Glasgow, John Barrett, Thornliebank, Glasgow, Madge Barrett, Thornliebank, Glasgow, Maria Barrett, Thornlibank Glasgow, Stephen Barrett, Peterborough, Canada, Alan Barrie, Guildford, Surrey, David Barrie, Erskine, Gordon Barrie, Rutherglen, Glasgow, Kevin Barron, Cheltenham, Gloucestershire, Kevin Barron, Cheltenham, Gloucestershire, Neil Barron, Luton, Bedfordshire, Robert Barron, Lutton, Justin Barry, Sydney, Australia Kevin Barry, Gallowgate, Glasgow, Mike Bartik, Dunfermline, Tony Bartlett, Alva, Clackmannanshire, Kelly Barton, Dundee, Elizabeth Bashir, Cardonald, Glasgow, Jav Bashir, Paisley, Stinder Bassi, Bearsden, Charlene Bauld, Drumoyne, Lanarkshire, Ben Bavis, Hong Kong, Mark Bavis, Hong Kong, Alan Baxter, Inverness, Colin Baxter, Cleland, Lanarkshire, Craig Baxter, Carluke, Craig Baxter, Carluke, Davy Baxter, Perth, Gerry Baxter, Bonnybridge, Stirlingshire, Glen Baxter, Woodburn, Dalkeith, Grant Baxter, Dalkeith, Isla Baxter, Inverness, Jordan Baxter, Inverness, Lauren Baxter, Inverness, Liam Baxter, Inverness, Sharon Baxter, Inverness, Marc Bean, Bishopbriggs, Glasgow, Craig Beaton, Stenhousemuir, David Beaton, Portree, Isle of Skye, Drew Beaton, Stepps, Lanarkshire, Frances Beaton, Surrey, Iain Beaton, Bellshill, Lanarkshire, Iain Beaton, Portree, Isle of Skye, John Beaton, Lochcarron, Ross-shire, Lorraine Beaton, Stenhousemuir, Niamh Beaton, Surrey, Nicola Beaton, Stenhousemuir, Rosie Beaton, Stepps, Lanarkshire, Ross Beaton, Pirbright, Surrey, Scott Beaton, Stenhousemuir, Alexis Beattie, Clydebank, Alexis Beattie, Clydebank, Conor Beattie, Croftfoot, Lanarkshire, Daniel Beattie, Croftfoot, Danny Beattie, Irvine, Ayrshire, Debbie Beattie, Irvine, Ayrshire, Iain Beattie, Bonhill, Dunbartonshire John Beattie, Bishopbriggs, Glasgow, Stephen Charles Beattie, Glasgow, Yvonne Beattie, Frank Beck, James Beck, Helensburgh, Pamela Beck, Whitburn, John Beckett, Glasgow, Judy Beckett, Glasgow, Robert Beckett, Easterhouse, Glasgow, Tam Beckett, Glasgow, Hugh Beedie, Peebles, Soskia Beetham, London, Gordon Begbie, Dalkeith, Ryan Begbie, Dalkeith, David Beggans, East Kilbride, Sean Beggans, East Kilbride, Mark Begley, Garry Begley, Glasgow, Sean Begley, Kildare, Thomas Begley, New Stevenson, Ayrshire, Grant Belizaire, Bath, Samuel Joseph Belizaire, Bath, Adam Bell, Invergordon, Alana Bell, Possilpark, Glasgow, Alison Bell, Isle of Harris, Charlie Bell, Rockingham, Western Australia, Chris Bell, Motherwell, Colin Bell, Falkirk, Daniel Bell, Invergordon, David Bell, Wemyss Bay, Eddie Bell, Ayrshire, Greg Bell, Ian Bell, Joclynne Bell, Motherwell, Joe Bell, Clydebank, John Paul Bell, Joseph Bell, Blantyre, Kay Bell, Lauren Bell, Invergordon, Margaret Bell, Ayrshire, Rian Bell, Richard Bell, Falkirk, Stevie Bell, Glasgow, Thomas Bell, Livingston, Gina Belton, Fife, John Belton, Seville, Sally Belton, Fife, Alexander Bender, California, USA, Gary Benjamin, Thornliebank, Jim Benkelly, Cardonald, Glasgow, Frank Bennedetti, East Kilbride, Wullie Bennet, Milton, Glasgow, Ann Bennett, Whitby, Ontario, Canada, Cheryl Bennett, Kilsyth, Christopher

Bennett, Rutherglen, Colin Bennett, Leven, David Bennett, Jack Bennett, Faifley, Jack Bennett, Janine Bennett, Airdrie, Jennifer Bennett, Shotts, Martin Bennett, Cumbernauld, Michael Bennett, Leven, Mick Bennett, Newton Mearns, Glasgow, Scott Bennett, Faifley, Clydebank, Tam Bennett, Newton Village, Dalkeith, Tony Bennett, Clydebank, Billy Bennie, Glasgow, Carol-Anne Benson, Glasgow, Fiona Bensoussane, Bellahouston, Hassan Bensoussane, Bellahouston, Steven Bentley, Thornliebank, Glasgow, Scott Benzie, Aberdeen, Stefan Bergin, Edinburgh, Bernett, East Lothian, Jack Berrie, Glasgow, Angela Berry, Blackhill, Angela Berry, Glasgow, David Berry, Stirling, Frances Berry, Garrowhill, Glasgow, Frank Berry, Blackhill, James Berry, Bargeddie, Lanarkshire, John Berry, Saltcoats, Michael Berry, Glasgow, Patrick Berry, Garrowhill, Glasgow, Katie Berryman, Drumsagard Village, Glasgow, Steven Berryman, Drumsagard Village, Glasgow, David Best, Cambuslang, Glasgow, David Best, Eastfield, Davie Best, Rutherglen, Glasgow, Elaine Best, Eastfield, Elizabeth Best, Eastfield, Stephen Best, Clarkston, Marie Bett, Dunfermline, Derek Bettie, Ayr, Cristopher Bettly, Coatbridge, Ellen Bettly, Coatbridge, Maryrose Beveridge, Fife, Steven Bevis, Bernd Beyer, Erlangen Germany, Brugie Bhoy, Glasgow, Dukesy Bhoy, Lesmahagow, Jammy Bhoy, Stevenston, Ayrshire, John Bhoy Murdoch, Kenny Bhoy, Ruchazie, Glasgow, The Bhoys, Bridgehouse, Norwich, Wilson Bhoys, Largs, Karen Bias, Kilmarnock, Ryan Bias, Kilmarnock, James Agustus Vincent Bickam, London, Alec Bickerstaff, Paisley, Sean Bigal, Manchester, Katriona Biggar, Motherwell, Allana Biggins, Barrowfield, Lanarkshire, Joe Biggins, Barrowfield, Lanarkshire, Alexander Bill, Pollok, Glasgow, Theresa Bill, Pollok, Glasgow, Conor Billings, Offaly, Ireland, Roslyn Billings, Offaly, Ireland, Andrew Binnie, Denny, David Binnie, Denny, George Binnie, Shieldhill, Falkirk, Katie Binnie, East Kilbride, Pauline Binnie, Bonnybridge, Stirlingshire, Robert Binnie, Bonnybridge, Stirlingshire, Stacey Binnie, Glasgow, Joe Biolik, Edinburgh, Martey Bird, Springburn, Mikey Bird, Springburn, Glasgow, Neil Bird, Dundee, Andrew Birnie, Northampton, Paul Birnie, Essex, Graeme Birrell, Pittenweem, Fife, Mark Birrell, Glasgow, Steve Birrell, Royal Estate Sandringham, Audrey Bisland, Calton, John Bisland, Calton, Alistair Bisset, Jamestown, Ryan Bissett, Perth, Ryan Bissett, Perth, Andrew Black, Dumfries, Anthony Black, Irvine, Colin Black, Eastleigh, Colin Black, Glasgow Celtic Supporters Club, Colin Black, Lerwick, Derek Black, Carluke, Dizzy Black, south-west Glasgow, Ian Black, Greenock, Ian Black, Shetland, Jacqueline Black, Isleburgh, Shetland, James Black, Dumbarton, Jamie Black, Dumbarton, Jamie Black, Lerwick, Jim Black, Prestwick, Joe Black, Shetland, John Black, Dundee, John Black, Paisley, Kathleen Black, Carluke, Kieran Black, Glasgow, Kieran (Wee Man) Black, Kings Park, Glasgow, Liz Black, Dumbarton, Liz Black, Glasgow, Michael Black, Stornoway, Ross Black, Livingston, Scott Black, Lerwick, Siannon Black, Dumbarton, Stewart Black, Livingston, Stewarty Black, Livingston, Thomas Black, Glasgow, Thomas (TJ) Black, south-west Glasgow, Tom Black, Prestwick, Vicki Black, Cumbernauld, Blackburn, Port Glasgow, John Blacker, Castlemilk, Glasgow, Thomas Blacker, Castlemilk, Glasgow, William Blacker, Castlemilk, Glasgow, Willie Blacker, Castlemilk, Glasgow, John Blackett, Cathkin, Lanarkshire, Morgan Blackie, Kilwinning, Jane Blacklock, Gorebridge, The Blacks, Maryhill, George Blackshaw, Glasgow, John Blackshaw, Glasgow, George Blackshore, Glasgow, Raymie Blackstock, Linwood, Ryan Blades, Coatbridge, Alastair Blain, Kilmacolm, George Blain, Shieldhall Ambulance Station, Shaun Blain, Allan Blair, Croy, Lanarkshire, Anthony Blair, Holytown, Charles Blair, Glasgow, Craig Blair, Castlemilk, Glasgow, Craig Blair, Elderslie, Renfrewshire, Craig Blair, Rutherglen, Glasgow, David Blair, Johnstone, Jim Blair, Blackhill, Jim Blair, Blackhill, Jim Blair, Provanmill, Glasgow, Joe Blair, Rutherglen, Glasgow, Joseph Blair, Rutherglen, Karen Blair, Germiston, Glasgow, Ryan Blair, Rutherglen, Glasgow, Zander Blair, Kirkintilloch, Gerry Blair Jnr, Blairhill, Coatbridge, Gerry Blair Snr, Blairhill, Coatbridge, Irene Blake, Renfrew, Liam Blake, Southport, Maureen Blake, Glasgow, Margo Blane, Glasgow, Andrew Blaney, Motherwell, Matthew Blaney, Motherwell, Seamus Og Blaney, Ballycastle, James Blenkinsop, Rosneath, Dumbartonshire, Ryan Bloomfield,

Kirkcaldy, Stevie Bloomfield, Kirkcaldy, Steven Bloomfield Jnr, Kirkcaldy, Donald Blue, Ardrishaig, Argyll, Francine Blues, Stirling, Gerry Blyth, Bargeddie, Lanarkshire, Gerry Blyth, Coatbridge, John Blyth, Glasgow, John Blyth, Glasgow, Stevie Blyth, Edinburgh, Kenneth Boa, Dumfries and Galloway, Gary Boag, Greenock, James Boardman, Dalbeattie, Kirkcudbrightshire, Rakhmet Bodeep, Govanhill, Glasgow, John Bogie, Glasgow, Tommy (Tim) Bogle, Johnstone Castle, Jong Boi, Glasgow, Mike Boil, USA, Cam Bolan, London, Claude Bolls, Amsterdam, Tosh Bolton, Bellshill, Agnes Bonar, Tarbolton, Craig Bonar, Glasgow, David Bonar, East Kilbride, Thomas Bond, Glasgow, Thomas Bonds, Glasgow, John Boner, Glasgow, Martin Boner, Glasgow, Sharon Boner, Glasgow, Allan Bonini, East Kilbride, Gary Bonini, Busby, Glenis Bonini, East Kilbride, Pauline Bonini, East Kilbride, Andy Bonnar, Greenock, David Bonnar, Greenock, David Bonnar, Isle of Man, Frank Bonnar, Barrow-in-Furness, Joe Bonnar, Greenock, Patrick Charles Bonnar, Northwood, Ryan Bonnar, Ibrox, Glasgow, Amy Bonner, Helensburgh, Christopher Bonner, Helensburgh, Jack Bonner, Helensburgh, Jamie Bonner, Helensburgh, Jamie Bonner, Helensburgh, Joshua Bonner, Helensburgh, Karen Bonner, Helensburgh, Kevin Bonner, Helensburgh, Lewis Bonner, Helensburgh, Martin Bonner, Gargunnock, Owen Bonner, Helensburgh, Patrick Bonner, Tillicoultry, Sarah Bonner, Helensburgh, Stuart Bonner, Yana Bonner, Yvonne Bonner, Tillicoultry, Darren Booie, Greenock, Ally Booth, Glasgow, Bryan Booth, Newton Mearns, Jim Boots, Clydebank, David Borland, Clydebank, Derek Borland, Carfin, Lanarkshire, Raymond Borland, Glasgow, Padge Boston, Aty Boswell, Craigneuk, Ishbel Boulton, East Wemyss, Fife, Shaun Bowers, Knightswood, Stephen Bowers, Knightswood, Stephen Bowers Junior, Knightswood, Lizzy Bowes, Glasgow, Don Bowie, Cumbernauld, Duncan Bowie, Australia, Elaine Bowie, Australia, Graham Bowie, Aberdeenshire, James Bowie, Watford, Shirley Bowie, Cumbernauld, Conner Bowman, Larkhall, Danny Bowman, Livingston, Jenni Bowman, Livingston, John Bowman, Winchburgh, West Lothian, Brian Boyce, Cumbernauld, Fraser Boyce, Ayrshire, Kevin Boyce, Glasgow, Marcus Boyce, Cumbernauld, Mark Boyce, Houston, Renfrewshire, Mary Boyce, Toryglen, Pauline Boyce, Glasgow, Sally Boyce, Peckham, London, Stephen Boyce, Cumbernauld, Veronica Boyce, Coatbridge, William Boyce, Croy, Lanarkshire, Eddie Boyce Jnr, Peckham, London, Eddie Boyce Snr, Peckham, London, Dickie Boyd, London, Ewan Boyd, Lenzie, Joseph Boyd, Chapelhall, Joseph Boyd, Chapelhall, Liam Boyd, South Armagh, Mary Boyd, Chapelhall, Lanarkshire, Mary Boyd, Chapelhall, Lanarkshire, Kieran-Paul Boyes, Whitburn, Rebekah Boyes, Whitburn, Bernie Boylan, Bathgate, David Boylan, Barrowfield, Frank Boylan, Leven, Sandra Boylan, Leven, Tam Boylan, Reading, Berks, Airen Boyle, Edinburgh, Andy Boyle, Kilwinning, Benny Boyle, Chapelhall, Billy Boyle, Greenock, Billy Boyle, Renfrew, Bossie Boyle, Coatbridge, Brendan Boyle, Shawlands, Glasgow, Brian Boyle, Hamilton, Brian Boyle, Hamilton, Caitlyn Boyle, Cumbernauld, Carol Boyle, Cumbernauld, Catherine Boyle, Glasgow, Catherine Boyle, Glasgow, Cecilia Boyle, Glasgow, Charles Boyle, Glasgow, Charlie Boyle, Paisley, Charlie Boyle, Wisp Green, Christopher Boyle, Clydebank, Danny Boyle, Edinburgh, David Boyle, Bishopbriggs, Glasgow, Dean Boyle, Kilmacolm, Renfrewshire, Erin Boyle, Kings Park, Glasgow, Esther Boyle, Glasgow, Evelyn Boyle, Clydebank, Gavin Boyle, Norway, Gerard Boyle, Glasgow, Gerry Boyle, Birmingham, Gerry Boyle, Kirkintilloch, Gerry Boyle, Motherwell, Gordon Boyle, Kilsyth, Isabell Boyle, Kirkintilloch, James Boyle, Renfrew, Jenni Boyle, Doncaster, Jimmy Boyle, Edinburgh, Joe Boyle, Bellshill, Joe Boyle, Johnstone, John Boyle, Bellshill, John Joe Boyle, Edinburgh, Jonjo Boyle, Bearsden, Joseph Boyle, Cumbernauld, Joseph Boyle, Lanton, Roxburghshire, Karen Boyle, Broxburn, Kerry Boyle, Bearsden, Kerryann Boyle, Kilsyth, Kevin Boyle, Clarkston, Kevin Boyle, Motherwell, Kevin Boyle, Springburn, Glasgow, Kevin Boyle, Sydney, Australia, Kieran Boyle, Kilmarnock, Kieran Boyle, Shawlands, Liam Boyle, Niddrie, Liz Boyle, Johnstone, Loraine Boyle, Motherwell, Lynda Boyle, Kincardine, Mairi Boyle, Bearsden, Martin Boyle, Kilmarnock, Martin Boyle, Kincardine, Matthew Boyle, Kirkintilloch, Matthew Boyle, Kirkintilloch,

Megan Boyle, Bearsden, Michael Boyle, Glasgow, Michael Boyle, Kilmarnock, Mick Boyle, Clydebank, Paddy Boyle, Edinburgh, Owen Boyle, North London, Paul Boyle, Glasgow, Paul Boyle, Glasgow, Paul Boyle, Paula Boyle, Kincardine, Robbie Boyle, Clydebank, Robert Boyle, Clydebank, Rosemarie Boyle, Cumbernauld, Stephen Boyle, Milton, Steven Boyle, Edinburgh, Steven Boyle, Grangemouth, Steven Boyle, Surrey, Stevie Boyle, Glasgow, Tony Boyle, Edinburgh, Tracey Boyle, Cardonald, Glasgow, John Boyle Jnr, Possilpark, John Boyle Snr, Possilpark, Burke Boys, Belfast, Stephen Brace, Greenock, Patrick Bracken, Peterhead, Aberdeenshire, Kelly Brackenridge, Linwood, Renfrewshire, Darren Bradey, Coatbridge, Bill Bradley, Whitehaven, Charles Bradley, Glasgow, Christopher Bradley, Bellshill, Coleen Bradley, Riddrie, Lanarkshire, David Bradley, Cumbernauld, Eddie Bradley, Bonnybridge, Stirlingshire, Eddie Bradley, Bonnybridge, Stirlingshire, Elizabeth Bradley, Port Glasgow, Gerry Bradley, Greenock, Gerry Bradley, Wishaw, Ian Bradley, Port Glasgow, James Bradley, Old Kilpatrick, John Bradley, Bellshill, Karen Bradley, Glasgow, Kevin Bradley, Port Glasgow, Liam Bradley, Castlemilk, Liam Bradley, Co. Derry, Lynette Bradley, Glasgow, Mariclare Bradley, Wishaw, Martin Bradley, Barrhead, Glasgow, Paul Bradley, Blackwood, Cumbernauld, Rhona Bradley, Linlithgow, Annemarie Bradshaw, Ashwood Park, Glasgow, Conlen Bradshaw, Linwood, Jonathan Bradshaw, Ashwood Park, Glasgow, Lewis Bradshaw, Ashwood Park, Glasgow, Steven Bradshaw, Ashwood Park, Glasgow, Anthony Bradwick, Glasgow, Andy Brady, Angie Brady, Ashleigh Brady, Whiteinch, Connor Brady, Broxburn, Dola Brady, Drumnadrochit, Inverness-shire, Gary Brady, Lochee, Gary Brady, Lochee, Jackie Brady, Broxburn, John Brady, Whiteinch, Kenneth Brady, Mosspark, Kevin Brady, Anstruther, Kevin Brady, Coatbridge, Kevin Brady, Inverness, Kevin Brady, Livingston, Laura Brady, Inverness, Mark Brady, Inverness, Michael Brady, Kings Park, Paul Brady, Coatbridge, Paul Brady, Whiteinch, Rena Brady, Lochee, Roseanne Brady, Barrowfield, Rosina Brady, Lochee, Ryan Brady, Drumnadrochit, Inverness-shire, Stephen Brady, Alexandria, Stephen G. Brady, Cheshire, Steve Brady, Troon, Terry Brady, Bathgate, Timmy Brady, Bathgate, James Brady Jnr, Bellshill, James Brady Snr, Bellshill, Gus Braid, Glasgow, Gus Braid, Glasgow, Martine Braid, Glasgow, George Braithwaite and gang, Lochgelly, David Branagan, Glasgow, John Brand, St Andrews, Matthew Brander, Dunning, Peter Branigan, Glasgow, Donna Brannan, St Ninians, Ian Brannan, Glasgow, Kieran Brannan, Hamilton, Kitkat Brannan, Hamilton, Margaret Brannan, Dundee, Mark Brannan, Glasgow, Mark Brannan, Springburn, Glasgow, Morag Brannan, Glasgow, Tommy Brannan, Newmarket, Canada, Tony Brannan, Glasgow, James Brannen, Aviemore, James Brannen, Aviemore, Dale Brannigan, Cambuslang, Jade Brannigan, Cambuslang, Marcella Brannigan, Cambuslang, Thomas Brannigan, Cambuslang, David Brannon, Dundee, Thomas Braven, , Stevie Brawley, Bailleston, Carol Bray, Glasgow, David Bray, Glasgow, Laura Bray, Glasgow, Maureen Bray, Royston, Glasgow, Sophie Bray, Glasgow, Susan Bray, Glasgow, Jamie Bredin, Glasgow, Niall Bree, Glasgow, Andrea Breen, Stevenston, Andrew Breen, Stevenston, Christopher Breen, Kirkintilloch, Eamon Breen, Newtonards, Eddie Breen, Bishopton, James Breen, Jersey, James Breen, Stevenston, John Breen, Oakley, Fife, Kenny Breen, Livingston, Marc Breen, Motherwell, Michael Breen, Glasgow, Michael Breen, Newtonards, Paul Tomas Breen, Kirkintilloch, Robbie Breen, Kinlochleven, Thomas Breen, Stevenston, Wullie Breen, Livingston, Kirsty Bremner, Elderslie, Aaron Brenan, Glasgow, Harrison Brenan, Glasgow, Amy Brennan, Saltcoats, Barry Brennan, Dalmuir, Billy Brennan, Bathgate, Eon Brennan, Dalmuir, Gillian Brennan, Jamie Brennan, Motherwell, Mhairi-Louise Brennan, Coatbridge, Pamela Brennan, Motherwell, Paul Brennan, Cleland, Peter Brennan, Dumbarton, Sean Brennan, Saltcoats, Tam Brennan, Saltcoats, Vicky Brennan, Motherwell, Bernie Breslin, Dallas, Texas, George Breslin, Bonhill, Nicki Breslin, Balloch, Paul Breslin, Stirling, Peg Breslin, Balloch, Stephen Breslin, Bishopbriggs, Paul and Amanda Brett, Edinburgh, Peter Brice, Glasgow, Darren (Jimmy) McBride, Coatbridge, Declan Bridgeman, Glasgow, John-Paul Bridgeman, Glasgow, Patrick Bridgeman, Clydebank, Fiona Bridges, Ross-shire, Phil

Bridges, Ross-shire, Davie Brien, Buckie, John Brien, Kirkcaldy, Martin Briggs, Glasgow, Iain Brisland, Port Glasgow, Anthony Bristol, Glasgow, Debbie Bristol, Greenock, Bob Brodie, Malton, Hamilton, Lauren Brodie, Croy, Melissa Brodie, Croy, Stephan Brodie, Glasgow, Brian Brody, Cardonald, Adam Brogan, Huntingdon, Eugene Brogan, Aberdeen, Jim Brogan, Corby, Jim Brogan, Corby, Paul Brogan, Dunfermline Sharon Brogan, Dumbarton, Sharon Brogan, Middlesbrough, Aidan Brolly, Castlemilk, Glasgow, Ann Brolly, Castlemilk, Glasgow, Brian Brolly, Coatbridge, Eddie Brolly, Croftfoot, Glasgow, James Brolly, Marie Brolly, Castlemilk, Glasgow, Wully Brolly, Coatbridge, Annie Brooks, Byfield, Northants, David Brooks, Greenock, Swoon Broon, Lochee, Jim Brophy, Carluke, Jamie Bross, Girvan, Paul Brothey, Airdrie, Paul Brothey, Blackburn, Tom Brothey, Blackburn, Ryan Brough, West Lothian, William Brough, West Lothian, Alan Brown, Arbroath, Alan Brown, Allan Brown, Aberdeen, Ann Brown, Barrhead, Anne Brown, Levenvale, Dunbartonshire, Anthony Brown, Erskine, Bobby Brown, Dunfermline, Bradie Brown, Menzieshill, Dundee, Christine Brown, Croy, Chrisy Brown, Hamilton, Colin Brown, Fife, Conner Brown, Glasgow, Craig Brown, Aberdeen. Craig Brown, Condorrat, Cumbernauld, Crawford Brown, Bishopbriggs, Danny (Jnr) Brown, Bellshill, Danny (Jnr) Brown, Bothwell, David Brown, Glasgow, David Brown, Glasgow, David Brown, Mount Vernon, Glasgow, Davy Brown, London, Eric Brown, Beith, Francis Brown, Glasgow, Freddie Brown, Lytham, Lancs, Gary Brown, Bridgeton, George Brown, Glasgow, Gerry Brown, Dublin, Graham Brown, Lochgilphead, Hendy Brown, Glasgow, Henry Brown, Hamilton, I Brown, Montrose, Ian Brown, Stepps, Ian Brown, Stepps, Jack Brown, Linnview, Jacqueline Brown, Ayr, Jacqueline Brown, Bonkle, Jacqueline Brown, Bonkle, James Brown, Ayr, James Brown, Cumbernauld, James Brown, Glasgow, James Brown, Newmains, James (The Bhoy) Brown, Coatbridge, Jamie Brown, Alva, Jason Brown, Glasgow, Jenna Brown, Chapelhall, Jim Brown, Rotherham, John Brown, Ayr, John Brown, Newmains, John Brown, Stirling, Jonathan Brown, Chapelhall, Josh Brown, Castlemilk, Julie Brown, Bishopbriggs, Julie Brown, Stornoway, Western Isles, Kai Brown, Salisbury, Kenneth Brown, Stirling, Kevin Brown, Duntocher, Clydebank, Kevin Brown, Uddingston, Kirsty Brown, Lanark, Lachlan Brown, Ayr, Linda Brown, Newmains, Maggie Brown, Partrick, Mandy Brown, Falkirk, Margaret And Danny Brown, Bellshill, Mark Brown, Kirkintilloch, Max Brown, Erskine, Michelle Brown, Dumbarton, Michelle Brown, Newmains, Mollie Brown, Erskine, Peter Brown, Salisbury, Robert Brown, Cumbernauld, Robert Brown, Cumbernauld, Robert Brown, Glasgow, Robert Brown, Hamilton, Simon Brown, Menzieshill, Dundee, Stephen Brown, Beith, Stephen Bernard Brown, Bathgate, Steven Brown, Glasgow, Steven Brown, Menzieshill, Dundee, Stevie Brown, Linnview, Telly Brown, Auchinleck, Ayrshire, Terence Brown, Belfast, Ross Brown, Lochcarron, Robert Brown Jnr, Cumbernauld, Ali Brown Kyle, Lochalsh, Denise Browne, Glasgow, Kelly Browne, Erskine, Nathan Browne, Erskine, Grant Browning, Milton Keynes, Lee Ryan Browning, Belfast, Lee Ryan Browning, Belfast, Derek Bruce, Glasgow, Gillian Bruce, , Jim Bruce, , Kevin Bruce, Wishaw, Kirsty Bruce, Wishaw, James Bryan, Shotts, John Bryan, Blackburn Lancashire, Paul Bryan, Blackburn Lancashire, John Bryce, York, Robert Bryce, Gourock, Alan Bryden, Tollcross, Glasgow, Aiden Bryson, Glasgow, Ashly Bryson, Glasgow, Jim Bryson, Fernigair, Joshua Bryson, Greenock, Linzi Bryson, Greenock, Liz Bryson, Glasgow, Richard Bryson, Glasgow, Stephen Bryson, Derry, Stewart Bryson, Greenock, J-Man B-Screen, , Ann Bsharat, Whitby,Ontario,Canada, James Bucanan, London, Andrew Buchan, Pilton, Edinburgh, Drew Buchan, 'D' Shift, St Fergus, Fred Buchan, Pilton, Edinburgh, Barry Buchanan, Ayr, Charles Buchanan, Ayr, Jameseybhoy Buchanan, Glasgow, Jan Buchanan, Croy, Jim (Bucky) Buchanan, Glasgow, Joan Buchanan, Croy, John Buchanan, Croy, John Buchanan, Cumbernauld, John Paul Buchanan, Croy, John Paul Buchanan, Kilmarnock, Katie Buchanan, Croy, Kelly Buchanan, Lambhill, Glasgow, Mark Buchanan, Kilmarnock, Martin Buchanan, Lambhill, Glasgow, Sarah Buchanan, Dennistoun, Thomas Buchanan, Croy, Kelly Buchanan - Lilly, Lambhill,

Glasgow, Martin Buchanan - Lilly, Lambhill, Glasgow, Tommy Buckfast, Isle of Benbecula, Edwin Buckie, , Emily Buckie, , Gena Buckle, Grangemouth, Kevin Buckle, Grangemouth, Buckle, Grangemouth, Sean Buckley, Renton/West Dunbartonshire, Paul Budis, Bolton, Eddie Buggy, Shotts, Ross Bulloch, Falkirk, Conor Bulman, Larkhall, Billy Bunce, Craigshill, Alex Buntine, Melbourne, Australia, Collete Buntine, Port Glasgow, James Buntine, Port Glasgow, Sandy Burgess, Forress, Tam Burgess, Langside, Xander Burgess, Forress, John Burgoyne, Kelvindale, Marianne Burgoyne, Kelvindale, Paul Burgoyne, Kelvindale, Vincent Burgoyne, Kelvindale, Bill Burke, Austrialia, Chris Burke, Darnley, Glasgow, John Burke, Sheildhall, Johnny Burke, Sheildhall, Kevin Burke, Pollok, Patrick Burke, Glasgow, Patrick John Burke, , Peter Burke, Balornock, Glasgow, Richard Burke, Govan, Thomas Burn, Glasgow, Burn, Airdrie, John Burn(jnr), Milton Keynes, Baz, Jake And Danielle Burnett, Leicester, England, Campbell Burnett, Fort Augustus, Marea Burnett, Wick, Gloria Burnley, Glasgow, Annemarie Burns, Craigshill, Ann-Marie Burns, Airdrie, Billy Burns, Bo'Ness, Billy Burns, Glasgow, Bryan Joseph David Burns, Saltcoats, Charles Burns, Philadelphia, USA, Chris Burns, Portsmouth, England, Craig Burns, Tolcross Glasgow, Danny Burns, Bo'Ness, Danny Burns, Bo'Ness, Danny Burns, Coatbridge, David Burns, Airdrie, Dean Burns, Riddrie, Eddie Burns, Carntyne, Francis Burns, Baillieston, Gary Burns, Glasgow, George Burns, Burnside, Harry Burns, East Kilbride, Harry Burns, Knightswood, Harry Burns, Partick, Ian Burns, Riddrie, James Burns, Burnbank, James Burns, London, Jim Burns, Coatbridge, Jim Burns, Gorgie, Edinburgh, Jim Burns, London, Jim (The Tim) Burns, London, John Burns, Glasgow, John Burns, Hamilton, John Martin Burns, Moodiesburn, John Paul Burns, Lochgelly, Jonathan Burns, Glasgow, Jonathan Burns, Glasgow, Karen Burns, Glasgow, Kenny Burns, Cumbernauld, Kenny Burns, Cumbernauld, Kenny J. Burns, Cumbernauld, M Burns, Broxburn, Maria Burns, Bearsden, Maria Burns, Glasgow, Mark Burns, Newmains, Mark Burns, Port Seton, Mark Burns, Portseton, Martin Burns, Clydebank, Michael Burns, Glenrothes, Michael Patrick Burns, Saltcoats, Neil Burns, Parkhead, Paddy Burns, Glasgow, Paul Burns, Belfast, Paul Burns, Glasgow, Paul Burns, Glasgow, Paul Burns, Partick, Peter Burns, Airdrie, Peter Burns, Airdrie, Peter Burns, Leigh, Robert Burns, Glenrothes, Ryan Burns, Hamilton, Stevie Burns, Bathgate, Tam Burns, Port Seton, Tam Burns, Port Seton, Thomas Burns, Leigh, David Burns Jnr, Airdrie, Donnie Burns MBE, Croydon, Mr And Mrs W Burnside, Lochore, Fife, Mike Burnsley, Rome, Angela Burt, Falkirk, Deke Burt, , Jackie Burt, Glenrothes, Joe Burt, Falkirk, Kevin Burt, Falkirk, Kieran Burt, Falkirk, Thomas Burt, Sighthill, Edinburgh, Colin Burtwell, Cardiff, Danielle Butler, Los Angeles, Frank Butler, Los Angeles, Jack Butler, Dublin, Kevin Butler, Los Angeles, Davie Butterly, Glasgow, Joe Butterly, Glasgow, John Butterworth, Glasgow, Lara Butterworth, Glasgow, Charles Buttworth, Glasgow, Paul Byars, Paisley, Ben Byrne, Saltcoats, Ben Byrne, Saltcoats, Bernie Byrne, Ayrshire, Clare Byrne, Cardonald, Demi Byrne, Anderston, Glasgow, Gordon Byrne, Cardenden, Jerry Byrne, Rugby, John Byrne, Bishopbriggs, John Byrne, Castlemilk, John Byrne, Castlemilk, Glasgow, John Byrne, Glasgow, Kieran Byrne, Bellshill, Mark Byrne, Glasgow, Martin Byrne, Anderston Glasgow, Michael Byrne, Drumchapel, Nicky Byrne, Corby, Reece Byrne, Anderston, Glasgow, Reece Byrne, Anderston, Glasgow, Reece Demi Byrne, Anderston Glasgow, Shaun Byrne, Saltcoats, Stephen Byrne, Cardonald, Thomas Byrne, Glasgow, James Byrnes, Danderhall.

Sam C, Welwyn Garden City. James C Cassidy, Ontario Canada, Gavin Cabrey, Paisley, Ed Cadden, Old Kilpatrick, John Cadden, Dalmuir Emerald, Kevin Cadden, Bathgate, Luke Cadden, Old Kilpatrick, Martin Cadden, Aberdeen, Matt Cadden, Motherwell, Scott Cadden, Drumchapel, Sharon Cadden, Aberdeen, Terry Cadden, Bathgate, Kate Cadden, Bathgate, Michael Caddis, Prestwick, Samuel Caddock, Prestwick, Gillian Cadenhead, Motherwell, John Cadenhead, Motherwell, John Cadenhead, Motherwell, Katie Cadenhead, Motherwell, Isabelle Cadzow, Motherwell, Melanie Cahir, Glasgow, Kieran Cain, Bellshill, Cain, Bathgate, Sandra Caine, Southampton, Steven Cains, Linlithgow, Ryan Caird, Reading,

Kevin Cairnduff, Cumbernauld, Declan Peter Cairney, Blantyre, Emma Cairney, Ayr, Gerry Cairney, Yoker, James A. Cairney, Leicester, Jim Cairney, Larkhall, Joanne Cairney, Kirkintilloch, Joanne Cairney, Kirkintilloch, John Cairney, Coatbridge, Jonathan Cairney, Larkhall, Steven Cairney, Denny, Alex Cairns, Camberwell, Ann Cairns, Cleland, Barry Cairns, Glasgow, Betty Cairns, Irvine, Brendan Cairns, Kilmarnock, Chris Cairns, Abronhill, Cumbernauld, Danny Cairns, Glasgow, Joe Cairns, Ferryside, Joe Cairns, Langley, Berks, John Cairns, West Lothian, John Cairns, West Lothian, John 'Jc' Cairns, Ayr, Leslie Cairns, Ferryside, Meghan Cairns, West Lothian, Nicola Cairns, Glasgow, Paul Cairns, Coatbridge, Peter Cairns, Baillieston, Peter Cairns, Glasgow, Peter Cairns, Glasgow, Peter Cairns, Welwyn Garden City, Herts, Ramie Cairns, Cumbernauld, Scott Cairns, Ayr, Sean Cairns, Jersey, Channel Islands, Sharon Cairns, Croy, Thomas Cairns, Jersey, Channel Islands, William Cairns, Clydebank, Kate Calaghan, Hamilton, David Calder, Buckie, Sean Calderwood, Linwood, Aidan Caldow, Motherwell, Stephanie Caldow, Motherwell, Andrea Caldwell, Mount Vernon, Glasgow, Cathie Caldwell, Parkhead, Glasgow, Chris Caldwell, Castlemilk, Colin Caldwell, Redcraig Mauchline, John Caldwell, Parkhead , John Caldwell, Parkhead, Glasgow, Kenny Caldwell, Kilsyth, Skye Caldwell, Mount Vernon, Glasgow, Thomas Caldwell, Mount Vernon, Glasgow, Thomas Caldwell, Mount Vernon, Glasgow, Carol Calenti, Potters Bar, Hertfordshire, Vince Calenti, Potters Bar, Hertfordshire, Vincent Calenti, Potters Bar, Collie Caleydoyle, Cyprus, David Call, Glasgow, Mary Call, Glasgow, Alison Callaghan, Greenock Scotland, Catherine Callaghan, Glasgow, Charles Callaghan, Hamilton, Ged Callaghan, Bathgate, James Callaghan, Easterhouse, James Hendrick Callaghan, Glasgow, John Callaghan, Glasgow, John Callaghan, Hamilton, Kate Callaghan, Holyrood High, Katie Callaghan, Furlongs, Lee Callaghan, Falkirk, Lisa Callaghan, Cumbernauld, Lyn Callaghan, Dublin, Lynn Callaghan, Dublin, Micheal Callaghan, Greenock, Neil Callaghan, Kirkintilloch, Patrick Callaghan, Glasgow, Paul Callaghan, East Kilbride, Phil Callaghan, Torquay, Ross Callaghan, Gourock, Stephanie Callaghan, Hamilton, Steven Callaghan, Chertsey, Steven Callaghan, Surrey, John Callahan, East Kilbride, John Callahan, Glasgow, Michelle Callahan, Motherwell, Scott Callahan, Dun Church, William Callahan, Glasgow, Nicky Callan, Drumchapel, Michael Callegan, Motherwell, Mark Calliper, Falkirk, Kevin Calliter, Falkirk, Jamie Callum, Glasgow, Ben Calvert, Paisley, Jan Calvert, Paisley, Laura Calvert, Paisley, Brendan Calvey, Fernieside, Kate Cambell, Cumbernauld, Mark Cambell, Glasgow, James Cambridge, Blantyre, Alana Cameron, Kilmarnock, Amy Cameron, Clydebank, Bertie Cameron, Ross-shire, Calum Cameron, Kilmarnock, Calum Cameron, Paisley, Colin Cameron, Anniesland, Colin Cameron, Anniesland, Glasgow, Colin Cameron, Whitecrook C/Bank, Don Cameron, Durham, Eddie Cameron, Kilmarnock, Iain Cameron, Cessnock, Glasgow, Jimmy Cameron, Dundee, John Cameron, Irvine, Ayrshire, John Cameron, Johnstone, Lynn Cameron, Barrhead, Ronnie Cameron, Montrose, Sandra Cameron, Bargeddie, Sandra Cameron, Montrose, Stewart Cameron, Queenslie, Stuart Cameron, Bridgehouse, Norwich, Suzi Cameron, Leeds, The Camerons, Thurso, The Camerons, Cambuslang, Angus Camerson, Isle of Skye, Lynne Camerson, Glasgow, Adrian Campbell, Chicago, Usa, Alan Campbell, Blackpool, Alan Campbell, Overtown, Wishaw, Alison Campbell, Port Glasgow, Allan Campbell, Dumbarton, Ami Campbell, Glasgow, Andra Campbell, Bathgate, Andrew Campbell, Airdrie, Angela Campbell, Larkhall, Brian Campbell, Linwood, Paisley, Brogan Marie Campbell, Livingston, Carol Ann Campbell, Kilmarnock, Chloe Campbell, Glasgow, Colin Campbell, Glasgow, Colin Campbell, Sandyhills, Daniel Campbell, Glasgow, David Campbell, Glasgow, David Campbell, Linwood, Paisley, Davie Campbell, Coatbridge, Dean Campbell, Heanor, Donald Campbell, Springboig Glasgow, Emily Campbell, Paisley, Errol Campbell, Fintree, Dundee, Frank Campbell, Coatbridge, Gary Campbell, Heanor, Gary Campbell, Renfrew, Gary Thomas Campbell, Jersey, Channel Islands, Iain Campbell, Lennoxtown, Iain Paul Campbell, Lennoxtown G66, Iain Paul Campbell, Lennoxtown G66, Ian Campbell, Baberton Mains, Ian Campbell, Baberton Mains Park, Ian Campbell,

Highlander Pub, Paderborn, Germany, Ian Campbell, Lanark, J. David Campbell, Red Deer, Alberta, Canada, J.David Campbell, Red Deer, Alberta, Canada, Jacky Campbell, Blantyre, Jake Campbell, Millerston, James Campbell, Glasgow, James Campbell, Provanhall, James Campbell, Pumpherston, Jamie Campbell, Kilwinning, Jamie Campbell, Liverpool, Jason Campbell, East Kilbride, Jim Campbell, Boc Brinsworth, Jim Campbell, Kingspark, Joan Campbell, Kilmarnock, Joe Campbell, Livingston, Joe Campbell, Richmond, Surrey, John Campbell, Linwood, Paisley, John Campbell, Polbeth, John Campbell, Scotstoun, John Joseph Campbell, South Uist, Johnny Campbell, Roag, Skye, Joshua Campbell, Birmingham, Julie Campbell, Heanor, Katie Campbell, Linwood, Kirsty Campbell, Kingspark, Lauren Campbell, Kilmarnock, Leanne Campbell, Kingspark, Liam Campbell, Shieldhall, Lisa Campbell, Stepps, Lisa Campbell, Stepps, Lynsey Campbell, Linwood, Lynsey Campbell, Linwood, Lynsey Campbell, Linwood, M. Campbell, South Uist, Margaret Campbell, Glasgow, Margaret Mary Campbell, Glasgow, Mark Campbell, LA., Martin Campbell, Glasgow, Michael Campbell, Glasgow, Mike Campbell, Richmond, Natalie Campbell, Kingspark, Patrick Campbell, Liverpool, Paul Campbell, Bathgate, Paul Campbell, Bermuda, Paul Campbell, Glasgow, Paul Campbell, Heanor, Paul Campbell, Heanor, Paul Campbell, Renfrew, Ronald Campbell, Canada, Ronnie Campbell, Kilmarnock, Roseann Campbell, Liverpool, Ross Campbell, Erskine, Ross Campbell, Glasgow, Steven Campbell, Polbeth, Terry Campbell, Liverpool, Thomas Campbell, Glasgow, Tony Campbell, Scotstoun, Tosh Campbell, Wishaw, Valerie Campbell, Kilmarnock, Wullie Campbell, Coatbridge, Wullie Campbell, Whifflet, Coatbridge, Zac Campbell, Kilmarnock, Ronnie Campbell Jnr, Kilmarnock, Skye Campbell-Gillen, Newton Mearns, Campbell Camron, Garry Camron, Glasgow, Stephen Camron, Nairn, Danny Canavan, High Blantyre, Paul Canavan, Livingston, Anna Candlish, Aberdeen, Jacqline Cann, Fife, Jimmy Canney, Greenock, Brendan Canning, Australia, Charles Canning, Motherwell, Erin Canning, Carntyne, Helen Canning, Carntyne, John Canning, Airdrie, Jonathan Canning, Bellshill, Maureen Canning, Motherwell, Michael Canning, Milton Of Campsie, Paddy Canning, Carntyne, Sean Canning, Airdrie, Stephen Canning, Knightswood, Vinny Canning, Carntyne, Alex Cannon, Port Glasgow, Alex Cannon, West Mersea, Essex, Alice Cannon, Glasgow, Brian Cannon, West Mersea Essex, Conner Cannon, Ireland, Jackie Cannon, Glasgow, Joe Cannon, Glasgow, Joe Cannon, Shettleston Glasgow, Lorraine Cannon, Greenock, Myles Cannon, Gortahork, Donegal, Neil Cannon, Maltby, South Yorkshire, Nikki Cannon, Falkirk, Pat Cannon, London, Peter Cannon, Glasgow, Peter Cannon, Glasgow, Rose Cannon, Gortahork, Donegal, Sean Cannon, Glasgow, Shaun Cannon, Glasgow, Thomas Cannon, Airdrie, Brian Cantwell, Perth, Sean Cantwell, Deans , Martin Canty, Plymouth, Brian Capaldi, Glasgow, Gerry Capaldi, Coatbridge, Gerry Capaldi, Coatbridge, Shaun Cappey, Coatbridge, Damien Cappie, Coatbridge, Daniel Cappie, Liverpool, Lynn Cappie, Sean Cappie, Coatbridge, Neil Carberry, Dunfermline, Neil Carbrry, Dunfermline, Thomas Cardigan, Glasgow, Irene Cardle, Lytham, Lancs, Irene Cardle, Lytham, Lancs, Joe Cardle, Lytham, Lancs, Joe Cardle, Lytham, Lancs, Joe Cardle, Lytham, Lancs, JoJo Cardle, Lytham, Lancs, Scotty Cardle, Lytham, Lancs, Paul Cardno, England, Jane Cardoo, East Kilbride, Ryan Cardoo, East Kilbride, Gillian Care, Glasgow, Mary Care, Glasgow, Matthew Care, Nicola Care, Glasgow, David Carey, Coatbridge, Ian Cargill, Elgin, Sean Cargill, Dumbarton, Debbie Carla, Dave, Stepps, Adeline Carlin, East Kilbride, Graham Carlin, East Kilbride, John Carlin, Coventry, Joseph Carlin, Glasgow, Laura Carlin, Clydebank, Liam Carlin, Viewpark, Mark Carlin, Seville, Mary Carlin, Clydebank, Peter Carlin, Darnley, Glasgow, Ronald Carlin, Giffnock Glasgow, Ronald Carlin, Romford Essex, Ross Carlin, Bishopbriggs, Sharon Carlin, Clydebank, Tony Carlin, Paisley, Frankie Carling and Mary Carling, Motherwell, Ronnie Carlton, Coatbridge, Vinny Carlton, Barrhead, Mark Carlyle, Bathgate, Ann Carmichael, Swanley, Annette Carmichael, Riddrie, Esther Carmichael, Port Glasgow, Ian Carmichael, Houston, Texas, Jane Carmichael, Dundee, Laura Carmichael, Dundee, Louise Carmichael, Houston, Texas,

Nathan Carmichael, Drumoyne, Peter Carmichael, Riddrie, Peter Carmichael, Riddrie, Peter Carmichael, Swanley, Raymond Carmichael, Carmyle, Duncan Carmichael Jnr, Craigshill, Maria Carmyle, Glasgow, Alan Carney, Ireland, John Carnwath, Springburn, Mark Carole, Irvine, Lara Caroll, Falkirk, Kerry Carpenter, Rosyth Fife, Paul Carpenter, Coatbridge, Abby Carr, Cumbernauld, Ailidh Carr, Cumbernauld, Amy Carr, Falkirk, Betty Carr, , Chris Carr, Alexandria, Clare Carr, Seoul, South Korea, Derek Carr, Saltcoats, Derek Carr, Shawlands, Frank Carr, Falkirk, Gerry Carr, Alexandria, Grant Carr, Kirkintilloch, Jamie Carr, Cumbernauld, Jim Carr, Bishopbriggs, Joe Carr, Glasgow, John Carr, Barlanark, John Carr, Coatbridge, John Carr, Isle of Man, John Carr, Kirkintilloch, Lucy Carr, Balornock, Glasgow, Margaret Carr, Coatbridge, Martin Carr, Glasgow, Melanie Carr, Springburn, Mr. Lorne Carr, Leith, Peter Carr, Jersey, William Carr, Aberdeen, George Carr, Falkirk, Fay Carrick, Luton, Fintan Carrick, Welwyn Garden Coty, Liz Carrick, Maryhill, Glasgow, Lynn Carrick, Drumchapel, Peter Carrick, Ruchill, Glasgow, Sonny Carrick, Clydebank, Mike Carrie, Wisbech, Alex Carrigan, South Shields, Amanda Carrigan, Yoker, Glasgow, Anthony Carrigan, Glasgow, Callum Carrigan, Shoreham-By-Sea, Catherine Carrigan, Shoreham-By-Sea, Christopher Carrigan, Yoker, Glasgow, Gerry Carrigan, Yoker, Glasgow, Jacqueline Carrigan, Yoker, Glasgow, Joseph Carrigan, Castlemilk, Glasgow, Joseph Carrigan, Shoreham-By-Sea, Tamzin Carrigan, Shoreham-By-Sea, David Carrol, Cumbernauld, Paul Carrol, Cumbernauld, Arthur Carroll, Linwood, Christopher Carroll, Dundee, Daniel Carroll, Glasgow, Debbie Carroll, Linlithgow, Gillian Carroll, Linwood, Iain Carroll,Airdrie, Iain Carroll, Erskine, Jamie Carroll, Aviemore, Jimmy Carroll, Dundee, Joe Carroll, Dartford, Kent, Kelly Anne Carroll, Possilpark, Kevin Carroll, Tollcross, Lee Carroll, Dundee, Martin Carroll, Airdrie, Megan Carroll, Aviemore, Mick Carroll, Law, Paul Carroll, Drumchapel, Paul Carroll, Drumchapel, Paul Carroll, Linlithgow, Rob Carroll, Falkirk, Roseanne Carroll, Possilpark, Stephen Carroll, Summerston, Glasgow, Terry Carroll, Renfrew, Tommy Carroll, Aviemore, Tony Carroll, Newstevenston, Colin Carruthers, Paisley, Pamela Carruthers, Bishopbriggs, Stuart Carruthers, Greenock, Murdo Carshalton, Surrey, Jenni Carstairs, Kirkcaldy, Mary Cartlon, Parkhead, Barry Cartwright, Glasgow, Peter Cartwright, Glasgow, David Carty, Kilmarnock, Craig Caryle, Carluke, Caroline Case, Wishaw, John Casey, Highlander Pub, Paderborn, Germany, Rod Casey, Corby, Steve Casey, Corby, Stephen Casey, Walthamstow, London, Rab Cassells, Symington, Martin Casserly, Townhead, Michael Cassiday, Eastbourne, Big Mick Cassidy, Alexandria, Brian Cassidy, Glasgow, Craig Cassidy, Drumchapel, Eddie Cassidy, Johnstone, Elaine Cassidy, Girvin, Gerry Cassidy, Coatbridge, Huey Cassidy, Yeading, Ian Cassidy, Royston, James Cassidy, Girvan, James Cassidy, Old Kilpatrick, Jim Cassidy, Girvan, Kevin Cassidy, Irvine, Macaulay Cassidy, Eastbourne, Margaret Cassidy, Glasgow, Margaret Cassidy, Possilpark, Glasgow, Mark Cassidy, Bellshill, Michael & Maureen Cassidy, Linnview, Riva Cassidy, Eastbourne, Tony Cassidy, Sweden, Wee Owen Cassidy, Alexandria, Grant Cassie, Inverness, Henry Cassie, Inverness, Jenny Cassie, Ross-Shire, Pamela Cassie, Ross-shire, Tommy Castle, Dunfermline, Stephanie Cathcart, Rutherglen Glasgow, David Cation, Kennoway, Michael Caughey, Corby, Robert Caughey, Viewpark, Uddingston, Sharon Caughey, Viewpark, Uddingston, Daniel Caulfield, Coatbridge, Raymond Caulfield, Coatbridge, Shane Caulfield, Broxburn, Val Caulfield, Broxburn, Heather Caullay, East Kilbride, John Cavan, Irvine, Richard Cavana, Helensburgh, Brian Cavanagh, Leicester, Jamie Cavanagh, Cumbernauld, Pat Cavanagh, Linwood, Sean Cavanagh, Leicester, Martin Cawley, Edinburgh, Eddie Caywood, Newcastle, William Celland, Airdre, William Cessen, Glasgow, Brian Chalmers, Renfrew, David Chalmers, Yoker, Iain Chalmers, Lenzie, Karen Chalmers, Musselburgh, Lisa Chalmers, Peterhead, Paul Chalmers, Dumfries, Sandy Chalmers, Inverness, Vic And Betty Chamberlain, Lochgelly, Fife, Joseph Chambers, L/Cpl Brian Chambers, Kilmarnock, Liam Chambers, Wishaw, Scott Chambers, Wishaw, Lisa Channing, Glasgow, Stuart Chap, Dunfermline, Scott Chaplin, Fife, Clare Chapman, Carrick Knowe, Paul Chapman, Renfrewshire, Kris Charalambous, Torrance, Lindsay Charalambous, Torrance, Paul

Charalambous, Torrance, James Charles, Rosyth, Fife, Lorraine Charles, Rosyth, Fife, Ross Charles, Rosyth, Fife, Stephanie Charles, Rosyth, Fife, Gary Charmers, Aberdeen, Chic Charnley, Possilpark, Glasgow, Gary Charnley, Coatbridge, Gary Charnley, Townhead, Coatbridge, Bill Charters, Fresno, California, Darren Charton, , Ayisha Chaudry, Blantyre, Vicky Chaudry, Blantyre, Angela Cheney, Uddingston, Jonathan Cheshire, Plymouth, Devon, Brian Chesney, Falkirk, Peter Chesney, Falkirk, Ronan Chesney, Falkirk, Big Chieffy, Duke Street, Anna Chisholm, Motherwell, Donnie Chisholm, Inverness, Neil Chisholm, Inverness, Tricia Chisholm, Glasgow, Andrew Chislett, Kilburn, Colette Chorley, Belfast, Billy Chorlton, , Sharron Chorlton, , Brodie Christie, Buckie, Davey Christie, Kirkcaldy, Dylan Christie, Buckie, Gary Christie, Edinburgh, Graham Christie, Aberdeen, Ian Christie, Greenock, Ian Christie, Kilmalcom, James Christie, Greenock, Jane Christie, Airdrie, Kelly Christie, Kirkcaldy, Leslie Christie, Northfleet, Nicola Christie, Glasgow, Christie, Glasgow, David Christy, Airdrie, James Church, Kirkintilloch, Jim Church, Kirkintilloch, John Church, Corby, Stephen Cichon, Livingston, Joe Cimlin, Kent, Joe Claghan, Motherwell, Bill Claire, Broxburn, Dominic Claire, Blackburn, Nicola Claire, Broxburn, Connelly Clan, Corby, Howley Clan, Livingston, Stanton Clan, Govan, Robert Clancy, Croydon, Surrey, Liz Clare, Boghall, Aaron Clark, Rutherglen, Alan Clark, Coatbridge, Amy Clark, Rutherglen, Andy Clark, Goodyear, Chloe Clark, Kettering, Chris Clark, Kirkintilloch, Clare Clark, Stirling, Danny Clark, Kettering, Darren Clark, San Francisco, California, David Clark, Elgin, David Clark, Glasgow, Gemma Clark, Simshill, Graeme Clark, Simshill, Hamish Clark, St Ninians, Joe Clark, Glasgow, Joe Clark, Watford, London, John Clark, Kirkintilloch, Jon Clark, Greenlaw, Jon Clark, Greenlaw Bank, Yoker, Joseph Clark, Clydebank, Kenny Clark, Rutherglen, Kevin Clark, Forgewood, Kristopher Clark, Simshill, Lewis Clark, Hillhead, Kirkintilloch, Lynsey Clark, Rutherglen, Mag Clark, Bannockburn, Mick Clark, Leicester, Niki Clark, Dalmuir, Paul Clark, Coatbridge, Pip Clark, Elgin, Robert Clark, Rutherglen, Robert Clark, Rutherglen, Ron Clark, Aberdeen, Speedy Clark, Dumfries, Steven Clark, Motherwell, Tam Clark, Goodyear, Thomas Clark, Maryhill, Wendy Clark, Corkerhill, Alex Clarke, Cumbernauld, Brian Clarke, Airdrie, Charlie Clarke, Saltcoats, Christopher Clarke, Glasgow, Eddie Clarke, Rainham, Essex, Jeff Clarke, Girvan, Joe Clarke, Diss, John Clarke, Bristol, Kevin Clarke, Glasgow, Mark Clarke, Glasgow, Ryan Clarke, Girvan, Sharon Clarke, Girvan, Siobhan Clarke, Gourock, Stacey Clarke, Glasgow, Stephen Clarke, U.S.A, Tommy Clarke, Carntyne, Glasgow, Tony Clarke, Edinburgh, Eddie Clarke Jnr, Rainham, Essex, Ross Clarkin, Hamilton, Danielle Clarkson, Motherwell, Alexander Clasper, Glasgow, Richard Class, Newton Mearns, Tony Clavering, Glasgow, Charleen Clay, Stoneyburn, Gary Clay, Stoneyburn, John Clay, Stoneyburn, Kevin Clay, Stoneyburn, Melissa Clay, Stoneyburn, Denis Clayton, Burdiehouse, Gordon Clayton, Overtown, Grant Clayton, Bearsden, Aaron Cleary, Belfast, Hugh Cleary, Govan, Glasgow, Mark Cleary, Belfast, Martin Cleary, Belfast, Patrick Cleary, Dumbarton, Sarah Cleary, West Buckland, Devon, Sammi Clegg, Kilbirnie Ayrshire, Sean Cleghorn, Newcastle, Brian Cleland, Glasgow, Peter Cleland, West Calder, Richie Cleland, , John Cleland Snr, , Davie Clelland, East Kilbride, Amy Clements, Cranhill, Brian Clements, Cambuslang, Christopher Clements, Cambuslang, Liam Clements, Cranhill, Nicola Clements, Cranhill, Stephen Clements, Viewpark, Tom Cleray, West Buckland, Devon, Fraser Clews, Carfin, Colin Cliff, Crosslee, Joanne Cliffe, East Kilbride, Shane Cliffe, East Kilbride, Catriona Clifford, Peebles, Gary Clifford, Shotts, John Clifford, , Jonathan Clifford, Wishaw, Mark Clifford, Shotts, Pauline Clifford, Alexandria, Sheona Clifford, Peebles, Scott Clinis, Dun Church, Diane Clinton, Wirral, James Clinton, Croy, Peter Clinton, Croy, Sadie Clinton, Rockaway Beach New York, Stuart Clinton, Aberdeen, Jim Clocherty, Paisley, Pat Clocherty, Corby, Northants, James Closh, Airdrie, Joseph Clougherty, London, Ian Club, Falkirk, Norrie Clucas, Kirkintilloch, Derek Cluderay, Ayr, David Clunie, Muthill, Perthshire, Joe Clyde, Neilston, Sylvia Clydesdale, Kilwinning, Bruce Cnfrey, Peebles, Dennis Coal, Dumbarton, Eddie Mcintosh, Coatbridge, Ricky Coates, Glasgow, Karen Coats, Airdrie, Karen Coats,

Chapelhall, Karen Coats, Julian Cobby, Ibiza, Russell Cochran, Paisley, Annlouise Cochrane, Croy, Davie Cochrane, Coatbridge, Margaret Cochrane, Bannockburn, Stephen Cochrane, Tranent, East Lothian, Tam Cochrane, Moodiesburn, Dougie Cockburn, West Lothian, Conner Cocken, Glasgow, John Cocker, Corby, Andrew Cockinham, Glasgow, Paul Cockran, Glasgow, Tom Cockran, Carlo Cocozza, Hamilton, Liz Cocozza, London, Stefano Cocozza, Glasgow, Auld John Coffield, Easterhouse, James Coffield, Germiston, Jim Cogann, Dundee, Piero Coia, Armadale, A. Coldfield, Erskine, John Coldfield, Glasgow, John Cole, Tamworth, Surrey, Katie Cole, Venice, Lewis Cole, Glasgow, Aiden Colefield, Erskine, Amanda Coleman, Armadale, West Lothian, Archie Coleman, Coatbridge, Chris Coleman, Armadale, West Lothian, Kane Coleman, Govan, Glasgow, Kathleen Coleman, Govan, Glasgow, Pauline Coleman, Bridgeton, Glasgow, Richard Coleman, Ireland, Scott Coleman, Edinburgh, Sean Coleman, Govan, Glasgow, Kevin Colhoun, Glasgow, Jenn Colin, Stanford Le Hope, Essex, Ann Colinson, Hawick, Danny Coll, Croftfoot Glasgow, Franny Coll, Gorbals, Stevie Coll, Burnbank, Sanghi Colla, Alexandria, Kathleen Collie, , Fraser Collier, Dunfermline, Anthony Colligan, Toryglen, Vance Colligan, Shawlands, Brian Collins, Moodiesburn, Chris Collins, Tenerife, Christopher Collins, Dumbarton, Craig Collins, Greenock, David Collins, Jersey, Dougie Collins, Walthamstow, London, Greg Collins, Moodiesburn, Jim Collins, Coatbridge, Jim Collins, Coatbridge, Joe Collins, Wishaw, John Collins, Hamilton, John Collins, London, Kenneth Collins, Port Glasgow, Mark Collins, Springboig, Martin Collins, Jersey, Paul Collins, Dumbarton, Paul Collins, New York, Stevie Collins, Co. Down, Collins, Darvel, Claire Collinson, Hawick, Lee Collinson, Bellshill, Patrick Collum, Glasgow, Shannon Collum, Govanhill, Jerry Colouzme, Royston, Bobo Colston, Brasil, David Colston, Bellshill, David Colston, Sheffield, Matthew Colston, Bellshill, Mark Colvin, Lytham, Lancs, Edward Comerford, Dunfermline, James Comerford, Bathgate, James Comerford, , Liam Compson, East Lothian, Dan Comrie, Stirling, Mick Comrie, Stirling, Anne-Marie Conachy, Ashley Conachy, Brian Conachy, Mosspark, Christopher Conachy, Mosspark, Chris Conaghan, Stevenson, Iain Conaghan, Hamiltonhill, Sean Conaghan, New York, Tony Conaghan, New Jersey, Tony Conaghan, New Jersey, Tony Conaghan Snr, Fort Lauderdale, Peter Conaline, Edinburgh, John Conboy, Forfar, Blair Condie, Cowie, Liz Condie, Cowie, Dionne Condron, Glasgow, Martin Condron, Bellshill, Paul Condron, Glasgow, Angelo Conetta, Glasgow, Steve Congalton, Brendan Conlan, Grimsby, Andrew Conlan , Jnr, Drumchapel, Andrew Conlan , Snr, Drumchapel, Glasgow, Paul Conlin, Erskine, Paul J Conlin, Bangkok, Johnnie Conlon, Port Said, Egypt, Leanne Conlon, Whithorn, Tony Conlon, Blantyre, Owen Connachan, Glasgow, Owen Connachan, Glasgow, Jerry Connacon, Greenoak, Kevin Connacon, Greenoak, Mary Connally, , Michael Connally, , Paul Connally, Glasgow, Rachel Connally , Davie Connarty, Coatbridge, Davie Connarty , Liam Connaughton, Ayr, Sean Connaughton, Ayr, Anne Marie Connell, Shotts, Brenda Connell, Royston, Hugh Connell, North Lanarkshire, Hugh Connell, North Lanarkshire, Hugh Connell, North Lanarkshire, Ian Connell, Glasgow, John Connell, Wirral, Merseyside, Martin Connell, Shotts, Paul Connell, Royston, Richard Connell, Shotts, Alan Connelly, Glasgow, Avril Connelly, Ruthenglen, Claire Connelly, Cambuslang, Darren Connelly, Glasgow, Gerry Connelly, Clydebank, Jack Connelly, Corby, Jack Connelly, Lochfoot, Jackie Connelly, Lochfoot, Jacqueline Connelly, Glasgow, James Connelly, Glasgow, James Connelly, Knightswood, Glasgow, James Connelly, Kincardie, Jamie Connelly, Corby, Jill Connelly, Lochfoot, John Connelly, Glasgow, John Connelly, Michael Connelly, Blackpool, Paul Connelly, Glasgow, Robert Connelly, Glasgow, Scott Connelly, Tollcross, Shaun Connelly, Stef Connelly, Possil, Tracy Connelly, Lochfoot, David Conner, Aberdeen, Mark Conner, Pat Conner, Glasgow, Sandra Conner, Berlin, Conner, Paisley, Jim Connick, Paisley, Jim Connick, Paisley, Amy Connolly, Clones Co. Monaghan, Ireland, Andy Connolly, Leith, Edinburgh, Andy Connolly, Leith, Barbara Connolly, California, Billy Connolly, Maidavale, Daniel Connolly, Chertsey Surrey, Danny Connolly, Clones, Co. Monaghan, Ireland, Dericka Connolly, Clones, Co.

Monaghan, Ireland, Eamonn Connolly, Bishopbriggs, Erica Connolly, Clones, Co. Monaghan, Ireland, Frank Connolly, Darlington, Co Durham, James Connolly, Cambuslang, Jim Connolly, Springhill, Joe Connolly, Drumchapel, John Connolly, Australia, John James Connolly, Motherwell, Megan Connolly, Clones, Co. Monaghan, Ireland, Michael Connolly, Bishopbriggs, Patrick Connolly, Dumbarton, Paul Connolly, Cathcart, Ryan Connolly, Springhill, Sean Connolly, East Kilbride, Stevie Connolly, Cumbernauld, Thomas Connolly, California, Jessica Connon, Glasgow, Joe Connon, Glasgow, Joseph P. Connon, Glasgow, Linda Connon, Glasgow, Alec Connor, London, Arthur Connor, Fort Sask, Alberta, Canada, Chaanach Connor, Newcastle, Daniel Connor, Stepps, Denise Connor, Paisley, Duncan Connor, Wishaw, Graham Connor, Peebles, Hugh Connor, Newbury, Berks, Ivene Connor, Aberdeen, Jacqueline Connor, Newbury, Berks, Janice Connor, Glasgow, Jim Connor, Edinburgh, Jim Connor, Edinburgh, John Connor, Peebles, Kevin Connor, Cumbernauld, Kevin Connor, Paisley, Kieran Connor, Glasgow, Linda Connor, Paisley, Louise Connor, Edinburgh, Louise Connor, Edinburgh, Mark Connor, Craigend, Mhairi and Meghan Connor, Newmains, Michelle Connor, Glasgow, Michelle Connor, Newbury, Berks, Morag Connor, Glasgow, Morag Connor, Newbury, Berks, Owen Connor, Helensburgh, Sean Connor, Glasgow, Stephen Connor, Glasgow, T Connor, Glasgow, T Connor, Tollcross, W Connor, Glasgow, W Connor, Tollcross, Marie Will You Marry Me Connor Brady, Stockport, Cheshire, Betty Conroy, Glasgow, Declan Conroy, West Lothian, Kevin Conroy, West Lothian, Kyle Conroy, West Lothian, Martin Conroy, Dunbar, East Lothian, Martin Conroy, West Lothian, Martin Conroy, Whitburn, Peter Conroy, West Lothian, Willaim Conroy, Renton, Marco Conte, Baillieston, Paul Conte, Baillieston, Gerry Convery, Largs, Lynne Convery, Port Glasgow, Michael Convery, Largs, Thomas Convery, Linthouse, Colin Conway, , Craig Conway, Highlander Pub, Paderborn, Germany, Frances Conway, Drumchapel, Isobel Conway, Cumbernauld, Lynne Conway, Cumbernauld, Shaun-Paul Conway, Cumbernauld, Steven Conway, Irvine, Mary Conwell, Srabane, N.Ireland, Patrick Conwell, Strabane, N. Ireland, Stephen Conwell, Strabane, N. Ireland, Charlie Coogans, Coatbridge, Michael Coogans, Coatbridge, David Cook, Menstrie, Steven Cook, Hawick, Wendy Cook, Eastriggs, E Cooley, Glasgow, Andrew Coolter, Glasgow, Gary Cooney, Coatbridge, Kieran Cooney, Dechmont, Marcella Cooney, Dechmont, Mary Cooney, Uphall, Sally Cooney, Dechmont, Stephen Cooney, Dechmont, Stevie Cooney, Uphall, Ashley Cooper, Nitshill, Brenda Cooper, Alloa, Brenda Cooper, Brian Cooper, Glenburn, Elaine Cooper, East Kilbride, Les Cooper, Coatbridge, N Cooper, Montrose, Tommy Cooper, Inverness, Tracy Cooper, Glasgow, Johnny Cooper, Nitshill, John Cooper Jnr, Nitshill, David Coote, Duntocher, Colin Copeland, Glasgow, John Copeland, Dennistoun, David Corcoran, , John Corcoran, Balloch, Jenny Cordiner, Aberdeen, Jim Core, , Kevin Core, Paisley, Paul Corey, Edinburgh, Tom Corkeran, Paisley, Sara Cormack, Beith, Ayrshire, Leesa Cornett, Edinburgh, Kevin Corr, Paisley, Ashley Corrigan, Milton, Christine Corrigan, Milton, Jim Corrigan, Irvine, Michael Corrigan, Edinburgh Univ, Paul Corrigan, Irvine, Paul Corrigan, Sheffield, Stephen Corrigan, Andrew Corrigan Edinburgh Univ, James Corry, Airdrie, Andy Cosgrove, Canada, Charlie Cosgrove, Blackwood, Danny Cosgrove, Hamilton, Jake William Cosgrove, Eastbourne, Sussex, John Cosgrove, Dunfermline, John Cosgrove, Giffnock Glasgow, Marion Cosgrove, Hamilton, Mark Cosgrove, Midlands, Tony Cosgrove, Giffnock, Glasgow, Markie Costelllo, USA, Amy Costello, Linwood, Paisley, Andrew Costello, Paisley, Brian Costello, Linwood, Paisley, Jodie Costello, Linwood, Paisley, Kevin Costello, Paisley, Linda Costello, Boness, Mark Costello, Wishaw, Sheena Costello, Linwood, Paisley, Lisa Cottia, Kent, Lisa Cottis, Sittingbourne, Kent, Angie Coulbeck, Grimsby, Arran Coull, Leven, Arran Coull, Leven, Dougie Coull, Lossiemouth, John Coull, Paisley, John Coull, Paisley, Alexander Coulter, Paisley, John Coulter, Newmains, John Patrick Coulter, Newmains, Steven Coulter, Wishaw, Stanley Coulter (Patsy), Carfin, Brian Courtney, Calton, Glasgow, Mick Court, Nottingham, Mick Courtney, Airdrie, Stephen Courtney, Glasgow, Mac Cousins, Killearn, Nicholas Cousins, Killearn, John Couttie, Luton, Bedfordshire, Billy Cowan,

Ardrossan, Caleb Cowan, Fife, Jamie Cowan, Ardrossan, Janet Cowan, Whitecrook, Clydebank, John Cowan, Ardrossan, John Cowan, Kirkcaldy, Kieran Cowan, Ardrossan, Lisa Cowan, Ardrossan, Mark Cowan, Glasgow, Michael Cowan, Ardrossan, Rena Cowan, Clydebank, Sean Cowan, Ardrossan, Bunty Cowe, Moffat, Graeme Cowe, Hereford, Wullie Cowe, Uddingston, Darren Cowie, Kincardine, Alastair Cox, Cardiff, Claire Cox, Glasgow, Elaine Margaret Cox, Carfin, John Cox, Yoker, Mark Cox, Glasgow, Mark Cox, , Michael Cox, Coatbridge, Michael Cox, Yoker, Sheryl Cox, Glasgow, Paul Coxson Jnr, Glasgow, Anne-Marie Coyle, Cambuslang, Glasgow, Anthony Coyle, Glasgow, Anthony Coyle, Kings Park, Austin Coyle, Cambuslang, Glasgow, Caitlin Coyle, Uddingston, Charlie Coyle, Kings Park, Claire Coyle, Cambuslang, Clare Coyle, Cambuslang, Declan Coyle, Philadelphia, USA, Gerry Coyle, Glasgow, Gerry Coyle, Glasgow, Harry Coyle, Stirling, Henry Coyle, Kilsyth, James Coyle, Condorrat, Cumbernauld, Joanne Coyle, Cambuslang, Glasgow, John Coyle, Glasgow, Josh Coyle, Wishaw, Kevin Coyle, Cambuslang, Glasgow, Louise Coyle, Uddingston, Mathew Coyle, Kilsyth, Mick Coyle, Cumbernauld, Nicola Coyle, Cumbernauld, Patrick Coyle, Kilsyth, Scott Coyle, Carmyle, Sean Coyle, Cambuslang, Glasgow, Sean Paul Coyle, Cambuslang, Shaun Coyle, Carmyle, Stevie Coyle, Carmyle, Stevie Coyle, Glasgow, Paul Coyne, Glasgow, Peter Coyne, Glasgow, Gary Craig, Banff, Bill Craig, Glasgow, Bryan Craig, Fairview, Alberta, Canada, Courtney Craig, Possilpark, David Craig, Anderston, Glasgow, David Craig, Clydebank, David Craig, Livingston, George Craig, Possilpark, Gerry Craig, East Kilbride, Jennifer Craig, Standburn, John Craig, Hamilton, Kirsten Craig, Possilpark, Michelle Craig, Anderston, Glasgow, Michelle Craig, Spain, Oliver Craig, Ayrshire, Robert Craig, Wishaw, Stacy Craig, Beith, Steven Craig, Glasgow, Steven Craig, Glasgow, Stuart Craig, Dumfries, Thomas Craig, , Tommy Craig, Stirling, Tony Craig, Dumbarton, Gillian Craigie, London-Originally Cambuslang, John Crainey, Croy, Alice Crainie, Croy, Archie Crainie, Croy, Dianne Crainie, Croy, Julie Crainie, Edinburgh, Mae Crainie, Croy, Marie.T. Crainie, Croy, Martin Crainie, Croy, Martin Crainie (Spike), Croy, William Crainie(Worlds Best Dad), Croy, Anne Craney, Uddingston, Steven Craney, Uddingston, Butch Crangle, , Neil Cranhan, Hastings, Sandra Cranhan, Hastings, Pete Cranie, Seville, Gary Crankshaw, Partick, Glasgow, David Cranston, Ayr, David Craughwell, Wimbledon, Steven Craven, Andrew Crawford, Gartcosh, Brendan Crawford, Stirling, Brian Crawford, Cumbernauld, Callum Crawford, Kennoway, Fife, Conner Crawford, Glasgow, David Crawford, Glasgow, david Crawford, Rutherglen, Emma Crawford, Johnstone, Francis Crawford, Airdrie, Ger Crawford, Milngavie, Gerry Crawford, Kennoway, Fife, James Crawford, Croy, John Crawford, Cambuslang, Kenny Crawford, Glenrothes, Lorna Crawford, Coatbridge, Martin Crawford, Cumbernauld, Michelle Crawford, Johnstone, Micky Crawford, , Ross Crawford, Glasgow, Tony Crawford, Chapel, Michael Crawlands, Inverkeighing, Teresa Crawley, Edinburgh, Clare Creighton, Paisley, Yvonne Creighton, Paisley, Dolina Cremin, Menstrie Clacmananshire, Jim Cremin, Menstrie, Jim Cremin, Menstrie, Clacmananshire, Jim Cremin, Menstrie Clacmananshire, Kevin Creswell, East Kilbride, Russell Crighton, 'D' Shift, St Fergus, John Crilly, Livingston, John Crilly, Livingston, Martin Crilly, Paisley, Paul Crimmins, Earlsdon, Coventry, Nigel Crisp, Strathaven, Frank Croall, Coatbridge, Allan Crockett, Erskine, Eileen Crockett, Erskine, Michael Crocock, Castlemilk, Glasgow, Sam Crombey, Irvine, Michelle Crombie, Glenrothes, Paula Crombie, Glasgow, Mark Crosbie, Glasgow, Bertie Crosby, Dundee, Lesley Crosby, Dundee, Mark Crosby, Glasgow, Mark Crosby, Glasgow, Paul Crosby, Corby, Alison Cross, London, William Crossack, Paisley, David Crossan, Cathcart, Graeme Crossan, Knightswood John Crossan, Airdrie, John Crossan, Glasgow, Mark Crossan, Gorbals, Glasgow, William Crossan, Knightswood, Robert Crothers, Blantyre, David Crotty, Ray Crouch, Yucatan N16 Stokie Tour, Barry Crowley, Mullingar, Ireland, Daragh Crowley, Westmeath, Ireland, Sean Crowley, Liverpool, The Crown Bar, Bellshill, Albert Croy, Beechmount, Ross Croy, Inverness, Mark J Cruden, Newton Mearns, Glasgow, Paul Cruickshanks, Glasgow, Stewart Cruickshanks, Falkirk, Alec Crum, , Jim Crum, Baillieston,

John Crum, Jim Cryans, East Kilbride, Sean Cryans, Thatcham, Paul Culbert, Leven, Fife, Paul Cameron Culbert, Leven, Fife, Gavin Cullan, Falkirk, Jordan Cullan, Falkirk, Kenneth Cullan, Falkirk, Kevin Cullan, Falkirk, Thomas Cullan, Wigan, Dean Cullas, Falkirk, Andrea Cullen, Airdrie, Catherine Cullen, Drumchapel, Derrick Cullen, Perth, John P Cullen, Maynooth, Ireland, Kimberly Cullen, Drumchapel, Lawrence Cullen, Seville, Stephen Cullie, East Kilbride, Mark Cullinane, Ardrossan, Jamie Cullins, Jersey, Jamie Cullins, Jersey, Helen Cullion, Livingston, John Cullion, Livingston, Michael Cullis, Falkirk, Len Culverwell, Bournemouth, Taylor Cumings, Denny, Roy Cumming, Silverton, Dumbarton, Walter Cumming, Airdrie, Jimmy Cummings, St Ninians, John Cummings, Priestfield, Edinburgh, Margaret Cummings, Priestfield, Edinburgh, Talyor Cummings, , Tommy Cummings, St Ninians, Daniel Cummiskey, East Kilbride, Julie Cummiskey, East Kilbride, Paul Cummiskey, East Kilbride, Sinead Cummiskey, East Kilbride, Christopher Cuningham, Barrhead, James Cuningham, Ardrossan, Gerry Cunniham, Hillington, Becky Cunning, Glasgow, Joe Cunning, Glasgow, Aaron Cunningham, Glasgow, Cammy Cunningham, Coventry, Carolann Cunningham, Glasgow, Caroline Cunningham, Linwood, Catherine Cunningham, Knightswood, Claire Cunningham, Linwood, Craig Cunningham, Livingston, Craig Mirin Cunningham, Livingston, Damian Cunningham, Highlander Pub, Paderborn, Germany, Eddie Cunningham, Gallowgate, Glasgow, Frank Cunningham, Springburn, Gary Cunningham, Cruden Bay, Gary Bunkle Cunningham, Brisbane Australia, Ian Cunningham, Fife, James Cunningham, Ardrossan, James Cunningham, Ardrossan, Joanne Cunningham, Pollokshields, Glasgow, John Cunningham, Linwood, John Paul Cunningham, Glasgow, John Paul Cunningham, Linwood, Kristopher Cunningham, Glasgow, Mark Cunningham, Glasgow, Mark Cunningham, Springburn, Paul Cunningham, Highlander Pub, Paderborn, Germany, Peter Cunningham, Port Glasgow, Stephen Cunningham, Greenock, Alec Cunniskey, Hamilton, Brian Curley, Cambuslang, Glasgow, Colin Curley, Glasgow, Damien Curley, Rutherglen, Ena Curley, Cardross, Graeme Curley, East Kilbride, Graeme Curley, East Kilbride, James Curley, Drumchapel, Kayleigh Curley, Cambuslang, Glasgow, Marion Curley, Cambuslang, Glasgow, Tony Curley, Cambuslang, Glasgow, Emma Curran, Govan, Frank Curran, Broxburn, Frank Curran, Broxburn, Owen Curran, Kings Park, Glasgow, P.J. Curran, Kings Park, Glasgow, Pat Curran, Newton Mearns, Paul Curran, Kings Park, Glasgow, Stephen Curran, Kings Park, Glasgow, Veronica Curran, Kings Park, Glasgow, Alan Currie, Glasgow, Alan Currie, Rosehill, Alex Currie, Motherwell, Alix Currie, Bothwell, Allen Currie, Kirkintilloch, Andrew Currie, Glasgow, Angela Currie, Rosehill, Billy Currie, Holytown, Cameron Currie, Cowdenbeath, Carol-Anne Currie, Rosehill, Claire Currie, Inverness, Colin Currie, Cumbernauld, Duncan Currie, Kelty, Eddie Currie, Viewpark, Emma Currie, Bothwell, Frank Currie, Glasgow, Gary Currie, Rosehill, Gordon Currie, Ballingry, Gordon Currie, Ballingry, Graeme Currie, Rosehill, Jim Currie, Viewpark, John Currie, Driffield, Margaret Currie, Holytown, Neil Currie, Rosehill, Paul Currie, Stenhousemuir, Rab Currie, Cowdenbeath, Rita Currie, Viewpark, Ross Currie, Cardonald, Glasgow, Tam Currie, Viewpark, Wullie Currie, Garrowhill, Glasgow, Barry Currier, Wishaw, Stuart Currier, Wishaw, John Currin, Ballieston, Allan Curtis, Lochgilphead, Argyll, Emma Curtis, Lochgilphead, Argyll, Jeff Curtis, Ardrishaig, Julie Curtis, Lochgilphead, Argyll, Mark Curtis, Co Kildare, Ireland, Stephen Curtis, Kilsyth, Vickie Curtis, Lochgilphead, Argyll, Andy Curwen, Aberdeen, Kenneth Cushen, Moodiesburn, Charile Custien, Inverness, Calum Cuthbert, Glasgow, Colin Cuthbert, Glasgow, Paul Cuthbert, Glasgow, Steven Cuthbert, Glasgow, Paul Cuthill, Dundee.

Shug D, Temple. Joseph Dabernig, Motherwell, Jagdeep Dagon, Glasgow, Manjit Dagon, Glasgow, Donato D'Agrosa, Eyemouth, Arlene Dahlstrom, Linwood, Sarah Clair Dahlstrom, Linwood, Paul Dailey, Hamilton, Eddie Daily, Lenzie, Gavin Dales, Glenrothes, Danny Daley, Cork, John-Paul Daley, Glasgow, Martin Daley, Northampton, Michael Dall, Australia, Elena Dallas, Clydebank, Stephen Dallas, Clydebank, Angela Dallimore, Royston,

Claire Dalrymple, Dumbarton, Jamie Dalrymple, Dumbarton, Jayne Dalrymple, Dumbarton, Stevie Dalton, Portsmouth, Cathy Daly, Hamilton, Chris Daly, Bellshill, Joe Daly, USA, John Daly, Milton, Glasgow, Karen Daly, Glasgow, Karen Daly, Springburn, Glasgow, Keiran Daly, Craigneuk, Wishaw, Paul Daly, Bearsden, Paul Daly, Hamilton , Thomas Daly, Bishopbriggs, Thomas Daly, Gorbals, Tommy Daly, Bishopbriggs, William Daly, Cadder, Glasgow, Billy Dalziel, New Stevenston, Joanne Dalziel, Greenock, James (Cookie) Daniel, Milton, Glasgow, Jordan Daniel, Garngad, Robert Daniel, Possilpark, Glasgow, Ronald (Bonzo) Daniel, Milton, Glasgow, Lynne Darby, Carntyne, Glasgow, Brian Darbyshire, Leven, Stephen Dargan, Govan, Gareth Dargie, Aberdeen, Ian Darragh, Govan, Paul Darren, Cleland, Mark Darroch, , Matthew Darroch, Newlands, Glasgow, Tommy Darroch, Easterhouse, Glasgow, William Darroch, Kings Park, Glasgow, Jackie Dass, Nairn, Disco Dave, Temple, Anne Marie Davenport, Glasgow, Bridget Davenport, Glasgow, Joanne Davenport, Glasgow, John Paul Davenport, Glasgow, Peter Davenport, London, Ryan James Davenport, Glasgow, Betty Davey, Paisley, Betty Davey, Paisley, Ciara Davey, Belfast, Connor Davey, Belfast, Francine Davey, Belfast, John Davey, Glasgow, Ronny Davey, Glasgow, Ronny Davey, Glasgow, Tony Davey, Glasgow, Mark David, Howwood, Ann-Marie Davidson, Glasgow, Archie Davidson, Bannockburn, Atholl Davidson, Inverness, Atholl Davidson, Inverness, Barry Davidson, Glasgow, Cailean Davidson, Inverness, Caroline Davidson, Bannockburn, Cath Davidson, Lochgelly, Fife, Cordelia Davidson, Livingston, Fiona Davidson, Gorbals, Glasgow, Harry Davidson, Glasgow, Janette Davidson, Carntyne, Glasgow, Jordan Davidson, Saltcoats, Kevin Davidson, Paisley, Renfrewshire, Liam Davidson, Erskine, Renfrewshire, Liam Davidson, Lochgelly, Fife, Liam Davidson, Stonehaven, Mark Davidson, Glenrothes, Fife, Michael Davidson, Glasgow, Ned Davidson, East Kilbride, Owen Davidson, East Kilbride, Owen Davidson, Stonehaven, Paul Davidson, Erskine, Renfrewshire, Paul Davidson, Ross-shire, Paul Davidson, Winchburgh, Rena Davidson, Blantyre, Robert Davidson, Edinburgh, Stewart Davidson, Haddington, Tony Davidson, Erskine, Renfrewshire, Wee John Davidson, Pollock, Wolf Davidson, Longriggend, Zara Davidson, Edinburgh, Liam Davidson Jnr, Lochgelly, Fife, Granny Margaret Davie-Haggarty, Penilee, Chris Davies, Inverness, Jimmy Davies, Leven, Kenny Davies, London, Colin Davis, Campbeltown, Hugh Davis, Dalkeith, Isabel Davis, Glasgow, Nick Davis, Wishaw, Nicola Davis, Belfast, Gary Davison, Glasgow, Arthur Davren, Bathgate, Helen Daw, Glasgow, Thomas Dawkins, San Francisco, Thomas Dawson, Ruchill, Glasgow, W. Dawson Milne, Aberdeen, Angus Day, Inverness, Billy Day, Glasgow, Callum Day, Inverness, Elizabeth Day, Inverness, Gail Day, Rosyth, Martin Day, Inverness, Ryan Day, Inverness, Gordon Deaas, Kirkcaldy, John Deacons, Bromley, David Deaker, Glasgow, Paul Dealey, Glasgow, Jordan Dean, Glasgow, Thomas Dean(jnr), Stevenston, Kevin Deane, Galashiels, Maureen Deane, Peterson Park, Michael Deane, Bothwell, Bill Deans, Eastwood, Sandy Deas, Leven,   Chris Decleyn, Barlornock, Ryan Decleyn, Barlornock, Mik Deegan, Stevenson, Gerard Deehan, Barrhead, Michael Deehan, Barrhead, Michael Deeney, Helensburgh, Pat Deery, St Ninians, Pat Deery, St Ninians, Joe Degg, Glagow, Thomas Degnan, Cumbernauld, Jim Deigan, Coatbridge, Jim Deighan, Big Tree CSC, Coatbridge, John Deighan, Coatbridge, Pat Deighan, Port Glasgow, Dan Delamere, Dalkeith, Paul James Delamere, Edinburgh, David Delaney, Cumbernauld, Donjie Delaney, Bicester, Willie Delaney, Bicester, John Delissen, Bathgate, Julie Dell, Glasgow, Lydia Delmeistro, Kirkcaldy, Michael DeMarco, Portobello, David Dempsey, Mossblown, Gary Dempsey, London, Joe Dempsey, Auchinlock, John Dempsey, Croy, John Dempsey, Hamilton, Kevin Dempsey, Kilbirnie, Patrick Dempsey, Glasgow, Paul Dempsey, Croy, Paul Dempsey, Croy, Rudi Dempsey, London, Shannon Dempsey, Croy, Bobby Dempster, Bearsden, Glasgow, D Dempster, Montrose, Douglas Dempster, Montrose, Karen Dempster, Ronnie Dempster, Glasgow, Stephen Dempster, Wigan, Kevin Dempsy, Kilbirnie, Lisa & Ryan Denholm, Bonnybridge, Betty Dennehy, Stirling, Jack Dennison, Clydebank, Maxine & Reni Dennistoun, Glasgow, Scott Densea, Aberdeen, Kay Denton,

Glasgow, Ally Dermidy, Bridge of Allan, Ally Dermidy, Bridge Of Allan, Mikie Derrick, Alloa, Steven Derycaer, Bellshill, Andrea Devaney, Uphall, Andrew Devaney, Uphall, Billy Devaney, Broxburn, Cheryl Devaney, Uphall, Daniel Devaney, Uphall, Danielle Devaney, Uphall, Jennifer Devaney, Uphall, Julie Devaney, Uphall, Kevin Devaney, Uphall, Mae Devaney, Broxburn, Mary Devaney, Broxburn, Michael Devaney, Broxburn, Paul Devaney, Coatbridge, Daniel Devanney, Hamilton, David Devenay, Port Glasgow, Paul Devenay, Port Glasgow, Kathleen Deveney, Linwood, Gary Devenney, Chapelhall, Airdrie, Melissa Devenny, Clydebank, Naomi Devenny, Drumchapel, Jack Devi ne, Glasgow, Jim Devin, Street, Adam Devine, Kenilworth, Warwickshire, Adam Devine, Kenilworth, Warwickshire, Andy And Kate Devine, Coatbridge, Barry Devine, Chapelhall, Airdrie, Bernard Devine, Alloa, Carly Devine, Liverpool, Charley Devine, East Kilbride, Charley Devine, East Kilbride, Charlie Devine, Stirling, Chris Devine, Gourock, Conor Devine, Lennoxtown Glasgow, Davy Devine, Bellshill, Ethel Devine, Stirling, Gary Devine, Pollok, Hugh Devine, Wishaw, Jack Devine, East Kilbride, James Devine, S.Wales, Jim Devine, Greenock, John Devine, East Kilbride, John Devine, Hamilton, Karen Devine, Barlanark, Glasgow, Kevin Devine, Alva, Kevin Devine, Easterhouse, Lee Devine, Derry, Lee Devine, East Kilbride, Lee Devine, East Kilbride, Liam Devine, Kenilworth, Warwickshire, Mallaidh Devine, Derry, Martin Devine, Glasgow, Maura Devine, Fleet, Hampshire, Patricia Devine, Stirling, Paul Devine, Glasgow, Robert Devine, Kenilworth, Warwickshire, Ryan Devine, Wishaw, Sandra Devine, East Kilbride, Shauna Devine, Derry, Terry Devine, Lennoxtown Glasgow, Thomas Devine, Auckland, New Zealand, Tilda Devine, Glasgow, Tilda Devine, Oldham, Gordon Devitt, Old Drumchapel, Glasgow, Ryan Devitt, Old Drumchapel, Glasgow, Andrew Devlin, Paisley, Arron Devlin, Glasgow, Bernie Devlin, Worthing, Sussex, Brian Devlin, Corby, Northants, Brogan Devlin, Corby Northants, Derek Devlin, Inverness, Derek Devlin, Inverness, Eoin Devlin, In Seville!!!, Gerry Devlin, Blantyre, Helen Devlin, Corby, Northants, John Devlin, Garngad, John Devlin, Garngad, Glasgow, John Devlin, Glasgow, Scotland, John Joe Devlin, Wildwood New Jersey Usa, Kayleigh Devlin, Corby, Northants, Mark Devlin, Condorrat, Cumbernauld, Michael Devlin, Edinburgh, Michelle Devlin, Blantyre, Pamela Devlin, Blantyre, Paul Devlin, Corby, Paul Devlin, Glasgow, Pauline Devlin, Lincolnshire, Phil Devlin, Craigton, Glasgow, Ryan Devlin, Craigton, Glasgow, Ryan Devlin, Craigton, Glasgow, Stephen Devlin, Blantyre, Tom Devlin, Fort Lauderdale, Florida, Tony Devlin, West Belfast, Tracey Devlin, , Michael Devlin Jnr, Edinburgh, Brian Devlin, Jnr, Corby, Northants, Steven Devline, Kilmarnock, Aston Dewar, Glasgow, Derek Dewar, Deaconsbank, Glasgow, Gerry Dewar, Alloa, Rab Dewar, Clayton-le-Moors, Ronan Dewar, Clayton-le-Moors, William Dewar, Clayton-le-Moors, Angela Diamond, Cardonald, David Diamond, Irvine, Des Diamond, Cardonald, Gerard Diamond, Coatbridge, James Diamond, Port Glasgow, Kenny Diamond, Glasgow, Kyle Diamond, Glasgow, Louise Diamond, St. Austell, Neil Diamond, Cardonald, Aidan Dick, Dunoon, Amanda Dick, Rutherglen, Bobby Dick, Coatbridge, Brendan Dick, Dunoon, Gary Dick, Largs, Gavin Dick, Glasgow, Gordon Dick, Melbourne, Australia, Julie Dick, Peebles, Logan Dick, Dumbarton, Mary Dick, Glasgow, Robert Dick, Coatbridge, Alison Dickie, East Kilbride, Brian Dickie, Ayr, Alan Dixie Dickson, Govanhill, Bill Dickson, Kirkaldy, Dale Dickson, Baillieston, Gary Dickson, Glasgow, Jean Dickson, Prestwick, John Dickson, Baillieston, Laura Dickson, Isle Of Mull, Linda Dickson, , Louise Dickson, Glasgow, Maggie Dickson, Hamilton, Marc Dickson, Glasgow, Michael Dickson, Royston, Micky Dickson, Glenferness, Micky Dickson, Glenferness, Rhys Dickson, Coatbridge, Scot Dickson, Prestwick, Stephen Dickson, Glasgow, Stephen Dickson, Royston, Tegan Dickson, Glasgow, Tommy Dickson, Prestwick, Tommy Dickson, Seville, Vicky Dickson, Prestwick, Wiliam Dickson, Glasgow, Aidso Digney, , Steven Dignon, Basingstoke, Alex Dillon, Denny, Denise Dillon, Mossend, Eric Dillon, Clydebank, Jaci Dillon, Maryhill, Glasgow, James Dillon, Milton, Jim Dillon, Lochee, Dundee, Matt Dillon, Erskine, Michael Dillon, Greenock, O Dillon, , Pauline Dillon, Maryhill, Glasgow, Steven Dillon, Coatbridge, Dillon, Stirling, Franco DiNardo,

Kirkintilloc, Peter Dingwall, Hamilton, Scott Dipiazza, Sutton, Surrey, Steven Dirom, Dumfries, Maureen Diver, Glasgow, Peter Diver, Scarborough, Anthony Divers, Kings Park, John Joseph Divers, Canning Town, London, Martin Divers, Scunthorpe, Paul Divers, Glasgow, Paul Divers, Summerston, Stacey Divers, Scotland, Stephen Divers, Dalmuir, Tony Divers, Livingston, John Divine, Carluke, John Divine, , Paul Diving, Glasgow, Anthony Dixon, Bellsmyre, Dumbarton, Bernadette Dixon, Dumbarton, Brian Dixon, Greenock, Cara Dixon, Toryglen, Darren Dixon, Airdrie, James Dixon, Toryglen, John Dixon, Clydebank, Jonathon Dixon, Cumbernauld, Laura Dixon, Lochgelly, Paul Dixon, , Paul Dixon, Blantyre, Rebecca Dixon, Greenock, Robert Dixon, Glasgow, Ross Dixon, Glasgow, Ryan Dixon, Greenock, Stephen Dixon, Glasgow, Tony Dixon, Dumbarton, Andrew Doak, Port Glasgow, Kierron Doak, Port Glasgow, Louise Doak, Kilwinning, Lynda Doak, Glasgow, Wullie Doak, Shieldhall Ambulance Station, Gerry Dobbin, Colchester, Essex, Thomas Dobbin, Wishaw, Elaine Dobbins, Glasgow, Danny Dobie, Perth, Danny Dobie, Perth, Eddie Dobie, Craigend, Glasgow, Brian Doc, Greenock, Craig Doc, Easterhouse, John Doc, Cumbernauld, John Doc, Greenock, Paul Doc, Easterhouse, Paul Doc, Easterhouse, Scott Doc, Easterhouse, Shug Doc, Easterhouse, Willy Doc, Kirky, Scott Docerty, Easterhouse, Alan Docherty, Bathgate, Andrew G. Docherty, Stranraer, Bernadette Docherty, Dumbarton, Billy Docherty, Cumbernauld, Billy Docherty, Dumbarton, Bilzer Docherty, Riddrie, Brian Docherty, Croftfoot, Brian Docherty, Wishaw, Caroline Docherty, Inverness, Chelsea Docherty, Drumoyne, Chris Docherty, Dumbarton, Chris Docherty, Gourock, Ciaran Docherty, Inverness, Ciaran Docherty, Inverness, Colin Docherty, Oldbury, West Midlands, Craig Docherty, Easterhouse, Daniel Docherty, Uddingston, Daniel Docherty, Uddingston, Darren Docherty, Drumoyne, David Docherty, Coatbridge, Donna Docherty, Uddingston, Florence Docherty, Crookston, Frank Docherty, Poulton-le-Fylde, Frankie Docherty, Poulton-le-Fylde, Gary Docherty, Gary Docherty, Dumbarton, Ge Docherty, Uddingston, Gemma Docherty, Dumbarton, Gemma Docherty, Renton, George Docherty, Poulton-le-Fylde, Georgia Docherty, Poulton-le-Fylde, Gerry Docherty, Campbelltown, Gerry Docherty, Campbeltown, Gerry Docherty, Coatbridge, Gillian Docherty, Stirling, Helen Docherty, Gorbals, J Docherty, Burnside, Jackie Docherty, Greenock, James Docherty, Uddingston, James 'Big Doc' Docherty, Uddingston, Jim Docherty, Enfield, Middlesex, Joe Docherty, Sandyhills Glasgow, John Docherty, Gorbals, John Docherty, Larbert, John Docherty, Stirling, Josephine C. Docherty, Stranraer, Karen Docherty, Coatbridge, Kevan Docherty, Cumbernauld, Kevin Docherty, Kevin Docherty, Cambernauld, Kevin Docherty, Coggeshall, Essex, Kevin Docherty, Cumbernauld, Kevin Docherty, Dumbarton, Liam Docherty, Glasgow, Lynne Docherty, Lenzie, Mairi-Claire Docherty, Coatbridge, Malcolm Docherty, Alness, Margaret Docherty, Dennistoun, Mari-Claire Docherty, Coatbridge, Mark Docherty, Coatbridge, Mark Docherty, Lenzie, Marti Docherty, Coatbridge, Martin Docherty, Crosshill, Glasgow, Martin Docherty, Greenock, Martin John Docherty, Sandyhills Glasgow, Maxine Docherty, Falkirk, Michael Docherty, Bishopbriggs, Michael Docherty, Larbert, Michael Docherty, Maryhill, Michelle Docherty, Coatbridge, Michelle Docherty, Greenock, Nicola Docherty, Drumoyne, Nicola Docherty, Saltcoats, Noris Docherty, Ayr, Patricia Docherty, Bargeddie, Patricia Docherty, Uddingston, Paul Docherty, Denny, Paul Docherty, Easterhouse, Paul Docherty, Larbert, Paula Docherty, Coatbridge, Pete Docherty, Niigata, Japan, Pete Docherty, Niigata, Japan, Richard Docherty, Crookston, Robert Docherty, Saltcoats, Robert Docherty, Saltcoats, Robert Docherty, Tain, Ryan Docherty, Crookston, Sadie Docherty, Poulton-le-Fylde, Scott Docherty, Crookston, Scott Docherty, Easterhouse, Sean Docherty, Inverness, Sean Docherty, Inverness, Sean Docherty, Paisley, Shannon Docherty, Inverness, Shannon Docherty, Inverness, Shawn Docherty, Broxburn, Sheralee Docherty, Greenock, Shuggie Docherty, Coatbridge, Shuggy Docherty, Easterhouse, Siobhan Docherty, Dumbarton, Stephanie Docherty, Greenock, Stephen Docherty, Govan, Steve, Marie & Conal Docherty, Abu Dhabi, Steven Docherty, East Kilbride, Steven Docherty, Glasgow, Thomas Docherty,

Glasgow, Tommy Docherty, Majorca, Tracy Docherty, Cumbernauld, Tricia Docherty, Coatbridge, William Docherty, Middlesbrough, James Docherty (Doc), Blantyre, Richard Docherty Jnr, Port Glasgow, Richard Docherty Snr, Port Glasgow, Mya Docherty-Thompson, Coatbridge, Reece Dock, Paisley, Robert Dock, Paisley, Alan Dockerty, Greenock, Brodie Dockerty, , Frank Dockerty, Paisley, John Dockerty, Coatbridge, John Dockerty, Larbert, Lee Dockerty, Greenock, Marie Dockerty, Glasgow, Michael Dockerty, Larkhall, Neil Dockerty, Greenock, Steven Dockerty, Glasgow, Aisling Doherty, Paisley, Andy Doherty, Jordanhill, Ann Marie Doherty, Glasgow, Anna Doherty, Blackpool, Ashley Doherty, Hamilton , Badger Doherty, Scotstoun, Brian Doherty, Chelmsford, Brian Doherty, Glasgow, Caolan Doherty, Derry City, Charlene Doherty, Newton Mearns, Ciara Marie Doherty, Blackpool, Dale Martin Doherty, Elderslie, Daniel Doherty, Newton Mearns, Donna Doherty, Glasgow, Elaine Doherty, Germany, Erin Mary Doherty, Elderslie, Frank Doherty, Knightswood, Gemma Doherty, Uddingston, Gerry Doherty, Barlanark, Gillian Doherty, Port St Lucie, Florida, James Doherty, Knightswood, Glasgow, Joe Doherty, Glasgow, John Doherty, Derry City, John Anthony Doherty, Blackpool/Donegal, John Patrick Doherty, Glasgow, Kieran Joseph Doherty, Hamilton , Laura Doherty, Glasgow, Lauren Taylor Doherty, Blackpool, Laurence Doherty, Paisley, Lee Doherty, Broxburn, Liz Doherty, Knightswood, Louise Doherty, Anniesland, Louise Doherty, Anniesland, Glasgow, Martin Doherty, Downpatrick, N. Ireland, Michael Doherty, Cathcart, Glasgow, Michael Doherty, Coatbridge, Mick Doherty, Airdrie, Mick Doherty, Lanarkshie, Mick Doherty, Lanarkshire, Mike Doherty, Bellshill, Monica Doherty, Linwood, Muirne Doherty, Hamilton , Neil Doherty, Jordanhill, Nicola Doherty, Rutherglen, Patrick Doherty, Germany, Paul Doherty, Broxburn, Paul Doherty, Knightswood, Paul Doherty, Newton Mearns, Pauline Doherty, Summerston, Phil Doherty, Mitchum, Surrey, Riona Doherty, Hamilton , Ronnie & Kevin Doherty, Mississauga, Ontario Canada, Ryan Doherty, Jordanhill, Sarah Doherty, Paisley, Sean Doherty, Glasgow, Teresa Doherty, Blackpool/Tipperary, Alex Dolan, Greenock, Alex Dolan, Greenock, Christopher Dolan, Clydebank, Conner Dolan, Blackburn, Denny Dolan, Blackburn, Jake Dolan, Perth, John Joseph Dolan, Colne, Lancashire, Lucy Dolan, Gourock, Marc Dolan, Greenock, Michael Dolan, Clydebank, Michael Dolan, Glasgow, Michelle Dolan, Clydebank, Mick Dolan, Clydebank, P. Dolan, Coulport, Shelby Dolan, Glasgow, Stephen Dolan, Baillieston, Tamzin Dolan, Greenock, Veronica Dolan, Barrhead, William Dolan, Glasgow, Big Dom, Govan, Patrick Domman, Glasgow, Thomas Don, Braehead, Bonhill, Lana Donaghey, Garngad, Anthony Donaghue, Glasgow, David Donaghue, Glasgow, David Donaghue, Glasgow, Fay Donaghue, Robroyston, Glasgow, Harry Donaghue, Bishopbriggs, Glasgow, Kenny Donaghue, , Lorraine Donaghue, Glasgow, Natalie Donaghue, Robroyston, Glasgow, Neil Donaghue, Bishopbriggs, Glasgow, Paul Donaghue, Glasgow, Paul Donaghue, Glasgow, Paul Donaghue, Robroyston, Glasgow, Clodagh Donaghy, Belfast, Paddy Donaghy, Belfast, Craig Donald, Kilwinning, John Donald, Ayr, Louis Donald, Alva, Trevor Donald, , Daniel Donaldson, Glasgow, Davie Donaldson, Milton of Campsie, Davie Donaldson, Milton of Campsie, Denise Donaldson, Ayr, Grant Donaldson, Blairdardie, Ian Donaldson, St Andrews, Peter Donaldson, Kilsyth, Ryan Donally, Glasgow, Terry Donally & Family, Coatbridge, Amy Donegan, Cowdenbeath, Audrey Donegan, Cowdenbeath, Joy Donegan, Cowdenbeath, Leonard Donegan, Govan, Stephen Donegan, Cowdenbeath, Ashley Donelli, Easterhouse, Glasgow, Craig Donelli, Easterhouse, Glasgow, Alan Donnachie, Glasgow, Brendan Donnachie, Port Glasgow, Bruce Donnachie, Spain, Carol Donnachie, Wishaw, Cathie Donnachie, Motherwell, Chink Donnachie, Greenock, Claire Donnachie, Port Glasgow, David Donnachie, Garngad, Francis Paul Donnachie, Motherwell, Frank Donnachie, Motherwell, James Donnachie, Netherton, Jean Donnachie, Garngad, John Donnachie, Garngad, Jonathan Donnachie, Greenock, Kevin Donnachie, Cleland, Maxine Donnachie, Garngad, Pat Donnachie, Gorbals, Sharon Donnachie, Motherwell, Sharon Donnachie, Motherwell, Sharon Donnachie, Troon, Stevie Donnachie, Troon, Tim

Donnachie, Gosport, Hampshire, Tim Donnachie, Gosport, Hampshire, Tony Donnachy, Glasgow, Paul Donnahoe, Ardrossan, Thomas Donnakey, Canada, Billy Donnall, Watford, Gerry Donnally, Glasgow, Joan Donnally, Wishaw, John Donnally, Glasgow, Michael Donnally, Glasgow, Pat Donnally, Steve Donnel, Renfrew, Billy Donnell, Luton, Alistair Donnelly, Glasgow, Bernard Donnelly, New Cumnock, Brandan Donnelly, Rutherglen, Brendyn Donnelly, Ballingry, Fife, Catherine Donnelly, , Chirs Donnelly, Falkirk, Colm Donnelly, Renfrew, Damien Donnelly, Viewpark, Daniel Donnelly, Renfrew, Eamon Donnelly, Morecambe, Fergus Donnelly, Stranraer, Gordon Donnelly, Ballingry, Fife, Iona Donnelly, Stranraer, Jack Donnelly, East Kilbride, James Donnelly, Cambuslang, Jim Donnelly, Bishopbriggs, Jim Donnelly, Kings Park, Glasgow, Joanne Bernadette Donnelly, Airdrie, Joe Donnelly, Morecambe, Joe Magners Donnelly, Glengormley, John Donnelly, Airdrie, Jonathan Donnelly, Glasgow, Justine Donnelly, Renfrew, Katie Anna Donnelly, Glasgow, Kev Donnelly, Glasgow, Kevin Donnelly, Kings Park, Glasgow, Kevin Donnelly, New Cumnock, Kirstin Donnelly, Blantyre, Lizanne Donnelly, Rutherglen, Louise Donnelly, Dundee, Margaret Donnelly, Ballingry, Fife, Margaret Donnelly, Calderbank, Airdrie, Martin Donnelly, Glasgow, Maureen Donnelly, Blantyre, Michael Donnelly, Blantyre, Michael Donnelly, Cumbernauld, Mickey Donnelly, Stranraer, Niall Donnelly, Stranraer, Nicole Donnelly, Ballingry, Fife, Pat Donnelly, Blantyre, Paul Donnelly, Dunfermline (West Fife Celts), Rob Donnelly, Bedworth, Samantha Donnelly, Govan, Seamus Donnelly, Stranraer, Sean Donnelly, Dundee, Shane Donnelly, Glengormley, Stephen Donnelly, Cookstown, Steven Donnelly, Cardonald, Susan Donnelly, Cambuslang, Thomas Donnelly, Bramalea, Canada, Tony Donnelly, Glasgow, Joe Donnelly Jnr, , Elaine Donnolly, Glasgow, Andrew Donoghue, Whitburn, Frances Donoghue, Denny, Stirlingshire, Ged Donoghue, Germany, Heather Donoghue, Whitburn, Margaret Donoghue, Whitburn, Mark Donohoe, Glasgow, Martin Donohoe, Glasgow, Mike Donohoe, Lytham, Lancs, Paul Donohoe, Ardrossan, Vince Donohoe, Lytham, Lancs, Jason Donovan, Burnt Island, Tom Libby Donowho, Dumfries, Tom Libby Donowho, Gerrard Doohan, Glasgow, Barry Doolan, Moodiesburn, Dick Doolan, Nottingham, John Doolan, Largs, Stephen Doonan, East Kilbride, Tommy Doonin, Blantyre, Bob Doran, Jersey, Channel Islands, Carly Doran, Govan, Cash Doran, Govan, Christopher Doran, Kilwinning, Conner Doran, Paisley, Evelyn Doran, East Kilbride, Frank Doran, Paisley, Jama Doran, Govan, Jim Doran, Bolton, Kieran Doran, Kilwinning, Michael Doran, Kilwinning, Pat Doran, Govan, Ryan Doran, East Kilbride, Sadie Doran, Sunny Govan, Sean Doran, Derry City, Sean Doran, Jersey, Channel Islands, William Doran, East Kilbride, Bob Doreen, Jersey, Davy Doris, Airdrie, Ian Dornan, High Peak, Peter Dornan, Renfrew, Jeff Doroh, Glasgow, John Paul Dorrian, Scourie, Gerald Dosange, Glasgow, Robert Dott Jr, Vancouver, Canada, Robert Dott Snr, Vancouver Island, Canada, Bartie Dougal, Eyemouth, David Dougal, Newtongrange, Ian Dougal, Dumbarton, Robert Dougal, Dumbarton, Barry Dougall, Cambuslang, Michelle Dougall, Leven, Frank Dougan, Crookston Glasgow Will Be In Seville On, John Dougan, Manchester, Phil Dougan, Clydebank, Sean Paul Dougan, Cumbernauld, Stephen Dougan, Whitecrook, Kevin Dougans, East Kilbride, Paul Dougans, East Kilbride, Kitsy Dougherty, Clydebank, Glasgow, Noreen Dougherty, Clydebank, Glasgow, Paul Dougherty, Kirkintilloch, Stephen Dougherty, Renfrew, Barney Douglas, Hawick, Erin Douglas, Currie, Joe Douglas, Overtown, Michael Douglas, Galashiels, Michael Douglas, Selkirk, Mick Douglas, Skelmersdale, Lancashire, Patrick Douglas, Hawick, Paul Douglas, Dumbarton, Paul Douglas, Glasgow, Paul Douglas, Newmarket, Canada, Ronnie Douglas, Uddingston, Ronnie Douglas, Uddingston, Walter Douglas, Dumbarton, John Dougrie, Glasgow, Adam Dow, Tamworth, Surrey, Jim Dow, Hamilton, Kevin Dow, Hamilton, Scott Dow, Tamworth, Surrey, Ellen Dowds, East Kilbride, Jerry Dowds, Glasgow, Steven Dowds, C-Hill, Lynn Dowe, Falkirk, Alex Dowie, Sandyhills, Glasgow, Kelly Dowie, Mayfield, Liz,Stacey And Kelly Dowie, Mayfield, Andrew Dowing, Coatbridge, Andrew Dowling, Motherwell, Ian Dowling, Bonnyrig, Martin Dowling, Linwood, Paul Down, Glasgow, Shaun Down,

Glasgow, Bridget Downen, St Louis, Marian Downes, Birmingham, Colin Downey, Scarborough, Hugh Downey, Belfast, Jamie Downey, Glasgow, Martine Downey, Glasgow, Corbet Downie, Grangemouth, David Downie, Glasgow, Dianne Downie, Renfrew, Edward Downie, Renfrew, John Downie, Blairgowrie, John Downie, Glasgow, Kayleigh Downie, Grangemouth, Roger Downie, Bellshill, Scott Downie, Glasgow, Tahnee Downie, Bathgate, Downie, Grangemouth, James Downing, Carmyle, Tahiti, Elaine Downs, Muirhead, James Downs, East Kilbride, Andrew Doyle, Stirling, Christopher Doyle, Hamilton, Claire Doyle, High Burnside, Clarelouise Doyle, Motherwell, Colin Doyle, Dundee, Colin Doyle, Livingston, Daniel Doyle, Fullarton Park, Glasgow, Danny Doyle, Fullarton Park, Glasgow, David Doyle, Baillieston, Frank Doyle, Bellshill, Frank Doyle, Bishopbriggs, Glen Doyle, Renfrew, Graham Doyle, Dundee, Ian Doyle, Birmingham, Jamie Doyle, Dumfries, Jasper Doyle, Dumfries, Jim Doyle, Bo'ness, Jim Doyle, Bo'ness, Jim Doyle, Bo'ness, John Doyle, Clydebank, John Doyle, Melbourne, Australia, Johnny Doyle, Drumchapel, Johnny Doyle, Fullarton Park, Glasgow, Johnny Sparky Doyle, Halfway, Jospeh Doyle, Glasgow, Kevin Doyle, Bo'ness, Linda Doyle, Glasgow, M Doyle, Slough, Mary Doyle, Glasgow, Michael Doyle, Bo'ness, Stephen Doyle, Springburn, Stevie Doyle, McVicar Printers, Tracy Doyle, Bridgeton, Michael Dragonis, East Kilbride, Brian Dragoonis, East Kilbride, Brian Dragoonis, East Kilbride, Chris Dragoonis, East Kilbride, Christopher Dragoonis, East Kilbride, Michael Dragoonis, East Kilbride, Micheal Dragoonis, East Kilbride, James Drain, Cumbernauld, Jimmy Drain, North London, Steven Drain, Clydebank, Val Drain, North London, Heather Drant, Paisley, Ronald Draws, Dunfermline, Jonny Drennan, Portsmouth, Drennan, Govan, Dougie Dreuer, Orkney, David Drew, Cardowan, Brian Drummond, Irvine, David Drummond, Helensburgh, Graham Drummond, Springburn, Jean Drummond, Helensburgh, Joan Drummond, Helensburgh, Mark Drummond, East Kilbride, Matt Drummond, East Kilbride, Matthew Drummond, Glasgow, Matthew Drummond, Glasgow, May Drummond, East Kilbride, Paul Drummond, Irvine, Ross Drummond, Helensburgh, Willie Drummond, Australia, Eddie Drumond, Wolverhampton, Ross Drumond, Glasgow, Joanne Drury, London, Jane Dryden, Glasgow, Heather Drymen, West Dumbartonshire, Eddie Ducey, Hamilton, Eddie Ducey, Hamilton, Joseph Duckett, Glasgow, Brian Duddy, Wishaw, Davy Duddy, Wishaw, Hugh Duddy, Wishaw, James Duddy, Port Glasgow, Joe Duddy, Kinning Park, Monica Duddy, Kinning Park, Tam Duddy, Motherwell, Billy Duff, Fife, Cara Duff, Nairn, Sean Duff, Drummy, Duff, Dundee, Christina Duffin, Bathgate, K. Duffin, Glasgow, Paul Duffin, London, Tony Duffin, Rutherglen, Adrian Duffy, Shotts, Allan Duffy, Saltcoats, Ann Duffy, Clarkston, Annmarie Duffy, Culdaff, Co Donegal, Billy Duffy, Saltire Court, Edinburgh, Brian Duffy, Paisley, Ciaran Duffy, Govanhill, Craig Duffy, Erskine, Danielle Duffy, Lennoxtown, Danielle Duffy, Lennoxtown, Danny Duffy, Govanhill, Francis Duffy, County Donegal, Frankie Duffy, Neilston, Gerry Duffy, Co. Monaghan Ireland, Glo Duffy, Lennoxtown, Gloria Duffy, Lennoxtown, Jamie Duffy, Newmains, Jim Duffy, Oxgangs, Joe Duffy, Lennoxtown, Joe Duffy, Lennoxtown, Joe Duffy, Peterborough, John Duffy, Culdaff, Co Donegal, John Duffy, Pollok, Kevin Duffy, Govan Hill, Glasgow, Kevin Duffy, South Africa, Louise Duffy, Stirling, Martha Duffy, Port Glasgow, Martin Duffy, Bangalore, India, Martin Duffy, Cumbernauld, Michelle Duffy, Clones Co. Monaghan Ireland, Paul Duffy, Hamilton, Paul Duffy, Linwood, Paul Joseph Duffy, Bishopbriggs, Phil Duffy, Big Tree CSC, Coatbridge, Phil Duffy, Coatbridge, Sam Duffy, Bathgate, Sean Duffy, Crookston, Sean Duffy, Govanhill, Sharon Duffy, , Stephanie Duffy, Lennoxtown, Steven Duffy, Possilpark, Glasgow, Tommy Duffy, Bathgate, William Duffy, Glasgow, Chris Dugan, Glasgow, James Dugan, Hamilton, Kevin Dugan, Bathgate, Sean Dugan, Bathgate, Eamonn Duggan, East Kilbride, Joe Duggan, Glasgow, Liz Duggan, Glasgow, Paul Duke, Greenhills, Angela Dulk, Clydebank, Thomas Dulk, Clydebank, Marian Dumma, Kelso, Wull Dumma, Kelso, T Dummalty, St Annes, Amanda Dunbar, Nitshill, Glasgow, Chic Dunbar, Manchester, Craig Dunbar, Cambuslang, David Dunbar, Nitshill, Glasgow, Dod Dunbar, Bishopmill, Elgin,

Dod Dunbar, Islay, Liam Dunbar, Manchester, Lorraine Dunbar, London, Marie Dunbar, London, Sandra Dunbar, Nitshill, Glasgow, Scott Dunbar, London, Alan Duncan, Saltcoats, Billy Duncan, Barrow in Furness, Brian Duncan, Glasgow, Carol Duncan, Isleburgh, Shetland, Casey Duncan, Arbroath, Chic Duncan, Glasgow, Chris Duncan, Ralston, Paisley, Gordon Duncan, Banknock, Ilona Duncan, Ireland, Isabel Duncan, Barrow in Furness, Josh Duncan, Ralston, Paisley, Julie Duncan, Barrow in Furness, Karen Duncan, Arbroath, Kenny Duncan, Stornoway, Liam Duncan, Cumbernauld, Linda Duncan, Glasgow, Nicola Duncan, Barrow in Furness, Pamela Duncan, Barrow in Furness, Rosie Duncan, Glasgow, Avid Dundas, Milton Keynes, Jack Dundas, Knightswood, Glasgow, Marc Dundas, Milton Keynes, Tom Dundas, Manila, William Dundas, Milton Keynes, Helen Dunese, Glasgow, Harry Dunion, Glenrothes, Fife, Kevin Dunion, Anstruther, Fife, Philip Dunion, Markinch, Fife, Andrina Dunlop, Whitburn, West Lothian, Andy Dunlop, Stepps, Angela Dunlop, Whitburn, West Lothian, Anne Dunlop, East Kilbride, Anne Dunlop, New York, Archie Dunlop, Whitburn, West Lothian, Billy Dunlop, Bonnybridge, Carol Anne Dunlop, Whitburn, West Lothian, Claire Dunlop, East Kilbride, David Dunlop, Carradale, Derek Dunlop, Edinburgh, John Dunlop, Dunfermline, Keira Dunlop, Dunfermline, Manus Dunlop, Whitburn, West Lothian, Margaret Dunlop, Whitburn, West Lothian, Maria Dunlop, Temple Anniesland, Mark Dunlop, Cork, Martina Dunlop, Cork, Matt Dunlop, Glasgow, Paul Dunlop, Coatbridge, Paula Dunlop, East Kilbride, Robert Dunlop, East Kilbride, Sharon Dunlop, Glasgow, Sharon Dunlop, Glasgow, Steven Dunlop, Coatbridge, Brian Dunn, Fife, Brian Dunn, Glasgow, Catrina Dunn, Paignton, Devon, Chris Dunn, Dundee, Chris Dunn, Dundee, Colin Dunn, Glenrothes, Drew Dunn, Blackburn, George Dunn, Ayrshire, George Dunn, Whitby Ontario Canada, Jennifer Dunn, Glasgow, Jenny Dunn, Dundee, Jenny Dunn, Dundee, Joe Dunn, Lincolnshire, John Dunn, Port Glasgow, Kevin Dunn, Luton, Mary Dunn, Lincolnshire, Mick Dunn, Barrhead Glasgow, Mick Dunn, East Kilbride, Paul Dunn, Glasgow, Pauline Dunn, Cumbernauld, Peter Dunn, Elderslie, Russell Dunn, Bo'Ness, James Dunnachie, Kilmarnock, Lorraine Dunnachie, Prestwick, Hugh Dunne, Drumchapel, Glasgow, James Dunne, Drumchapel, Glasgow, Mick Dunne, Barrhead, Pauline Dunne, Cumbernauld, Simon Dunne, Stirling, Trevor Dunne, Tallaght, Dublin, Callum Dunnion, York, Connor Dunnion, York, James Dunsmeir, Ayr, Thomas Dunsmere, Cambuslang, Wullie Dunsmore, Boness, Jim Dunsmuir, Eastfield, Dunsmuir, Glasgow, Paul Dunwoodie, Bournemouth, Dick Duran, Nottingham, John Durkin, Falkirk, Charlie Durnan, Renfrew, Paul Durnan, Kirkintilloch, Jean Durning, Coatbridge, Kim Durning, Coatbridge, Mr.James Duthie, Phoneix House,Glasgow, Gerard Dutton, Glasgow, Chris Dwyer, Milngavie, Chris Dwyer, Milngavie, Andrew Dyke, Peterhead, Andy Dyke, Perth, Oz, Michael Lovatt Dyke, Erskine, Greg Dykes, Glasgow, James Dykes, Galston, Mark Dykes, Kings Park, Glasgow, Shug Dylon, Cowdenbeath, Francis Dynan, Australia, Jim Dynan, Australia, Stephen Dynes, Glasgow.

Craig E Morrison, Greenock. Alan Eadie, Bishopbriggs, George Eadie, Milngavie, Glasgow, Hugh Eadie, Kingswells, Aberdeen, Ken Eadie, Largs, Tricia Eadie, Largs, Joycy Ealing, John Earlie, Salsburgh, John Jnr Earlie, Salsburgh, Karen Earlie, Whitburn, Kathleen Earlie, Salsburgh, Bernie Early, Rotterdam, Claire Louise Early, Wishaw, Davie Early, Wishaw, Holly Marie Early, Wishaw, Jodie Early, Wishaw, Jordan Early, Wishaw, Kieran Early, Wishaw, Marina Early, Wishaw, Marina Early, Wishaw, Grace Easdale, Port Glasgow, George Easdale Snr, Port Glasgow, Jennifer East, East Calder, Willie Eastcroft, Kinlochbervie, Marie Easter, Leven, Anthony Easterhouse, Glasgow, Anton Easterhouse, Glasgow, Jordan Easterhouse, Glasgow, Sharon Easterhouse, Glasgow, Craig Easton, Falkirk, Hazel Easton, Clackmannanshire, Kevin Easton, Leven, Michael Easton, Leven, Robert Easton, Falkirk, Stephanie Easton, Leven, James Eastwood, East Kilbride, Davie Eccles, Glasgow, Joan Eccles, East Kilbride, Kenny Eccleson, Cumbernauld, Kenny Eccleson, Cumbernauld, Andy Ecosse, Paisley, Big Eddie, Pollok, Tony Eddie, Glasgow,

Debbie Edelsten, Kings Park, Declan Edelsten (Jnr), Kingspark, Gavin Eden, Perth, Australia, Jamie Eden, Perth, Australia, Gary&Sharon Edgar, Seville,Spain, Gordon Edgar, Greenock, Graham Edgar, Dumfries, Graham Edgar, Dumfries, Laura Edgar, Dunipace, Big Gav Edinburgh, , Paul Edmonson, Castlemilk, Fred Edwards, Doncaster, Fred Edwards, Doncaster, Richard Edwards, Oban, Amanda Egan, Stirling, Eddie Egan, London, Karen Egan, Motherwell, Margaret & Michael Egan, Glasgow, Mark Egan, Cleland, Mark Eileen, Glasgow, Dessie Elder, Ballymena, Gavin Elder, Glasgow, Gillian Elder, Glasgow, Kathryn Elder, Dumbarton, Lewis,Alison&Scott Elder, Kirkintilloch/Glasgow, Lynsey Elder, Dumbarton, Sharon Elder, Dumbarton, Steven Elle, Stirling, Benny Elliot, Ballycastle Co.Antrim, Kris Elliot, Glasgow, Martin Elliot, Kirklandneuk, Benny Elliott, Coatbridge, Jane Elliott, Dundee, John Elliott, Newarthill Lanarkshire, Kevin Elliott, Keighley, Mickey Elliott, London, Paul Elliott, Inverness, Ross Elliott, Nairn, Alun Ellis, Edinburgh, Arthur Ellis, Edinburgh, Mark Ellis, Blackpool, Susan Ellis, Kirkcaldy, Steven Elly, Stirling, Steven Elmes, Frimley Green, Surrey, Dean Elrick, Bearsden, Lorraine Else, Corby, Northants, Brian Emans, Baillieston, Tam Emans, Baillieston, Assumption Club Emerald Room, Coventry, Daniel Emerson, Glasgow, Mick Enzmann, Corby, Gail Erskin, Scotstoun, Glasgow, John Erskine, Armadale, Robert Espie, Toryglen, Pauline Esposito, U.S.A, Steven Esposito, U.S.A, Tony Esposito, U.S.A, Jim Esson, St Fergus, Jonathan Esson, Hamilton, Jordan Esson, Hamilton, Marcus Ethen, Hamilton, Peter Etherson, Bishopbriggs, Peter Etherson, Bishopbriggs, Peter Etherson, Ruchill, Alex Evan, Glasgow, Mary Evan, Aimee Evans, Arbroath, Pat Evans, Sheffield, Nicola Ewart, Partick, Catherine Ewing, Knightswood, Glasgow, James Ewing, Coatbridge, John Ewing, Forres, Jonathan Ewing, Denny, Jonnie Ewing, Dunipace, Ryan Ewing, Kilmarnock, Stephen Ewing, Coatbridge, Theresa Ewing, Portumna, County Galway, Grace Easdale, Port Glasgow, George Easdale Snr, Port Glasgow, Jennifer East, East Calder, Willie Eastcroft, Kinlochbervie, Sutherland, Marie Easter, Leven, Fife, Anthony Easterhouse, Glasgow, Anton Easterhouse, Glasgow, Jordan Easterhouse, Glasgow, Sharon Easterhouse, Glasgow, Craig Easton, Falkirk, Hazel Easton, Clackmannanshire, Kevin Easton, Leven, Fife, Michael Easton, Leven, Fife, Robert Easton, Falkirk, Stephanie Easton, Leven, Fife, James Eastwood, East Kilbride, Davie Eccles, Glasgow, Joan Eccles, East Kilbride, Kenny Eccleson, Cumbernauld, Andy Ecosse, Paisley, Big Eddie, Pollok, Glasgow, Tony Eddie, Glasgow, Debbie Edelsten, Kings Park, Declan Edelsten (Jnr), Kingspark, Gavin Eden, Perth, Australia, Jamie Eden, Perth, Australia, Gary and Sharon Edgar, Seville, Spain, Gordon Edgar, Greenock, Graham Edgar, Dumfries, Graham Edgar, Dumfries, Laura Edgar, Dunipace, Big Gav, Edinburgh, Paul Edmonson, Castlemilk, Glasgow, Fred Edwards, Doncaster, Fred Edwards, Doncaster, Richard Edwards, Oban, Amanda Egan, Stirling, Eddie Egan, London, Karen Egan, Motherwell, Margaret and Michael Egan, Glasgow, Mark Egan, Cleland, Mark Eileen, Glasgow, Dessie Elder, Ballymena, Gavin Elder, Glasgow, Gillian Elder, Glasgow, Kathryn Elder, Dumbarton, Lewis, Alison and Scott Elder, Kirkintilloch, Lynsey Elder, Dumbarton, Sharon Elder, Dumbarton, Steven Elle, Stirling, Benny Elliot, Ballycastle, Co. Antrim, Kris Elliot, Glasgow, Martin Elliot, Kirklandneuk, Renfrewshire, Benny Elliott, Coatbridge, Jane Elliott, Dundee, John Elliott, Newarthill, Lanarkshire, Kevin Elliott, Keighley, Yorkshire, Mickey Elliott, London, Paul Elliott, Inverness, Ross Elliott, Nairn, Alun Ellis, Edinburgh, Arthur Ellis, Edinburgh, Mark Ellis, Blackpool, Susan Ellis, Kirkcaldy, Steven Elly, Stirling, Steven Elmes, Frimley Green, Surrey, Dean Elrick, Bearsden, Lorraine Else, Corby, Northants, Brian Emans, Baillieston, Glasgow, Tam Emans, Baillieston, Glasgow, Assumption Club Emerald Room, Coventry, Daniel Emerson, Glasgow, Mick Enzmann, Corby, Gail Erskin, Scotstoun, Glasgow, John Erskine, Armadale, West Lothian, Robert Espie, Toryglen, Glasgow, Pauline Esposito, USA, Steven Esposito, USA, Tony Esposito, USA, Jim Esson, St Fergus, Jonathan Esson, Hamilton, Jordan Esson, Hamilton, Marcus Ethen, Hamilton, Peter Etherson, Bishopbriggs, Glasgow, Peter Etherson, Bishopbriggs, Glasgow, Peter Etherson, Ruchill, Glasgow, Alex Evan, Glasgow, Mary Evans, Aimee Evans, Arbroath, Pat Evans, Sheffield,

Nicola Ewart, Partick, Catherine Ewing, Knightswood, Glasgow, James Ewing, Coatbridge, John Ewing, Forres, Jonathan Ewing, Denny, Jonnie Ewing, Dunipace, Stirlingshire, Ryan Ewing, Kilmarnock, Stephen Ewing, Coatbridge, Theresa Ewing, Portumna, County Galway, Antony Ezziane, Calton, Glasgow, Karima Ezziane, Baillieston, Glasgow.

Michael Faccenda, Tony Faccenda, Cumbernauld, Jackie Fagan, Motherwell, Michelle Fagan, Motherwell, Patrick Fagan, Canada, Peter Fagan, Bo'ness, Willie Fagan, Armadale, John Fagan, Carfin, John Fagan Junior, Carfin, Colin Fagen, Airdrie, Adam Fahim, Hawick, Emma Faichney, Falkirk, Andy Fairfield, Gorbals, Glasgow, Agnes Fairlie, Chapelhall, Lanarkshire, Arthur Fairlie, Airdrie, Brian Fairlie, Chapelhall, Lanarkshire, John Fairlie, Bothwell, Kathryn-Anne Fairlie, Livingston, Paul Fairlie, Livingston, Peter Fairlie, Livingston, Raymond Fairlie, Easterhouse, Glasgow, Steven Fairlie, Livingston, Mike Fairs, Glasgow, Billy Falconer, Arbroath, Mike Falconer, Arbroath, Francis Fallan, Shotts, Lanarkshire, Jane Fallan, Shotts, Lanarkshire, Joe Fallan, Whitburn, Danny Fallen, Luton, Bedfordshire, Peter Fallen, Luton, Bedfordshire, Barry Fallens, Stirling, Steven Fallens, Milburn, John Faller, Greenock, Robbie Faller, Greenock, Brian Fallon, Bathgate, Charles Fallon, Glasgow, George Fallon, Coatbridge, John Fallon, Brixham, Devon, Margaret Fallon, Abu Dhabi, UAE, Paul Fallon, Glasgow, Sean Fallon, Glasgow, Shaun Fallon, Corby, Atley Family, Glasgow, Binn Family, Port Glasgow, Brenan Family, Irvine, Cassidy Family, Glasgow, Cassidy Family, Motherwell, Connally Family, Glasgow, Daw Family, Doherty Family, Maple Court, Dunn Family, Port Glasgow, Foley Family, Burnside, Gallagher Family, Athy, Co. Kildare, Garner Family, Northants, Gill Family, Nottingham, Granger Family, Yoker, Haynes Family, New Zealand, Howard Family, Lumphinnans, Fife, McGeown Family, Greenock, McGinley Family, Glasgow, McGowan Family, Donegal & Glasgow, Meechan Family, Isle of Skye, Mullin Family, Glasgow, Omizik Family, Glasgow, Rea Family, Portsoy, Aberdeenshire, Sweeney Family, Old Kilpatrick, Sweeny Family, Glasgow, McManus Famliy, Glasgow, Alan Fanking, Port, Glasgow, Eric Fanking, Port, Glasgow, Mary Fanking, Port Glasgow, Roz Fanking, Port Glasgow, Stevie Fanking, Port Glasgow, John Fanning, Parkhouse, Glasgow, Eck Farmer, Leslie, Fife, Elizabeth Farmer, Toronto, Canada, Harry Farmer, South Armagh, Pete Farmer, Wellington, New Zealand, Peter Farmer, Wellington, New Zealand, Frankie Farnin, Bellshill, Colin Faron, Pitlochry, Perthshire, Mark Farquire, Glasgow, John Farrall, Glasgow, Aileen Farrell, Bridgeton, Glasgow, David Farrell, Garrowhill, Glasgow, Derek Farrell, Lochelly, Fife, Emma Farrell, Drumoyne, Glasgow, James Farrell, Dennistoun, Glasgow, James Farrell, Grangemouth, Jamie Farrell, Grangemouth, John Farrell, Dennistoun, Glasgow, John Farrell, East Kilbride, Joseph Henry Farrell, Craigbank, Margaret Farrell, Glasgow, Martin Farrell, East Kilbride, Megan Farrell, Grangemouth, Michael Farrell, Drumoyne, Pat Farrell, Glasgow, Paul Farrell, Poleglass, Belfast, Peter Farrell, Chapelhall, Scott Farrell, Grangemouth, Sean Farrell, Drumoyne, Sean Farrell, Shettleston, Shug Farrell, Carmyle, Glasgow, Michael Farren, Glasgow, Tom Farren, Bangor, Colin Farron, Perthshire, Louis Farry, Ireland, Sean Farry, Ireland, Andy Fathers, Oldbury, West Midlands, Marie Fathers, Oldbury, West Midlands, James Fawns, Fife, James Fealey, Kieran Fealy, Glasgow, Jessica Feaney, Spain, Mark Daniel Fearnon, Pollok, Glasgow, Alan Feechan, Blantyre, Lorraine Feegan, Wishaw, Frank Feely, South Armagh, James Feely, Turiff, Aberdeenshire, Billie-Jo Feeney, Linthouse, Glasgow, Danny Feeney, Dundee, Lisa Feeney, Tullibody, Marc Feeney, Mount Vernon, Glasgow, Willie Feeney, Larkhall, John Fegan, Coatbridge, Brian Feighan, Coatbridge, Paul Feighan, Bonnybridge, Sean Feighan, Belfast, Stephen Feighan, Bonnybridge, David Fellgee, Glasgow, Arthur Fellowes, Preisthill, Glasgow, Susanne Fellowes, East Kilbride, Thomas Fellowes, Preisthill, Glasgow, Bryan Fennessey, Coatbridge, Paul Fennessey, Coatbridge, Bobby Fenton, Johnstone, Ralph Fenton, Glasgow, Aiden Hendrik Ferguson, Elgin, Alex Ferguson, Eastbourne, Andy Ferguson, Rockingham, Western Australia, Angie Ferguson, Belfast, Ashleigh Ferguson, Port Glasgow, Baby Ferguson, Castlemilk, Barry

Ferguson, Benderloch, Craig Ferguson, Craigend, Danny Ferguson, Castlemilk, Gerard Ferguson, Croy, Gordon Ferguson, Falkirk, Ian Ferguson, Craigend, Jackie Ferguson, Port Glasgow, Jason Ferguson, Beanhill, Milton Keynes, Jim Ferguson, Motherwell, Leanne Ferguson, Aberdeen, Liz Ferguson, Livingston, Mairanne Ferguson, Glenrothes, Margaret Ferguson, Castlemilk, Glasgow, Mark Ferguson, Uddingston, Paul Ferguson, Craigend, Paul Ferguson, Schuh, Peter Ferguson, Edinburgh, Roselyn Ferguson, Falkirk, Sheila Ferguson, Paisley, Stephen Ferguson, Bracknell, Berks, Stevie Ferguson, Caithkin, Tam Ferguson, Glenrothes, Thatch Ferguson, Cowie, Stirlingshire, Thomas Ferguson, Cowie, Stirlingshire, Tracy Ferguson, East Kilbride, Broghan Fern, Coatbridge, James Fern, Coatbridge, Kelly Fern, Coatbridge, Leanne Fern, Coatbridge, Leeanne Fern, Coatbridge, Lewis Fern, Coatbridge, Scon Fern, Shawhead, Coatbridge, Stephen Fern, Coatbridge, Lee Fernandes, Stirling, Kevin Fernie, Dennyloanhead, Stirlingshire, Sean Fernon, Gerry Ferns, Liverpool, Stephen Ferns, East Kilbride, Stephen Ferns, East Kilbride, Thomas Ferns, Kirkintilloch, The Ferns Pub, Fernbank, Livingston, Annie Ferrie, Bellshill, Brandon Ferrie, Carfin, Brian Ferrie, Carfin, Daniel Ferrie, Bellshill, Elaine Ferrie, Wishaw, Lewis Ferrie, Carfin, Daniel Ferrier, Bonnyrigg, Gregor Ferrier, Edinburgh, Mark Ferrier, Bonny-rigg, Mark Ferrier, Paisley, Paul Ferrier, Paisley, Stuart, Linda, Martin And Ryan Ferrier, Penicuik, Paul Ferrin, Belfast, Eddie Ferris, Erskine, Joe Ferris, Erskine, Lynne Ferris, Erskine, John Ferrol, Torquay, Robert Ferrol, Airdrie, Brian Ferry, Hamilton, Eleanor Ferry, Hamilton, Gerald Ferry, Glasgow, Gerald Ferry, Glasgow, Haigh Ferry, West Kilbride, Hugh Ferry, Hamilton, Jamie Ferry, Kirkintilloch, Mark Ferry, Easterhouse, Glasgow, Monica Ferry, Motherwell, Pedro Ferry, Moat, Edinburgh, K. Fiddler, Grangemouth, Jo Field, Dennistoun, Glasgow, Tony Fielding, Sauchie, Emma Fife, Aberdeen, Kimberly Fife, Aberdeen, Matt Fife, Aberdeen, Ryan Fife, Aberdeen, Colin Findlaker, Killmarnock, Alistair Findlay, Kilsyth, Bridget Findlay, Rawyards, Airdrie, Connor Findlay, Rawyards, Airdrie, Darren Findlay, Rawyards, Airdrie, Erin Findlay, Livingston, Jack Findlay, Rawyards, Airdrie, James Findlay, Kilsyth, John Findlay, Abbotsford, Joseph Findlay, Livingston, Keith Findlay, Montrose, Lindsey Findlay, Glasgow, Lynn Findlay, Dunoon, Mike, James, Jack Findlay, Peterhead, Nancy Findlay, Lennoxtown, Tam Findlay, Govan, Glasgow, James Christopher Findley, Airdrie, John Findley, Ballysillan, Belfast, Marcus Findley, Coatbridge, Samuel Findley, Glasgow, Fran Findon, Sydney, Australia, Caitlin Finegan, Glasgow, Jim Finegan, Glasgow, Sean Finegan, Glasgow, Paul Finesy, Coatbridge, Darragh Finglas, Dublin, Brian Finigan, Glasgow, Scott Finlay, Torrance, Craig Finlayson, St Ninians, Stirling, Christopher Finley, Glasgow, William Finley, Falkirk, Sandra Finn, Camberwell, Surrey, Paul Finnel, Paisley, Bernie Finnerty, Balornock, Glasgow, Chic Finnetty, Perth, Tomas Finney, Lorraine Finnie, Edinburgh, Tricia Finnie, Edinburgh, Catrina Finnigan, Inverness, Chris Finnigan, Inverness, Christopher Finnigan, Inverness, David Finnigan, East Kilbride, Jimmy Finnigan, Inverness, Jimmy Finnigan, Inverness, John Finnigan, Kincraig, Inverness-shire, Michael Finnigan, Barrhead, Michelle Finnigan, Inverness, Robert Finnigan, Craigend, Glasgow, Ushka Finnigan, Inverness, John Finningan, Coatbridge, James Finnley, Glasgow, Andrew Fisher, Ardrossan, Anthony Fisher, Coatbridge, Claire Fisher, Carluke, Colin Fisher, Brent Bravo, Drew Fisher, Wishaw, George Fisher, Ardrossan, James Fisher, Carluke, James Fisher, Glasgow, James Fisher, Parkhouse, Jill Fisher, Blandford, Dorset, Jim Fisher, Wishaw, Melissa Fisher, Hawick, Michael Fisher, Motherwell, Nikki Fisher, Wishaw, Robert Fisher, Glasgow, Fisher, Carluke, Billy Fitch, Leicester, Billy Fitch, Blackpool, Bobby Fitch, Provanmill, Glasgow, David Fitch, Provanmill, JP Fitch, Provanmill, Glasgow, Megan Fitch, Leicester, Stephen Fitch, Tony Fitch, Coatbridge, Greens Fitness, Giffnock, Mark Fitzgerald, Paisley, Andrew Fitzpatrick, Johnstone, Anthony Fitzpatrick, Bearsden, Brian Fitzpatrick, Bonnybridge, Chloe Fitzpatrick, Aberdeen, Daniel Fitzpatrick, Johnstone, Eddie Fitzpatrick, Glasgow, Ellen Fitzpatrick, Johnstone, Gavin Fitzpatrick, Torrance, Hugh Fitzpatrick, Glasgow, John Fitzpatrick, Aberdeen, Joseph Fitzpatrick, Pollok, Glasgow, Kevin Fitzpatrick, Aberdeen, Kevin Fitzpatrick, Torrance, Liam Fitzpatrick, Torrance, Martin

Fitzpatrick, Bearsden, Glasgow, Paul Fitzpatrick, Ballycastle, Co.Antrim, Paul Fitzpatrick, Johnstone, Paul Fitzpatrick, Pollokshields, Glasgow, Paul Fitzpatrick, Pollokshields. Glasgow, Sean Fitzpatrick, Aberdeen, Sian Cara Fitzpatrick, Aberdeen, Siobhan Fitzpatrick, Johnstone, Tommy Fitzpatrick, Pollok, Glasgow, Collin Fitzsimmons, Musselburgh, Declan Fitzsimmons, Castlemilk, Glasgow, Gillian Fitzsimmons, Abronhill, Cumbernauld, James Fitzsimmons, Glasgow, Kevin Fitzsimmons, Musselburgh, Michael Fitzsimmons, Abronhill, Michelle Fitzsimmons, Musselburgh, Vinny Fitzsimmons, Ardrossan, Bernie Flaherty, Falkirk, Frankie Flaherty, Falkirk, Joshua Flaherty, Falkirk, Kevin Flaherty, Falkirk, Mark Flaherty, Falkirk, Bobby Flanagan, Bathgate, Denis Flanagan, Glasgow, James Flanagan, Glasgow, John M Flanagan, Oldham, Marie Flanagan, Glasgow, Mellissa Flanagan, Castlemilk, Glasgow, Stephen Flanagan, Oldham, Steven Flanigan, Motherwell, Tommy Flanigan, Motherwell, Mark Flaningan, Paisley, Matthew Flaningan, Paisley, Janice Flannagan, Charlie Flannigan, Airdrie, Joe Flannigan, Tannochside, Lanarkshire, John Flannigan, Bathgate, Terry Flannigan, Bathgate, Andy Flaws, Shetland, Bruce Flaws, Stirling, Jeni Flaws, Shetland, Konrad Flaws, Shetland, Marcus Fleet, Gallowgate, Glasgow, Allan Fleming, Yoker, Glasgow, Andrew Fleming, Edinburgh, Billy Fleming, Lochgelly, Fife, Claire Fleming, Stirling, Daniel Fleming, Clydebank, Eirinn Fleming, Gallowgate, Glasgow, Jim Fleming, Barmulloch, Glasgow, Jim Fleming, Fuengirola, Jim Fleming, Fuengirola, John Fleming, North Belfast, Judith Fleming, Johnstone, Linda Fleming, Carrickhill, Belfast, Margaret Fleming, Glasgow, Peter Fleming, Clydebank, Ryan Fleming, Mosspark, Glasgow, Sammyjo Fleming, Dominican College, Fortwilliam, Belfast, Sinead Fleming, St Gemmas High School, Belfast, Stephen Fleming, Ayrshire, Tess Fleming, Livingston, Wullie and Maureen Flemin, Cranhill,Glasgow, Debbie Flemington, Darnley, Laura Flemington, Darnley, Glasgow, Alexander Flemming, Glasgow, Angela Flemming, Glasgow, Claire Flemming, Glasgow, Frank Flemming, Glasgow, Liz Flemming, Glasgow, Martin Flemming, Glasgow, Peter Flemming, Clydebank, Robert Flemming, Glasgow, Ryan Flemming, Glasgow, Billy Fletcher, Summerston, Glasgow, Conor Fletcher, Summerston, Glasgow, James Fletcher, Loughborough, Leicestershire, Karen Fletcher, Drumoyne, Glasgow, Michael Fletcher, Falkirk, Emma Flockhart, West Calder, K Flood, Glasgow, Jade Florence, Govanhill, Kevin Florence, Inverness, Kieran Florence, Inverness, Danny Flynn, Barlanark, Glasgow, Francis and Anne Flynn, Uphall, West Lothian, Jennifer Flynn, Irvine, Joe Flynn, Perth, Joe David Flynn, Perth, John Flynn, Adelaide, South Australia, Julie-Anne Flynn, Perth, Kevin Flynn, Prestwick, Louis Paul Flynn, Perth, Martin Flynn, Linwood, Renfrewshire, Max John Flynn, Perth, Michael Flynn, Edinburgh, Paddy Flynn, St Ninians, Stirling, Patric Flynn, Glasgow, Paul Flynn, Greenock, Paul Flynn, Greenock, Paul David Flynn, Perth, Ryan Flynn, Easterhouse, Glasgow, Sean Flynn, Coventry, Sean Flynn, Irvine, Shannon Flynn, Irvine, Shaun Flynn, Glasgow, Stefan Flynn, Greenock, Stephen Flynn, Glasgow, Tony Flynn, William Flynn, Greenock, Willie Foeley, Hamilton, Qurious Fogg, Q_Fogg1981@hotmail.com, Mark Folan, Port Glasgow, Ryan Folan, Port Glasgow, Alison Foley, Elderslie, Christine Foley, Elderslie, Christine Foley, Elderslie, John Foley, Stenhousemuir, Pat Foley, Elderslie, Stephen Foley, Paisley, Steven Foley, Johnstone, Terry Foley, Sciennes, Paul's Folks, Hamilton, Drew Folland, Derry, Northern Ireland, Jack Folland, Derry, Matthew Folland, Derry, Michael Folland, Edinburgh, Billy Forbes, Cumbernauld, Danielle and Lauren and Toni Forbes, Glasgow, Isabel and Joe Forbes, Glasgow, James Forbes, Govanhill, Glasgow, Kevin Forbes, Derry, Scott Forbes, Coatbridge, Wee Joe Forbes, Glasgow, Eddie Ford, Wishaw, Harry Ford, Worthing, Sussex, Kevin Ford, The Inch, Edinburgh, Scott Ford, Jersey, Michael Forker, Sutton Coldfield, West Midlands, Eirinn Forkin, Bolton, Kevan Forkin, Bolton, Bill Forrest, Monifieth, Claire Forrest, Cambuslang, Glasgow, Danny Forrest, Austria (but Wishaw at heart), Kevin Forrest, Uphall, West Lothian, Mark Forrest, Castlemilk, Willie Forrest, Monifieth, David Forrester, Clayton-le-Moors, Frank Forrester, Riddrie, Harris Forrester, Garrowhill, Glasgow, Robert Forrester, Cumbernauld, Alexander Forster, Stirling, Michael Forster, Canada,

Michael Forster, Canada, Christopher John Forsyth, Hartlepool, Craig Forsyth, Lesmahagow, Michael Forsyth, Hartlepool, Patrick Forsyth, Dennistoun, Glasgow, Tiny Forsyth, Falkirk, Mark Fossett, Newton Mearns, Anne Foster, Glasgow, Bob Foster, Govan Hill, Glasgow, Robert Foster, Edinburgh, Thomas Foster, Govanhill, Glasgow, David Fotheringham, Kirkcaldy, James Fotheringham, Kirkcaldy, Mark Fotheringham, Lanark, Lyes Foussi, Sighthill, Beduff Fox, Bedworth, Brendan Fox, Bangor, Gerald Fox, Commonhead, Ian Fox, Glasgow, James Fox, Annan, Joe Fox, Moodiesburn, John Fox, Falkirk, John Fox, Santa Ponsa, Mallorca, Kieran Fox, London, Mark Fox, Hawick, Scotland, Paul Fox, Falkirk, Robert Fox, Robert Fox Jnr, Croftfoot, Glasgow, Stevie Fox, Glasgow, The Foxes, Oban, Paul Foxs, Hamilton, Jade Foy, Paisley, Jodie Foy, Paisley, John Foy, Cumbernauld, Kevin Foy, Livingston, Michelle Foy, Leon,Spain, Ryan Foy, Livingston, Gordon Fraiser, Sheryl Fraiser, Allan Frame, Busby, Glasgow, Allan Frame, Glasgow, Amanda Frame, Coatbridge, Gerry Frame, Airth, Lesley Frame, Inverness, Pater Frampton, Bathgate, Steven France, Denny, John Francis, Coatbridge, Paul Francis, Glasgow, Alexander Fraser, Inverness, Andy Fraser, Beauly, Barry Fraser, Caitlin Fraser, Inverness, Carol Fraser, Edinburgh, Cheryl Fraser, Stepps, Corrina Fraser, Inverness, Darryl Fraser, Lhanbryde, Morayshire, Eck Fraser, Baillieston, Glasgow, Freddie Fraser, Priesthill, Glasgow, Gary Fraser, Edinburgh, Gerry Fraser, Darnley, Glasgow, Iain C Fraser, Tobermory, Isle Of Mull, James Fraser, Inverness, James L. Fraser, Inverness, John Fraser, Springburn, Kevin Fraser, Inverness, Lindsay Fraser, Arbroath, Michelle Fraser, Inverness, Nicky Fraser, Glasgow, Sean Fraser, Glasgow, Shirelle Fraser, Arbroath, Stephen Fraser, Inverness, Alan Frasier, Andrew Frasier, Inverness, Dawn Frasier, Inverness, Ewan Frasier, New Zealand, Tony Frasier, Glasgow, Stephen Frazer, Gorebridge, Lisa Freeburn, Sauchie, William Freeland, Danderhall, Gordon Freezer, Inverness, Jim Freezer, Inverness, Freezer, New Zeland, Darryl French, Brent Bravo, Gary French, Fife, Paddy French, Fife, Ross French, Fife, Roy French, Fife, Eddie Frew, Muirhead, James Frew, Clarkston, Glasgow, John Frew, Blantyre, Peter Gerard Frew, Bellshill, Tracey Jenna Frew, Stevenson, Caitie Friel, Coatbridge, Chris Friel, Cambuslang, Glasgow, Christopher Friel, Cambuslang, Glasgow, Eleanor Friel, Sandyhills, Glasgow, Franny Friel, Croy, Lanarkshire, Gerry Friel, Rutherglen, Hammy Friel, Cambuslang, Joe Friel, Blackheath, London, John Friel, Kilsyth, John Friel, Kilsyth, Jonathan Friel, Kilsyth, Jonathan Friel, Kilsyth, Lauren Friel, Coatbridge, Mark Friel, Glasgow, Natalie Friel, Blackheath, London, Paul Friel, Coatbridge, Pauline Friel, Coatbridge, Robin Friel, Cambuslang, Tony Friel, Glasgow, Tony Friel, Rutherglen, Glasgow, Vincent Friel, Glasgow, William Friel, Croy, Lanarkshire, Matthew Frizzel, Crouch End, London, Gary Fullarton, Newmains, Wishaw, Robert Fullarton, Newmains, Wishaw, Rob Fuller, Swindon, Tom Fuller, Swindon, Gary Fullerton, Wishaw, Ross Fullerton, Courthill, Aaron Fulton, Falkirk, Carol Fulton, Falkirk, Caroline Fulton, Fernhill, Cathrine Fulton, Girvan, Helen Fulton, Fernhill, Lanarkshire, Jim Fulton, Falkirk, Rab Fulton, Fernhill, Lanarkshire, Dan Fury, Saltcoats, Matthew Fyfe, Kincorth, Aberdeen.

Cora Gaffey, Deaglan Gaffey, Keith Gaffey, Liam Gaffey, Mark Gaffey, Tiarna Gaffey, Kevin Gaffney, Glasgow. Mags Gaffney, Uddingston, Martin Gaffney, Port Glasgow, Sandra Gage, Douglas, Isle of Man, Ian Gair, Largs, Paddy Galagher, Croy, Dom Galasso, Glasgow, Alex Galbraith, Kirkintilloch, Gordon Galbraith, Paisley, Kieran Galbraith, Coatbridge, Michael, J. Galbraith, Stenhousemuir, Michael John Galbraith, Larbert, Steff Gall, Glenrothes, Andy Gallacher, Newton Mearns, Ann Gallacher, Glasgow, Anne Gallacher, Glasgow, Annie Gallacher, Clydebank, Brian Gallacher, Drumchapel, Glasgow, Brian Gallacher, Glasgow, Charles Gallacher, Drumchapel, Colin Gallacher, Wishaw, Craig Gallacher, Clydebank, Craig Gallacher, Wishaw, Danny G. Gallacher, Dennistoun, Glasgow, Darren Gallacher, Pitlochry, Declan Gallacher, Dunblane, Declin Gallacher, Glasgow, Derek Gallacher, Paisley, Elaine Gallacher, Corby, Euan Gallacher, Greenock, Hugh Gallacher, Wishaw, Ian Gallacher, Gourock, James Gallacher, Dumbarton, Jason Gallacher, Wishaw, John

Gallacher, Airdrie, John Gallacher, Clydebank, John Gallacher, Glasgow, John Gallacher, Wishaw, Jordan Gallacher, Balornock, Glasgow, Jordan Gallacher, Glasgow, Karen Gallacher, Kevin Gallacher, Bathgate, Kevin Gallacher, Bishopbriggs, Kevin Gallacher, Glasgow, Kevin Gallacher, Glasgow, Kevin Gallacher, Wishaw, Kieran Gallacher, Clydebank, Laura Gallacher, Paisley, Lauren Gallacher, Glasgow, Lyall Gallacher, Greenock, Mark Gallacher, Airdrie, Nathan Gallacher, Clydebank, Paul Gallacher, Glasgow, Paul Gallacher, Plains, Ross Gallacher, Glasgow, Scott Gallacher, Gourock, Sean Gallacher, Glasgow, Shaun Gallacher, Alloa, Shaun Gallacher, Glasgow, Sophie Gallacher, Stuart Gallacher, Greenock, Susan Gallacher, Paisley, Tony Gallacher, Jersey, William Gallacher, Falkirk, Willie Gallacher, Bosnia, Winnie Gallacher, Seville, Adrian Gallagher, Merrylee, Glasgow, Alan Gallagher, Bishopbriggs, Angela Gallagher, Renfrew, Annemarie Gallagher, Glasgow, Annie Gallagher, Eire, Anthony Gallagher, Newton Mearns, Brian Gallagher, Irvine, Brian Gallagher, Kuwait, Bryan Gallagher, Doune, Caitlin Gallagher, Moodiesburn, Carol Gallagher, Oxgangs, Charlie Gallagher, Letterkenny, Co. Donegal, Ireland, Christie Gallagher, Erskine, Ciaran Gallagher, Ardrossan, Claire Gallagher, Coatbridge, Colin Gallagher, Airdrie, Colin Gallagher, Athy Co Kildare, Colin A. Gallagher, County Kildare, Ireland, Connie Gallagher, Mosspark, Danny Gallagher, Muirhead, Darby Gallagher, Paisley, Darryl Gallagher, Airdrie, David Gallagher, Balornock, David Gallagher, Balornock, David Gallagher, Dundee, Frank Gallagher, Airdrie, Gamon Gallagher, Falkirk, Gerry Gallagher, Barlanark, Jade Gallagher, Ardrossan, Jayde Gallagher, Dumfries, Jim Gallagher, Merrylee, Joe Gallagher, Castlemilk, John Gallagher, Baillieston, John Gallagher, Bromley, Kent, John Gallagher, Glasgow, John Gallagher, Norside, Joseph Gallagher, Ashton Under Lyne, Kevin Gallagher, Airdrie, Kevin Gallagher, Glasgow, Kevin Gallagher, Merrylee, Kevin Gallagher, Muirhead, Kieran Gallagher, West End of Glasgow, Laureen Gallagher, Moodiesburn, Lauren Gallagher, Johnstone, Linda Gallagher, Ardrossan, Maggie Gallagher, Wishaw, Margaret, Martin and Megan Gallagher, Chapelhall, Marie Gallagher, Edinburgh, Marie Gallagher, Glasgow, Marie Gallagher, Mossblown, Mark Gallagher, Ardrossan, Mark Gallagher, East Kilbride, Mark Gallagher, Glasgow, Martin Gallagher, Govanhill, Glasgow, Mary Gallagher, Merrylee, Michael Gallagher, Barrowfield, Michael Gallagher, East Kilbride, Michael Gallagher, Glasgow, Neil Gallagher, Glasgow, Owen Gallagher, Glasgow, Pat Gallagher, Torquay, Paul Gallagher, Crosshill, Glasgow, Paul Gallagher, Glasgow, Paul Gallagher, Milton, Paul Gallagher, Newton Mearns, Peter Gallagher, Kuwait, Pig Gallagher, Falkirk, Ross Gallagher, Glasgow, Scooby Gallagher, Barrowfield, Scotty Boy Gallagher, Spittal, Sean Gallagher, Glasgow, Shaun Gallagher, Torquay, Siobhan Gallagher, Moodiesburn, Stephen Gallagher, Burnside, Stephen Gallagher, Hamilton, Stephen Patrick Gallagher, Newton Mearns, Steve Gallagher, Aberdeen, Teresa Gallagher, Castlemilk, Thomas Gallagher, Glasgow, Tommy Gallagher, Glasgow, Tony Gallagher, Dumfries, Tony Gallagher, Newton Mearns, William Gallagher, Chapelhall, Airdrie, Zoe Gallagher, Glasgow, Gallagher, Coatbridge, Eoghan Gallagher-Ahmad, Dungannon, Kerry Gallahan, Glasgow, Amanda Gallgher, Johnstone, Alan Galloway, Coleford, Hilda Galloway, Coleford, Ian Galloway, Troon, Jamie Galloway, Pat Galloway, Glasgow, Paul Galloway, Bangor, Paul Galloway, Bangor, Co.Down, Rhys Galloway, Troon, Ross Galloway, Coleford, Ross Galloway, Motherwell, George Galvey, Glasgow, KFC Gang, Belfast, Ireland, Yan Gangorgold, Greenock, Chris Gannon, Uddingston, David Gannon, Grangemouth, Gerald Gara, Melbourne, Australia, Kevin Gara, Mosspark, Michael Gara, Melbourne, Australia, Brian Garden, Inverness, David Garden, Cardonald, Glasgow, David Garden, Inverness, Freddie Garden, Inverness, Jessie Garden, Inverness, Keith Garden, Loanhead, Steven Garden, Girvan, Paul Gardiner, Greenock, Stephen Gardiner, Greenock, Tracey Gardiner, Livingston, Yvonne Gardiner, Livingston, Brian Gardner, Glasgow, Chris Gardner, Glasgow, Christopher Gardner, Glasgow, Elizabeth Gardner, Gallowgate, George Gardner, Denny, Gerry Gardner, London, Kirsty Marie Gardner, Glasgow, Patrick Gardner, Glasgow, Peter Gardner, Glasgow, Kevin Garety, Damien Garland, Kim Garland, Glasgow,

189

Alex Garner, Co. Kildare, Ireland, Clare Garner, Co. Kildare, Ireland, Darren Garner, Livingston, George Garner, Denny, George Garner, Greenock, Paul Garner, Denny, Jamsie Garrigan, Glenrothes, Archie Garrity, Irvine, Kevin Garrity, Omagh, Gerry Gatens, Corby, Gerry Gatens, Corby, Northants, Rory Gatens, Corby, Stevie Gather, Glasgow, David Gattens, Glasgow, Andy Gaughan, Hamilton, Carol Gaughan, Buckhaven, John Gaughan, Kingspark, Glasgow, Tracey Gaughan, Kirkintilloch, George Gauldie, Arbroath, Angus, Donnay Gault, Easterhouse, Glasgow, Michael Gault, Easterhouse, Glasgow, Bill Gavin, Falkirk, Brian Gavin, Armadale, Iain Gavin, Falkirk, Julie Gavin, Northfield, Edinburgh, Malcolm Gavin, Armadale, West Lothian, Michael Gavin, Greenock, Thomas Gavin, Maryhill, Andy Gay, Queenslie, Danny Gaynor, Glasgow, Katie Gedath, Glasgow, Jamie Geddes, Cardenden, Fife, Janet Geddes, London, Jim Geddes, Barrhead, Joanne Geddes, Helensburgh, Sarah Geddes, Helensburgh, Dougie Gellan, Pollokshields, Glasgow, Dave Gemell, Edinburgh, Andy Gemmell, Port Glasgow, Chris Gemmell, Cambuslang, David Gemmell, Plains, Airdrie, Martin Gemmell, Ardrossan, Tony Geoghegan, Baillieston, Glasgow, Sarah Georgia, Peterhead, Craig Geraghty, Methven, Perth, Paul Gerard, Coventry, Brian Gerrard, Ayr, David Gerrard, Ayr, Laura Gerrard, Mossblown Ayr, Robert Gerrard, Glasgow, Anne Getty, Kirkintilloch, Aldo Giamblanco, Leith, Edinburgh, Giovanni Giamblanco, Leith, Edinburgh, Alessio Giannandrea, Stirling, Sandy Giannandrea, Stirling, Peter Giannottie, Kings Park, Glasgow, Joe Gibb, Castlemilk, Glasgow, Mark Gibb, Glasgow, Stephan Gibb, Penicuik, Ross Gibbon, Hawick, Michael Gibbons, Milton, Glasgow, Harry Giblin, Hamilton, Mark Giblin, Hamilton, Patrick Giblin, Barrhead, Glasgow, Arlene Gibson, Foxbar, Ashleigh Gibson, Gorebridge, Bobby Gibson, Banbury, Oxfordshire, Damian Gibson, Mount Vernon, Glasgow, George Gibson, Foxbar, Paisley, Jacqueline Gibson, Patna, Ayrshire, James Gibson, Maryhill, Glasgow, James Gibson, Twechar, Jaqueline Gibson, Patna, Ayrshire, Liam Gibson, Clydebank, Mark Gibson, Paisley, Ross Gibson, Bearsden, Ryan Gibson, Gorebridge, Taylor Gibson, Maryhill, Glasgow, Tony Gibson, London, Scott Giggal, Falkirk, Susana Gil Serna, Madrid, Hugh Gilbert, Langside, Glasgow, Davy Gilday, Glasgow, Declan Gilday, Glasgow, Flyer Gilday, Barrhead, Glasgow, Patrick Gilday, Renfrew, David Gildea, Paisley, Saoirse Gildea, Thornliebank, Glasgow, Steve Giles, Rochester, Kent, Stevie Gilespie, Croy, Chic Gill, Cowdenbeath, Conor Gill, Cowdenbeath, Kieran Gill, Cowdenbeath, Sean Gill, Glasgow, Steven Gill, Glasgow, Tony Gill, Glasgow, Arlene Gillan, Spain, Charles Gillan, Glasgow, David Gillan, Glasgow, John Gillan, Barrhead Glasgow, Lynn and Stan Gillan, Irvine, Mark Gillan, Cambuslang, Mark Gillan, Glasgow, Mary Gillan, The Gillans, Kilwinning, Robert Gillchrist, Airdrie, Ann Gillen, Anne Gillen, Newton Mearns, John Gillen, Glasgow, Kevin Gillen, Barrhead, Liam Gillen, Newton Mearns, Mark Gillen, Newton Mearns, Nicole Gillen, Newton Mearns, Patrick Gillen, Blantyre, Ryan Gillen, Newton Mearns, Chris Gillespe, Glasgow, Arthur J. Gillespie, Glasgow, Brian Gillespie, East Kilbride, Brian Gillespie, East Kilbride, David Gillespie, Switzerland, David Gillespie, Zurich, Gerry Gillespie, Johnstone, Graeme Gillespie, Majorca, Graeme Gillespie, Majorca, Janine Gillespie, Hull (originally Aberdeen), Jim Gillespie, Aldershot, John Gillespie, North Wales, Melissa Gillespie, Glasgow, Paul Gillespie, Toryglen, Glasgow, Paul Gillespie, Toryglen, Ross Gillespie, East Kilbride, Stephen Gillespie, Luton, Bedfordshire, Brendan Gillian, Glasgow, Brian Gillian, Govanhill, Glasgow, Brooke Gillian, Govanhill, Glasgow, Jake Gillian, Basford, Notts, Jennifer Gillian, Clydebank, Jim Gillian, Govanhill, Mark Gillian, Govanhill, Rorie Gillian, Wishaw, Ali Gillies, Inverness, Jim Gillies, Brian Gilliespe, Glasgow, Carolann Gilligan, Linwood, Chris Gilligan, Larkhall, John Gilligan, Linwood, Lindsay Gilligan, Linwood, Mena Gilligan, Linwood, Daniel Gilliland, Glasgow, Jim Gillis, Glasgow, Stuart Gillis, Alloa, Martin Gilliss, Alloa, Andy Gillon, Inverness, Gail Gillon, Inverness, Kevin Gillon, Wishaw, Mick Gillon, Wishaw, Charlotte Gillooly, Airdrie, James Gillooly, Airdrie, James Gillooly, Airdrie, Marjory Gillooly, Airdrie, Mark Gillooly, Airdrie, Steven Gilluley, Hamilton, Daniel Gilmartin, Gourock, Eddie Gilmartin, Parkhead, Edward Gilmartin, Parkhead, Hugh

Gilmartin, Largs, Davie Gilmore, Hamilton, John Gilmore, Maidstone, Kent, John Dillon Gilmore, Kilwinning, Andrew Gilmour, Coatbridge, Anthony Gilmour, Glasgow, Davie Gilmour, Coatbridge, Jim Gilmour, Ullapool, Marion Gilmour, Blantyre, Martin Gilmour, Broxburn, Sharon Gilmour, Castlemilk, Glasgow, William Gilmour, Motherwell, Willie Gilmour, Erskine, Craig Gilroy, Blackpool, Gaynor Gilroy, Glasgow, Laura Ann Gilroy, Blackpool, Natasha Gilroy, Glasgow, Scott Gilroy, Blackpool, Heather Gilruth, Mount Vernon, Karen Gilruth, Rosyth, Fife, Ryan Girvan, Crookston, Glasgow, Drew Glacken, Cleland, Eileen Glancy, Easterhouse, James Glancy, Bearsden, James Glancy, Bearsden, John Glancy, Dumfries, Marie Glancy, Bearsden, Mark Glancy, Bearsden, Mark Glancy, Bearsden, Michael Glancy, Bearsden, Rosaleen Glancy, Kelvindale, Stewart Glancy, Hamilton, Theresa Glancy, Linthouse, Chris Glasgow, Haddington, Kenny Glasgow, Haddington, Paul Glasgow, Haddington, Sharon Glasgow, Cumbernauld, Danny Glass, Luton, Tam Glass, Alloa, Clackmannanshire, Brian Glen, Bathgate, Christopher Glen, Bathgate, Gary Glen, Grangemouth, Gerard Glen, Bathgate, James Glen, Mossend, James Glen, Vernon, BC, Canada, William Glen, Holytown, Wullie Glen, Craigend, David Glenn, Barrhead, John Glenn, Glasgow, John Glenn, Glasgow, Shirley Glenn, York, Chalrotte Glennie, Milton Keynes, David Glennie, Kendal, Lezli-An Glennie, Milton Keynes, Rachel Glennie, Milton Keynes, Stewart Glennie, Milton Keynes, Louise Glover, Bellshill, Scott Glover, Drumchapel, Glagsow, Jim Glovern, Coatbridge, Ellen Glynn, Tranent, East Lothian, Patrick 'Sonny' Glynn, Tanent, East Lothian, Sean Glynner, Texas - Usa, Martin Godfrey, Stenhousemuir, Stephen Godley, Moodiesburn, Glasgow, Leanne Godsell, Livingston, Liam Godsell, Livingston, Win Godsell, Livingston, Graham Godsman, Inverness, Sadie Goff, Knightswood, Kevin Gogarty, Bellshill, Willie Goggans, Irvine, Andy Goldie, The Dale, Christopher Goldie, Cambuslang, Conor Goldie, Blackburn, West-Lothian, Daniel Goldie, Easterhouse, Dennis Goldie, Camelon, John Goldie, Clydebank, David Goldie Jnr, Cambuslang, David Goldie Snr, Cambuslang, Erin Goldthorp, Elderslie, Lauren Goldthorp, Elderslie, Gerard Gonley, Falkirk, J Goodhall, Prestonpans, Jamie Goodliffe, Boston, Usa, George Goodwillie, Tullibody, Amanda Goodwin, Barrhead, Andrew Goodwin, Barrhead, Darren Goodwin, Barrhead, Holly Goodwin, Kilmarnock, Laura Goodwin, Viewpark, Paula Goodwin, Glasgow, Taylor Goodwood, Edinburgh, Foxy Goodyear, Caroline Goold, Cumbernauld, Allan Gordon, Rutherglen, Allan Gordon, Rutherglen, Ann-Marie Gordon, Johnstone, Brid Gordon, Baltinglass, Co. Wicklow, Craig Gordon, Rutherglen, David Gordon, Haddington, Davy Gordon, Bonhill, Eggy Gordon, Athlone, Co. Westmeath, Gary Gordon, Leeds, George Gordon, Govanhill, Glasgow, Grant Gordon, Glasgow, Jack Gordon, Paisley, Jim Gordon, Springburn, Joe Gordon, Johnstone, John Gordon, Glasgow, Laura Gordon, Johnstone, Margaret Gordon, Inverness, Mel Gordon, Athlone, Co. Westmeath, Micky Gordon, Ballymena, Philip Gordon, Baltinglass, Co. Wicklow, Philip Gordon, Johnstone, Pierce Gordon, Kilkenny, Co Kilkenny, Ross Gordon, Carmyle, Samantha Gordon, Paisley, Samuel Gordon, Paisley, Samuel Gordon, Paisley, Sandie Gordon, Leeds, Sean Gordon, Cricklewood, London, Wullie Gordon, Bellshill, Wullie Gordon, Bellshill, Gerard Gormally, Glasgow, Clark and Janet Gorman, Stevenston, James Gorman, Edinburgh, Kieran Zap Gorman, Livi, Maureen Gorman, Glasgow, Sharon Gorman, Ardrossan, Finny Gormley, Wishaw, Maggie Goss, Wishaw, Andy Goudie, Robbie Goudie, Wully Goudie, Charlie Gourley, Barnton, Siobhan Gourock, Derek Govan, Drumchapel, Scott Govan, Drumchapel, Danielle Gow, Glasgow, Tracey Gow, Grangemouth, Claire Gowen, Northampton, The Gows, Thurso, Gareth Gracie, Bearsden, Andy Gracy, Alan Grady, Isle of Man, Eddie Grady, Newton Mearns, Glasgow, Martin Grady, Johnstone, Andrew Graham, Dunfermline, Andrew Graham, Lockerbie, Anne Graham, Paisley, Anthony Graham, Blantyre, Audrey Graham, Grangemouth, Bobby Graham, Tullibody, Brian Graham, Gorbals, Glasgow, Catherine-Ann Graham, Blackwood, Cumbernauld, Christie Graham, Paisley, Christine Graham, Carluke, Christopher Graham, Gorbals, Glasgow, Colin Graham, Paisley, David Graham, Kilbirnie, Donna Graham,

Glasgow, Donna Graham, Wellhouse, Glasgow, Edward Graham, Saltcoats, Frankie Graham, Garrowhill, Glasgow, Gordon Graham, Blackwood, Cumbernauld, Iain Graham, Lockerbie, James Graham, Lockerbie, Jamie Lee Graham, Wellhouse, Glasgow, Jordan Graham, Glasgow, Jordan Graham, Josey Graham, Gorbals, Glasgow, Kathleen Graham, Blantyre, Liam Graham, Parkhead, Glasgow, Michael Graham, Airdrie, Natasha Graham, Glasgow, Paul Graham, Brisbane, Australia, Paula Graham, Airdrie, Pauline Graham, Glasgow, Peter Graham, Glenrothes, Peter Graham, Lerwick, Ross Graham, Paisley, Roy Graham, Lockerbie, Shuggie Graham, Australia, Stephen Graham, Barrhead, Stephen Graham, Gorbals, Glasgow, Steven Graham, Tam Graham, Aberdeen, Tam Graham, Kirkintilloch, Victoria Graham, Lockerbie, Wendy Graham, Debenhams, Glasgow, Stewart Grain, Hawick, Grant Granger, Yoker, Ryan Granger, Fuengirola, Adam Grant, Maryhill, Angus Grant, Gourock, Bill Grant, 'D' Shift, St Fergus, Bobby Grant, Holytown, Brian Grant, Bellshill, Brian Grant, London, Claire Grant, Glasgow, Colette Grant, Holytown, Danny Grant, Eastfield, Derek Grant, LInlithgow, Derek Grant, Linlithgow, George Grant, Rafford, Moray, Jackie Grant, Nairn, James Grant, Hamilton, Joe Grant, Airdrie, Joseph Grant, Chapelhall, Airdrie, Kyle Grant, Airdrie, Larsson Grant, Jersey, Liam Grant, Holytown, Lindsay Grant, Rafford, Moray, Lorraine Grant, Chapelhall, Lorraine Grant, Chapelhall, Maggie Grant, Jersey, Mairi Grant, Wishaw, Mark Grant, Hamilton, Mark Grant, Hamilton, Mel Grant, Alness, Nettie Grant, Glasgow, Nichola Grant, Coatbridge, Nickie Grant, Coatbridge, Nigel Grant, Inverness, Paul Grant, Coatbridge, Rachel Grant, Glasgow, Richard Grant, Nairn, Ross Grant, Blantyre, Ross Grant, Stoneyburn, Sharon Grant, Holytown, Sharron Grant, Airdrie, Theresa Grant, C-Hill, Amanda Grassie, Royston Glasgow, Derek Grassie, Royston, Glasgow, Chloe Grattan, Perth, Australia, Jamie Grattan, Perth, Australia, Margaret Grattan, Perth, Australia, Margaret Grattan, Pollok, Glasgow, Samantha Grattan, Pollok, Glasgow, Chelsea Gray, Bridgetown, Colin Gray, Bellshill, Craig Gray, Linlithgow, Craig Gray, Linlithgow, Danny Gray, Alloa, David Gray, Clarkston, Glasgow, Dom Gray, Shotts, Eddie Gray, Alloa, Frank Gray, Bridgetown, Franky Gray, Bridgeton, G. Gray, Bridgetown, Gary Gray, Glasgow, Jim Gray, Hamilton, Joe Gray, Kilsyth, John Gray, Houston, Jordon Gray, Kilsyth, M Gray, Easterhouse, Paul Gray, Cathcart, Glasgow, Paul Gray, Glasgow, Stephen Gray, Patrick, Terry Gray, Lumphinnans, Fife, Tom Gray, Deltona, Florida, USA, Wez Gray, Johnstone, Wully Gray, Blackburn, West Lothian, Paul Greechan, Chryston, Glasgow, Joseph Greed, Glasgow, Angela Green, Craigend, Charlotte Green, Greenock, Danny Green, Paisley, David Green, Stevenston, Dominic Green, Motherwell, Gary Green, Santa Ponsa, Majorca, Jack Green, Coatbridge, Jake Green, Glasgow, James Green, Glasgow, James Green, Glasgow East End, James Green, Greenock, John Green, Kilsyth, John Green, Bridgeton, Kelly Green, Galashiels, Kenny Green, Port Glasgow, Laura Green, Stenhousemuir, Liam Green, Craigend, Mark Green, Glasgow, Matty Green, Galashiels, Maureen Green, Galashiels, Michael Green, Balmore, Nicky Green, Craigend, Nicola Green, Galashiels, Robert Green, Craigend, Stephan Green, Glasgow, Steven Green, Glasgow, Bobby Greenan, Hamilton, Gemma Greenan, Blantyre, Lauren Greenan, Hamilton, Mark Greenan, Hamilton, Peter Greenan, Hamilton, Rab Greenan, Scotstoun, Sean Mark Greenan, Hamilton, Vicky Greenan, Hamilton, Peter Greenan (Snr), Hamilton, Joe D. Greenfield, Glasgow, Allan Greenlees, Houston, Jim Greenlees, Dunfermline, Steven "The Bhoy" Junior Greens, Penicuik, Steven "The Bhoy" Senior Greens, Penicuik, Iain Greenshields, Yemen, Alec Greenwell, Cambuslang, Glasgow, Sean Greenwood, Nottingham, Seanie Greenwood, Nottingham, Alex Greer, Peterborough, Cara Greer, Cumbernauld, Martin Greer, Cumbernauld, Paul Greer, Glasgow, David Gregg, Western Australia, Tommy Grehan, Dennistoun, Glasgow, Derek Greig, Scotstoun, Glasgow, Eammon Greig, Belfast, Jim Greig, Bishopsgate, Glasgow, J. Grey, Bellshill, Lanarkshire, Mark Grey, London, Martin Grey, Motherwell, Erin Gribben, Airdrie, Kathleen Gribben, Corby, Northamptonshire, Matthew Gribben, Airdrie, Stephen Gribben, Corby, Charles Grier, Saltcoats, Colin Grier, Saltcoats, Jim Grier, Australia,

Johnny Grier, Saltcoats, Pat Griffen, Bannockburn, Stirling, Derek Griffin, Dagenham, Essex, Francis Griffin, Croy, Lanarkshire, James Griffin, Hamilton, Jim Griffin, Hastings, Sussex, Kieran Griffin, Fanad, Donegal, Ireland, Michael Griffin, Fanad, Donegal, Ireland, Raymond Griffin, Belfast, Sheila Griffin, Fanad, Donegal, Ireland, Geraldine Griffiths, Glasgow, Kirsty Griffiths, Coatbridge, Shirley Grimshaw, Dagenham, Essex, Chris Gritton, Rome, Fran Grogan, Kirkshaws, Coatbridge, Marie Grogan, Falkirk. Megan Grogan, Coatbridge, Stephen Grogan, Coatbridge, Andy Gronneberg, Milton Keynes, Stuart Gross, Austrialia, Jason Groves, Glasgow, Liam Grubb, Fife, Gary Guckel, Glasgow, Tracey Guest, Grangemouth, Daniel Gunn, Rotherham, S. Yorkshire, Frank Gunn, Newmains, James Gunn, Easterhouse, Karen Gunn, Rotherham, Tanya Gunn, Rotherham, Gary Gutherie, Glasgow, Daniel Guthrie, Kings Park, Glasgow, Garry Guthrie, Kings Park, Glasgow, Geraldine Guthrie, Balornock, Gerry Guthrie, Edinburgh, Gerry Guthrie, Kings Park, Glasgow, James Guthrie, Airdrie, John Guthrie, Shawlands, Glasgow, Lauren Guthrie, Ballornock, Liam Guthrie, Cadder, Ryan Guthrie, Kings Park, Glasgow, Tom Guthrie, Irvine, Ayrshire, Andrew Guy, Airdrie, Juergen Gwozdz, Berlin.

Cassie H, Glasgow. Vincent H. McCann, East Kilbride, Gary Hackett, East Kilbride, Carolanne Haffie, Clydebank, Chris Hagan, Kirkintilloch, Paul Hagen, Bonnybridge, Richard Hagen, Coatbridge, Brian Hagerty, Falkirk, John Paul Hagerty, Coatbridge, Granda James Haggarty, Penilee, John Haggarty, Penilee, Lee Haggarty, Penilee, Ryan Haggarty, Penilee, Caitlin Haggerty, Johnstone, Cheryl Haggerty, Johnstone, Eddie Haggerty, Dumbarton, Erin Haggerty, Johnstone, Geo Haggerty, Invergordon, Grahame Haggerty, Invergordon, Jack Haggerty, Glasgow, James Haggerty, Invergordon, J.D. Haggerty, Dumbarton, John Haggerty, Dumbarton, Kevin Haggerty, Penilee, Owen Haggerty, Johnstone, Tom Hagney, Morecambe, Shaun Hailstones, Newton Mearns, Eric Hainay, Girvan, John Haines, Coventry, Ben Hainey, Newarthill, Brian Hainey, Edinburgh, Paul Haintree, London, Daive Haircut, Glasgow, Davie Haircut, Glasgow, Margaret Halbert, Larkhall, Sandra And James Halbert, Glasgow, Wullie Halbert, Larkhall, Dave Halcrow, Kettering, Duncan Haldane, Glasgow, Paul, Bryan, Paul and Michael Haldane, Glasgow, Duncan Haldane Snr, Glasgow, Lee Haldene, Glasgow, Danny Hale, Belfast, Matthew James Haley, Glasgow, Stephen Haley, Newmains, Ally Halford, Motherwell, Gary Halford, Motherwell, Mari-Ann Halford, Motherwell, Wullie Halford, Motherwell, Alistair Hall, Scotland, Andy Hall, Kent, Chris Hall, Alloa, Cyril Hall, Sittingbourne, Kent, James Hall, Mallorca, Spain, June Hall, Garthamlock, Laura Hall, Seville, Megan Cara Hall, Glasgow, Michael Hall, Majorca, Spain, Moira Hall, Edinburgh, Pat Hall, Viewpark, Rosemary Hall, Sittingbourne, Kent, Ryan Hall, Portugal, Stuart Hall, Sittingbourne, Kent, Tam Hall, Overtown, Duncan Halldean, Glasgow, Davie Halley, Clydebank, Derek Halley, Glenrothes, Fife, Scotland, Raymond Halley, Fife, Joanne Halliday, Bishopbriggs, Kevin Hallihan, Cork, Margaret Anne Hallon, Motherwell, Aaron Hamill, Cowie, Alan Hamill, Thornliebank, Billy Hamill, Corby, Carol Hamill, Belfast, Colleen Hamill, Stirling, Des Hamill, Coatbridge, Francis Hamill, Glasgow, James Hamill, Belfast, Joseph Hamill, East Kilbride, Lee Hamill, Stirling, Mark Hamill, Airdrie, Mark Hamill, Glasgow, Michael Hamill, Stewarton, P. J. Hamill, Corby, Patrick Hamill, Belfast, Paul Hamill, Coatbridge, Steven Hamill, Stirling, Taylor-Rose Hamill, Cowie, James Hamill Jnr, Glasgow, James Hamill Jnr, Glasgow, James Hamill Snr, Glasgow, Betty Hamilton, Billy Hamilton, Edinburgh, Brenda Hamilton, Glasgow, Chic Hamilton, Airdrie, Chris Hamilton, Kilmarnock, Claire Hamilton, Rosneath, Conner Hamilton, Glasgow, Dionne Hamilton, Garry Hamilton, Irvine, Gary Hamilton, Wishaw, Gerard Michael Hamilton, Honor Hamilton, Glasgow, James Hamilton, Summerston, Jim Hamilton, Barrhead, Jim Hamilton, Paisley, John Hamilton, Airdrie, John Hamilton, Larkhall, Kevin Hamilton, Berwick-upon-Tweed, Kyle Hamilton, Airdrie, M. Hamilton, Stirling, Marcus Hamilton, New York, Morag Hamilton, London, Wullie Hamilton, Edinburgh, Myles Hamilton, Falkirk, Neil Hamilton, Edinburgh, Nikki Hamilton, Hillpark,

Glasgow, Owen Hamilton, Australia, Owen Hamilton, Bellshill, Paul Hamilton, Glasgow, Roy Hamilton, St Andrews, S. Hamilton, Falkirk, Wullie Hamilton, Denny, Cheryl Hamlin, Jersey, Carl Hammell, Belfast, James Hammell, Belfast, Patrick Hammell, Belfast, Bernie Hamnet, Stevenston, Sean Hamnet, Stevenston, Frank Hampson, Rutherglen, Raymond Hampson, Rutherglen, Ryan Hand, Saltcoats, Chucks Haney, Stirling, Neil Haney, Coatbridge, Ryan Haney, Bellshill, Stephen Haney, Mossend, Willie Hanguy, Grangemouth, Jim Hanley, Blantyre, Martin Hanley, London, Tam Hanlin, Dundonald, Anna Hanlon, Glasgow, Chas Hanlon, Glasgow, Denise Hanlon, Alloa, Joe Hanlon, Glasgow, John Hanlon, Glasgow, Michael Hanlon, Edinburgh, Paul Hanlon, Falkirk, Paul Hanly, Bellshill, Jade Hanna, Alexandria, Laura Hanna, Alexandria, Laura Hanna, Alexandria, Lynsey Hanna, Alexandria, Claire Hannah, Glasgow, George Hannah, Pollok, John Hannah, Bellshill, John Hannah, Irvine, K. Hannah, Cowdenbeath, Linda Hannah, Glasgow, Ray Hannah, Addiewell, West Lothian, Robert Hannah, Glasgow, Tony Hannah, Shetland, Wullie Hannah, Glasgow, Brian Hannan, Bathgate, Dave Hannan, London, Kieran Hannaway, Coatbridge, Kay Hannot, Stevenston, Tam Hannson, Denny, Michael Hanrahan, Glasgow, Mick Hanrahan, Glasgow, Amanda Hanson, Kilwinning, Stephen Hanway, Bargeddie, Lindsay Hap, Glasgow, Garry Haq, London, Jimmy Haran, Crookston, Glynis Harcus, Shetland, Cheryl Hardie, Grangemouth, George Hardie, Glasgow, Glenn Hardie, Grangemouth, Jamie Hardie, Livingston, John Hardie, Glasgow, John David Hardie, Glasgow, Martin Hardie, Glasgow, Maureen Hardie, Glasgow, Paul Hardie, Greenock, Shaun Hardie, Grangemouth, Stephen Hardie, Garngad, Yvonne Hardie, Grangemouth, Alison Hardy, Clydebank, Freddy Hargreaves, Westburn, Charles Harkin, New York, Frances Harkin, Saltcoats, Jack Harkin, New York, Kevin Harkin, Glasgow, Kevin Harkin, New York, Liz Harkin, New York, Mary Harkin, New York, Ryan Harkin, New York, Sophie Harkin, Clydebank, Tracy Harkin, New York, Billy Harkins, Emlea, Kent, Donna Harkins, Bridge Of Weir, Gary Harkins, Bridge Of Weir, James Harkins, Partick, James Harkins, Springburn, John Harkins, Kent, Kevin Harkins, Johnstone, Lizzy Harkins, Kent, Marie Harkins, Rutherglen, Martin Harkins, Rothesay, Mary Harkins, Broxburn, Matt Harkins, Bridge Of Weir, Michael Harkins, Stockport, Mark Harkins, Leith, Saskia Harkins, Kent, Kris Harley, Fife, Paul Harley, Coatbridge, Lawrie Harmon, Pollok, Glasgow, James Harnett, Stevenston, James Harnett Jnr, Stevenston, Michael Harnett, Stevenston, Colin Harper, Airdrie, David Harper, Bathgate, David and Gail Harper, Tillicoultry, James Harper, Glasgow, Laura Jane Harper, Coatbridge, Michael Harper, Steven Harper, Rosyth, Rhiannon Harrigan Popowicz, Middlesex, Neil Harrington, Greenock, Ruth Harrington, Greenock, Bryan Harris, Roslin, Midlothian, Bryan Harris, Roslin, Christopher Harris, Glasgow, George Harris, Barrhead, John Harris, Dundee, John Harris, Glasgow, Laura Harris, Stockton-on-Tees, Lily Harris, Cheltenham, Lucy Harris, Cheltenham, Michael Harris, Bonnybridge, Olivia Harris, Stockton-on-Tees, Raymond Harris, Glasgow, Richard Harris, Roslin, Tom Harris, London, Tony Harris, Prestonpans, Willie Harris, Edinburgh, Christopher Harrison, Bourtreehill, Jim Harrison, Belfast, Kevin Harrison, Saltcoats, Mark Harrison, Greenock, Caitlyn Hart, Castlemilk, Helen, Martin, Karen, Martin, Sean +Paddy Hart, Bonnybridge, Jacci Hart, Castlemilk, James Hart, Kilmarnock, Jim Hart, Linwood, Norman Hart, Glasgow, Peter Hart, Motherwell, Ray Hart, Bangalore, India, Robert Hart, Troon, Rose Hart, Glasgow, Scott Hart, East Kilbride, Thomas Hart, Exmouth, Yvonne Hart, Barrhead, Austin Harte, Madrid, Stevie Harte, Galway, Joe Hartie, Coatbridge, Jack Hartley, Leeds, David Harty, Glasgow, Angela Harvey, Greenock, Christopher Harvey, Greenock, Derek Harvey, Chard, Elaine Harvey, Rutherglen, Gerald Harvey, Rutherglen, James Harvey, Broxburn, James Paul Harvey, Newhaven, Jim Harvey, Blackpool, John Harvey, Greenock, Jordan Harvey, Chard, Keith Harvey, Hamilton, Margaret Harvey, Greenock, Michael Harvey, Chard, Pat Harvey, Clydebank, Rab Harvey, Glasgow, Robert Harvey, Rutherglen, Scott Harvey, Millport, Sharon Harvey, Edinburgh, Stephen Harvey, Isle of Wight, Steven Harvey, Beverley, Matthew Harvie, Mount Florida, Richard Harvie, Hamilton, Tony Harvie,

Hamilton, Chloe Hassan, Johnstone, Declan Hassan, Johnstone, Paul Hastie, St Fergus, Ross Hastie, Arbroath, Stephen Hastie, Inverness, Steven Hastie, Greenock, Lee Haston, Dumfries, Mark Hattie, Kirkintilloch, Martin Hattie, Kirkintilloch, Ann-Marie Hatton, Glasgow, Denise Hatton, Glasgow, Paul Hatzeman, McVicar, Printers, Dessie Haughian, Lurgan, Emmet Haughian, Lurgan, Emmet Haughian, Lurgan, Kieran Haughian, Airdrie, Liam Patrick Haughian, Airdrie, Niall Haughian, Lurgan, Nicole Haughian, Airdrie, Alison Haughin, Coatbridge, Conor Havelin, Anderston, Glasgow, Wullie Havelin, Anderston, Glasgow, Justine Hawes, Norwich, The Hawk, Patrick, Glasgow, Charley Kennedy Hawkes, Witham, Essex, James Hawkins, London, Tam Hawthorn, East Kilbride, Anton Hawthorne, Viewpark, Geraldine Hawthorne, Viewpark, Kieran Hawthorne, Viewpark, Mark Hawthorne, Viewpark, Adele Allison Hay, Hunterhill, Paisley, Alex Hay, Balloch, Andrew Hay, Haldane, Andy Hay, Pembrokeshire, Davida Hay, Haldane, Kara Louise Hay, Hunterhill, Paisley, Kenny Hay, Duns, Berwickshire, Lisa Hay, Pembrokeshire, Natasha Irene Hay, Hunterhill, Paisley, Rebecca Hay, Pembrokeshire, Robbie Hay, Pembrokeshire, William Hay, Bearsden, Michelle Hayburn, Perthshire, Andy Hayes, Glasgow, Caroline Hayes, Johnstone, Jackie Hayes, Hamilton, Mark Hayes, Paisley, Paul Hayes, Glasgow, Sarah Hayes, Glasgow, Shaun Hayes, Telford, Tommy Hayes, Glasgow, Vincent Hayes, Methil, Carol Hayley, Glasgow, Lee Hayley, Glasgow, Matt Hayley, Glasgow, Daniel Haynes, Douglas Haynes, New Zealand, Jessica Mary Haynes, Coatbridge, Darren Hayton, Motherwell, Donna Hayton, Motherwell, Sandra Hayton, Motherwell, Kelsay Hazard, Glasgow, Kia Hazard, Glasgow, Charlie Hazelton, Largs, Richard Head, Bollsover, Adele Healey, Liverpool, John Healey, Coatbridge, Sandra Healey, Motherwell, Andrew Healy, Glasgow, Des Healy, Didcot, Oxfordshire, Katrina Healy, Gilmerton, Edinburgh, Mark Healy, Bishopbriggs, Michael Healy, Edinburgh, Michael Healy, Holytown, Nancy Healy, Gilmerton, Edinburgh, Paddy Healy, Gilmerton, Edinburgh, Peter Healy, Kilsyth, Rose Healy, Edinburgh, Stephen Healy, Paisley, Tim Healy, London, Yvonne Healy, East Kilbride, Brendan Heaney, Belfast, Jamie Heaney, Glasgow, John Heaney, Whitburn, Lisa-Marie Heaney, London, Mark Heaney, Livingston, Ross Heaney, Bonnybridge, Philip Heapburn, Nairn, Jim Hearns, Glasgow, Richie Hearns, Glasgow, Mark Heavey, Irvine, Jacklyn Heckles, Isle of Lewis, Jayne Heckles, Benbecula, Eugene Heenan, Kenny Heenan, Denny, Stevie Heenan, Alness, James Heeney, Hillington, Margaret Heeney, Ibrox, Glasgow, Stephen Heeney, Glasgow, Andrew Heeps, Grangemouth, Christopher Heeps, Grangemouth, John Heeps, Grangemouth, Gary Heffron, Glasgow, Peter Heffron, Yeading, Austin Hegarty, Wakfield, Nick Heggarty, Germany, Ashleigh Heggie, Livingston, Craig Heggie, Livingston, Lauren Heggie, Livingston, Angela Hempstead, Bo'ness Home, Brian Henaghen, Edinburgh, Julie Henaghen, Edinburgh, Alison Henderson, Dunfermline, Archie Henderson, Glasgow, Barry Henderson, Salsburgh, Brian Henderson, Partick, Chris Henderson, Cumbernauld, Craig Henderson, Edinburgh, Craig Henderson, Glasgow, Don Henderson, Wales, Gary Henderson, Ge Henderson, Viewpark, Jimmy Henderson, Stevenston, Lesley Henderson, Peebles, Mark Henderson, Linwood, Renfrewshire, Martin Henderson, Lochore, Fife, Mick Henderson, Falkirk, Paul Henderson, Hamilton, Paul Henderson, Milton Keynes, Paul Henderson, Newarthill, Rena Henderson, Stevenston, Roy Henderson, Dumfries, Shay Henderson, Armadale, Stevie Henderson, Kirkintilloch, Austin Hendren, Hatfield, Hertfordshire, Jim Hendren, Dumbarton, Willie Hendren, Balornock, Ally Hendry, Paisley, Brian Hendry, Shotts, Dave Hendry, Rochester, David Hendry, Glasgow, David Hendry, Greenock, Hannah Hendry, Jimmy Hendry, Glenboig, Lynnie Hendry, Paisley, Marc Hendry, Barrowfield, Glasgow, Margaret Hendry, Greenock, Mark Hendry, Erskine, Melissa Hendry, Greenock, Nicole Hendry, Greenock, Patrick Hendry, Clydebank, Paul Hendry, Acton, London, Paul Hendry, Cambuslang, Paul Hendry, Greenock, Paul Hendry, Paisley, Tam Hendry, Govanhill, Glasgow, William Hendry, Glasgow, Anthony Hennery, Glasgow, Hennery, Glasgow, Sarah Hennessy, Whitson, Martin Hennigan, Glasgow, Jack Henrik, Hathaway, Kettering, Aidan Henry, Linwood, Alan

Bundy Henry, Livingston, Big Eamonn Henry, Ballymurphy, Belfast, Chris Henry, Greenock, Christopher Henry, Glasgow, James Henry, Cumbernauld, L Henry, Maureen Henry, Glasgow, Nathan Henry, Glasgow, Neil Henry, East Kilbride, Derek Henshaw, Glasgow, Ross Henshelwood, Langside, Billy Hepburn, Kinning Park, Glasgow, Billy Hepburn, Rutherglen, Christopher Hepburn, Rutherglen, Flo Hepburn, Gordon Hepburn, Greenock, James Hepburn, Glasgow, Mary Hepburn, Glasgow, Pauline Hepburn, Grangemouth, Steven Hepburn, Grangemouth, Karl Herbert, South Armagh, Neil Herbert, Corby, Vikki Hercus, Annan, Connor Herd, Glenrothes, Donald Herd, Cupar, Gail Herd, Cupar, Kenny Herd, Glasgow, Kenny Herd, Glenrothes, Matthew Herd, Cupar, Rowan Herd, Cupar, Sarah Herd, Glenrothes, Billy Heron, Ross-shire, David Heron, Coatbridge, Davie Heron, Port Glasgow, Russell Heron, Govan, Sean Heron, Twinbrook, Belfast, Tony Heron, Twinbrook, Belfast, Sean Anthony Herriot, Saudi Arabia, Marty Heter, Leicester, Robbie Hetherington, Gateshead, Steph Hetherington, East Kilbride, Karen Hewer, Italy, Angela Hickey, Bridgeton, Barry Hickey, Cork, Brian Hickey, Motherwell, Eileen Hickey, Motherwell, John Hickey, Banbridge, County Down, Alex Higgins, London, Andrew Higgins, Glasgow, Anne Higgins, Wishaw, Billy Higgins, Huntly and Paisley, Corrie Higgins, , Derek Higgins, Stevenston, Elizabeth Higgins, Dunoon, Ian Higgins, Baillieston, James Higgins, Port Glasgow, Jay Higgins, Port Glasgow, Jeanette Higgins, Port Glasgow, Joe Higgins, Port Glasgow, John Higgins, Carmyle, Glasgow, John Higgins, Dunoon, John Higgins, Renfrew, John and Michael Higgins, Inch Lea, Renfrew, Joseph Higgins, Easterhouse, Joseph A Higgins, Cumbernauld, Joseph Anthony Higgins, Port Glasgow, Kieran Higgins, Dunoon, Lynn Marie Higgins, Port Glasgow, Mark Higgins, Motherwell, Mary Higgins, Glasgow, Michael Higgins, Renfrew, Myra Higgins, Port Glasgow, Pally Higgins, Glasgow, Pat Higgins, Port Seton, Paul Higgins, Glasgow, Paul Higgins, Port Seton, Paul Henrik Higgins, Port Glasgow, Paul T. Higgins, Port Seton, Phil Higgins, Airdrie, Roseanne Higgins, Glasgow, Ryan Higgins, Greenock, Sean Higgins, Glasgow, Sean Patrick Higgins, Port Glasgow, Shawn Higgins, Glasgow, Steven 'Higgie' Higgins, Drumchapel, Glasgow, Higgins, Lanark, Ann-Marie High, Craigavon, James And Ronnie Highfield, Gold Post Glasgow, Stefan Highton, Ballymena, Paul Higins, Greenock, Margaret Higney, Oshawa, Ontario, Martin Higney, Croy, Sarah Hilditch, Larbet, Dan Hilferty, Glasgow, Danny Hilferty, St Bees, John Hilferty, Greenock, John Paul Hilferty, Greenock, Archie Hill, Tadworth, Charlie Hill, Tadworth, Christopher Hill, Airdrie, Dermot Hill, Scotstoun, Helen Hill, Scotstoun, Iain Hill, Campbeltown, Isabell Hill, Port Glasgow, John Hill, Linthouse, John Hill, Josh Hill, Tadworth, Katie Hill, Luton, Luke Hill, Luton, Peter Hill, Scotstoun, Sam Hill, Tadworth, Tommy Hill, Port Glasgow, Tony Hill, London, John Hillhouse, Moodiesburn, Robert Hillhouse, Glasgow, Joe Hillington, Shawlands, Carol Hillis, Scotstoun, Thomas Himan, Canada, Drew Hinde, Glasgow, Alan Hinds, Sandyhills, Glasgow, Iain Hinds, Clacton-on-Sea, Jimbob Hinds, Twechar, John Hinds, Clacton-on-Sea, John Paul Hinds, Clacton-on-Sea, Lewis Hinds, Erskine, Samuel Hinds, Clacton-on-Sea, Allan Hington, Sighthill, Anton Hinton, Sighthill, Scott Hinton, Sighthill, Willie Hipson, Maryhill, Scott Hislop, Hallside, Glasgow, Kevin Hoddy, Stoke-on-Trent, John Hodge, Suffolk, Lynne Hodge, Ayr, Michael Hodge, Greenock, Nicola Hodge, Greenock, Yvonne Hodge, Greenock, Aiden Hoenigmann, Tranent, Andrew Hoey, Newport, South Wales, Mary Hoey, Easter Queenslie, Peter Hoey, Newarthill, Marie Hoffmann, Annan, Derek Hogan, Lochee, Joe Hogan, Drumchapel, Ryan Hogan, Slamannan, Caron Hogg, Bonnyrigg, Christopher Hogg, Bonnyrigg, Daniel Hogg, Bonnyrigg, Frank Hogg, Glenrothes, Robert Hogg, Saltire Court, Edinburgh, Stephen Hogg, Bonnyrigg, Scott Hoggan, Glasgow, David Holden, Ballycastle, Co Antrim, Paul Holden, Aberdeen, Ronnie Holden, Ballycastle, Co Antrim, Andy Holder, Maryhill, Andy Holder, USA, Michelle Holiday, Glasgow, Adam Holland, Ayr, George Holland, Greenock, Julia Holland, Helensburgh, Mechelle Holland, Greenock, Shirley Holland, Greenock, Kerry Holliday, Glasgow, Lee Hollinger, Glasgow, Craig Hollingsworth, East Kilbride, Jim Hollinsworth,

Knightswood, Glasgow, Graham Hollston, Motherwell, Frank Hollywood, Lothian, Linda Hollywood, Lothian, Rachael Holman, Linwood, Ciaran Holmes, Knightswood, Eamonn Holmes, Glasgow, Elizabeth Holmes, Gary Holmes, Glasgow, Mark Holmes, Knightswood, Sian Holmes, Drumchapel, Andrew Holms, Lochgilphead, Gav Holms, Lenzie, Morris Holms, Lenzie, John Home, Inverness, Marc Honeyman, Cranhill, Barrie Hood, Dunbar, Raymond Hood, Hamilton, Robert Hood, Inverness, Rosann Whannel And Donna Hoodless, Whithorn, Frank Hoolahan, Uddingston, Frank Hoolahan, Uddingston, Caitlin Hoolighan, Glasgow, Christine Hoolighan, Glasgow, Clair Hoolighan, Glasgow, Hugh Hoolighan, Glasgow, Yvonne Hooman, Livingston, Yvonne Hooman, Livingston, James Hope, Cambuslang, Davy Hopkins, Drumchapel, Tommy Hopkins, Paisley, Shanna Hopley, Paisley, Anthony Horan, Cumbernauld, Kevin Horan, Kelty, Mike Horan, Catterick, Tommy Horan, Cumbernauld, T. Horbit, Grangemouth, Martin Horn, Irvine, Jamie Hornall, High Bonnybridge, Derek Horne, Grangemouth, Paul Horne, Glasgow, George Horsburgh, Bannockburn, Joanne Horsburgh, Johnstone, Tommy Horsfield, Ross-shire, R. Hosie, Bristol, Helen Housley, Cambuslang, Rosemary Housley, Cambuslang, Anton Houston, Linwood, Danny Houston, Glasgow, David Houston, Ilford, Essex, Gail Houston, Kirkcaldy, Jane Houston, Knightswood, Glasgow, Jayne Houston, Johnstone, John Houston, Hamilton, Kenneth Houston, Johnstone, Kirsty Houston, Paisley, Renfrewshire, Martin Houston, Drumchapel, Sean Houston, Glenrothes, Sharon Houston, Hamilton, Stephen Houston, Johnstone, Kevin Houten, Peebles, Elaine Howard, Lumphinnans, Davina Howarth, Symington, Stephen Howarth, Symington, Alan Howden, Cowie, Christine Howden, Cowie, Tommy Howden, Cowie, Mark Howdine, Glasgow, Mark Howe, Rosyth, Gloria Howie, Falkirk, Neil Howie, Fordwich, Kent, Fraser Howley, Livingston, Donnie Hoxy, Morrison, Jason Hoye, Craigavon, Amanda Huggen-Kiz, USA, Adien Hughes, Ardrossan, Alan Hughes, Chorley, Barry Hughes, Glasgow, Ben Hughes, Hamilton, Chad Hughes, Edinburgh, Chris Hughes, Hamilton, Chris Hughes, Nottingham, Christiaan Hughes, Rutherglen, Christopher Hughes, Edinburgh, Ciaran Hughes, Belfast, Colette Hughes, Rutherglen, Connor Hughes, Chorley, Damien Hughes, Cumbernauld, David Hughes, Edinburgh, David Hughes, Neilston, Dominic Hughes, Rutherglen, Ellie Hughes, Glasgow, Gareth Hughes, Cumbernauld, Gerald Hughes, Glasgow, Gerry Hughes, Ralston, James Hughes, Airdrie, James Hughes, Hamilton, Joe Hughes, Ardrossan, John Hughes, Neilston, John Hughes, London, Jordan Hughes, Erskine, Kevin Hughes, Port Glasgow, Kevin John Hughes, Haddington, East Lothian, Lesley-Anne Hughes, Cowdenbeath, Liz Hughes, Greenock, Lorraine Hughes, Hamilton, Mairi Hughes, Springburn, Marion Hughes, Wishaw, Mark Hughes, Carlisle, Mark Hughes, Glasgow, Mark Hughes, Kilbirnie, Mark Hughes, Musselburgh, Martin Hughes, Carlisle, Martin Hughes, , Moira Hughes, Edinburgh, Thomas Hughes, C/O Of Ann Summers, Liverpool, Natalie Hughes, Baillieston, Natalie Hughes, Glenboig, Owen Hughes, Stirling, Paddy Hughes, The Cairn, Paul Hughes, Barrhead, Paul Hughes, Glasgow, Paul Hughes, Glasgow, Paul Hughes, Riddrie, Glasgow, Paul Hughes, Singapore, Paula Hughes, Glasgow, Peter Hughes, Kettering, Peter Hughes, Wishaw, Peter Hughes, , Richard Hughes, Bournemouth, Scott Hughes, Govan, Sean Hughes, , Stephanie Hughes, East Kilbride, Stephen Hughes, South Armagh, Stevie Hughes, Edinburgh, Stevie Hughes, Falkirk, Tam Hughes, Edinburgh, Tam Hughes, Glasgow, Tony Hughes, Johnstone, Tony Hughes, Maryhill, Tony Hughes, Wishaw, Tam Hughes Jnr, Edinburgh, Amanda Hugnkiz, Burlington, Iowa, Scooby Huhges, Stirling, Joe Humble, Kirkcaldy, Ian Robert Hun, Whalsay, Alan Hunnam, East Lothian, Chris Hunt, Dundee, Jake Hunt, Dundee, Kevin Hunt, Dundee, Liam Hunt, Dundee, Alan Hunter, Govanhill, Andrew Hunter, Whitburn, Andy Hunter, Norwich, Angus Hunter, Glasgow, Billy Hunter, Strathaven, Calum Hunter, Kirkcaldy, Calum Hunter, Norwich, Carolann Hunter, Coatbridge, Chloe Hunter, Cumbernauld, Claire Hunter, Edinburgh, Eddie Hunter, Bath, Euan Hunter, Coatbridge, Gloria Hunter, Norwich, James Hunter, Burlington, Ontario, James Hunter, Norwich, Jamie Hunter, Glasgow, Jayne Hunter, Edinburgh, Jim Hunter,

Boness, Jim Hunter, Bo'Ness, Kerry Hunter, Paisley, Lauren Hunter, Toryglen, Linda Hunter, Edinburgh, Peds Hunter, Livingston, Peter Hunter, Glasgow, Phyllis Hunter, Harthill, Raymond Hunter, Edinburgh, Stewart Hunter, harthill, Ted Hunter, Bathgate, Alexander Hunting, Dunning, Matthew Hurding, Kirkcaldy, Cameron Hurkins, Clydebank, Robert Hurrell, Port Glasgow, Michael Finbar Hurton, Calderwood, East Kilbride, John Huskie, Glenrothes, Ron Huskie, Fife, Cherie Huson, Isle of Benbecula, Ibrar Hussain, Manchester, James Hustis, , Gordon Huston, Montrose, Kevin Hutchens, Stonehaven, Jim Hutcheson, Battlefield, Ian Hutchinson, Kettering, Ian Hutchinson, Kettering, Michael Hutchinson, Glasgow, Rob Hutchinson, Kettering, Thomas Hutchinson, Hamilton, Viv Hutchinson, , Anna Hutchison, Granton, Edinburgh, Bazza Hutchison, Kilwinning, John B Hutchison, South Nitshill, Glasgow, John C Hutchison, Easterhouse, Glasgow, Leah Hutchison, Kirkintilloch, Lynsey-Anne Hutchison, South Nitshill, Glasgow, Michele Hutchison, Castlemilk, Martin Hutchy, Cumbernauld, Andrew Hutton, Glasgow, Blair Hutton, Alloa, Ian Hutton, Jersey, Karen Hutton, Alloa, Kenny And Paul Hutton, Townhead, Coatbridge, Ryan Hutton, Alloa, Terry Hutton, Dunfermline, Joseph Hyland, Glasgow, Corey Hynds, Wishaw, Ashleigh Hynes, Provanhall, Brian Hynes, Provanhall, Ryan Hynes, Provanhall, Victor Hynes, London, Harry Hyslop, Port Glasgow.

Rab Ideer, Clydebank. Chris Idziak, Tillicoultry, Chris Idziak, Tillicoultry, Danny Imrie, Kinglassie Fife, Lyndon Inch, Plockton, Rebecca Inch, Plockton, Bill Inchinan, , Macy Inchinan, , George Ingham, Glasgow, Duncan Inglis, Taiwan, Alan Ingram, Girvan, Danielle Ingram, Girvan, Kevin Ingram, Ayr, Billy Innes, Perth, Brian Innes, Parkhead, Brian Innes, Ruchill, Glasgow, Callum Innes, St Ninians, Carol Innes, Conon Bridge, Chris Innes, Cawdor, Chris Innes, Inverness, Kenneth Innes, Ruchill, Glasgow, Maria Innes, Parkhead, Tony Innes, Glasgow, Suse Inoz, Sydney, Australia, Nick Ioannou, Bearsden, Glasgow, Neil Ireland, Irvine, Noel Ireland, Irvine, Paul Ireland, West Belfast, Northern Ireland, Parwez Irshad, Tokyo, Japan, Alex Irvine, Glasgow, Andrea Irvine, Haghill, Andy Irvine, Haghill, Darren Irvine, London, John Irvine, Coldstream, John Irvine, Girvan, Mary Irvine, Haghill, Oliver Irvine, Dornoch, Patricia Irvine, Whitecrook, Sarah Irvine, Dornoch, Robert Irvine Jnr, Bromley, David Irving, Glasgow, John Irving, Kingspark, Neil Irving, Glasgow, John Irving Jnr, Kingspark, Johnny Irwin, Jersey, Jonny Irwin, Jersey, Channel Islands, Joe Isaac, Port Glasgow, Luke Isaac, Port Glasgow, Ruth Isaac, Port Glasgow, Stephanie Isaac, Port Glasgow, Eddie Isaku, Anderston Glasgow, Aisha Issac, Leeds, Shawn Issac, Leeds, Terry Ivany, Inverness.

Alan Jack, Cumbernauld. Allan Jack, Cumbernauld, Caitlin Jack, Rutherglen, Denise Jack, Rutherglen, Ryan Jack, Rutherglen, Alex Jackson, Carluke, Claire Jackson, Motherwell, David Jackson, Greenacres, Gerry Jackson, Craigneuk, Graeme Jackson, East Kilbride, Jackie Jackson, Grangemouth, Jim Jackson, Coatbridge, Paul Jackson, Grangemouth, Ross Jackson, Greenock, Scott Jackson, Greenock, Scott Jackson, Greenock, Sean Jackson, Carluke, Steve Jackson, Dundee, James Robert Jackson-Brown, Glasgow, Big Jake, Kirkintilloch, Chrisie James, Airdrie, Derek James, Pollok,Glasgow, Mark James, Pollok,Glasgow, Kevin James McArthur, Dumbarton, Brian Jamieson, Dennistoun, Gary Jamieson, Perth, Western Australia, Joe Jamieson, Port Glasgow, Kirsty Jamieson, Port Glasgow, Mark Jamieson, Hamilton, Paul Jamieson, London, Sarah Jamieson, Fife, Andrew Japp, London, Eddie Japp, Wishaw, Fraser Jardine, Hyndland, Joe Jardine, Barrhead, Joe Jardine, Barrhead, Kerrianne Jardine, Irvine, Mick Jardine, Ibiza, Robert Jardine, Irvine, Scott Jardine, Whitburn, Hugh Jarse, Lesbia, Andrew Jarvie, East Kilbride, Andrew Jarvis, Barrowfield, Chelsey Jarvis, West Lothian, Edward Jarvis, Barrowfield, Steven Jarvis, Glasgow, Ali Jasim, Bellshill, Usman Javed, Grangemouth, Ian Jay, Millwall, Peckham, Hugh Jaynous, Parkhead, Peter Jaysbury, Alloa, Heywood Jeblome, Dallas City, Illinois, Graham Jeffers, Corby, Northants, Aidan Jeffrey, Lumphinnans, Tracy Jeffrey, Aberdeen,

Wullie Jeffrey, Gallowgae, Brian Jelly, Bournemouth, Angela Jenkins, Perth, W Australia, John Jenkins, Maryhill, Glasgow, John Jenkins, Perth, W Australia, Martin Jenkins, Motherwell, Michelle Jenkins, Bellshill, Paul Jenkins, Maryhill, Glasgow, Robbie Jenkins, Perth, Western Australia, Ross Jenkins, Perth, W Australia, Vickie Jenkins, Bathgate, Willie Jenkins, Perth, W Australia, Mary Jenkinson, Low Waters, The Jobsons, Bothwell, Bernard Johannesen, Carmyle, Roger Johansson, Stockholm, Anthony John, Glasgow, Lorna John, Dumbarton, Maureen John, Glasgow, Rhys John, Oban, Seville 5 John, Martin, Willie, Alan Johnson, Cumbernauld, Jim Johnson, Preswick, John Johnson, Glasgow, Lauchlin Johnson, Carmyle, Tahiti, Laura Johnson, Stornoway, Western Isles, Linda Johnson, Grangemouth, Phil Johnson, Bracknell, Johnson, Glasgow, Adam,Claire,Dylan,Ryan And Alix Johnston, Bo'ness, Ben Johnston, Moffat, Byron Nicholas Johnston, Ayr, Carol Johnston, Baillieston, Glasgow, Dale Johnston, Loanhead, Davie Johnston, London, Diddler Johnston, , Ewan Johnston, Ibrox, Glasgow, Fran Johnston, Rushden, Northants, Frank Johnston, Drumchapel Glasgow To Benalmadena, G Johnston, Montrose, Gary Johnston, Loanhead, Reiss Johnston, Provenmill, Reiss Johnston, Provenmill, Riagan Christopher Johnston, Ayr, Steven Johnston, Wishaw, Susi Johnston, Govanhill, William Johnston, Parkhead, Kelly Johnston, Baillieston, Glasgow, Diddler Johnston Jnr, , Billy Johnstone, Glasgow, Calum Johnstone, Kilmarnock, Craig Johnstone, Lesmahagow, David Johnstone, Leven, Derek Johnstone, Coatbridge, Frankie Johnstone, Nottingham, Gavin Johnstone, Leslie Fife, Ged Johnstone, Milton, Glasgow, John Johnstone, Milton, Glasgow, Paul Johnstone, Peterhead, Paul Johnstone, Saltcoats, Sam Johnstone, Maryhill, Glasgow, Sean Johnstone, Johnstone, Tam Johnstone, Plymouth, William Johnstone, Bridgeton , Jai Jolly, Whithorn, Leanne Conlan, Tyler Jolly, Whithorn, Barry Jones, Bridge of Weir, Bobbie Jones, East Kilbride, Brian Jones, Glasgow, Charles Jones, Glasgow, Charles Jones, Mosspark, Chris Jones, Glasgow, Christine Jones, Hamilton, Craig Jones, Wishaw, Damon Jones, Castle Douglas, Daniel Jones, Glasgow, Daniel Jones, Mosspark, David Jones, Blackburn, David Jones, Shieldhill, Davy Jones, Blackburn, Deborah Jones, Glasgow, Francis Jones, Broxburn, Gareth Jones, Glasgow, Gary Jones, Brighton, Kerry Jones, Shieldhill, Kevin Jones, Glasgow, Kevin Jones, Mosspark, Lee Jones, Blackburn, Lynne Jones, Shieldhill, Michael Jones, Arbroath, Nicola Jones, Easterhouse, Robert Jones, Hamilton, Ross Jones, Shieldhill, Stephen Jones, Wishaw, Glenda Jordan, Wishaw, Hugh Jordan, Belfast, Jack Jordan, Glasgow, Jason Jordan, Mosspark, Karen Jordan, Enfield, Middlesex, Maxine Jordan, Wishaw, Paul Jordan, Livingston, Peter Jordan, Kirkintilloch, Eddie Jordon, London, David Joseph, , Richie Journeaux, Sydney, Australia, Kevin Joyce, Bearsden, Harry R. Jumpjet, Biggin Hill, Kent, Dion Junor, Peterhead, Wayne Junor, Peterhead, Frank Jurczick, Glasgow, Edmond Jurczyk, Larkhall, Frank Jurszyk.

Robert K, B'Dairde. Frank. K. Airney, Grangemouth, John Kaleta, Cowdenbeath, Gerry Kaluzny, Garngad, Laura Kaluzny, Garngad, Susan Kaluzny, Garngad, Tracey Kaluzny, Garngad, Andrew Kane, Eastleigh, Chris Kane, Blantyre, Garry John Kane, Coatbridge, Gerald Kane, Alexandria, Gerald Kane, Renton, Dunbartonshire, James Kane, Hamilton, Jimmy Kane, , Joe Kane, Bletchley, Milton Keynes, Kevin Kane, Blantyre, Kevin Kane, Cleland, Kevin Kane, Denny, Michael Kane, Dumfries, Michael Kane, Isle of Bute, Tam Kane, Ardrossan, Willie Kane, Denny, Mathew Kanuskas, Uddingston, Matt Kanuskas, Uddingston, Sara Kaskonas, Glasgow, Claire Kavan, Glasgow, Paul Kavanagh, Garrowhill, Glasgow, Paul Kavanagh, Glasgow, Paul Kavanagh (Rac), Garrowhill, Brian Kay, Glasgow, Fraser Kay, Dunfermline, Danni Kaye, Airdire Xx, Danni Kaye, Airdire Xx, Alan Kayes, Cumbernauld, James Kealy, Glasgow, Eamon Kean, Greenford, Donna Keane, Armadale. West Lothian, Tom Keane, Irvine, Daniel Keaney, Glasgow, Dennis Keany, Glasgow, Patrick Keany, Glasgow, Kevin Kearney, Motherwell, Paul Kearney, Kilmarnock, Frank Kearns, Maryhill, Gary Kearns, Renton, Robert Kearns, Glasgow, Sammy Kearns, Stepps, Glasgow, Andrew Keating, Garrowhill, Maureen Keating, Garrowhill, Thomas Keating,

Garrowhill, Gerald Keatings, Wishaw, Gerry Keatings, Wishaw, Meireade Keatings, Wishaw, Shovan Keatings, Wishaw, Richie Keaton, Cork, Nick Keaveny, East Kilbride, Eamonn Kedney, London, Eamon Keegan, Portadown, Northern Ireland, Jamie Keegan, Royal Tunbridge Wells, Jim Keegan, Royal Tunbridge Wells, Michael Keegan, Cumbernauld, Paul Keegan, Liverpool, Andria Keelan, East Kilbride, Cameron Keen, Bothwell, Michael Keen, Bothwell, Bruce James Keenan, Glasgow, Cathie Keenan, Linwood, Chris Keenan, Cumbernauld, Chris Keenan, , David Keenan, Anderston, Gary Keenan, Perth, W Australia, Holly Keenan, Cumbernauld, Jacqueline Keenan, , Jim Keenan, Bellshill, Lee Keenan, Cumbernauld, Pat Keenan, , Paul Keenan, Farmecastle Court, Paul Keenan, Farmecastle Court, Paul Keenan, Farmecastle Court, Paul Keenan, Farmecastle Court, Paul Keenan, Preston, Paul Keenan, Rutherglen, Glasgow, Paul Keenan, Rutherglen, Peter Keenan, North Blackhill, Kaley Keeney, Glasgow, Nicola Keeney, Glasgow, Ben Keggan, Dunfermline, Tommy Keicher, Cowdenbeath, Doug Keighley, Sydney, Australia, Ryan Keily, East Kilbride, Nid Keirnan, Lincoln, Alan Keith, Greenock, Alan Kelly, Yoker, Glasgow, Alan Kelly, Yoker, Glasgow, Albert Kelly, Stevenston, Albert Kelly, Stevenston, Andy Kelly, Barrhead, Angela Kelly, Glasgow, Anne Kelly, East Kilbride, Barry Kelly, Govanhill, Bessie Kelly, Uddingston, Big Joe Kelly, Easterhouse, Brendan Kelly, Coatbridge, Brian Kelly, Tollcross, Glasgow, Brian Kelly, Yoker, Glasgow, Cain Kelly, Glasgow, Caroline Kelly, Drumchapel, Catherine Kelly, Liverpool, Chris Kelly, Bathgate, Chris Kelly, Knightswood, Glasgow, Chris Kelly, Motherwell, Christopher Kelly, Baillieston, Christopher Kelly, Glasgow, Christopher Kelly, Knighstwood, Glasgow, Christopher Kelly, Woodfield, Cian Kelly, Glasgow, Claire Kelly, Glasgow , Dalmarnock, Colum Kelly, Belfast At Home Watching The Game, Craig Kelly, Clydebank, Daniel Kelly, Cumbernauld, David Kelly, Chapelhall, Elaine Kelly, Cumbernauld, Elaine Kelly, Cumbernuald, Elizabeth Kelly, Larbert, Ellen Kelly, Sandhills, Francis Kelly, Dundee, Frank Kelly, Baillieston, Frank Kelly, Wigan, Frankie Kelly, Erskine, Frankie Kelly, Milton, Glasgow, Gary Kelly, Dundee, Gary Kelly, Fort William, Glen Kelly, Hamilton, Greame Kelly, Lisburn, NI, Hugh Kelly, Paisley, Ian Kelly, Glasgow(At Seville On 2St May), Ian Kelly, Glasgow(At Seville On 2St May), Jack Kelly, Linwood, James Kelly, Ayr, James Kelly, Cambuslang, James Kelly, Glasgow, Jamie Kelly, Coatbridge, Jennifer Kelly, Drumchapel, Joe Kelly, Glasgow, John Kelly, Bellshill, John Kelly, Eastbourne, John Kelly, Erskine, John Kelly, Erskine, John Kelly, Springboig, John Paul Kelly, Springboig, Jordan Kelly, Easterhouse, Jordy Kelly, West Lothian, Jordy Kelly, West Lothian, Joseph Kelly, Ballycastle, Joseph Kelly, Clydebank, Joseph Kelly, Easterhouse, Kathleen Kelly, Baillieston, Kevin Kelly, Alloa, Kevin Kelly, Bothwell, Kharis Kelly, Dundee, Louise Kelly, Coatbridge, Lyndsey Kelly, Dundee, Mack Kelly, Glasgow, Mack Kelly, Glasgow, Maggi Kelly, Crossgates, Fife, Mark Kelly, Uddingston, Martin Kelly, Govan, Martybhoy Kelly, Seville, Michael Kelly, Bearsden, Michael Kelly, Bowmore Islay, Michael Kelly, Clydebank, Michael Kelly, Islay, Michael Kelly, Islay, Michael Kelly, Possilpark, Mick Kelly, Kirkintilloch, Mikey Kelly, West Lothian, Owen Kelly, Alloa, Paige Kelly, Dundee, Patrick Kelly, Glasgow, Paul Kelly, Alloa, Paul Kelly, Baillieston, Paul Kelly, Balornock, Paul Kelly, Dundee, Paul Kelly, East Kilbride, Paul Kelly, London, Paula Kelly, Dublin, Philip, Eileen, Roisin & Danny Kelly, East Kilbride, Philomena Kelly, Belfast At Home Watching The Game, Richard Kelly, Baillieston, Ricky Bhoy Kelly, Drovers Gallogate, Ricky Bhoy Kelly, Drovers Gallowgate, Rosa Kelly, Glasgow, Ryan Kelly, Blantyre, Sarah Kelly, Belfast, Scott Kelly, Belfast, Sean Kelly, Bathgate, Sean Kelly, Edinburgh, Shannon Kelly, Falkirk, Shannon Kelly, Knighstwood, Glasgow, Shannon Kelly, Knightswood, Glasgow, Shaun Kelly, Darnley, Shaun Kelly, Glasgow, Shaun Kelly, Glasgow, Stephen Kelly, Alloa, Stephen Kelly, Falkirk, Steven Kelly, Clydebank, Tam Kelly, Barton on Humber, Thomas Kelly, Hartlepool, Tommy Kelly, Sandhills, Tony Kelly, Cambuslang, Vinny Kelly, Darnley, Wib Kelly, West Lothian, William Kelly, Cheltenham, Yvonne Kelly, Blantyre, Terence Kelly Jnr, Ashford, Paul Kelly Jr., Yoker, Glasgow, Terence Kelly Snr, Ashford, Alison Kelman, Motherwell, Peter Kelson, Bathgate, Peter Kelson, ,

Stephen Keltie, Coatbridge, Andy Kemp, Orkney, Didle Kemp, Stirling, Nora Kemp, 227A Rannoch Road Perth Scotland, Nora Kemp, Letham, Perth, Sinead Kemp, Stirling, William Rattray Kemp, 227A Rannoch Road Perth Scotland, William Rattray Kemp, Letham, Perth, Alan Kenedy, Wishaw, John Kenedy, Glasgow, Alex Kenmore, Renfrew, Maria Kenn, Dunfermline, Frankie Kennan, Shotts, Jeg Kennan, Whitson, Alan Kennedy, Newmains, Allan Kennedy, Hamilton, Anthony Kennedy, Glasgow, Anthony Kennedy, Kilsyth, Bill Kennedy, Glasgow, Billy Kennedy, Rosshead, Boab Kennedy, Strathaven, Caroline Kennedy, Airdrie, Chris Kennedy, Bellahouston, Dean Kennedy, New Stevenston, Donna Kennedy, Glasgow, Eddie Kennedy, Caldercruix, Fiona Kennedy, Santa Ponsa, Mallorca, Gary Kennedy, Glasgow, Gerry Kennedy, Cumbernauld, James Kennedy, Airdrie, James Kennedy, Glasgow, Jamie Kennedy, Glasgow, Kim Kennedy, Coatbridge, Leanne Kennedy, Fort William, Lorraine Kennedy, Cardonald, Marie Kennedy, , Mark Kennedy, Kirkintilloch, Mary Kennedy, Caldercruix, Matthew Kennedy, Glasgow, Megan Kennedy, Carmyle, Mia Kennedy, Airdrie, Michael Kennedy, Airdrie, Michael Kennedy, Coatbridge, Michael Kennedy, Fort William, Michael Kennedy, Livingston, Pablo Kennedy, Albert Hotel ,Gourock, Paul Kennedy, Ayr, Paul Kennedy, Coatbridge, Pedro Kennedy, Albert Hotel ,Gourock, Peter Kennedy, Glasgow, Rab Kennedy, Strathaven, Ross Kennedy, Bromley, Ross Kennedy, Cumbernauld, Sony Kennedy, Coatbridge, Stephen Kennedy, Prestwick Ayrshire, Stevie Kennedy, Cairneyhill, Fife, William Joseph Kennedy, Glasgow, James Kenney, Dumbarton, Arlene Kenny, Dundee, Ashleigh Kenny, Dumbarton, Bobby Kenny, Kirkintilloch, Brian Kenny, Perth, George Kenny, Maryhill, Jamie Kenny, Riddrie, Jim Kenny, Gorbals, Liam Kenny, Kirkintilloch, Lisa Kenny, Riddrie, Paul Kenny, Glasgow. Thomas Keown, Glasgow, John Kernan, Whitecrook, Liam Kernan, Whitecrook, Adam Kerr, Girvan, Aidan Kerr, Bargeddie, Alan Kerr, Seville, Alanah Kerr, Glasgow, Alex Kerr, Greenfield, Glasgow, Alexander Kerr, Greenfield, Glasgow, Alexander Kerr, Greenfield, Glasgow, Allan&Susie Kerr, Grangemouth, Amander Kerr, Greenfield, Glasgow, Angela Kerr, Knightswood, Billy Kerr, Errogie Street, Easterhouse, Billy Kerr, Glasgow, Bryce Kerr, Fuengirola, Bryce Kerr, Fuengirola, Christina Kerr, Glasgow, Clare Kerr, Glenrothes, Colin Kerr, Bargeddie, Craig Kerr, Glasgow, Daniel Kerr, London, Darren Kerr, Airdrie, Ethel Kerr, Parkhead, Gary Kerr, Glasgow, Geraldine A. Kerr, Motherwell, Grahame Kerr, Lochee, Ian Kerr, Portugal, Jake Kerr, Barrhead, James Steven Kerr, Glasgow, Jim Kerr, Paisley, John Kerr, Garrowhill, John Kerr, Paisley, John Kerr, Rutherglen, Julie Kerr, Cambuslang, Kevin Kerr, Elderslie, Kevin Kerr, Glasgow, Kevin Kerr, Knightswood, Liz Kerr, Bargeddie, Luke Kerr, Greenfield, Glasgow, Lynn Kerr, Garrowhill, Marc Kerr, Glasgow, Marie Kerr, Cambuslang, Mary Kerr, Garrowhill, Matthew Kerr, Greenfield, Glasgow, Matthew Kerr, Greenfield, Glasgow, Patrick Kerr, Motherwell, Peter Kerr, Glasgow, Reece Kerr, Glasgow, Robert Kerr, Portugal, Scot Douglas Kerr, York, Steven Kerr, Easterhouse, Stuart Kerr, Bermuda, Suzanne Kerr, York, Tony Kerr, Brisbane, Australia, William Kerr, Denniston, Aidan Kerrigan, Airdrie, Alex Kerrigan, South Shields, Anne Marie Kerrigan, Falkirk, Bradley Kerrigan, Falkirk, Brett Kerrigan, Falkirk, Cassie Kerrigan, Falkirk, Craig Kerrigan, South Shields, Jackie Kerrigan, Cardonald, Jackie Kerrigan, Falkirk, Joe Kerrigan, Carmunnock, Laraine Kerrigan, South Shields, Maureen Kerrigan, Falkirk, Megan Kerrigan, South Shields, Stacey Kerrigan, South Shields, Robert Kerry, Glasgow, Kiki Kershaw, Renfrew, Sam Kershaw, Renfrew, Martin Kery, Ardrossan, Christine Kettell, Bedworth, Jamie Kettle, Glasgow, Sam Kettle, Glasgow, Thomas Kettle, Govan, Brendan Keyes, Yucatan N16 Stokie Tour, Michael Keyes, Carlisle, Niall Keyes, Carlisle, Pat Fintan Keyes, Yucatan N16 Stokie Tour, Sharron Keyes, Stokie, Sharron Keyes, Yucatan N16 Stokie Tour, Norman Keys, Renfrew, Samiul Khan, Bearsden, Glasgow, Steven Khan, Blantyre, Gregor Khun, Kilmarnock, Eddie Kidd, East Kilbride, Phil Kidd, Northampton, Gary Kielty, Falkirk, Adam Kiely, Bellshill, Deborah Kieran, Diane Kiernan, Cumbernauld, Daniel Kilbride, Govan, Gary Kilcullen, Cardonald, Glen Kilcullen, Glasgow, John Robert Kilcullen, Cardonald, Laura Kilcullen, Gateshead, Mark Kilcullen, Gateshead, Sandra Kilcullen,

Gateshead, Sandra Kilcullen, Glasgow, Donna Kilday, Armagh, Harry Kilday, Cumbernauld, Neil Kilday, Easterhouse, Rab Kilday, Easterhouse, Rab Kilday, Easterhouse, Stephen Kilday, Viewpark, Stephen Kilday, Viewpark, Robert Kilday Jr, Easterhouse, Robert Kilday Jr, Easterhouse, Brady Kilgallon, Torrevieja, Spain, James Kilgallon, Torrevieja, Spain, Joe Kilgallon, Corby, Mark Kilgallon, Corby, Willie Kilgallon, Corby, Northants, Willy Kilgallon, Cottingham, Market Harbro, Danny Killfertey, Cumbria, Barbara Killoran, Paisley, Mark Kiln, London, Roy Kilner, Peebles, Wullie Kilpatrick, Overtown, Lynda Kiltie, Crookston, Richard Kimble, Hermosa Beach, California, William Kimmet, Glasgow, David Kincaid, Kirkintilloch, Ross Kincaid, Alexandria, Scott Kincaid, Kirkintilloch, Carol King, Glasgow, Heather King, Darvel, James King, Lanarkshire, Jamie King, Bellshill, John King, Kirkcaldy, Julie King, Broxburn, Mick King, Port Glasgow, Mike Stena King, Aberdeen, Robert King, Motherwell, Scott King, Falkirk, Scott W. King, Preisthill, Glasgow, Sean King, Cleland, William King, Nottingham, Joan Kinloch, Hamilton, Craig Kinnear, Lochgelly, Graeme Kinnear, Drybridge, James Kinnon, Yoker, Jason Kinnon, Yoker, Kevin Kinnon, Yoker, James Kinnon, Dad, Yoker, Stuart Kinsey, Northampton, John Kirby, Gillian Kirk, Glasgow, Ian Kirk, Easterhouse, Michael Kirk, Seville, Willie Kirk, Saltire Court, Edinburgh, George 'Cookie' Kirk, Gorbals, Lynn Kirkham, Grangemouth, Willie Kirkland, Linwood, Colin Kirkpatrick, Burlington Canada, Mark & Ryan & Mark Kirkpatrick, Craigend, Stephen Kirkson, Wishaw, Kyle Kirkswood, Dalkeith, Darren Kirkwood, Hamilton, Ian Kirkwood, Motherwell, James Kirkwood, Hamilton, James Kirkwood, Kilmarnock, James Kirkwood, Kilmarnock, Ronnie Kirkwood, Pollok, Michaela Kite, Drumchapel, Robert Kivlichan, Galashiels, Conner Klin, Glasgow, Peter Kline, Glasgow, Paddy Jimmy Knockhill, Renfrew, Garry Knotts, Gorbals, Ian Knotts, Dennistoun, Lauren Knotts, Dennistoun, James Knox, Glasgow, Paul Konopate, Westerwood, Jo Kraske, Edinburgh, Joe Kraske, East Lothian, Michael Kraske, Wallyford, Michael Kraske, East Lothian, Brian Kreel, Northampton, Angela Kristmanns, Paisley, Davy Kristmanns, Paisley, Stefan Kristmanns, Paisley, Kristoffer, Alloa, Tracey Kriton, Annan, Izzy Krykant, Grangemouth, Martin Kuhn, Kilmarnock, Rhianna Kurimbux, Freuchie, Margaret Kurzepa, Sandyhills, Glasgow, Margaret Kurzepa, Sandyhills , Glasgow, Callum Kyle, Nitshill, Glasgow, Derek Kyle, Kirkconnel, Josephine Kyle, Airdrie, Shaun Kyle, Law Port, Glasgow, Stephen Kyle, Ballymena.

Kyle Lacatus, Co Tyrone, Northern Ireland. Pam Lacey, Dundee, Pat Laferty, Airdrie, Brendan Lafferty, Paisley, Ciaran Lafferty, Perthshire, Cornelius Lafferty, Coatbridge, David Lafferty, Cleland, Donna Lafferty, Viewpark, Donna Lafferty, Viewpark, Frank Lafferty, Carmyle, Frank Lafferty, Scotstoun, Greg Lafferty, Cambuslang, Helen Lafferty, Coatbridge, Ian Lafferty, Arbroath, James Lafferty, Jim Lafferty, Arbroath, Kieran Lafferty, Louise Lafferty, Bannockburn, Mandy Lafferty, Coatbridge, Marie Lafferty, Scotstoun, Glasgow, Marie Lafferty, Scotstoun, Mark Lafferty, Airdrie, Megan Lafferty, Coatbridge, Nicola Lafferty, Cleland, North Lanarkshire, Nicole Lafferty, Coatbridge, Robert Lafferty, Garthamlock, Stevie Lafferty, Wishaw, Terry Lafferty, Coatbridge, Frank Laffety, Scotstoun, Glasgow, John Laffey, Glasgow, Tony Laffey, Glasgow, Eric Laidlaw, Hillhouse, Andy Laing, Stirling, David Laing, , Stefan Lair, , Alan Laird, Falkirk, Christina Laird, Robroyston, John Laird, Kilmacolm, Stefan Laird, Kilmacolm, Craig Laisman, Helensburgh, Kevin Lally, Clydebank, Reece Lally, Clydebank, William Lally, Bathgate, Brian Lamb, Crewkerne, Somerset, Darrel Lamb, Livingston, Joe Lamb, Denny, Joe Lamb, Denny, Scott Lamb, Livingston, Angela Lambell, Kirkintilloch, Charles Lambert, Greenock, Charlie Lambert, Greenock, Gregor F. Lamberton, Blantyre, Karen Lambie, Glasgow, Amy Lambrou, Stirlingshire, Andreas Lambrou, Stirling, Colette Lambrou, Stirlingshire, Joe Lammond, Dunfermline, Ronnie Lammond, Dunfermline, James Lamon, Castlemilk, Elizabeth Lamont, Glasgow, Ewen Lamont, Inverness, George Lamont, Doncaster, Luke Lamont, Glasgow, Madeline Lamont, Glasgow, Margaret Lamont, Glasgow, Margaret Lamont, Partick, Mark Lamont, Muirend, Tony Lamont, Glasgow, William Lamont, Glasgow, Kevin Lanaghan,

Glasgow, Frank Lancey, , Andrew Lang, London, Marianne Lang, Drumchapel, Michael Lang, Ilford, Robert Lang, Paisley, Steven Lang, Glasgow, Steven Lang, Kennishead, Tracy Lang, Barrhead, Bob Lang Jr, Ontario, Canada, Bobby Lang Snr, Ontario, Canada, Dodge Langan, Glasgow, Willie Langford, Falkirk, Mark Langlin, Glasgow, John Langton, Newarthill, John W. Langton, Newarthill, Jamie Lannigan, Airdrie, Martin Lannigan, Coatbridge, Paul Lannigan, Airdrie, Reece Lannigan, , Arthur Lappin, Yucatan N16 Stokie Tour, Christina Lappin, Govan, Ciaran James Lappin, Govan, Evelyn Lappin, Clarkston, Gerry Lappin, Pollok, Ian Lappin, Clarkston, James Lappin, Govan, James Lappin, Govan, Lorraine Lappin, Govan, Tina Lappin, Govan, Norma Large, Clackmannan, William Large, Clackmannan, Gary Larkin, East Kilbride, Gary Larkin, Frimley Green, Surrey, John Larkin, Frimley Green, Sheryll Larkin, Shortroods, Paisley, David Larmour, Hillington, Karen Larne, Caroline Larsson, East Kilbride, Zag Larsson, Jersey, Paul Lattin, Glasgow, Gerard Lauchlan, Mount Vernon, Gerard Lauchlan, Mount Vernon Mvtf, Ryan Lauder, Sydney, Australia, Ryan Lauder, Sydney, Australia, Patrick Laughland, Glasgow, Cathy Laurence, Birmingham, Ian Laurenson, Holmsgarth, George Laurie, Summerston, Glasgow, Rosemary Laurie, Glasgow, Stephen Laurie, Bathgate, Warner Laurie, Spain, Bob Lauterhahn, Wannaque, New Jersey, USA, Christine Lavell, Irvine, John Lavell, Irvine, Gerry Lavelle, Shettleston, Joe Lavelle, Shettleston, Tony Lavelle, Falkirk, Michelle Laverie, Glasgow, James Laverty, Kieran Laverty, Bill Lavery, Hamilton, Brian Lavery, Bathgate, Damien Lavery, Motherwell, Damien Lavery, Motherwell, Gerard Lavery, Hamilton, Gerard Lavery, Hamilton, Hugh Lavery, Blackwood, Hugh Lavery, Blackwood, Lee Lavery, Toryglen, Mark Lavery, Newport, Pagnell, Tam Lavery, Dennistoun, Glasgow, William Lavery, Hamilton, William Lavery, Hamilton, Caroline Lavin, Bo'ness, Jon Lavin, Stirling, Varry Lavin, Stirling, Craig Law, Village, Gerard Law, Glasgow, Gerrard Law, Alexandria, Lyndsay Law, Moodiesburn, Lyndsay Law, Moodiesburn, Shug Law, East Kilbride, Colin Lawlor, Clackmannan, David Lawlor, Welwyn Garden City, Andrew Lawlor , Snr, Drumchapel Glasgow To Benalmadena, Kathy Lawrence, Birmingham, Alex Lawrie, South Side, Edinburgh, George Lawrie, Lochgell, Fife, Alex Lawson, Cumbernauld, Charlene Lawson, Kirkcaldy, David Lawson, Port Glasgow, Davie Lawson, Port Glasgow, Davy Lawson, Port Glasgow, Gary Lawson, Aberdeen, John Lawson, Bishopbriggs, Kevin Lawson, Glasgow, Mark Lawson, Robroyston, Paul Lawson, Milton Keynes, Paul Lawson, Robroyston, Stevie Lawton, Blackburn, Liam Laycock, Inverness, Le Grice, Bathgate, Anthony Le Huquet, Jersey, Martin Leadbetter, Pumpherston, Michael Leary, Coatsbridge, Archie Leckie, , Archie Leckie, Creiff, Perthshire, Brian Leckie, Paisley, Catherine Leckie, Paisley, Ciaran Leckie, Paisley, John Leckie, Paisley, Phil Leckie, Uddingston, Tam Ledingham, Rosneath, Carol Lee, Motherwell, Chris Lee, The Cairn, Claire Lee, Irvine, Gerry Lee, Motherwell, Jack Lee, Prestwick, Jon Lee, Prestwick, Jordan Lee, Prestwick, Kristan Lee, Sunderland, Mark Lee, Irvine, Mark Lee, Motherwell, Michael Lee, Irvine, Michael Lee, Prestwick, Peter Lee, Irvine, John "Collins" Leebody, Possill, Connor Leech, Trenton, Billy Lees, Bonhill, Jude Lees, Galashiels, Kevin Lees, Pat Lees, Salisbury, Rikki Lees, St Andrews, Robert Lees, Mid Caulder, Robert Lees, Stanhope,New Jersey, USA, Siobhan Lees, St Andrews, Paul Leese, Glasgow, Finlay Legatte, Tollcross, Alastair Leggate, Hamilton, Dylan Leggate, Hamilton, Lorna Leggate, Hamilton, Francis Lehmann, Blantyre, Kieran Francis Lehmann, Blantyre, Allan Leighton, Rosyth, Alan Leitch, Govan Derek Leith, Ayr, Derek & Rhonda Leith, Ayr, Derek & Rhonda Leith, Ayr, Finlay Leith, Pollok, Rhonda Leith, Ayr, Carousel Bar Leith CSC Bhoys, Barry Leitham, Perth, Matthew Leitham, Perth, , Raymond Leitham, Perth, Brian Lellan, Southampton, Bru Lenadoon, Barry Lenaghan, Govan, Glasgow, Barry Lenaghan, Gerard Lenaghan, Castlewellan, Co Down, David Lenihan, Renfrew, Francis Lenihan, Renfrew, Barry Lennon, Darvel, Ayrshire, Brian Lennon, Coatbridge, Frank Lennon, Knebworth, Herts, Kenneth Lennon, Kilmarnock, Pat Lennon, Wishaw, Ryan Lennon, Kilmarnock, Steven Lennon, Falkirk, Bill Lennox, Reading, Graham Lennox, Dumfries, Karen Lennox, Lesmahagow, Linda Lennox, Glasgow, Graham Lenox, Dumfries, David Lenton, Bannockburn, Ela Lentz,

Tallahassee, Florida, Russ Lentz, Tallahassee, Florida, Russ Lentz, Tallahassee, Florida, Sean Lentz, Tallahassee, Florida, Brian Leonard, Glasgow, Carl Leonard, Wigan, John Leonard, Shotts, Jordan Leonard, Wigan, K. Leonard, Wigan, Kieran Leonard, Paul Leonard, Shotts, Dean Leslie, Lochgelly Fife, Ronny Leslie, Glasgow, Stephen Leslie, Greenock, Ben Lester, Bellshill, Chris Lester, Bellshill, Christopher Lester, Bishopbriggs, David Lester, Bishopbriggs, Frank Lester, Knightswood, Glasgow, Irene Lester, Bellshill, Marc Lester, Bellshill, Alexander Lettersoak, Antony Levell, Glasgow, Michael Leville, Newry, Yannis Levisassonis, Athens., Aaron Lewis, Sittingbourne, Kent, Aidan Lewis, Condorrat, Gordon Lewis, Hartlepool, Gordon Lewis, Hartlepool, Kieran Lewis, Condorrat, Kieran Lewis, Condorrat, Lana Lewis, Newport, South Wales, Liam Lewis, Sittingbourne, Kent, Miss Lewis, Glasgow, Paul Lewis, Wishaw, Ricky Lewis, West Kilbride, James Lewsley, Kirkintilloch, John Lewsley, Kirkintilloch, Billy Leydon, Bonhill, Harry Liddell, Kings Park, Darri Liddle, Westhill, George Liddle, Glasgow, John G Liddle, Wells, James Lieser, Parkhead, Glasgow, Jimmy Lightbody, Methven, Perth, Karen Lightfoot, Arbroath, Jim Lilley, East Kilbride, Alan Lillis, Sligo, Cheryl Lilly, Glasgow, James Lilly, Glasgow, Marty Lilly, Lambhill, Glasgow, Nikki Lilly, Glasgow, John Linagan, Stirling, Mary Linagan, Stirling, Sean Lincoln, Johnstone, Tony Lindin, East Kilbride, Andrew Lindsay, Coatbridge, Barry Lindsay, Wishaw, Diane Lindsay, Coatbridge, Jamie Lindsay, Bourtreehowl, Jeg Lindsay, Ayr, Joanne Lindsay, Glasgow, Lana Lindsay, Wigtownshire, Paula Lindsay, Glasgow, Sarah Lindsay, Wigtownshire, Stephen Lindsay, Coatbridge, Stevie Lindsay, Coatbridge, William Lindsay, Wigtownshire, William Lindsay, Wigtownshire, Gerry Liney, Linwood, Kevin Liney, Linwood, Suzanne Liney, Linwood, Edward Linich, Mount Annan, Paddy Linton, West Belfast , Gillian Linwood, Connie Lipton, Par, Wullie Lipton, East Kilbride, Mark Liptrot, Bellshill, Malc Lise, East Calder, Craig Lister, Bannockburn, Rhiannon Lister, Sandyhills, Glasgow, William Lister Jr, Penicuik, Chris Little, Dumbarton, Dale Little, Glasgow, Peter Little, Cawdor, Robert Little, Greenock, John Livingston, London, Michael Livingston, Norfolk, Angela Livingstone, Glasgow, Colin Livingstone, Croftfoot, Glasgow, Peter Livingstone, Glasgow, Amy Loader, Glasgow, Martin Loader, Blackpool, Alan Lochhead, Milton Keynes, Thomas Lochhead, Westbury, Thomas Lochhead Snr, Linwood, James Lochhhead, New Zealand, Brian Lochinver, Sutherland, Bush Lochinver, Sutherland, Dave Lochinver, Sutherland, Shaune Lochinver, Sutherland, Willie Lochinver, Sutherland, Martin Lochran, Coatbridge, Ped Lochran, Coatbridge, Craig Lockhart, Glasgow, Grant Lockhart, Dalkeith, Marc Lockhart, Dalkeith, Ross Lockhart, Simshill, Glasgow, Andrew Lockhead, Glasgow, Drew Lockhead, Glasgow, Kevin Lockhead, Glasgow, Andrew Logan, Cumbernauld, Andrew Logan, Cumbernauld, Chas Logan, Glasgow, Davie Logan, East Kilbride, Graham Logan, Cumbernauld, Ian Logan, Edimburgh, James Logan, Jason Logan, Glasgow, Jaye Logan, Glasgow, John Logan, Bishopbriggs, Lorraine Logan, Cumbernauld, Mew Logan, Glasgow, Susan Logan, Glasgow, Susan Logan, Glasgow, John Logue, East Kilbride, Anthony Lomax, Denny, Elroy London, Stirling, Gary Long, Bishopbriggs, Martyn Long, Dalry N-Ayrshire, Sara Lopes, Southampton, Lynn Lopez, Fort William, Stephen Lopez, Fort William, Caroline Loran, Coatbridge, Michelle Loran, Coatbridge, Jean Lou, Grangemouth, Adam Louden, Woodburn,Dalkeith, Darren Louden, Castlemilk, Grant,Andrew.Stephanie Louden, Woodburn ,Dalkeith, Maureen Louden, Woodburn,Dalkeith, Liam Loudon, Perth, Western Australia, Michael Lough, Glenrothes, Barry Loughlin, Port Glasgow, John Loughlin, Blackpool, John Loughlin, Coatbridge, Peter Loughlin, Port Glasgow, Ryan Loughlin, Port Glasgow, Billy Loughran, Glasgow, Darby Loughran, Glasgow, Jim Loughran, Irvine, Joan Loughran, Coatbridge, John Loughran, Dundee, Stephen Loughran, Whitecross, William Loughran, Glasgow, Michael Louty, Callander, Andy Love, Paisley, Derek Love, Livingston, George Love, Kilmarnock, Jean Love, Uddingston, Jordan Love, Kilmarnock, Mark Love, Bishopbriggs, Richard Love, Paisley, Stephen Love, Barcelona, Spain, William Love, Alloa, Owen Lovelock, Hamilton, Allan Loveman, Portland/Greenock, James Loveman, Portland/Greenock, Michael

Loverstone, Glasgow, Darren Loves Elaine, Clydebank, Jacqueline Low, Viewpark, Andy Lowe, Stirling, Andy Lowe, Fallin, John Lowe, Stirling, David Lowrie, Glasgow, Gordon Lowrie, Shettleston, Glasgow, Pat Lowrie, Balmore, John Lubanski, Glasgow, Graeme Luby, Cardonald, Emma Lucas, Johnstone, Marcello Luisi, Glasgow, Marcello Luisi, West Dunbartonshire, James Luke, Motherwell, John Luke, Motherwell, Chris Lumsden, Denny, Louise Lumsden, Falkirk, Steven Lumsden, Denny, Brian Lundie, Baillieston, Stephen Lundrigan, Hartlepool, Stephen Lunge, Glasgow, Jade Lurinsky, Barmulloch, Christopher Lusk, Ayr, Craig Lusk, Peebles, Liam Lusk, Alexandria, Michael Lusk, Alexandria, Owen Luton, Hawaii, David Lyall, Hawick, Alec Lyle, Barmulloch, Glasgow, Rab Lyle, Barmulloch, Glasgow, Robert Lyle, Barmulloch, Glasgow, Zooney Lyle, Barmulloch, Glasgow, Noreen Lynagh, Calton, Glasgow, Jim Lynas, Richmond, Surrey, Ali Lynch, Bedford, Bambi Lynch, Kingspark, Glasgow, Barry Lynch, Cambuslang, Caroline Lynch, Bathgate, Charles Lynch, Greenock, Chris Lynch, Port Glasgow Harp C.S.C., Colin Lynch, Glasgow, Donna Lynch, Paisley, Ed Lynch, Glasgow, Eddie Lynch, Port Glasgow C.S.C., Garry Lynch, Wishaw, Gerald Lynch, Bedford, Gillian Lynch, Greenock, Julie Lynch, Ruchill, Kate Lynch, Mossend, Kev Lynch, Airdrie, Kevin Lynch, Coatbridge, Kevin Lynch, Gorbals, Kieran Lynch, Croftfoot, Liam Lynch, Croftfoot, Liam Lynch, Glasgow, Liam Lynch, West Lothian, Liam Lynch, West Lothian, Mark Lynch, Mossend, Michael Arthur Lynch, Greenock, Mick Lynch, Govanhill, Mick Lynch, Ruchill, Niamh Lynch, West Lothian, Norman Joseph Lynch, Glasgow, Norrie Lynch, Kings Park, Glasgow, Oliver Lynch, , Paul Lynch, Bathgate, Paul Lynch, Croftfoot, Paul Lynch, , Paul (Zoke) Lynch, Milton, Glasgow, Peter Lynch, Bathgate, Phil Lynch, Ibrox, Sean Lynch, Bathgate, Stephen Lynch, Mossend, Tommy Lynch, Glasgow, Lynch, Bedford, Isaac & Josh Lyndsey, London, Marty Lynsey, Belfast, Edward Lyon, Milton, Glasgow, James (Tiger) Lyon, Milton, Glasgow, Johnny Lyon, Milton, Glasgow, Joseph Lyon, Milton, Glasgow, Martin Lyon, Milton, Glasgow, Stephen Lyon, Milton, Glasgow, Denis Lyons, Bishopbriggs, Eddie Lyons, Milton, Glasgow, Edward Lyons, East Kilbride, James Lyons, Milton, Glasgow, Jamie Lyons, Kincardine, John Lyons, Milton, Glasgow, Ruth Ann Lyons, Hamilton, Thomas Lyons, Coatbridge, Tony Lyons, Cumbernauld, Veronica Lyons, Bishopbriggs, Andy Lyttle, Reading, Steve Lyttle, Reading.

Denise M, Kilsyth. John M Edelsten, Kingspark, Arabella M Johnston, Ayr, Alison M Smith, Jersey, Channel Islands., Claire Mac, Tullibody, Jimmy Mac, Erskine, Kenny Mac, Tullibody, Kevin Mac, Donald, Alan Mac Donald, East Kilbride, John Mac Donald, London, Lynne Mac Donald, East Kilbride, Murdie Mac Dougall, Rutherglen, Martin Macafferty, Hamilton, Jospeh Macaleer, Glasgow, Kelly MacAleer, Royston, Mark MaCallister, Forest Hill, Mick Macallister, Inverness, Sean Macallister, Bangkok, Caitlin MacAngus, Tain, Conall MacAngus, Tain, Rab Macaree, Riddrie, Bethani Macari, Rosyth, Danielle Macari, Lochgelly, Dougie Macari, Rosyth, Greg Macari, Lochgelly, Fife, Martyn Macari, Lochgelly, Paul Macari, Lochgelly, Ralph Macari, Lochgelly, Ross Macari, Rosyth, William Macari, Lochgelly, Charlotte Macaulay, Glasgow, Colette Macaulay, Knightswood Glasgow, Garry Macaulay, Glasgow, James Macaulay, Rutherglen, Kieran Macaulay, Knightswood Glasgow, Robert Macaulay, Knightswood Glasgow, Sadie Macaulay, Lambhill Glasgow, Mark Macauley, Bellshill, Alex Macbain, East Kilbride, The Macbeans, Glasgow, Cathrine MacCaller, Glasgow, Joseph MacCaller, Glasgow, Neil MacCaskill, Inverness, Brian MacCormick, Irvine, Brian MacCormick, Irvine, Christine Maccormick, Fort William, Joan Maccormick, Fort William, John Paul Maccormick, Fort William, Shane Maccormick, Fort William, Duncan MacCrae, Isle of Benbecula, Alan MacCuish, Polmont, Alan Maccuish, Polmont, Alan Macdonald, Glasgow, Alisdair MacDonald, South Uist, Angus MacDonald, Fort William, Angus Macdonald, South Uist, Ashleigh Macdonald, Inverness, Bill Macdonald, Inverness, Bryan MacDonald, Fort William, Calum MacDonald, Johnstone, Cath Macdonald, Inverness, Cavey MacDonald, Isle of Benbecula, Chris Macdonald, Dumbarton, Craig MacDonald, Livingston, Craig MacDonald, Livingston, David Macdonald, Dumbarton, Di

205

Macdonald, Grangemouth, Drew Macdonald, Troon, Gary Macdonald, Dumbarton, Gary MacDonald, East Kilbride, Geraldine Macdonald, Dumbarton, Gillian MacDonald, Fort William, Gordon MacDonald, Johnstone, Hughena MacDonald, South Uist, Iain MacDonald, Stenhousemuir, Jamie MacDonald, , Jessie Ann MacDonald, South Uist, John Macdonald, London, Kevin Macdonald, Burntisland, Kimberley Macdonald, Plockton, Mackie MacDonald, Livingston, Malcolm Macdonald, Partick, Glasgow, Mark MacDonald, Perth, Niall MacDonald, Quarter, Oighrig MacDonald, South Uist, Paul MacDonald, Fort William, Sandy Macdonald, Kinlochleven, Stuart MacDonald, Argyll, Tony Macdonald, Coatbridge, Tony Macdonald, Kilmarnock, Sandy Macdonals, Amsterdam, Shirley Macdonlad, Inverness, Andrew MacDougall, South Uist, Bob Macdougall, Hereford, Richard MacDougall, Wick, Samantha MacDougall, Inverness, Murphy MacEachen, Western Isles, Innes Maceachen O.B.E., Oban, Alasdair Macfarlane, London, Karen MacFarlane, Motherwell, Stewart Macfarlane, Cowie, Drew Macfie, Blantyre, Johnny MacGowan, Cathcart, Calum MacGregor, Edinburgh, Calum MacGregor, Edinburgh, Casey MacGregor, Edinburgh, Darcy MacGregor, Edinburgh, Karlie MacGregor, Edinburgh, David MacInnes, Stoneybridge, South Uist, Dawn MacInnes, County Derry, Northern Ireland, Ewen MacInnes, Stoneybridge, South Uist, Iain MacInnes, Stoneybridge, South Uist, John Macinnes, Hyndland, Iain William Macintosh, Nairn, Ryan MacIntosh, Coatbridge, Steven MacIntosh, Coatbridge, Jim MacIntyre, Scammadale, Donald MacIsaac, South Uist, Donald MacIsaac, South Uist, Gary Macisaac, Kingussie, Iain MacIsaac, South Uist, John Macisaac, Ayr, Katie MacIsaac, South Uist, Mary Rose MacIsaac, South Uist, Mathew MacIsaac, South Uist, Rachele MacIsaac, South Uist, David MacIver, North Uist, Ewen Maciver, Inverurie, Moira MacIver, Inverness, Tony MacIver, Inverness, John Mack, Glasgow, Kevin Mack, , Lynzie Mack, Menstrie, Mary Mack, Pollok, Tom Mack, Menstrie, Angus Mackay, Foxbar, Paisley, Ania MacKay, Isle of Benbecula, Daniel Mackay, Bishopbriggs, David Mackay, Foxbar, Paisley, Donald MacKay, Inverasdale, Emily Mackay, Bishopbriggs, Gary MacKay, Inverasdale, Hughie MacKay, Isle of Benbecula, Jamie Mackay, Bishopbriggs, Jamie Mackay, Bishopbriggs, Joan MacKay, Inverasdale, John-Paul Mackay, Paisley, Leanne MacKay, Inverasdale, Mark Mackay, Foxbar, Paisley, Mark Mackay, Foxbar, Paisley, Mark Mackay, Inverness, Ruauaidh MacKay, South Uist, Steven MacKay, Inverasdale, John Mackeddie, North Lincolnshire, Adam MacKenzie, Dunkeld, Callum MacKenzie, , Connor MacKenzie, , Gillian Mackenzie, Blackpool, Jennifer Mackenzie, Fort Augustus, John Mackenzie, Blackpool, John Mackenzie, Shetland, Kenny Mackenzie, Australia, Kirsty Mackenzie, Blackpool, Maggie MacKenzie, , Megan MacKenzie, , Natalie Mackenzie, Blackpool, Oliver MacKenzie, Ayrshire, Scott MacKenzie, Cawdor, Alan Mackie, Port Glasgow, Drew Mackie, Kennoway Fife, John Mackie, Cumbernauld, Margaret Mackie, Cumbernauld, Robert Mackin, Glasgow, Alan MacKinnon, Parkway Bar, Ally MacKinnon, Blairdardie, Grahame MacKinnon, Isle of Benbecula, Jamie Mackinnon, Ayr, Josh Mackinnon, Ayr, Lubo MacKinnon, Roddy's House, Roddy Mackinnon, Cathcart, Ryan MacKinnon, Milton, Alan Mackintosh, Inverness, Angus Mackintosh, Glasgow, Doug Mackintosh, Aberdeen, Scott Mackintosh, Inverness, Paul Mackle, Kilsyth, Kyle Mackrell, Yoker, Mary MacLachan, Mosspark, Morgan MacLachan, Mosspark, Andy MacLean, Colinton, David Maclean, Isle of Mull, Richard Maclean, Paisley, Colin MacLellan, East Kilbride, Lally MacLellan, Loch Portain, Alistair (Sam) Macleod, Cardonald Glasgow, Darren Macleod, Dornoch, David Macleod, Prestonpans, Eddie MacLeod, Royston, Hazel Macleod, Largs, Iain Macleod, Edinburgh, John MacLeod, Belfast, John Macleod, Blairdardie, Kay Macleod, Largs, Kay Macleod, Largs Ayrshire, Martin MacLeod, Clydebank, Ross MacLeod, South Uist, Shona Macleod, Glasgow, Steven Macleod, Ayr, Steven Macleod, Lairg, David Maclugash, Wigan, Margaret MacManus, Stockport, Adam MacMaster, Largs, John MacMaster, Largs, John Macmaster, Largs, Ryan MacMaster, Largs, Siobhan MacMaster, Largs, Susan MacMaster, Largs, Susan Macmaster, Largs, Andrew John MacMillan, Isle of Benbecula, Anne MacMillan, Isle of Benbecula, Colin MacMillan, South Uist, David

206

Macmillan, West Lothian, Iain MacMillan, Isle of Benbecula, Iona MacMillan, South Uist, John Macmillan, St Albans, Johnpaul MacMillan, Govan, Kenny Macmillan, Glasgow, Millie MacMillan, Isle of Benbecula, Sandra MacMillan, South Uist, Stephen MacMillan, Govan, Ryan Macmurray, Hamilton, Swally MacNally, Greenwich, Andrew Macnamara, Carmunnock, Philip "Maxi" MacNamara, Motherwell, Donald Macneil, Stornoway, Emma MacNeil, Invergordon, Hughie Macneil, Isle of Barra, Siobhan MacNeil, Invergordon, Gerry Macormick, Southampton Hampshire, Andy Macphee, Northwood Middlesex, Norman Macphee, Dumbarton, Aonghas MacPherson, Isle of Benbecula, Donald MacPherson, Aberdeen, Jamie Macpherson, Aberdeen, Andrew MacQuarry, North Uist, John MacQueen, Perth, John Macrae, Inverness, John MacRae, Springburn, Johnny Macrae, Inverness, Stephen MacReadie, Partick, Margaret Maculay, Clydebank, Ian Macverish, Leamington Spa, Derek Macvicar, Edinburgh, Jimmy Macwilliams, Stevenston, Christopher Madden, Edinburgh, Davie Madden, Northamptonshire, Donna Madden, Patna, Elizabeth Madden, Gary Madden, Linwood, Geo Madden, Springburn, Glasgow, Jim Madden, Julie Madden, Patna, Robert Madden, Edinburgh, Robert Madden, Edinburgh, Greg Madin, Glasgow, James Madin, Govern, Teresa Madin, Glasgow, Noel Magaw, Belfast, Barry Magee, Drumchapel, Micky Magee, Belfast, Shaun Magee, Drumchapel, Michael Magennis, Belfast, Bunty Maghera, , Frogger Maghera, , Ratty Maghera, , Liam Magill, West Belfast, Chris Maguire, Cumbernauld, Dorothy Maguire, Cumbernauld, Drew Maguire, East Kilbride, Gerry Maguire, Paisley, Jaki Maguire, Uddingston, John Maguire, Bellshill, John Maguire, Sidcup, Kent, Joseph Maguire, Renfrew, Kirsty Maguire, Irvine, Liam Maguire, Belfast, Ireland, New Lodge, Liam Maguire, London, Madge Maguire, Penilee, Glasgow, Paul Maguire, Kirkintilloch, Peter Maguire, Bellshill, Shane Maguire, Swords, Dublin, Tony Maguire, Irvine, Jibz Mahmood, Cathcart, Jim Mahon, Co Kildare, Ireland, Danny Mahoney, London, Kieran Maiden, Rossshire, Brian Mailer, Garrowhill, Glasgow, Steven Mailer, Garrowhill, Glasgow, Paul Mailey, Dornoch, Andy Main, Grangemouth, Michael Main, Carrickstone, Cumbernauld, Willie Main, Inverness, Claire Maine, East Kilbride, George Mainland, Shetland, Angela Mains, Greenock, Shereen Mains, Greenock, Stacey Mains, Greenock, Wilma Mains, Greenock, Craig Mair, Glasgow, Jim Mair, Darnley, John Mair, Glasgow, Keith Mair, Airdrie, Linda Mair, Cleland, Scott Mair, Coatbridge, Taylor Mair, Shawlands, Mark Maither, Milton, Glasgow, Paul Maither, Milton, Glasgow, Annemarie Maitland, Uddingston, Derek Maitland, Uddingston, Gemma Maitland, Uddingston, Robyn Maitland, Uddingston, Paul Makernen, Ladyton Bonhill, Lesley Malarkey, Rutherglen, Liam Malarkey, Rutherglen, Mad Max Doogan Malarkey, Glasgow, Shug Malarkey, Glasgow, Jason Malcolm, London, Robert Malcolm, Glasgow, Darren Maley, Gartharmlock, Terry Maley, Hartlepool, Mark Malfray, Bannockburn, Phillipe Malfray, St Ninians, Colin Malin, Livingstone, Jim Mallan, York, Alexis Malley, St Ninians, Margaret Malley, , Paul Malley, Irvine, Paul &Fiona Malley, Dunblane, Charles Mallice, Falkirk, Mary Mallice, Falkirk, Michael Mallin, Leven, Ross Mallinson, Killin, Brian Mallon, Twechar, Jacqueline Mallon, Twechar, James Mallon, Glasgow, Joe Mallon, Uphall, John Mallon, Morecambe, John Mallon, Morecambe, Kerry Mallon, Glasgow, Lisa Mallon, Glasgow, SarahAnne Mallon, Twechar, Stephen Mallon, Belfast, Danni Malloy, Blantyre, Tim Malloy, Penilee, Barry Malone, Castlemilk, Glasgow, Barry Malone, Spittal, Glasgow, Barry Malone, Spittal, Glasgow, James Malone, Clydebank, Jeremiah Malone, Greenock, Joe Malone, Clydebank, John Malone, Castlemilk, Glasgow, John-Paul Malone, Greenock, Kevin Malone, Castlemilk, Glasgow, Kevin Malone, Castlemilk, Glasgow, Larry Malone, Clydebank, Lisa Malone, Glasgow, Michael Malone, Greenock, Paul Malone, Greenock, Ronnie Malone, Greenock, Sean Malone, Castlemilk, Glasgow, Sean Malone, Greenock, Steven Malone, Clydebank, Thomas Malone, Castlemilk, Glasgow, Thomas Malone, Dumfries, William Malone, Glasgow, James Maloney, Rutherglen, Margaret Maloy, , Peter Maloy, Caldercruix, Danny Mancini, Grangemouth, Mick Mangan, Alloa, Claire Mann, Bo'Ness, Jock Mann, Forres, Tommy Mann, Bo'Ness, Ellen Mannion, Crook, Devon, Marie Mannion, Fae,

Motherwell, Tam Mannion, Denny, Charlie Manson, Broxburn, Jaffa Manson, Thurso, Fiona March, Pitenween, Fife, Elizabeth Marchetti, Toronto Canada, William Marenghi, Edinburgh, Chris Markie, Bristol, Adele Marley, Glasgow, Andrew Marley, Glasgow, Tricia Marley, Glasgow, Jim Marnell, North Queensferry, Andrew Marner, Turiff, Aberdeenshire, Matt Marner, Greenock, Patrick Marner, Greenock, Joe Marr, Clydebank, Michelle Marr, Tullibody, Robert Marr, Tullibody, Karon Marrow-Clews, Carfin, David Michael Marsh, East Kilbride, Adam Marshall, Coatbridge, Adam Robert Marshall, Coatbridge, Alan Marshall, Motherwell, Bob Marshall, Blackford, Claire Marshall, Coatbridge, Claire & Adam Marshall, Coatbridge, Colin Marshall, Perth, Craig Marshall, Glasgow, Dino Marshall, Bathgate, Graeme Marshall, Lennoxtown, Greig Marshall, Cowdenbeath, James Marshall, Avonbridge, Jonathan Marshall, Cumbernauld, Josh Marshall, Stepps, Kenny Marshall, Stepps, Martin Marshall, Basra, Iraq, Robert Marshall, Louden Tavern Glasgow, Tam & Helen Marshall, Coatbridge, William Marshall, Castlemilk, Kerry Marshel, Motherwell, Gary Marshell, Glasgow, Alex Martin, Hamiltonhill, Glasgow, Alex Martin, Hamiltonhill, Glasgow, Andy Martin, East Kilbride, Baz Martin, Denny, Stirlingshire, Billy Martin, St Andrews, Billy Martin, St Andrews, Colin Martin, Rochester, Danny Martin, Glasgow, David Martin, Glasgow, Derek Martin, Stamperland, Edward Martin, Livingston, Frank Martin, Glasgow, Gina Martin, Glasgow, Hayley Martin, , Ian Martin, Bannockburn, Ian Martin, Glasgow, Irene Martin, Falkirk, Jack Martin, Kingspark, James Martin, Glasgow, James Martin, Mary Hill, Jamie Martin, Airdrie, Joanne Martin, Drumchapel, John Martin, Glasgow, John Martin, Mary Hill, John Paul Martin, Dundee, John Paul Martin, Dundee, June Martin, Coatbridge, Kenny Martin, St Andrews, Liam Martin, Bognor Regis, West Sussex, Norman Martin, Inverness, Pat Martin, Coatbridge, Paul Martin, Arden, Paul Martin, Glasgow, Paul Martin, St Andrews, Paul Martin, St Andrews, Paul Martin, , Peter Martin, Ballifeary, Philip Martin, , Rab Martin, Ayr, Rab Martin, McVicar Printers, Ryan Martin, Glasgow, Sandy Martin, Sidcup, Stacey Martin, Motherwell, Stephen Martin, Coatbridge, Steve Martin, St Andrews, Steven Martin, London, Steven Martin, St Andrews, Susan Martin, Teresa Martin, Dumbarton, William Martin, Ayr, William Martin, Glasgow, Gary Marzella, Johnstone, Michael Marzella, Motherwell, Andrew Mason, Edenbridge, Kent, Jim Mason,Edenbridge, Kent, Matthew Massey, Bonnyrigg, Simon Massey, Palma de Mallorca, Anne Masterson, Glasgow, Raymond Masterson, Bannockburn, Stirling, Stewart Mathers, Balornock, Glasgow, Andrew Matherson, Stockbridge, Claire Matheson, Kincorth, Aberdeen, Daniel Matheson, Carrbridge, Inverness-Shire, Daniel Matheson, Carrbridge, Inverness-Shire, Isobel Matheson, Milngavie, Colin Mathieson, St Ninians, Donny Mathieson, Glasgow, Stephanie Mathieson, Easthall, Glasgow, Matty Matonti, Mid Calder, James Mattear, Ruchill, Glasgow, John Matthew, Edinburgh, John Matthew, Edinburgh, Debbie Matthews, Southsea, William Matton, , Chris Maughan, Giffnock, Stephen Maughan, Giffnock, Stephanie Maule, Spain, Michael Maun, Greenock, Mark Mavers, East Kilbride, Danny Maxell, Hamilton, Anthony Maxwell, Glasgow, Bobby Maxwell, Possilpark, Glasgow, Charlie Maxwell, Bannockburn, Darren Maxwell, Castle Douglas, James Maxwell, Clydebank, John Maxwell, Greenock, Kevin Maxwell, Clydebank, Kevin Maxwell, Greenock, Kevin Maxwell, Greenock, Paul Maxwell, Southsea, Philip Maxwell, Barrhead, Robert Maxwell, Possilpark, Glasgow, Steven Maxwell, Bellshill, William Maxwell, Clydebank, Gav C Maybole, , Jamie Mayes, Grafton, Jamie Mayes, Granton, Thomas Maze, Glasgow, Marc Mazzucco, Bearsden, Gerry Mc Auley, Brent Bravo, Louise Mc Avoy, Belfast, Paul Mc Breardy, Glasgow, Catherine Mc Bride, Ibrox, Joe Mc Bride, Coatbridge., Lorraine Mc Bride, Coatbridge, Mary Mc Bride, Govan, Mick McBride, Ibrox, Mick McBride, Ibrox, Paul McBride, Coatbridge, Sean McBride, Ibrox, Shannon Mc Bride, Coatbridge, Zoe McBride, Ibrox, Andrew Mc Cabe, Chapelhall, Bernadette Mc Cabe, Chapelhall, Ross McCabe, Chapelhall, Tom McCabe, Chapelhall, Paul McCaffery, Church Street/Glasgow, Steve McCall, Aberdeen, Gerald McCann, Carntyne. Glasgow, Paul McCann, Glasgow, Stevie McCarthy, Barrhead Glasgow, Mick McCarthy, Barrhead Glasgow, Stevie McCarthy

Jnr, Barrhead Glasgow, Liam McCormack, Blantyre.Glasgow, Kevin Mc Culloch, Glasgow, Kenneth McDaid, East Kilbride, Gerry McDonald, Burnbank ,Hamilton., Brian McLaughlin & Kevin McEvey, Scarborough C S C, Colin McEwan, Brent Bravo, Eddie Maureen And Edward Jnr McEwan, Pollok Glasgow, Amy Mc Fadden, Falkirk, Patrick McFadden, Dunfanaghy, Tony McFadden, Falkirk, Stephen McGill, Coatbridge, Dan M Gowan, Clydebank,Thomas Mc Gregor, Cambuslang, Gerry Mc Guire, Cambuslang, John McHenry, Ballycastle Co.Antrim, Wullie McIlear, Brent Bravo, Franny McKee, Brent Bravo, Michael McKeown, Manchester, Jean McKinney, Craigend, Kathleen McKinney, Glasgow, Jama McLaughlin, Coatbridge, Daniel McMaster, Oban Argyll, Harry McMaster, Oban Argyll, Jennie M Master, Oban Argyll, Leanne McMaster, Oban Argyll, Eileen McTeague, Helensburgh, James Joseph McTeague, Garelochhead, Michael McTeague, Ferryhill, Co Durham, Patrick McTeague, Weymouth, Dorset, Peter Joseph McTeague, Weymouth, Dorset, Ross Patrick McTeague, Weymouth, Dorset, James McTeague Snr, Helensburgh, John McAbe, Kent, John(Big Scooby) McCabe, Turf Lodge Belfast, Roshin McAbe, Kent, Caddie & Molly McAdam, Dennistoun, Frances McAdam, E/K, Gerry McAdam, Kirkintilloch, Jamie Mcadam, Dennistoun, John McAdam, Dennistoun, Kenny McAdam, Bonhill, Lee McAdam, Coatbridge, Lynne McAdam, East Kilbride, Stephen McAdam, Kirkintilloch, Ciaran McAlary, Kilrea, South Derry, NI , Paul McAleavey, Lomond Drive, Wishaw, Paul McAleavey, Lomond Drive, Wishaw, Paul McAleavey, Lomond Drive, Wishaw, Ml2, Paul McAleavey, Lomond Drive, Wishaw, Ml2, Gary McAleavy, Wishaw, Andrew McAleer, Erskine, PJ McAleer, Omagh, N Ireland, Tommy McAleer, Glasgow, Harry McAleese, Coatbridge, Paul McAleese, Coleraine, N. Ireland, Charlie McAlinden, Durham Celtic Ontario Canada, Kenny McAlindon, Perth, Christopher Mcalister, Clydebank, Russell McAllister, Drumchapel, Aidan McAllister, Wishaw, Allan McAllister, Aberdeen, Andrew McAllister, Greenock, Andrew McAllister, Greenock, Andrew McAllister, Greenock, Andrew Mcallister, Greenock, Annabella McAllister, Mosstodloch by Elgin, Billy McAllister, Greenock, Billy McAllister, Greenock, Billy McAllister, Greenock, Billy McAllister, Greenock, Cameron McAllister, Wishaw, Charlie Mcallister, Lanark, Christopher Mcalister, Aberdeen, Danny McAllister, Greenock, Danny McAllister, Greenock, Danny McAllister, Greenock, Dave McAllister, Dundonald Inn, Ayrshire, Gary Mcallister, Aberdeen, Gemma Mcallister, Milton Of Campsie, Gordan McAllister, Workington, Greg McAllister, Paisley, Ian McAllister, James McAllister, Elgin, James McAllister, Glasgow, Lorraine McAllister, Irvine, Mark Mcallister, Formerly Inverness Now London, Martin McAllister, Girvan, Paul Mcallister, Aberdeen, Paul McAllister, Aberdeen, Rab Mcallister, Drumchapel, Sean McAllister, Girvan, Shay McAllister, Hamilton, Stephen McAllister, Workington, Theresa McAllister, Port Glasgow, Tony Mcallister, Aberdeen, Tony McAllister, Greenock, Tony McAllister, Greenock, Tony McAllister, Greenock, Ainsley McAllum, Braehead, Bonhill, Michaella McAllum, Braehead, Bonhill, Christopher McAloon, Wishaw, Donna McAloon, Wishaw, Gerald McAloon, Manchester, James McAloon, Knightswood, James McAloon, Wishaw, Jim McAloon, Knightswood, Zara McAloon, Wishaw, Abbie McAlpine, Motherwell, Cloe McAlpine, Motherwell, Martin McAndrew, Leven, Richard McAndrew, Glasgow, Tomas McAndrew, Glasgow, Derek McAnenay, Norfolk, Colin McArdle, Lanark, Cynthia McArdle, Eastleigh, Edward McArdle, New Stevenston, Elizabeth McArdle, Glenrothes, John McArdle, Hamilton, Liz McArdle, New Stevenston, Martin McArdle, Glenrothes, Michelle McArdle, Glenrothes, Paul McArdle, Hamilton, Phil McArdle, Hamilton, Sharon McArdle, Hamilton, Tam McArdle, Hamilton, Martin McArdle Jnr, Glenrothes, Andrew McArthur, Auchtermuchty, Craig McArthur, Kirkintilloch, Kevin McArthur, Alexandria, Kevin Paul McArthur, Dumbarton, Tosh Mcarthy, Boghall, Brian McAtamney, Ayrshire, Anthony McAtear, Dumbarton, Frank McAtear, Dumbarton, Melissa McAtee, Kilmarnock, Sean McAtee, Denny, Ann McAteer, Kilcock, Co Kildare, Anne Marie McAteer, Gravesend, Kent,Francis McAteer, Kinross, Gerry McAteer, Falkirk, Jon McAteer, Kilcock, Co Kildare. Mandy McAuley, Seville, Brian McAuley, Edinburgh, Christopher McAuley, Ballycastle,

Daniel McAuley, Anderston, Glasgow, Daniel McAuley, Glasgow, Dave McAuley, Gorbals, Debbie McAuley, Motherwell, Emma McAuley, Motherwell, Gary McAuley, Belfast, Ireland, Gerry McAuley, Greenock, Gillian McAuley, Motherwell, Hugh McAuley, Anderston, Glasgow, Hugh McAuley, Glasgow, James Mcauley, Bellshill, Jamie Mcauley, Linwood, John McAuley, Bellshill, John McAuley, Co. Antrim, John McAuley, Motherwell, John m McAuley, Govan, Kathleen McAuley, Glasgow, Kathleen McAuley, Glasgow, Keith McAuley, Larkhall, Liz McAuley, Larkhall, Liz McAuley, Larkhall, Liz McAuley, Stirling, Mairead McAuley, Co. Antrim, Marc Mcauley, Blantyre, Marion McAuley, Anderston, Glasgow, Marion McAuley, Glasgow, Megan McAuley, Motherwell, Mick McAuley, Coatbridge, Paul Mcauley, Blantyre, Paul McAuley, Blantyre, Reagan McAuley, Motherwell, Rosalyn McAuley, Charing Cross, Glasgow, Rosalyn McAuley, Glasgow, Ross McAuley, Clydebank, Scott McAuley, Clydebank, Scott McAuley, Edinburgh, Sean McAuley, Edinburgh, Terry McAuley, Seville, Wullie Mcauley, Paisley, Keith Mcauley, Larkhall, Brian Mcauley Jnr, Kirkintilloch, Brian McAuley Snr, Edinburgh, Brian Mcauley Snr, Kirkintilloch, Brian McAvoy, Rutherglen, Carol McAvoy, Wishaw, Catherine McAvoy, Rutherglen, Charles McAvoy, Newmains, Claire Mcavoy, Rutherglen, Eddie McAvoy, Rutherglen, Edward Mcavoy, Rutherglen, James McAvoy, The Thorn, Johnstone, Jamie McAvoy, London, Niomi McAvoy, Newmains, Rowena McAvoy, Newmains, Tam McAvoy, Parkhead, Thomas McAvoy, Priesthill, Marian McBaide, Glasgow, Brian McBain, East Kilbride, Mick McBain, Renfrew, Andrew McBrearty, Musselburgh, Adam McBride, Glasgow, Andy McBride, Falkirk, Daniel McBride, Shawlands, Glasgow, Edward McBride, Old Kilpatrick, Edward McBride, Old Kilpatrick, Gary McBride, Greenock, Gerald McBride, Plumbridge, James McBride, Glasgow, James McBride, Mary Hill, Jamie McBride, Paisley, Jerrad McBride, Wishaw, John McBride, , Kenny McBride, Falkirk, Kenny McBride, Falkirk, Mark McBride, Gartcosh, Mary McBride, Blantyre, Mary McBride, Govan, Maureen McBride, Glasgow, Michael McBride, Muirend, Mick McBride, Ibrox, Mikey McBride, Saltcoats, Neil McBride, Snr Waterside, Paddy McBride, Old Kilpatrick, Paul McBride, Saltcoats, Robert Mcbride, Hamilton, Scott McBride, Barrhead, Shannon McBride, Old Kilpatrick, Simon McBride, Rome, Stephen McBride, Falkirk, Stephen McBride, Glasgow, Stevie McBride, Falkirk, Teresa McBride, Old Kilpatrick, Tony McBride, Coatbridge, Vinny McBride, Blantyre, Vinny McBride, Willie McBride, Bowmanville, Canada, Colin McBurnie, Dumfries, Hazel McBurnie, Uphall, Ian McBurnie, Uphall, Samantha McBurnie, Uphall, Stuart McBurnie, Uphall, Angela McCabb, Edinburgh, Clare McCabe, Leighton Buzzard, Darryl McCabe, Glasgow, David McCabe, Hamilton, Davie McCabe, Irvine, Eddie McCabe, Croftfoot, Eimear McCabe, Belfast, Emma McCabe, Millerston, Glasgow, George Mccabe, Robroyston, Gerry McCabe, Milngavie, James McCabe, Millerston, Glasgow, John McCabe, Belfast, John McCabe, Dumfries, John McCabe, Duntocher, John McCabe, Glasgow, Joseph McCabe, Isle Of Bute, Kevin Mccabe, Robroyston, Liam McCabe, Glasgow, Martin Mccabe, Barrhead, Micheal McCabe, Hamilton, Mick McCabe, Eddlewood, Nicholas McCabe, Millerston, Paul McCabe, Bathgate, Peter McCabe, Prestonpans, Rab McCabe, Hamilton, Ross McCabe, Glasgow, Vicky McCabe, Parkhead, Glasgow, Dorothy McCabe, Glasgow, Thomas McCabe Snr, Glasgow, Alan McCafferty, Alexandria, Anna McCafferty, Hamilton, Anthony McCafferty, Welling, Barry McCafferty, Wishaw, Bernard McCafferty, Denny, Blair McCafferty, Dunblane, Bobo Lenni Lubo McCafferty, Hawksland, Brigette McCafferty, Glasgow, Chris McCafferty, Kirkintilloch, Chris McCafferty, Kirkintilloch, Chris McCafferty, Lanark, Craig Mccafferty, Kent, Daniel McCafferty, Hamilton, Davey McCafferty, Parkhead, Dennis McCafferty, Glasgow, Frank McCafferty, Canada, Frank McCafferty, Canada, Frank McCafferty, Denny, Gerard McCafferty, Denny, Grace McCafferty, Denny, James McCafferty, Denny, Jamie McCafferty, Fankerton, John McCafferty, Canada, John McCafferty, Fankerton, John McCafferty, Hamilton, Joseph McCafferty, Glasgow, Kevin McCafferty, Denny, Kevin McCafferty, Rutherglen, Martin Mccafferty, Nassau, Bahamas, Martin McCafferty, Rutherglen, Michael McCafferty, Cumbernauld, Paul McCafferty,

Glasgow, Paul McCafferty, Tollcross, Richie McCafferty, Greenock, Roddie McCafferty, Fife, Stephan McCafferty, Dumbarton, Thomas McCafferty, Glasgow, Tracy McCafferty, Glasgow, Eddie & Frances Mccaffery, Kirkintilloch/Glasgow, Charlie McCaffrey, Seville, Ged McCaffrey, Seville, Laurie McCaffrey, Lago,Cosenza,Italy87035, Louis McCaffrey, Holyrood High, Michael McCaffrey, Auchinairn, Glasgow, George McCahill, Port Glasgow, Joseph McCahill, Port Glasgow, Lynda H McCahill, Port Glasgow, Gary McCaig, Baillieston, Glasgow, Collette McCairn, Wishaw, Michael McCairn, Port Glasgow, Michelle McCairn, Port Glasgow, Lynne McCaldon, Motherwell, Chantell McCalin, Glasgow, Colin McCall, Glasgow, David McCall, Mosspark, John McCall, Castlemilk, Tracey McCall, Glasgow, Daniel McCallion, Glasgow, Teresa McCallon McCallion, Fraserburgh, Andrew McCallister, Dumbarton, Andrew Mccallum, Greenock, Gary McCallum, Glasgow, John McCallum, Helensburgh, John McCallum, Streatham Hill, Jordan McCallum, Carfin, Liam McCallum, Hamilton, Paul McCallum, East Kilbride, Ross McCallum, Hamilton, Ryan McCallum, Helensburgh, Sab McCallum, Bonhill, Sarah McCallum, Netherlee, Glasgow, Sarah McCallum, Netherlee, Glasgow, Scott McCallum, Glasgow, Tony McCallum, Paisley, McCallym, Edinburgh, Jason McCamley, Largs, Joe McCamley, Glasgow, Martin McCamley, Glasgow, Annie McCandlish, Isle of Benbecula, Katie McCandlish, Isle of Benbecula, Kelley McCandlish, Irvine, Maria McCandlish, Isle of Benbecula, Oighrig McCandlish, Isle of Benbecula, Alan McCann, Linlithgow, Alan McCann, Linlithgow, Andrew 'Sticky' McCann, East Kilbride, Andrew 'Sticky' McCann, East Kilbride, Andy McCann, Bishopbriggs, Glasgow, Anne McCann, Barrhead, Anne McCann, Glasgow, Annie McCann, Carrickhill Belfast, Bobby McCann, Glasgow, Christopher McCann, Hamilton, Clare McCann, Ripon, Craig Mccann, Tollcross, Debbie McCann, Glasgow, Eddie McCann, Glasgow, Ella McCann, Ripon, Evan McCann, Glasgow, Frank McCann, Stirling, Gerald & Cheryl McCann, Carntyne, Glasgow, Geraldine McCann, Derryadd, N Ireland, Gordon Mccann, Falkirk, Gordon McCann, Glasgow, Graeme McCann, Hamilton, Hugh McCann, Linlithgow, Iain McCann, Richmond, Jacqui McCann, Glasgow, James McCann, Glasgow, Jennifer McCann, Hamilton, John McCann, Catterick, North Yorkshire, John McCann, Dunfermline, Jordan Mccann, Glasgow Green, Jordan McCann, Stewartfield, East Kilbride, Kieren McCann, Armdale, Liam McCann, Bathgate, Lisa McCann, Dunfermline, Margaret McCann, Catterick, North Yorkshire, Mark McCann, Dumbarton, Martin McCann, Cardonald, Melanie McCann, Motherwell, Michael McCann, Glasgow, Michael McCann, Ripon, Michael McCann, Stewartfield, East Kilbride, Nick McCann, Carrick Knowe, Edinburgh, Paul McCann, Glasgow, Paul McCann, Glasgow, Peter McCann, Springboig, Robert McCann, Glasgow , Springburn, Rona McCann, Lanarkshire, Scotland, Scott McCann, Hamilton, Scott McCann, Larkhall, Shaun McCann, , Sinead McCann, Glasgow, Stephen McCann, Bathgate, Stephen Mccann, Bathgate, Stephen Mccann, Mcallen,Texas, Usa (Originally Paisley), Stephen McCann, Texas, Steven McCann, Glasgow, Tam McCann, Sigthill, Glasgow, Thomas McCann, Baillieston, Tony McCann, Bathgate, Tony Mccann, Bathgate, Vince McCann, Armdale, Vinnie Mccann, Netherlands, Wee Bru McCann, Ardrossan, Willy McCann, Hillhead, Glasgow, Craig McCarney, Bishopbriggs, Frank McCarnock, Coatbridge, Jamie McCarnock, Renton, John McCarrall, Cumbernauld, Kaye McCarrall, Cumbernauld, Liam McCarrall, Cumbernauld, William McCarrall, Cumbernauld, Alice McCarroll, Peterborough, Coco McCarroll, Hamilton, Daniel McCarroll, Peterborough, Alex McCarron, Seville, Brian McCarron, Milngavie, Brian McCarron, Milngavie, Chris McCarron, Milngavie, Chris McCarron, Milngavie, Eleanor McCarron, Motherwell, James McCarron, Uttoxeter, Staffs, James Paul McCarron, Motherwell, Michael McCarron, Uttoxeter, Staffs, Mick McCarron, Uttoxeter, Staffs, Stephen McCarron, Robroyston, Connor McCarry, Glasgow, John McCartan, N.Belfast, Maureen McCartan, N. Belfast, AGG McCarthy, Springboig, Amber McCarthy, Falkirk, Christina McCarthy, Glasgow, Danny McCarthy, Wishaw, Ian McCarthy, Partick, Janet Mccarthy, Maryhill,Glasgow, John McCarthy, Glasgow, Michael McCarthy, Falkirk, Nick McCarthy, London, Candy Mccartney, Gorbals, Glasgow, Christopher

McCartney, Ayrshire, Colin Mccartney, Cumbernauld Scotland, Darryn McCartney, Govan, Davie Mccartney, Gorbals, Glasgow, Joker McCartney, Barrhead, Paul Mccartney, Gorbals Glasgow, Scott McCartney, Clackmannanshire, Scott McCartney, Edinburgh, Stephen McCartney, Glasgow, Teresa Mccartney, Gorbals, Glasgow, Matthew McCartney Jnr, Cambuslang, Glasgow, Matthew McCartney Snr, Gorbals, Glasgow, Ross McCather, , Dominick Mccauley, West Calder, Gerry McCauley, Irvine, Lenny McCauley, Falkirk, Declan McCausland, Mosspark, John McCausland, Mosspark, Martin McCausland, Cushendall, Co Antrim, Sean McCausland, Mosspark, David McCay, Derry City, Damian Mcccourt, Irvine, Jason McCebb, Eastbourne, Stephen McCerman, Saltcoats, Billy McCernan, Glasgow, Stuart McCewan, Kilwinning, Alec McCib, , Paul McCinn, Glasgow, Brian McCivery, Glasgow, Kevin McClae, Kings Park, Ryan McClae, Kings Park, Steven McClafferty, Glasgow, Hugh McClaide, Kelty, Craig McClaire, Grangemouth, Stewart McClaire, Grangemouth, Callum McClane, Helensburgh, Charles McClann, Glasgow, McClare, Motherwell, Frank McClaren, Hailsham, George McClay, Rotherham, Joe McClay, Kings Park, M McClay, Kings Park, Raymond McCleans, Glasgow, Liz McClear, Motherwell, Joe McClearly, Dumbarton, Doreen McCleary, Irvine, Jim McCleary, Irvine, Kenny McCleary, Irvine, Andrew McCleland, Glasgow, Craig McClelland, David McClelland, David McClement, Bearsden, William McClinn, Glasgow, Andy McClintock, Crewe, Chris McClintock, Crewe, Lorraine McClintock, Crewe, Paul McClintock, Milton, Glasgow, Liam McClorey, Ilford, London, Mick McClorey, Ilford, London, Ryan McClorey, Folkestone, Alan McCloskey, Edinburgh, Bill McCloskey, Lochwinnoch, Bill McCloskey, Lochwinnoch, Chic McCloskey, Kilmarnock, Kevin McCloskey, Jersey, Kevin McCloskey, Kilmarnock, Fiona McCloud, Prestonpans, Kerry-Ann McCloy, Stenhousemuir, Paul McClung, Stirling, Jamie McClure, Ayr, Barry McClurg, Banknock, Joseph McClury, Knightswood, Andrew McCluskey, Larkhall, Annmarie McCluskey, Isle of Man, Carragh McCluskey, Glasgow, Claire McCluskey, Glasgow, Jamie McCluskey, Uddingston, Jodie McCluskey, Larkhall, Joseph McCluskey, Ballymena, Joseph McCluskey, Springburn, Margaret McCluskey, Glasgow, Mark Mccluskey, Larkhall, Martin McCluskey, Falkirk, Muir McCluskey, Glasgow, Paul McCluskey, Crieff, Robert McCluskey, Glasgow, Theresa McCluskey, Berwick-upon-Tweed, Tony McCluskey, Dartford, Tricia McCluskey, Glasgow, Anne McClymont, Port Glasgow, Michael McCoach, Australia, Alan McCole, Cumbernauld, Connor McCole, County Donegal, Connor McCole, Glasgow, Eileen McCole, County Donegal, Eoghan McCole, County Donegal, Mark McCole, Cumbernauld, Michael McCole, County Donegal, Neil McCole, Dumfries, Neil McCole, Greenock, Ryan McCole, Dumfries, Claire McColl, Coatbridge, James McColl, Milngavie, Rab McColl, Pollok, Allan McColm, Edinburgh, Colin McColm, Thurso, Paul McColm, Stevenage, Marie Mccomb, Ayr, Shaun McCombe, Dumfries, Stevie McComiskie, Methil, Stevie McComiskie, Methill, Mary McConalouge, Pollok, Michael McConnall, Glasgow, Jim McConnell, Cumnock, Lisa McConnell, Coatbridge, Lorna Mcconnell, Royston, Paula McConnell, Blantyre, Paula McConnell, Blantyre, Thomas McConner, Manchester, Aisling McConville, Belfast, Aisling McConville, Belfast, Ciaran McConville, Belfast, Ciaran McConville, Belfast, Declan McConville, Belfast, Declan McConville, Belfast, Gerard McConville, Belfast, Gerard McConville, Belfast, James McConville, Kingspark, Jim McConville, Wishaw, Laurence McConville, Kingspark, Mairead McConville, Belfast, Mairead McConville, Belfast, Michael McConville, Belfast, Michael McConville, Belfast, Brian McCooey, Coatbridge, Damien McCool, Dumbarton, Jake McCool, Motherwell, Caroline McCord, Glasgow, Steven McCord, Livingston, Thomas McCord, Clydebank, Andrew McCormack, Johnstone, Bobby McCormack, East Killbride, Caroline McCormack, Glenrothes, Fife, Charlie McCormack, Fife, Christopher McCormack, Glasgow, Conor McCormack, Cowdenbeath, Fife, Daniel McCormack, Glenrothes, Fife, Danny McCormack, Glenrothes, Fife, Daryne McCormack, Glenrothes, Fife, Declin McCormack, Kelty, Eddie McCormack, Fife, Eddie McCormack, Glasgow, Frank McCormack, , Gary McCormack, , Gary McCormack, Liverpool, Helen McCormack, T.T.

Blackburn, Irene McCormack, Glenrothes, Fife, Ish McCormack, Kelty, James McCormack, Cowdenbeath, Fife, James McCormack, Glenrothes, Fife, Jim McCormack, Girvan, Joe McCormack, Glenrothes, Fife, John McCormack, Glasgow, John McCormack, Milton, Glasgow, Kevin McCormack, Glasgow, Kevin McCormack, Glenrothes, Fife, Liam McCormack, Blantyre.Glasgow, Michael McCormack, Aberdeenshire, Nancy McCormack, East Killbride, Paul McCormack, , Sarah McCormack, Glenrothes, Fife, Sean McCormack, Airdrie, Sonia McCormack, Glenrothes, Fife, Spanky McCormack, Glasgow, Steven McCormack, Fife, Amanda McCormick, Mossend, Brian McCormick, Falkirk, Christopher McCormick, Glasgow, Gary McCormick, Paisley, Jim McCormick, Cumbernauld, Jimmy McCormick, Renfrew, Glasgow, Kevin McCormick, Wishaw, Kevin McCormick, Marika McCormick, Mossend, Mary Francis McCormick, Glasgow, Pat McCormick, Mossend, William Mccormick, Greenock, John McCormick Jnr, Paisley, John McCormick Snr, Paisley, Jackie Mccorry, Melbourne Australia, Damien McCourt, Irvine, Kieran McCourt, Irvine, Kieran Mccourt, Irvine, Lizzie Mccourt, Barlanark, Tony McCourt, Jervi, Bill McCowie, Erskine, Erin McCowie, Erskine, Liam McCowie, Erskine, Ryan McCowie, Erskine, Gary McCoy, Kilbirnie, Gary McCoy, Kilbirnie, Jon,June, Iain and Hana McCracken, Glasgow, Laurie McCracken, Paisley, Steven McCracken, Glasgow, William McCracken, Glasgow, Aiden McCrae, Condorrat, Alex McCrae, Highlander Pub, Paderborn, Germany, Calum McCrae, Stornoway, Colin McCrae, Highlander Pub, Paderborn, Germany, Agnes Mccready, Townhead, Coatbridge, Aileen And William Mccready, Bellshill, Connie Mccready, Dundyvan, Coatbridge, Gerry McCready, Wishaw, Hamilton And Aileen Mccready, Townhead, Coatbridge, Hugh And Agnes McCready, Bothwell, James McCready, Seville, John McCready, Wishaw, Kevin McCready, Wishaw, Liz, Jamie And Barry McCready, Glenboig, Mark And Korey McCready, Bellshill, Rab McCready, Wishaw, Sean McCready, Wishaw, Shannon Mccready, Dundyvan, Coatbridge, Tony McCrear, Cadder, John McCrickett, London, Ann-Marie McCrimmond, Glasgow, Paul McCroary, Sydney , Australia, Arlene McCrone, Armagh, Bobbie McCrone, Govan, Glasgow, Chloe McCrone, Govan, Courtney McCrone, Govan, Danny McCrone, Govan, Joe McCrone, Govan, Kelly Mccrone, Easterhouse, Kevin Mccrone, Easterhouse, Kevin Mccrone, Swinton, Martin McCrone, Govan, Mick McCrone, Govan, Peter McCrone, Crookston, Glasgow, Peter Mccrone, Crookston, Taylor Mccrone, Crookston, Caitlin McCrorie, Eaglesham, Catherine McCrorie, Eaglesham, Elise McCrorie, Eaglesham, Mark McCrorie, Eaglesham, Steven Mccrory, Cumbernauld, Damian Mccrossan, Motherwell, Thomas McCrossan, Clydebank, John McCrystal, Johnstone, Sarah McCrystal, Leven, Bill Mccue, Baillieston, Billy Mccue, Springhill, Connor Mccue, Glasgow, Connor McCue, Milton Keynes, Jacqueline Mccue, Glasgow, Joe McCue, Glasgow, Mark Mccue, Shotts, Michael McCue, Dunlop, Ayrshire, Patrick Mccue, Glasgow, Paul McCue, Eastbourne, Scott McCue, Edinburgh, Stuart Mccue, Uddingston, Fiona McCuish, Argyllshire, John McCullack, Livingston, Bobby McCullagh, Carnwadric, Johnboy McCullagh, Aidan McCullar, Port Glasgow, Andy Mcculloch, Baillieston, Andy McCulloch, Ratho, Bob McCulloch, Whitburn, Brian McCulloch, Kirkolm, Cheryl McCulloch, Cora McCulloch, Whitburn, George McCulloch, Glasgow, Helen Margaret McCulloch, Cadder, Glasgow, James Paul Aloysius Mcculloch, Langside, Glasgow, John McCulloch, Clydebank, Kev McCulloch, Hamilton, Kieran Paul McCulloch, Dumfries, Mary Magdala McCulloch, Cadder, Glasgow, Paul Mcculloch, Shawlands, Glasgow, Paul Richard McCulloch, Cadder, Glasgow, Pauline McCulloch, Whitburn, Peter McCulloch, Papanui, New Zealand, Tony McCulloch, East Kilbride, Gerry McCullock, Motherwell, John McCullock, Inverness, Paul McCullock, Glasgow, William McCully, Germiston, Georgia McCunnie, Glasgow, Jim Mccunnie, Bothwell, Liza McCunnie, Glasgow, Mark Mccunnie, Bothwell, Mark McCunnie, Glasgow, Morgan McCunnie, Glasgow, Frank McCurrach, Montrose, Ashley McCusker, Castlemilk, Graeme McCusker, Alloa, Graham McCusker, Castlemilk, Neil McCusker, Ramsgate, Kent, Stuart McCusker, Stirling, Thomas Mccusker, Bishopbriggs, Thomas Christopher McCusker, Bishopbriggs, Jackie McCutcheon,

Rutherglen, Paul McCutcheon, Mount Vernon, Glasgow, Sam McCutcheon, Mount Vernon, Glasgow, Tony Mccutcheon, Glasgow, Tony McCutcheon, Mount Vernon, Glasgow, Anthony McDade, Airdrie, Brian Mcdade, Edinburgh, Daniel McDade, Ayrshire, Jamie McDade, Glasgow, Mark McDade, , Pat Mcdade, Priesthill, Patrick Mcdade, Priesthill, Peter McDade, Wishaw, Philip Mcdade, Priesthill, Scott McDade, Bletchley, Stephen McDade, Airdrie, Tony McDade, Johnstone, Anne McDaid, Lenzie, Anthony Mcdaid, Pub In Glasgow, Brian Mcdaid, Derry, Brook McDaid, Paisley, Cecilia Mcdaid, Blantyre, Charlie McDaid, Letterkenny, Co. Donegal, Chris McDaid, Banbury, Oxfordshire, Colm McDaid, Letterkenny, Co. Donegal, Grace McDaid, Cumbernauld, James Mcdaid, Lenzie, John McDaid, Paisley, Michael McDaid, Livingston, Phillip Mcdaid, Lenzie, Stella McDaid, Fuengirola, Thomas Mcdaid, Fuengirola, Peter McDaide, Hamilton, Graham McDermid, Dumbarton, Jamie Mcdermid, Fife, Jim McDermid, Dumbarton, Melissa McDermot, Glasgow, Robert McDermot, Glasgow, Anthony McDermott, Motherwell, Billy McDermott, Glasgow, Derrick McDermott, Hamilton, Jordan McDermott, Glasgow, Kathleen McDermott, Gorbals, Natalie McDermott, Hamilton, Paul McDermott, Glasgow, Tony McDermott, London, Wayne McDermott, Sligo, Gerrt McDevit, Glasgow, Carole Anne McDevitt, Lennoxtown, Charlie McDevitt, Milton, Dumbarton, Charlie McDevitt, Milton, Dumbarton, Conor Mcdevitt, Simshill Glasgow, Gerry McDevitt, Glasgow, Mark McDevitt, Greenock, Mary Mcdevitt, Simshill Glasgow, Sean Mcdevitt, Simshill Glasgow, Steven McDiarmid, , Eve McDill, Shetland, Liam McDill, Shetland, Megan McDill, Shetland, Annemarie McDonagh, Lambhill, Glasgow, Brian McDonagh, Linlithgow, Brian McDonagh, Linlithgow, Daniel McDonagh, Paisley, Edith McDonagh, Linlithgow, Edith McDonagh, Linlithgow, John Mcdonagh, Glasgow, Martin McDonagh, Linlithgow, Martin McDonagh, Linlithgow, Alan McDonald, Andrew McDonald, Dalbeattie, Andrew McDonald, Troon, Angus McDonald, , Ashley McDonald, Witham, Essex, C McDonald, Fort William, Carol McDonald, Glasgow, Carol McDonald, , Carol-Anne McDonald, Alexandria, Cathy McDonald, Glasgow, Chris McDonald, Irvine, David McDonald, Dalbeattie, Gary McDonald, Clydebank, Gerald McDonald, Derry, Gwen McDonald, Barrow in Furness, James Mcdonald, Cranhill, James McDonald, Islington, London, Jim McDonald, Barrow in Furness, Joe McDonald, Glasgow, Joe McDonald, Glasgow, Joy McDonald, Galway, Ireland, K McDonald, Glasgow, Kaygan McDonald, Galway, Ireland, Kenny McDonald, Paisley, Kirsty McDonald, Dalbeattie, Kris McDonald, Dalbeattie, Lynsey McDonald, Glasgow, Martin McDonald, Islington, London, Mary McDonald, Falkirk, Matthew McDonald, Inverness, Nicola McDonald, Dalbeattie, Peter McDonald, Bannockburn, Stirling, Robin McDonald, Galway, Ronan McDonald, Derry, Ross McDonald, Milton, Sammy McDonald, Greenock, Scot McDonald, Port Glasgow, Sean McDonald, Galway, Ireland, Sherry McDonald, Inverness, Steph McDonald, Irvine, Steven McDonald, Glasgow, Stevie McDonald, Glasgow, William McDonald, Glasgow, Elizabeth McDonna, Glasgow, Peter McDonna, Partick, Bryan McDonnell, Dublin, Ian&Julie McDonnell, Gallowgate, Glasgow, Stuart McDonnell, Croftfoot, Stuart McDonnell, Croftfoot , Alister McDougal, Johnstone, Robert McDougal, Argyle, Alan McDougall, Crosshill, Brian McDougall, Springburn, Glasgow, Charlie Mcdougall, Rutherglen, Dannielle McDougall, Springburn, Glasgow, David McDougall, Springburn, Glasgow, Fiona McDougall, Glasgow, Frances McDougall, Glasgow, James McDougall, Springburn, Glasgow, Mark McDougall, Springburn, Glasgow, Michael McDougall, Glasgow, Pat McDougall, Mossend, Patrick McDougall, Glasgow, Paul McDougall, Springburn, Glasgow, Scott McDougall, Kirkintilloch, Scott McDougall, Kirkintilloch, Graham McDowall, Glasgow, Graham McDowall, , Mark McDowall, Pat McDowall, Methil, Christine McDowell, Blairhall, James McDowell, Blairhall, Jonathan McDowell, Glasgow, Jordan McDowell, Blairhall, Martin McDowell, Basildon, Nicola McDowell, Blairhall, Patrick McDowell, Clyde Bank, Robert McDowell, Airdrie, Thomas McDowell, Yucatan N16 Stokie Tour, Tom McDowell, Belfast, Tony McDre, Glasgow, Danny McDuff, Leicester, Gary McDuff, Leicester, Jeff McDuff,

Leicester, Louie McDuff, Leicester, David McEewan, Glasgow, Martin Mcelroy, Falkland, Fife, Mike McElroy, Naoimh McElroy, Ireland, Thomas McElroy, Cumbernauld, Thomas McElroy, Cumbernauld, Tom McElroy, Grangemouth, Dada McElwee, Port Glasgow, Ernie Mcelwee, Port Glasgow, Jim McElwee, Greenock, Stan McElwee, Port Glasgow, John McEnemy, Fife, Paddy Mcenhill, Rosyth, Sean McEniff, Renfrew, Richard McEnore, Glasgow, Brian McEnroe, Motherwell, Shanade McEnroe, Motherwell, Thomas McEnroe Jnr, Glasgow, Stephanie McEnroy, Glasgow, Bridgeton, Andi McEntee, Nottingham, Lisa McEntee, Nottingham, Pat McEntee, Crossmaglen, Paul McErlane, Auchinlock, N McEvoy, , Paul McEvoy, Glasgow, Tony McEvoy, Alec McEwan, Glasgow, Brian McEwan, Partick Glasgow, Caitlin McEwan, Girvan, Chloe McEwan, Hamilton, Christopher McEwan, Glasgow, Colin McEwan, Greenock, Craig Mcewan, Partick Glasgow, Derek McEwan, Cumbernauld, Eve McEwan, Hamilton, Fergus McEwan, , Frank McEwan, Clydebank, James McEwan, Glasgow, Jenna Mcewan, Rutherglen, Jenna Mcewan, Rutherglen, Jenny & Josh McEwan, Alloa, John McEwan, Glasgow, Lewis McEwan, Hamilton, Mark Mcewan, Greenock, Michael McEwan, Kirkintilloch, Neale McEwan, Ayr, Paul McEwan, Motherwell, Paul McEwan, Paisley, Philip McEwan, Hamilton, Robert McEwan, Kilwinning, Vivian McEwan, Hamilton, Brian Mcewan Jnr, Partick Glasgow, Thomas McEwan Jnr, Ayr, Thomas McEwan Snr, Ayr, Robert McEwen, Glasgow, Amy McFadden, Denny, Brian McFadden, Glasgow, Danny McFadden, Glasgow, Denis Mcfadden, Linlithgow, Gerry Mcfadden, Kings Park Glasgow, Jackie McFadden, Kinning Park, Glasgow, Jimmy McFadden, Govanhill, Glasgow, Joe McFadden, Ibrox, Glasgow, John McFadden, Kinning Park, Glasgow, John McFadden, Motherwell, Joseph Patrick McFadden, Glasgow, Mary McFadden, , Michael McFadden, Glasgow, Neil McFadden, Glasgow, Owenie McFadden, Co Donegal, Owenie McFadden, Co Donegal, Paul McFadden, Glasgow, Paul McFadden, Gorbals, Paul McFadden, Reece McFadden, Motherwell, Reiss Mcfadden, Elderslie, Sarah McFadden, Holyrood Senior Sec, Glasgow, Stuart McFadden, Milton Keynes, Stuart McFadden, Milton Keynes, Tony McFadden, Denny, Ronald McFadgen, Coatbridge, Andy Mcfadyen, Livingston, Drew Mcfadyen, Edinburgh, Kerry McFadyen, Glasgow, Robert McFadyen, Stirling, Angela McFarlane, St Ninians, Caitlyn McFarlane, Wardie, Edinburgh, Elaine McFarlane, Lilybank, George McFarlane, Edinburgh, Iain McFarlane, Motherwell, John Mcfarlane, Blackwood, John McFarlane, Cumbernauld, John McFarlane, Cumbernauld, John McFarlane, St Ninians, Kevin McFarlane, Wardie, Edinburgh, Mick McFarlane, Dunfermline, Mick McFarlane, St Ninians, Mick McFarlane, St Ninians, Paul McFarlane, St Ninians, Sean McFarlane, Leith, Sean McFarlane, Westburn Village, Edinburgh, Steff McFarlane, Hamilton, Teresa McFarlane, St Ninians, Tracey McFarlane, Bishopbriggs, McFarlane, Livingston, Stuart McFarlane Jnr, Livingston, Stuart McFarlane Snr, Livingston, Darcy McFarlen, Livingston, Julie McFarlen, Livingston, Peter M'cFarlen, Croy, Colette McFaul, Coatbridge, Joe McFaul, Worthing, Kimberley McFaulds, Coatbridge, Martin McFaulds, Coatbridge, David McFeely, Wishaw, Paul McFeely, Wishaw, Paul McFeely, Wishaw, David McFeely Junior, Wishaw, David McFeely Junior, Wishaw, Robert McFenney, James Mcferran, Greenock, Peter McFlinn, Glasgow, McFly, Eastfield, Craig McFlynn, Glasgow, John McFlynn, King's Lynn, Kevin McFlynn, Keiren McFunny, Wishaw, Linda McG, Newcastle, Andrew McGachan, Ballingry, Andrew Mcgachan, Fife, Andrew Hayley Chloe and James McGachan, Ballingry Fife, George McGachey, Kilsyth, Gerry McGachy, Edmonton, John Mcgachy, Port Glasgow Harp C.S.C, Peter McGahan, Motherwell, Peter Mcgahan, Motherwell, Terry Mcgahan, New Jersey, Usa, Kenny McGaharon, Dumbarton, Steven McGaharon, Dumbarton, Ronnie McGain, Downpatrick, Amanda McGairy, Liverpool, Charles McGairy, Glasgow, Charles McGairy, Liverpool, Ellen McGairy, Glasgow, Michael McGairy, Liverpool, Paula McGairy, Liverpool, Stephen McGairy, Liverpool, Grant McGaley, Sandyhills, Jim McGalliard, Kirkintilloch, Paul McGalshan, Glasgow, Thomas McGann, Rutherglen, Tom McGann, Milngavie, Martin McGarby, Sutton, McGarby, Sutton, Martin McGardy, Sutton, McGardy, Sutton, James McGarigal, Glasgow, Clare McGarr,

Falkirk, Matt McGarr, Falkirk, Paul McGarr, Falkirk, Stephen McGarr, St. Ninians, Bridget Mcgarrell, Barmulloch, Colin McGarrell, Bathgate, John McGarrell, Garngad, Pauline McGarrell, Garngad, Edward Mcgarrell M.B.E, Barmulloch, John McGarrity, Drumchapel, Glasgow, Matthew McGarrity, Drumchapel, Glasgow, Brian McGarry, Glasgow, Dominic Mcgarry, India, Jim McGarry, John McGarry, Kirkintilloch, Linda McGarry, Kirkintilloch, Martin McGarry, Glasgow, Matthew McGarry, Glasgow, Nick McGarry, Windsor, Paul McGarry, Glasgow, Scott Mcgarry, East Kilbride, Tommy McGarry, Easterhouse, Tony Mcgarry, Cumbernauld, Gavin McGarth, Tallaght, Dublin, Rona Mcgarva, Cumnock, Tam McGarva, Penicuik, Charles McGarvey, Cumbernauld, Chic McGarvey, Cumbernauld, Chic McGarvey, Seville, Laura Mcgarvey, Crookston, Sean McGarvey, Denny, Stuart McGary, Coatbridge, George McGeachie, Bishopbriggs, Glasgow, George McGeachie, Robroyston, Glasgow, Gary Mcgeachy, Craigend, Gerry T Mcgeachy, Celbridge (Ireland) Ex-Stirling, Scott McGeachy, Possilpark, Sean Mcgeady, Maryhill, Glasgow, John McGeaghy, Campbelltown, Angela McGee, Paisley, Brian & Valerie McGee, Aberdeen, Cathie McGee, Laurieston, Daniel McGee, , Gerry Mcgee, Thornliebank, Gina McGee, Glasgow, Joseph McGee, Glasgow, Margaret McGee, Glasgow, Michael McGee, Edinburgh, Michael & Margaret McGee, Cambuslang, Monty McGee, Cambuslang, Patrick McGee, Edinburgh, Paul McGee, , Scott McGee, Glasgow, Scott McGee, Kilmarnock, Tom McGee, Simshill, Glasgow, William McGee, Elderslie, James McGeechan, Greenock, Mark McGeehan, Chapelhall, Scott McGeever, Grangemouth, Franny McGeoch, St Ninians, Gary McGeoch, St Ninians, Margaret McGeoch, Glasgow, Maureen Mcgeoch, Bishopbriggs, Ryan McGeoch, Glasgow, Robert McGeogh Jnr, Paisley, Martin McGeough, Coatbridge, Raymond McGeough, Coatbridge, Janet McGeowan, Glasgow, Lindsay McGeown, Glasgow, Stephen McGerty, Robroyston, Ciaran McGettigan, Elderslie, William McGettigan, Barrhead, Arthur G Mcghee, Kilwinning, Betty McGhee, Glasgow, Brian Mcghee, Elderslie, Brian McGhee, Johnstone, Brian McGhee, Johnstone, Caitlin McGhee, Milngavie, Charlie McGhee, Clydebank, Derek McGhee, East Kilbride, Gerry McGhee, Blackwood, John McGhee, Glasgow, John McGhee, Glasgow, Larry McGhee, Milngavie, Liam McGhee, Johnstone, Martin McGhee, Bellshill, Mary McGhee, Tranent, Neil McGhee, Cumnock, Neil McGhee, Tranent, Pat McGhee, Motherwell, Stephen McGhee, Newarthill, Steven McGhee, Duntocher, Stuart McGhee, Corby, Stuart McGhee, Corby, McGhee, Glynnis McGhhe, Tranent, Bryan McGhie, Cumbernauld, Jim McGhie, Greenock, K McGiffin, Patrick McGiffin, Eddie McGilfery, Clydebank, Aaron McGill, Lanarkshire, Alan McGill, Troon, Allison McGill, Airdrie, Ann McGill, Glasgow, Annmarie McGill, Netherton, Annmarie McGill, Netherton, Danny McGill, Springburn, Eamonn McGill, Lanarkshire, James McGill, Glasgow, Kevin & Julie McGill, The Scheme, Port Seaton, Paul McGill, Barrowfield, Neil McGilligan, Perth, Dylan McGillvray, Dalmuir, Adele McGinigle, Elderslie, Adele Mcginigle, Elderslie, John McGinlay, Glasgow, Jordan McGinlay, Bishopbriggs, Louise Mcginlay, Markinch, Fife, Thomas McGinlay, Glasgow, Andy Mcginley, Acre, Barry McGinley, Blyth, Cara Maria McGinley, Govanhill, Caroline McGinley, Bathgate, Caroline McGinley, Whitburn, Charlie McGinley, Edinburgh, Charlie McGinley, Gorbals, Conn Mcginley, Glasgow, Cullum McGinley, Glasgow, Danielle McGinley, Leicester, David McGinley, Clydebank, Jack McGinley, Glasgow, James McGinley, Blyth, Joe Bobby McGinley, Dalry, Ayrshire, John McGinley, Glasgow, John McGinley, Peniculk, Jude Thomas McGinley, Dennistoun, Keri Mcginley, Acre, Kieran McGinley, Coatbridge, Margaret McGinley, Wishaw, Marie Mcginley, Govanhill, Mark McGinley, Johnstone, Mark McGinley, Kirkintilloch, Matt McGinley, Johnstone, Michael McGinley, Toryglen, Michael McGinley, Whitburn, Neil McGinley, Anniesland, Glasgow, Patsy McGinley, Edinburgh, Patti McGinley, Edinburgh, Sean-Paul McGinley, Leicester, Steph McGinley, Leicester, Steven McGinley, Glasgow, Brian McGinn, Glasgow, Jim McGinn, Stevenston, John McGinn, Broxburn, Kelly McGinn, Glasgow, Kevin McGinn, Glasgow, Kevin McGinn, Glasgow, Kirsty McGinn, Glasgow, Mick McGinn, Coatbridge, Mick McGinn, Coatbridge, Paul

McGinn, Annemarie McGinnes, Newmains, Daniel McGinnes, Newmains, Elsa McGinnes, Newmains, George McGinnes, Newmains, Joseph McGinnes, Newmains, Kerry McGinnes, Elderslie, Maurice McGinnes, Newmains, Robert McGinnes, Elderslie, Robert McGinnes, Elderslie, Debra McGinness, Newcastle Upon Tyne, John McGinness, Newton Mearns, Kevin McGinnigle, Elderslie, Stephen McGinnigle, Livingston, Brian McGinty, Curry, Joe McGinty, Glasgow, Maureen McGinty, Glasgow, Michael McGinty, London, Paul McGivan, Fife, Paul McGivan(jnr), Fife, Lee McGiven, Glasgow, Paul McGlasen, Archie McGlashan, Bonhill, Gillian McGlashan, Carntyne, Lesley McGlashan, Carntyne, Paul McGlaughlin, Stephen McGlaughlin, Wishaw, Evelyn McGlinchey, Knightswood, John McGlinchey, John McGlinchey, Dubai, U.A.E., Lorraine McGlinchey, Fauldhouse, Barry McGloan, Maryhill, Glasgow, John McGlochlin, Andrew McGlocklin, Dundee, Alex McGlone, Bosnia, James McGlone, Killmarnock, Johnny McGloughlan, Bathgate, Connor McGlynn, Aberdeen, Daniel McGlynn, Glasgow, Dean McGlynn, Aberdeen, John McGlynn, Prestonpans, Lynda McGlynn, Prestonpans, Mark McGlynn, Glasgow, Paul McGlynn, Aberdeen, Rhaegan McGlynn, Aberdeen, Sandra McGlynn, Aberdeen, Scott McGlynn, Aberdeen, Brian McGodrick, Springboig, Danny Mcgoldrick, Wishaw, Janice McGoldrick, Wishaw, Kris McGoldrick, Milngavie, Melissa McGoldrick, Wishaw, Michael McGoldrick, Wishaw, Ryan McGoldrick, Torrance, Gary McGomary, Blackburn, Adam McGonagil, Edinburgh, John McGonigal, Bellshill, Craig McGonigle, Glasgow, Danny McGonigle, Glasgow, Danny McGonigle, Glasgow, Eddie McGonigle, Glasgow, Lyndsey Marie McGonigle, Glasgow, Mhari-Ann McGonigle, Dunoon, Nancy McGonigle, Glasgow, Patrick McGonigle, Southampton, Teresa Mcgonigle, Glasgow, Terry McGonnell, Jersey, Alex McGoogan, Cumbernauld, Liz McGookin, Glasgow, Tom McGoran, Adelaide, Australia, Tom McGoran, Adelaide, Australia, Tom McGorren, Glasgow, Graham McGougan, Muthill, Perthshire, Ian McGougan, Limerick, Ireland, Margaret- Ann McGourlick, Linwood, Mary McGourlick, Linwood, Thomas McGourlick, Linwood, Ann McGovern, Mary Hill, Connor McGovern, Maryhill, Donna McGovern, Greenock, James McGovern, Maryhill, James McGovern, Maryhill, John McGovern, Perth, John McGovern, Glasgow, Kara McGovern, Alexandria, Les McGovern, Springburn, Malcolm Mcgovern, Lochgelly, Paul McGovern, Springburn, Glasgow, Sam McGovern, Glasgow, Seamus McGovern, Newlands, Shaun McGovern, Pollock, Terence Graham McGovern, Aberdeen, Andy McGowan, Staines, Andy McGowan, Staines, Blair McGowan, Tamworth, Surrey, Bradley McGowan, Glasgow, Brian McGowan, Leeds, Caitlin McGowan, Coltness, Wishaw, Cula McGowan, Castlemilk, Glasgow, James McGowan, Glasgow, Jenny McGowan, Glasgow, Jim McGowan, Glasgow, Jim McGowan, Glasgow, Joe McGowan, Glasgow, John McGowan, Glasgow, Jonathan McGowan, Glasgow, Joseph McGowan, Glasgow, Joseph Patrick McGowan, Bishopbriggs, Glasgow, Kevin McGowan, Coatbridge, Kevin (Sep) McGowan, Coatbridge, Kevin Frank McGowan, Buncrana, Lauren McGowan, Coatbridge, Michael McGowan, Glasgow, Michael D McGowan, Billericay, Essex, Neil McGowan, Newton Mearns, Noel McGowan, Ballycastle, Paul McGowan, Ballycastle, Paul McGowan, Luton, Beds, Pete McGowan, Glasgow, Ryan McGowan, Austrialia, Shaun McGowan, Coatbridge, Steven McGowan, Glasgow, Steven McGowan, Shotts, Stevie McGowan, Dennistoun, Terry McGowan, Castlemilk, Glasgow, Tony McGowan, France, Tony McGowan, Glasgow, Tony McGowan, Lanarkshire, Betty McGrady, Coatbridge, Hugh McGrady, Coatbridge, James McGrady, Coatbridge, Jim McGrady, Coatbridge, Josh McGrady, Coatbridge, Kieran McGrady, Coatbridge, Lorraine McGrady, Coatbridge, Mark McGrady, , Mark McGrady, Coatbridge, Mark McGrady, Coatbridge, Paul McGrady, Coatbridge, Sue McGrady, Coatbridge, Thomas McGrady, Coatbridge, Jamie McGrael, Glasgow, Sharon McGrager, Glasgow, Jamie McGrail, Glasgow, Laura McGrall, Glasgow, Michael McGrame, Glasgow, Beth McGrane, Chapelhall, Beth Mcgrane, Chapelhall, Brian McGrane, Chapelhall, Brian McGrane, Chapelhall, Benny McGrath, Salou, Spain, Charlie McGrath, Glasgow, Colin McGrath, Condorrat, Cumbernauld, Elizabeth McGrath, Condorrat, Jim McGrath, GreenFeild, John McGrath,

Condorrat, Cumbernauld, Kevin McGrath, Glengormley, Mark McGrath, Tallaght, Dublin, Noel McGrath, Maghera, Shug McGrath, Govan, Glasgow, Thomas McGrath, Glasgow, John McGrath Jnr, Condorrat, Cumbernauld, Gary McGrattan, Swinton, James McGrattan, Kilbirnie, Paul McGrattan, Kilwinning, Gary McGratten, Whiteinch, Hugh McGraw, Coatbridge, Ian (Mogadon) McGraw, Florida Park, Langside, Mark McGraw, Coatbridge, Martin McGraw, Thorntonhall, Martin McGread, Mount Vernon,Glasgow, Gerry McGread Jnr., Mount Vernon,Glasgow, Tam McGreary, Dundee, Alex McGreavey, Edinburgh, Jolene McGreevy, Glengormley, Kevin McGreevy, Glengormley, Terri McGreger, Dundee, Nicholas Peter McGreggor, Glasgow, Andy McGregor, Port Glasgow, Drew McGregor, Fiona McGregor, Frank McGregor, Castlemilk, John McGregor, Bannockburn, Kevin McGregor, Lochee Dundee, Mark McGregor, Port Glasgow, Mary McGregor, Port Glasgow, Neil McGregor, Bannockburn, Rebekah McGregor, Glasgow, Ryan McGregor, Dundee, Sean McGregor, Bellshill, Sharon McGregor, Lochee, Steven McGregor, Greenock, Stevie McGregor, St Ninians, Stuart McGregor, Glasgow, Brian McGreskin, Shettleston, Glasgow, Allan McGroarty, Saddleworth, Chris McGroarty, Perth, Glen McGroarty, Johannesburg, Harry McGroarty, Saddleworth, Liam McGroarty, Perth, Martin McGroarty, Kirkcaldy, Paddy McGroarty, Bishopbriggs, Pat McGroarty, Perth, William McGroarty, Midsomer Norton, Somerset, Anthony McGrogan, Dumbarton, D McGrogan, Dumbarton, Damien McGrogan, Dumbarton, Ian McGrogan, Port Glasgow, Daniel McGrory, Penicuik, Dermot McGrory, Penicuik, Eddie Mcgrory, Dublin, John Paul McGrory, Gorbals, Manus McGrory, Royston, Tom McGrory, Milngavie, Tony McGrory, Glasgow, Tony McGrory, Govanhill, Andrew McGrotty, Cirencester, Kieran McGrotty, Chapelhall, Paul McGrotty, Carluke, Paul McGrotty, Carluke, Gerard McGroyie, Glasgow, Daniel McGuckin, Livingston, Dominic McGuckin, Cumbernauld, Danielle McGuigan, Glasgow, David McGuigan, Livingston, Eddie Mcguigan, Calderbank, Francis McGuigan, Bannockburn, Hugh McGuigan, Livingston, James McGuigan, Law Village, James 'Gigsy' McGuigan, Coventry, Jamie McGuigan, Linlithgow, Jamie McGuigan, Linlithgow, Jimmy McGuigan, Barrhead, Joe McGuigan, Motherwell, Liz McGuigan, Barlanark, Maria McGuigan, Barlanark, Mark McGuigan, East Kilbride, Megan McGuigan, Glasgow, Nicole McGuigan, Glasgow, Paul McGuigan, Greenock, Pete McGuigan, Glasgow, Pete McGuigan, Rutherglen, Peter McGuigan, Motherwell, Scott McGuigan, Glasgow, Yvonne McGuigan, Cumbernauld, McGuigan, Glasgow, Amy McGuiness, Airdrie, Claire McGuiness, Glasgow, Danny McGuiness, Airdrie, Emma McGuiness, Douglas, Harry McGuiness, Jack McGuiness, James McGuiness, Fernhill, Joe McGuiness, Brighton, John McGuiness, Halfway, John McGuiness, John McGuiness, Mary McGuiness, Glasgow, Mathew McGuiness, Paisley, Megan McGuiness, Paul McGuiness, Livingston, Rachael McGuiness, Douglas, Beryl McGuinnes, Motherwell, Jimmy McGuinnes, Motherwell. Stephen McGuinnes, Byfleet, Buddy McGuinness, Crofton Park, London, Charlie McGuinness, Coltness, Wishaw, Ciaran McGuinness, Airdrie, George McGuinness, Broomhill, Jacqueline McGuinness, Glasgow, James McGuinness, Glasgow, Jim McGuinness, Dunure, Ayrshire, John McGuinness, Jordan McGuinness, Airdrie, Lawrence McGuinness, Lanark, Maria McGuinness, Dunure, Ayrshire, Patrick Mcguinness, Coatbridge, Paul McGuinness, Shotts, Stevie Arch McGuinness, Dublin, Tracey McGuinness, Ruchazie, Glasgow, Andy McGuinniety, Drogheda (Eire), Lorraine McGuinniety, Linthouse, Glasgow, Brian McGuire, Denny, Catherine McGuire, Glasgow, Collette McGuire, Coatbridge, Danny McGuire, Bellshill, Darren McGuire, Hamilton, Gary McGuire, Glasgow, Ian McGuire, Montrose, Jack McGuire, Angus, James Mcguire, Nj, Usa, James McGuire, Rutherglen, Jamie McGuire, Glasgow, Joe McGuire, Hamilton, John McGuire, Bonnybridge, Johnny McGuire, Dunipace, Libby McGuire, Chapelhall, Mark McGuire, Hamilton, Mark McGuire, Martin McGuire, Glasgow, Mary McGuire, Rutherglen, Matthew McGuire, Denny, Mick McGuire, Raploch, Nicola McGuire, Maryhill, Paul McGuire, Hamilton, Paul McGuire, Viewpark, Philip McGuire, Rutherglen, Rita McGuire, Nj, Usa, Robert McGuire, Glasgow, Ryan Mcguire, Nj, Usa, Susan McGuire, Warwick, T

McGuire, Glasgow, William McGuire, Carmyle, Yvonne McGuire, Camelon, Thomas McGuire Jnr, Glasgow, Thomas McGuire Snr, Glasgow, Mark McGull, Glasgow, Jim McGurk, Stirling, John McGurk, Greenock, Matthew McGurk, Inverness, Florida, John McHale, Aviemore, Gary McHarg, Borehamwood, Herts, Holly McHarg, Borehamwood, Herts, Hugh McHarg, Borehamwood, Herts, Conor Mchenry, Ballycastle, Sean Mchenry, Ballycastle, Liam McHugh, Linlithgow, Angela McHugh, Glasgow, Angela McHugh, Glasgow, Catherine McHugh, Newcastle, Catherine McHugh, Newcastle, Celia McHugh, Airdrie, Colin McHugh, Glasgow, Courtney McHugh, Glasgow, David McHugh, Dalmuir, Gerry McHugh, Edinburgh, Helen McHugh, Glasgow, John McHugh, Linlithgow, John McHugh, Linlithgow, Jonathan McHugh, Glasgow, Jonathan McHugh, Glasgow, Laura McHugh, Glasgow, Laura McHugh, Glasgow, Liam McHugh, Linlithgow, Lisa McHugh, Glasgow, Michael McHugh, Newcastle, Michael McHugh, Newcastle, Michelle McHugh, Glasgow, Mick McHugh, Sligo, Nick Mchugh, Sligo, Patrick McHugh, Newcastle, Patrick McHugh, Newcastle, Terry McHugh, Belfast, Wullie McILear, Wullie McIlear, Brent Bravo, Wullie McIlear, Greenock, John McIhatton, Pontefract,W/Yorkshire, George McIllroy, Aviemore, Lisa McIllroy, Belfast, Frank McIlroy, Cardonald, Jamie McIlroy, Barrhead, Jim McIlroy, Port Glasgow, John McIlroy, Elaine McIlveney, Clydebank, Angela McIlwraith, Newton Mearns, Gary McIlwraith, Newton Mearns, Glasgow, Gary McIlwraith, Newton Mearns, Tracy McIlwraith, Newton Mearns, Aidan McInally, Belfast, Alan McInally, Invergordon, Brian McInally, Bishopbriggs, Christina McInally, Belfast, David McInally, Glasgow, Jordan McInally, Invergordon, Shug McInally, Belfast, Tania McInally, Belfast, Vincent McInally, Glasgow, Daniel McInnes, Edinburgh, Fiona McInnes, Edinburgh, Ian McInnes, Cupar, Fife, Paul McInnes, Saltcoats, Willie McInnes, Saltcoats, James McInstrey, Glasgow, Claire McInstry, Glasgow, Alex Mcintosh, Bo'ness, Alice McIntosh, Isle of Benbecula, Analeise McIntosh, Isle of Benbecula, Aonghas McIntosh, Isle of Benbecula, Bill McIntosh, Johannesburg, Christina McIntosh, Isle of Benbecula, Colin McIntosh, Dundonald, Ayrshire, Davy Mcintosh, Boc Carfin, Derik McIntosh, Isle of Bebecula, Derik McIntosh, Isle of Benbecula, Eddie McIntosh, Coatbridge, Eric Mcintosh, Giffnock, James McIntosh, Dundonald, Ayrshire, Liam Mcintosh, Bo'ness, Megan McIntosh, Isle of Benbecula, Pauline Mcintosh, Bo'ness, Rachael Mcintosh, Bo'ness, Ross McIntosh, Glasgow, Sharon McIntosh, Dundonald, Ayrshire, Stephan McIntosh, Coatbridge, Stephen McIntosh, Coatbridge, Stephen Mcintosh, Coatbridge, Steven McIntosh, Glasgow, Terry McIntosh, Dundonald, Ayrshire, Terry McIntosh, Edinburgh, Agnes Mcintyre, Corby, Northants, Alan McIntyre, Pollock, Andy McIntyre, Ibrox, Barry McIntyre, Braehead, Billy McIntyre, Southampton, David McIntyre, Glasgow, Gordon Mcintyre, Essex, John McIntyre, Greenock, Jose McIntyre, Port Glasgow, Joseph McIntyre, Eastleigh, Mark McIntyre, Greenock, Megan Mary McIntyre, Anderston Glasgow, Paul McIntyre, Bathgate, Paul McIntyre, Cumbernauld, Peter Mcintyre, Tollcross, Glasgow, Shona McIntyre, Grangemouth, Stefan Scott McIntyre, Anderston, Glasgow, Tam McIntyre, Harrogate, N.Yorks, Tyrone McIntyre, Port Glasgow, Hugh McInulty, Kelvindale, Lizzie McInulty, New Farm, Kilmarnock, Heather McIver, Dalneigh, Inverness, Jake McIver, Dalneigh, Inverness, Kirstie McIver, Dalneigh, Inverness, Mike McIver, Dalneigh, Inverness, Ryan McIver, Dalneigh, Inverness, Scott Mciver, Duntocher, James McIvor, Galston, James Mcivor, Galston, Nick McIvor, Dennistoun, Paul McIvor, Galston, Paul Mcivor, Galston, Stephen Mck, Kirkintilloch, Steven McKaren, Glasgow, Alison McKay, Blackpool, Andrew McKay, Bishopbriggs, Glasgow, Bridget McKay, Castlederg, County Tyrone, Charles McKay, Castlederg, County Tyrone, Christopher McKay, Glasgow, David McKay, Paisley, Duncan McKay, Motherwell, Ian McKay, Airdrie, James McKay, Glasgow, Jamie McKay, Hailsham, Jean McKay, Glasgow, Joe Mckay, Sandyhills, JP McKay, Glasgow, Kelly McKay, Castlederg, County Tyrone, Lorna McKay, Tain, Mark McKay, Tain, Natalie McKay, Castlederg, County Tyrone, Nick McKay, Broomhill, Nick "Varga" Mckay, Broomhill, Rab McKay, Corby, Rab Mckay, Corby, Northants, Stef McKay, Drumchapel, Stuart 'Malky' McKay, Perth, Stuart

'Malky' McKay, , Stevie Mckay And The Pollok Inn Team, Pollok, Andy McKay Snr, Bishopbriggs, Glasgow, Ronnie McKeane, Blackpool, Debbie McKechnie, Easterhouse, Glasgow, James McKechnie, Easterhouse, Jonny Mckechnie, A R Services, Franny McKee, Greenock, Jeremy McKee, Glasgow, Karen McKee, East Kilbride, Stephen Mckee, Banbury Oxon, Mary McKeen, Bellshill, Pam McKeeney, Duns, Kevin McKeeve, Bishopton, Mark McKeeve, Bishopton, Erin Marie McKeever, Greenfield, Harry Mckeever, Brantford Canada, John McKeever, Glasgow, Joseph Patrick McKeever, Milton, Stephen McKeever, Halway, Cambuslang, Jaz McKeirnan, Hamilton, William McKeirnan, , Arthur McKell, Rutherglen, Paul McKell, Dennistoun, Carol Mckellar, Campbeltown, Gail McKellar, Paisley, Jim McKellar, Baillieston, Jim McKellar, Baillieston, Mark McKellar, Drumchapel, Lesley McKellican, Buckhaven, Alan McKelvie, Mount Vernon, Christopher McKelvie, Barrhead, Christopher McKelvie, Barrhead, Daniel McKelvie, Barrhead, John McKelvie, Cambuslang, Kerry McKelvie, Barrhead, Hugh McKenan, Inverness, David McKendric Jnr, Carluke, David McKendric Snr, Carluke, Andy Mckendrick, Johnstone, Laura McKendrick, Johnstone, Liz McKendrick, Johnstone, Paul McKendrick, Johnstone, Robert McKendrick, Inverness, Robert McKendrick, Johnstone, Don McKenize, Campbeltown, Chris McKenna, Irvine, Claire McKenna, Linlithgow, Con McKenna, Paisley, Craig McKenna, Glasgow, Damien McKenna, Newmains, Euan McKenna, High Wycombe, Frank McKenna, Glasgow, Frank McKenna, High Wycombe, Frankie McKenna, Cumbernauld, George McKenna, Dundee, George McKenna, Johnstone, Gerry Mckenna, Maryhill, Harry McKenna, Glasgow, Ian McKenna, Saltcoats, Jake McKenna, Glasgow, Jennifer Mckenna, Kingspark,Glasgow, Jim McKenna, Sandyhills, Jimba Mckenna, Port Glasgow, John McKenna, Belfast, John McKenna, Cotridge, John McKenna, Highlander Pub, Paderborn, Germany, John Mckenna, Larbert, John Mckenna, Port Glasgow, Jordan McKenna, Coatbridge, Kathy McKenna, Stirling, Katia McKenna, Falkirk, Kelly Mckenna, Coatbridge, Kenneth Mckenna, Bailleston, Kenneth McKenna, Johnstone, Kenneth McKenna, Johnstone, Linda Mckenna, Linwood, Lisa McKenna, Glasgow, Maggie McKenna, Stirling, Mairi McKenna, Linlithgow, Mark McKenna, Newmains, Martin McKenna, Coatbridge, Matthew McKenna, Wishaw, Michael McKenna, Glasgow, Michelle McKenna, Wishaw, Nicola Mckenna, Cumbernauld, Ossie McKenna, Paisley, Paul McKenna, Corby, Peter McKenna, Linlithgow, Peter McKenna, Wishaw, Raymond McKenna, Coatbridge, Robert McKenna, Bermuda, Sean McKenna, Cowdenbeath, Snowy Mckenna, Zander McKenna, Stirling, Zanders McKenna, Stirling, Peter Paddy McKennan, Dundondald, Hugh McKenny, Glasgow, Paul McKenny, Uddingston, Alison McKenzie, Horsham, Ally McKenzie, Linlithgow, Ally McKenzie, Linlithgow, Brian McKenzie, Barrhead, Brodie McKenzie, Edinburgh, Cathrine Mckenzie, Govanhill, Chris McKenzie, Greenfield, Colin McKenzie, Glenrothes, Corrie-Louise McKenzie, Edinburgh, Courtney McKenzie, Balliston, Craig McKenzie, Stirling, Edward Mckenzie, Cambuslang, Gerry Mckenzie, Govanhill, Graeme McKenzie, Edinburgh, Hugh McKenzie, Alva, Hugh McKenzie, , James McKenzie, Stirling, Jayn Mckenzie, Palma De Mallorca, Joanne McKenzie, St Ninians, John Mckenzie, Govanhill, Kevin McKenzie, Basingstoke, Mark McKenzie, Stirling, Scott McKenzie, Dumfries, Sharon Mckenzie, Govanhill, Andrew McKeown, Hamilton, Andrew McKeown, Hamilton, Angela Mckeown, Rutherglen, Angela Mckeown, Rutherglen, Anthony McKeown, Bannockburn, Claire McKeown, Stirling, Dionne McKeown, Eastfield, Jim McKeown, Wishaw, John McKeown, Eastfield, John Paul McKeown, Ralston, John-Paul McKeown, Seville, Joseph Mckeown, Wigtown,Scotland, Karen McKeown, Seville, Kenny Mckeown, Newcastle, Kevin McKeown, Stirling, Mark Patrick McKeown, Motherwell, Neil McKeown, Glasgow, Paul McKeown, Wishaw, Robert McKeown, Glasgow, Robert McKeown, Glenfinnan, Sean McKeown, Eastfield, Stephen McKeown, Cumbernauld, Stephen McKeown, Glasgow, Thomas McKeown, Ballymena, Thomas Mckeown, Ballymena, Thomas Mckeown, Ballymena, County Antrim, Stewart McKergow, Troon, David McKernan, Bonhill, Gary Mckernan, Dumbarton, James McKernan, Bonhill, Paul McKernan, Bonhill, Paul McKernan,

Glasgow, Stewart Mckernan, Dumbarton, Graham McKernon, Saltcoats, Hazel McKernon, Saltcoats, Robin McKernon, Saltcoats, Steven McKernon, Saltcoats, Steven McKernon, Saltcoats, McKernon, Saltcoats, Cameron McKerracher, Glasgow, Joan McKerrin, Glasgow, Kevin McKerrn, Wishaw, Doreen Mckerrow, Glenrothes, Pete McKerry, Glasgow, Harper McKibbon, Harthill, James McKiddie, Benwell, Tam McKiddie, Cruddars Park, Christopher McKie, Dumfries, Janice McKie, Dumfries, Michael McKie, Dumfries, Natalie McKie, Falkirk, Nicole McKie, Flakirk, John McKIinley, Stenhousemuir, Kirsty McKIinley, Glasgow, Patricia McKinley, Glasgow, Ross McKIinley, Stenhousemuir, Fiona McKim, Paisley, Kevin McKimmie, Aberdeen, William McKindley, Alison McKinlay, Easterhouse, Glasgow, Allan McKinlay, Easterhouse, Glasgow, Bert Mckinlay, Milton, Glasgow, Brian McKinlay, Ayr, Gary McKinlay, Stirling, Ian McKinlay, Collingwood, Ian McKinlay, Collingwood, James McKinlay, Cumbernauld, Jamie McKinlay, Kintyre, Jason McKinlay, Cambuslang, John Paul McKinlay, Carluke, Kathleen McKinlay, Cumbernauld, Kevin McKinlay, Falkirk, Scott MCKinlay, Cumbernauld, Stuart McKinlay, Glasgow, William Mckinlay, Cumbernauld, William Mckinlay, Cumbernauld, William McKinlay, Stirling, Bill Mckinley, Coatbridge, Butch Mckinley, Coatbridge, Cathy Mckinley, Coatbridge, Ciar Mckinley, Glasgow, Karen Mckinley, Glasgow, Kayleigh McKinley, Glasgow, Mikaela Mckinley, Glasgow, Paul McKinley, Suzanne McKinley, Glasgow, Kyle McKinn, Aberdeen, Carol McKinney, Glasgow, Donny McKinney, Reading, Elaine Mckinney, Craigend, Gary Mckinney, Pollok, Lynn Mckinney, Greece, Jackie McKinnie, Glasgow, Lee McKinnie, Glasgow, Alan McKinnon, Milngavie, Carol McKinnon, Giffnock, Dougie Mckinnon, North Kelvinside, Gordon McKinnon, Westcliffe, Lorna McKinnon, Glasgow, Jackie McKinstrie, Wishaw, Danielle McKinstry, London, Michael McKinstry, Clydebank, Scott McKittrick, Bridgeton, Glasgow, John Paul McKiver, Glasgow, Kevin McKivor, Clydebank, John McKluskey, Hamilton, Kevin Mcknight, Mossblown, Andrew McLachlan, Rutherglen, David McLachlan, Isle of Bute, Gavin McLachlan, Paisley, George McLachlan, Airdrie, Jim McLachlan, Barrhead, Jim McLachlan, Wemyss Bay, Jim McLachlan, Weymss Bay, Joanne Mclachlan, Barrhead, Neal Mclachlan, Thornhill, Robbie McLachlan, Wemyss Bay, Rory McLachlan, Cambuslang, Willie McLachlan, Barrhead, Jim McLachlan Snr, Wemyss Bay, Bernard McLafferty, Renfrew, Robert McLafferty, , Nichola McLaine, Glasgow, Annemarie McLaren, Motherwell, Billy Mclaren, Bonhill, Ceri Anne McLaren, Motherwell, Frazer McLaren, Glenburn, Paisley, Jim McLaren, Motherwell, Karen McLaren, Westburn, Marion McLaren, Motherwell, Michael McLaren, Motherwell, Tracy McLaren, Maryhill, Wullie Mclaren, Bridgeton, Isabell Mclauchlan, Glasgow, Lisa Mclauchlan, Glasgow, Joe McLaughen, Glasgow, Ann Mclaughlan, Bellshill, Paul McLaughlan, , Stephen McLaughlan, Livingston, Alex McLaughlin, Cambuslang, Allan McLaughlin, Bishopton, Amanda McLaughlin, Clydebank, Barry McLaughlin, Ballieston, Benny McLaughlin, Seville, Bill (Liam) McLaughlin, Bellshill, Brian McLaughlin, Hyndland, Chris McLaughlin, Ballieston, Chrissie McLaughlin, Dalmuir, Claire & John Mclaughlin, Wellingborough, Northants, Damien McLaughlin, Glasgow, Damien McLaughlin, Glasgow, Danny McLaughlin, Glasgow, Danny McLaughlin, Del McLaughlin, Manchester, Elizabeth McLaughlin, , Geraldine McLaughlin, Calderbank Airdrie, Harry McLaughlin, Ballieston, Irene McLaughlin, Coatbridge, James Mclaughlin, Glasgow, Jennifer McLaughlin, Airdrie, Jim McLaughlin, Girvin, Jim McLaughlin, Kings Park, Jim 'Swampy' McLaughlin, Mount Ellen Golf Club, John & Claire Mclaughlin, Wellingborough, England, Jolene McLaughlin, Parkhall, Josh Mclaughlin, Rutherlgen, Glasgow, Kathleen McLaughlin, Co Donegal, Kevin Sean Mclaughlin, Glasgow, Lee McLaughlin, Gourock, Liam McLaughlin, Bishopton, Margaret McLaughlin, Glasgow, Margaret McLaughlin, Wishaw, Marie McLaughlin, Inverurie, Mark McLaughlin, East Kilbride, Mark McLaughlin, Paisley, Michael McLaughlin, Calderbank Airdrie, Michael McLaughlin, Co Donegal, Michael McLaughlin, East Kilbride, Michael McLaughlin, Kings Park, Michael Joseph McLaughlin, East Kilbride, Neil McLaughlin, Arden, Neil McLaughlin, Inverurie, Nichole McLaughlin, Coatbridge, Noddy McLaughlin, Wallingford, Owen

McLaughlin, Croydon, Patrick McLaughlin, East Kilbride, Paul McLaughlin, Luton, Paul McLaughlin, Paisley, Peter McLaughlin, Paisley, Peter McLaughlin, Paisley, Peter Mclaughlin, Paisley, Peter Mclaughlin, Paisley, Peter Mclaughlin, Paisley, Peter Mclaughlin, Paisley, Phil McLaughlin, Bishopton, Phil McLaughlin, East Kilbride, Rose McLaughlin, Cambuslang, Ross Mclaughlin, Port Glasgow, Ryan Patrick McLaughlin, East Kilbride, Sean McLaughlin, Johnstone, Shona McLaughlin, Co Donegal, Stephen Mclaughlin, Greenock, Stephen McLaughlin, South Carolina, Stephen McLaughlin, South Carolina, Syzanne McLaughlin, Inverurie, Tony McLaughlin, , Tony McLaughlin, Frinton on Sea, Wesley McLaughlin, Dalmuir, Yvonne McLaughlin, Coatbridge, Allan McLaughlin Jnr, Ballieston, Joe Mclaughlin Jnr, Kings Park, Glasgow, Allan McLaughlin Snr, Ballieston, Joe Mclaughlin Snr, Kings Park, Glasgow, Frank McLay, Rutherglen, Gary McLay, Paisley, Ann McLean, Glasgow, Brian McLean, Springburn, Colin Mclean, Blackwood, Danielle McLean, Newarthill, Darren Francis Mclean, Carfin, David McLean, Kilsyth, Donald McLean, Penilee, Eddie McLean, , Edward McLean, Jade McLean, Arden, James McLean, Stirling, Kenny McLean, Stirling, Marc McLean, Maryhill, Mark McLean, , Mark Mclean, Hamilton, Mary McLean, Croy, Kilsyth, Mary Jane McLean, Springburn, Murdo McLean, Broomhill, Nicole McLean, Kilsyth, Rab McLean, Stirling, Ross McLean, Fort William, Ryan McLean, Arden, Stephen McLean, East Kilbride, William McLean, 103 Sycamore Cres East Kilbride, Willie McLean, East Kilbride, David McLean, Patrick, David McLean Snr, Patrick, Kieran McLear, Larkhall, Ryan McLear, Larkhall, David McLearie, Alexandria, John McLeary, Overtown, Steven McLeavy, East Kilbride, Michelle McLees, Port Glasgow, Stephen McLees, Greenock, Jimmy Mcleish, Brent Bravo, Stephan McLeish, Glasgow, Stephen McLeish, Springboig, Susan McLeish, Glasgow, Susan McLeish, Springboig, Carly McLellan, Falkirk, Drew McLellan, Glasgow, Helen Mclellan-Cassidy, Accrington, Colin McLelland, Moodiesburn, Joe McLelland, Livingston, Neil Mclelland, Glasgow, Vikki McLelland, Livingston, Stuart Mclellen, Clydebank, Alistair McLeod, Cambuslang, Andy McLeod, Bishopbriggs, Callum McLeod, Dumbarton, Ellen McLeod, Possilpark, Fraser McLeod, Edinburgh, Jim Mcleod, Kilbirnie, Jimmy McLeod, Chubby's Bar, Wexford, Kenny McLeod, Maryhill, Glasgow, Lynsey Mcleod, Alloa, McLeod, Glasgow, Stuart McLeoud, Ayr, Shaun McLernon, Ralston, Stevie McLinn, Stewarton, Ross Mclintock, Svodne Dvory, Czech Republic, Ross Mclintock, Svodne Dvory, Czech Republic, Ross Mclintock, Svodne Dvory, Czech Republic, Steven McLoued, , Damian Mcloughlin, Ballycastle, Co Antrim, Des McLoughlin, Haddington, John McLoughlin, Niddrie, Edinburgh, Jordan McLoughlin, Niddrie, Edinburgh, Mark McLoughlin, Haddington, Victor McLulock, Stranraer, Jason McLurg, Dalbeattie, Barry McLuskey, King's Park, Jim McLuskey, Alva, Jimmy McLuskey, Govanhill, Glasgow, Stevie McLuskie, Airdrie, Brian McMacken, Bonnybridge, John McMacken, Bonnybridge, Pamela McMacken, Bonnybridge, Anne McMahon, Wishaw, Barry Mcmahon, Belfast, Brian McMahon, Wishaw, Collin Mcmahon, London, Eddie McMahon, Wishaw, Finlay Mcmahon, Milton Keynes, Francis McMahon, Paisley, Gerry McMahon, Bothwell, Gez McMahon, Bothwell, Ian McMahon, Birmingham, James McMahon, Wishaw, Jamie McMahon, Possil Park, Glasgow, Kevin Mcmahon, Milton Keynes, Lisa McMahon, Wishaw, Paul Mcmahon, Bonnybridge, Paul McMahon, Cambusnethan, Paul J McMahon, Seafield, Ricky Mcmahon, Maryhill, Sarah McMahon, Kirky, Steph McMahon, East Kilbride, Steven McMahon, Wishaw, Susan McMahon, Wishaw, Ted McMahon, Newmains, Terence Mcmahon, Birmingham, England, Terence Mcmahon, Birmingham,England, Alan McMahon Hay, Hunterhill, Paisley, Christie McManis, Motherwell, Danielle McManis, Motherwell, Francis McManis, Airdrie, Francis McManis, Motherwell, Michael McManis, Motherwell, Andrew McMann, Ipswich, Gary McMann, Glasgow, Kevin McMann, Milton Keynes, Marie McMann, Bonnybridge, Grant McMannus, Glasgow, Andy McManus, Milngavie, Andy Mcmanus, Milngavie, Arron McManus, Glasgow, Bert McManus, Grangemouth, Christopher Mcmanus, Balornock,Glasgow, David McManus, Haddington, Frank McManus, Motherwell, Franny McManus, Carfin, Gerry McManus, Milngavie, Harry McManus, Dundee, J McManus, Easter

House, Jamie McManus, Scotstoun, Glasgow, Jonny McManus, Glasgow, Matthew Mcmanus, Altofts, West Yorkshire, Michael McManus, Carfin, Michael McManus, Motherwell, Phil McManus, Birmingham, Scott McManus, Kilmarnock, Sean Mcmanus, Batley,West Yorkshire, Sean McManus, Birmingham, Winni McManus, Bellshill, David McMaster, Dundee, Paul McMaster, Glasgow, Paul McMaster, Kirkintilloch, Paul McMaster, Old Kilpatrick, Dean McMaster, Dundee, Mark McMeekin, Airdrie, Mark McMeekin, Airdrie, McMeekin, Glasgow, Andrew & Tasha Mcmenamin, Perth Australia, Chris McMenamin, Annan, Christopher McMenamin, Glasgow, Mark McMenamin, Annan, Anne McMenemy, Denny, Colin McMenemy, Glasgow, Michael McMenemy, Denny, Michael McMenemy, Glasgow, Michael McMenemy, Glasgow, Neil McMenemy, Burnside, Paul Mcmenemy, East Kilbride, Stephen McMenemy, Nottingham, Joseph McMeneny, Glasgow, John McMennmie, Stonehaven, John McMichael, Belfast, Michelle McMichan, Forres, Jim McMicheal, East Kilbride, Alex McMillan, Ayrshire, Alex McMillan, Paisley, Brian McMillan, Kilwinning, Chris McMillan, Kilbirnie Ayrshire, Gerry McMillan, Ardrossan, Gordon McMillan, Bromley, John McMillan, Linwood, Nina McMillan, Stevenson, Ricky McMillan, Glasgow, Stuart McMillan, St.Catharines, Ontario Canada, James McMillan Jnr, Greenock, Richard McMillan Jnr, Southampton, Ian McMillian, Paisley, Josh McMillian, Blackburn.West Lothian., Scott McMillan, Paisley, David McMinn, Bannockburn, Isa Mcminn, Bo'ness, Jamie Mcminn, Bo'ness, Lewis McMinn, Bannockburn, Lisa McMinn, Bannockburn, Edith McMonagle, Dumbarton, Neil & David McMonagle, Rutherglen, Ross McMonagle, Aviemore, Ross McMonagle, Aviemore, Scott Mcmonagle, Glasgow, Willie McMonagle, Dumbarton, Conor McMonagley, Glasgow, Ian Mcmorrin, Aberdeen, Brian McMullan, East Kilbride, Chloe McMullan, Dundee, Des McMullan, Glasgow, Emma McMullan, Glasgow, Gerry McMullan, Dundee, Joe McMullan, East Kilbride, Kieran McMullan, East Kilbride, Lee McMullan, Gglasgow, Liam McMullan, Dundee, Lisa Jane McMullan, Dundee, Lynda McMullan, Dundee, Malachy Mcmullan, Dublin, Mick McMullan, East Kilbride, Niall McMullan, East Kilbride, Paul McMullan, East Kilbride, Rose McMullan, Glasgow, Stephen McMullan, Denny, Steven Mcmullan, High Burnside, Tony McMullan, Banknock, Emma McMullen, Motherwell, Johnpaul McMullen, Coatbridge, Louise McMullen, Motherwell, Mark McMullen, Bearsden, Mary McMullen, Glasgow, Michael Mcmullen, Glasgow, Paul McMullin, Motherwell, Tommy McMullin, Motherwell, McMullin, Motherwell, Paul McMullins, , James McMultan, Livingston, James McMultan, Livingston, Mickey McMultan, Livingston, Mickey McMultan, Livingston, Scott McMurchie, Kirkton, Taylor McMurchie, Kirkton, Tom McMurchie, Perth, Paul Mcmurray, Paisley, William Mcmurray, Paisley, Robbie Mcmurtrie, Balornock, Andrew McNab, Hereford, Christopher McNab, Glasgow, Kenneth Mcnab, Dalgety Bay, George McNabey, Croydon, Scott McNabney, Alloa, Noel McNaboe, Cavan, Ireland, Ian McNair, Kenilworth, Warwickshire, Tom McNair, Kingspark, Brian McNairn, Irvine, Catlin McNairney, Haghill, Connor McNairney, Haghill, Aidan McNally, Motherwell, Andy McNally, Dorset, Catherine Ann McNally, Shotts, Chic McNally, Shettleston, Glasgow, Diarmid McNally, Condorrat, Gayle McNally, Cumbernauld, Jamie McNally, Motherwell, Jordan McNally, Ferguslie Park, Kevin McNally, Shettleston, Glasgow, Linzi McNally, Shettleston, Glasgow, Lorraine McNally, Shettleston, Glasgow, Martin McNally, Motherwell, Pat McNally, Corby, Rab McNally, Corby, Rab Mcnally, Corby, Northants, Sam McNally, Cumbernauld, Sean McNally, Johnstone, Tony McNally, Glenrothes, Gary Mcnamara, East Kilbride, Grant Mcnamara, East Kilbride, Anne McNamee, Glasgow, Daniel McNamee, Cambuslang, Michael McNamee, Glasgow, Paul McNamee, Glasgow, Peter McNamee, Paisley, Stevie McNamee, Edinburgh, Stevie McNamee, South Side, Gavin McNamere, Glasgow, Ali McNaught, East Kilbride, Joe McNaught, Glasgow, Joe McNaughton, , Sean McNaughton, Denny, Nathan Paul McNee, Merrylee, Glasgow, Paul McNee, Merrylee, Glasgow, Stephen Mcnee, Chapelhall, Alex McNeil, Drumchapel, Glasgow, Ashley McNeil, Sauchie, Ashley Mcneil, Sauchie, Billy McNeil, Perth, Colin McNeil, Motherwell, Drew McNeil, Drumchapel, Glasgow, Elizabeth McNeil, Drumchapel,

223

Glasgow, Jim Mcneil, Bishopton, John Mcneil, East Kilbride, John Mcneil, Portglasgow, Julie McNeil, Nitshill, Laura McNeil, Nitshill, Margaret McNeil, Drumchapel, Glasgow, Martin McNeil, Port Glasgow, Mick McNeil, Renfrew, Ned McNeil, Perth, Sandra Mcneil, Renfrew, Sean McNeil, Renfrew, Suzanne Mcneil, Portglasgow, Barry McNeill, New York City, Billy McNeill, Whitburn, Colin McNeill, East Kilbride, Dan McNeill, Bishopbriggs, Gary McNeill, Paisley, Mark McNeill, Co. Down, Paul McNeill, Paul McNeill, Blantyre, Robbie McNeill, Paisley, Ryan McNeill, Irvine, Sam McNeill, Kilmarnock, Stacey Mcneill, Whitburn, Tam McNeill Jnr, , Tam McNeill Snr, Senga Mcneilly, Easterhouse, Glasgow, Mcneilly, Easterhouse, Glasgow, Paul McNelis, Port Glasgow, Robert McNenemy, Peterhead, Aaron McNevin, Dundee, Annette McNicol, Balornock, James McNicol, Glasgow, Moya McNicol, Balornock East, Paula McNicol, Largs, Ian Mcniece, Kings Park, Glasgow, Andrew McNish, Darvel, Bernard McNulty, Paisley, Garry McNulty, Aberdeen, James McNulty, Mountcastle, Edinburgh, Kevin McNulty, Mountcastle, Edinburgh, Mark McNulty, Milngavie, Paul McNulty, Milngavie, Sam McNulty, Coventry, Sean McNulty, Bishopbriggs, Tony Mcnulty, Paisley & Huntly, Tony Mcnulty, Paisley & Huntly, Vincent McNulty, Bishopbriggs, Barry McPake, St Ninians, Charlie McPake, St Ninians, Eddie McPake, Lochee, Dundee, Erin McPake, Lochee, Dundee, Pedro Mcpake, Hamilton, Stephen McPake, Rutherglen, James McParland, Coatbridge, James McPeake, N. Belfast, Sandy McPhail, Corby, Angela McPhearson, Clydebank, Kris McPhedran, Cumbernauld, Ross McPhedran, Cumbernauld, Alex Duke McPhee, Port Glasgow, Sharn McPhee, Port Glasgow, Tam McPhee, Giffnock, Tam McPhee, Giffnock, Billy McPherson, Robroyston, Glasgow, Christopher McPherson, Paisley, Dyllan McPherson, Falkirk, Finlay McPherson, East Kilbride, Gordon Mcpherson, Greenock, Helen Mcpherson, Greenock, James McPherson, Denny, Jim McPherson, Corby, Jinky McPherson, Seville, Jon McPherson, East Kilbride, Raymond McPherson, Inverneshire, Sinead McPherson, Paisley, Stewart Mcpherson, Cumbernauld, Yvonne McPherson, Prestwick, Barry McPhilemy, Baillieston, Terry McPhilemy, Possil, James McPhillips, Boghall, West Lothian, Jim McPhillips, Bathgate, Mary McPhillips, Boghall, West Lothian, Mary McPhillips, , Peadar McPhillips, Dublin, Stephen McPhillips, Irvine, Ayrshire, David McPike, Glasgow, David McPike, Glasgow, Andrew McQuade, Cumbernauld, Anna Mcquade, Grangemouth, Anna McQuade, Grangemouth, Blair McQuade, Fife, Connor McQuade, Falkirk, Frankie McQuade, Harrington, Northhants, Iain Mcquade, Renfrew, Scotland+, Jack McQuade, Harrington, Northhants, James McQuade, Newmains, Lesley McQuade, Texas, Lyn Mcquade, Sighthill, Patrick McQuade, Bellshill, Roy McQuade, Texas, Ryan McQuade, Texas, Sara McQuade, Texas, Sarah McQuade, Glasgow, Shug McQuade, Falkirk, Tam McQuade, Blantyre, Tam Mcquade, Wishaw, Thomas Mcquade, Burnside, Tom McQuade, Blantyre, Ian Mcquat, Harrow, Middlesex, Breen McQueen, Falkirk, Callum Mcqueen, Currie, Midlothian, Gordon McQueen, Plymouth, Jack McQueen, Glasgow, Janet McQueen, Falkirk, Pamela Mcqueen, Currie, Midlothian, Ian McQuillan, Canada, Nick McQuillan, Glasgow, John McQuillian, Kirkintilloch, Sandy Mcquiston, Ayr, Mcquiston, Ayr, Conner McRae, Ana McRobert, Leicestershire, Anna McRobert, Melton Mowbray, David McRobert, Kilmarnock, Moray McRobert, Leicestershire, Murray McRobert, Melton Mowbray, Scott McSeueney, Shotts, Stephen McSeuney, Shotts, Anthony McShane, Preisthill, Glasgow, Billy McShane, Barrhead, Charlie McShane, Carfin, Declan Mcshane, Ballingry, Fife, Isabell Mcshane, Ballingry, Fife, James Mcshane, Ballingry Csc, Jazz McShane, Denniston, John McShane, Carfin, Lisa Mcshane, Felixstowe, Megan Mcshane, Ballingry, Fife, Norma McShane, Greenock, Pat McShane, Coatbridge, Colin McShannon, Bothwell, Gerry Mcsheffrey, Scotstoun, Jerry McSheffrey, Glasgow, John Mcsheffrey, Knightswood, Michael Sean McSherry, Glasgow, Vince McSherry, SE England, Vincent McSherry, Glasgow, Ross Mcskeane, Clarkston, David Mcsorley, Johnstone, Gary McSorley, Hackbridge, Kevin McSorley, Glasgow, Paul McSorley, Glasgow, Siobhan McSorley, Glasgow, Tom McSorley, Tadworth, Peter McSpadey, Coatbridge, John Jock McStay, Larkhall, Neil McSween, Oben, Benny McSwegan, Johnstone, Benny McSwegan,

Johnstone, Graeme Mctaggart, Glasgow, Mark McTaggart, Blantyre, Nicky McTaggart, Glasgow, Craig McTagggart, Glasgow, Jamie McTear, Glasgow, Jim McTear, Glasgow, Stacey McUrnon, Saltcoats, S McVay, Glasgow, Peter Mcverry, Whitburn, Robert McVerry, Whitburn, Daniel McVey, Ferguslie Park, Daryll McVey, Ferguslie Park, Davey Mcvey, Port Glasgow Harp C.S.C., Debbie Mcvey, Port Glasgow, Gerald McVey, Scotstoun, Gerald McVey, Scotstoun, Glasgow, John McVey, Coatbridge, Laura McVey, Scotstoun, Linda McVey, Scotstoun, Lisa McVey, Scotstoun, Paul McVey, Coatbridge, Sean McVey, Scotstoun,Chris McVicar, Erskine, Connor McVicar, Erskine, Craig McVicar, Erskine, George McVicar, Erskine, Hugh McVicar, Erskine, Kirstin McVicar, Erskine, Julie McWalter, Arbroath, Alec McWaters, Greenock, Gerrard McWilliam, Hogganfield, Martyn McWilliam, Hogganfield, Tommy McWilliam, Glasgow, A McWilliams, Partick, David McWilliams, Glasgow, Denise McWilliams, Paisley, Gary McWilliams, Coatbridge, Gerry McWilliams, Kilmarnock, Gerry Mcwilliams, Kilmarnock, J McWilliams, Govan, John McWilliams, Paisley, R McWilliams, Govan, Shuana McWilliams, Kilmarnock, Tominey McWilliams, Coatbridge, Stephen Meade, Rosyth, Robert Meaken, Bellshill, Laurence Meaney, Clacton on Sea, David Mearns, Hamilton, Garry Mearns, Stepps, Scott Mearns, Newton Mearns, John Mears, Leven, Charlie Meecham, Wishaw, Ashley Meechan, Wishawhill, Brodie Meechan, Garngad, Chris Meechan, Hamilton, Frank Meechan, Banff, Frank Meechan, Gilmerton, Edinburgh, Jamie Meechan, Bellshill, John Meechan, Uddingston, Jordan Daniel Meechan, Garngad, Kenny Meechan, Leith, Kerry Meechan, Gilmerton, Edinburgh, Nicole Meechan, Bellshill, Pat Meechan, Bellshill, Ryan Meechan, Hamilton, William Meechan, Tullibody, Willie And Tommy Meechan, Springburn, Anne Meehan, St Catharines, Canada, Gerry Meehan, St Catharines, Canada, Jacky Meehan, St Catharines, Canada, James Meehan, Cardonald, Kevan Meehan, Erskine, Paul Meehan, Edinburgh, Charles Meek, Glasgow, Eamon Meenan, Kingspark, Gary Meers, Kilwinning, Gary Meers, , Michael Meers, London, Marya Meighan, Inverness, Mark Meijle, Dumbarton, Craig Meikle, Leith, Edinburgh, Nathan Meikle, Milton, Glasgow, Stewart Meikle, Lesmahagow, David Meiklejohn, Torphins, Aberdeen, Emily Meiklejohn, Torphins, Aberdeen, Gary Meiklejohn, Kirkcaldy, Dougie Mekile, Denny, Linda Mel, Glasgow, Colin Meldrum, East Kilbride, Kenny Meldrum, Balloch, Charlie Mellon, Cambuslang, James Mellon, Ruchill, Glasgow, Jamie Mellon, Tullibody, Michael Mellon, Tullibody, Michael Sean Mellon, Peterlee, Co Durham, Ronnie Mellon, Tullibody, Clare Melly, Glasgow, Chris Stuart Melvile, Glasgow, Arlene Melville, Dullator, Lynne Melville, Gran Canaria, Duncan Melvin, Glasgow, Jim Melvin, Surrey, Jim Melvin, Surrey, Martin Melvin, Kinghorn, Ross Melvin, Glasgow, Steven Melvin, Glasgow, Brendan Memner, Motherwell, Ryan Memner, Motherwell, Eddie Men, Epping, Colleen Menham, Ballymoney, Jadzia Menham, Ballymoney, Mary Menham, Ballymoney, Megan Menham, Ballymoney, Claire Menzies, Glasgow, Derek Menzies, Glasgow, Fergus Mernagh, Chubby's Bar, Wexford, Martin Merrick, Bishopbriggs, Fraser Methven, Kinross, Kieron Methven, Kinross, Stephen Methven, Kinross, C Michaelson, Dundee, Barrie Middleton, Cambuslang, Gemma Middleton, Cambuslang, Hannah Middleton, Greenock, Lee Middleton, Port, Glasgow, Mark Middleton, Dunoon, Natalie Middleton, Port, Glasgow, Ross Middleton, Port, Glasgow, Eric Mike, Dumfries, Scott Milden, St Johnstone, Stewart Miles, Denny, Alan Mill, Angela Millar, Cardonald, Glasgow, Bobby Millar, Charles Millar, Motherwell, David Millar, Halkirk, Erin Millar, Tullibody, Gillian Millar, Paisley, Gordon Millar, Paisley, Grant Millar, Balloch, Jacqui Millar, Newton Mearns, James Millar, Mosspark, Glasgow, James Millar, Paisley, John Millar, Clydebank, John Millar, Kinning Park, Glasgow, Julie Millar, South Queensferry, Martin Millar, Paisley, Robbie Millar, Dunfermline, Scott David Millar, Dunfermline, Stephen Millar, Clydebank, Steven Millar, Tullibody, Tony Millar, Dalkeith, Tracey Millar, Paisley, Patrick Millarkie, Barrhead, Ian Millarvie, Hamilton, Michael Milld, Abronhill, Andy Miller, Helensburgh, Anne Miller, Wishaw, Anthony Miller, Newcastle-Upon-Tyne, Anton Miller, Darnley, Barry Miller, Denny, Caroline Miller, Newcastle-Upon-Tyne, Catherine Miller, Ayr, Chris Miller, Barrhead, Chris Miller, Whitburn,

Craig Miller, Kirriemuir, Daniel Miller, Newcastle-Upon-Tyne, David Miller, Glasgow, David Miller, Motherwell, David Miller, Newcastle-Upon-Tyne, Deborah Miller, Dunfermline, Derek Miller, Old Drumchapel, Ericka Miller, Paisley, Gary Miller, Blantyre, Gary Miller, Hamilton, Graeme Miller, Newton Mearns, J Miller, Kilsyth, Jimmy Miller, Egremont, John Miller, Glasgow, Kerry Ann Miller, Blantyre, Lisa Miller, Wishaw, Louise Miller, Paisley, Lynne Miller, Alexandria, Lynne Miller, Alexandria, Lynne Miller, Alexandria, Dunbartonshire, Michael Miller, Lochgelly, Michelle Miller, Lochgelly, Mick Miller, Glasgow, Paul Miller, Grangemouth, Paul Miller, Rutherglen, Pauline Miller, Wishaw, Rachael Miller, Paisley, Raymond Miller, Glasgow, Ronan Miller, Paisley, Sharon Miller, Glasgow, Sharon Miller, Glasgow, Stacey Miller, Glasgow, Stephanie Miller, Blantyre, Steven Miller, Law, Steven Miller, Law, Stevie Miller, Bar 67 Gallowgate, Stevie Miller, Motherwell, Stu Miller, Glasgow, Victoria Miller, Shotts, Andrew Milligan, Parkhead, James Milligan, Sunningdale, John Milligan, Glasgow, Kieran Milligan, Edinburgh, Kieran Milligan, Edinburgh, William Milligan, Edinburgh, William Milligan, Edinburgh, William Milligan, Oxgangs, Conor Milloy, Gourock, Andrew Mills, Glasgow, Davie Mills, Bury, Garry Mills, Abronhill, Harry Mills, Cambuslang, Brian Milne, Faifley, Chloe Milne, Maryhill, Glasgow, Colin Milne, Cumbernauld, Craig Milne, Falkirk, Craig Milne, Grangemouth, Dawson Milne, Aberdeen, Dean Milne, Airdrie, Demi Milne, Springburn,Glasgow, Elizabeth Milne, Glasgow, Graham Milne, Bicester, Graham Milne, Colchester, Jackie Milne, Springburn,Glasgow, Jacqui Milne, Armdale, West Lothian, Jane Milne, Maryhill,Glasgow, Jim Milne, Airdrie, John Milne, Cumbernauld, Neville Milne, Cumbernauld, Paul Milne, Maryhill,Glasgow, Stephanie Milne, Springburn,Glasgow, Tam Milne, Springburn,Glasgow, The Milnes, Robroyston, Simon Milroy, Glasgow, Steven Milroy, Glasgow, Steven Milroy Jnr, Glasgow, Shaun Milton, , Stevie Milton,   Aaron Mimnaugh, Motherwell, Airan Mimnaugh, Motherwell, Barry Mimnaugh, Cleland, Courtney Mimnaugh, Motherwell, Regan Mimnaugh, Motherwell, Ryan Mimnaugh, Motherwell, James Mimner, Motherwell, Kieran Minnery,   Glasgow, Sean Minnery, Glasgow, David Minnis, Kirkshaws, Coatbridge, Andy Mitchell, Brechin, Arlene Mitchell, Dreghorn, Baby Mitchell, Glasgow, Blair Mitchell, Stonehaven, Brian Mitchell, Clackmananshire, Brian Mitchell, Washington Court House, Ohio, Usa, Brian Mitchell, , Brian J Mitchell, Alva, Brian, Sara & Aidan Mitchell, Washington Ch., Ohio, Usa, Caryn Anne Mitchell, Baillieston, Chris Mitchell, Easterhouse, Connor Mitchell, Townhead, Coatbridge, Craig Mitchell, Stonehaven, Darren Mitchell, Kilwinning, David Mitchell, Baillieston, David John Mitchell, Baillieston, Fraser Mitchell, Glasgow, Gordon Mitchell, Dennistoun, James Mitchell, Quarryknowe, Joe Mitchell, Greenock, Kenny Mitchell, Brechin, Kevin Mitchell, Lennoxtown, Marie Mitchell, Baillieston, Mary Mitchell, Tarboltan, Ayrshire, Paul Mitchell, Glasgow, Peter David Mitchell, Ibrox, Scott Mitchell, Dumbarton, Stan Mitchell, Stonehaven, Stanley Mitchell, Stonehaven, Steven Mitchell, Falkirk, Tony Mitchell, Baillieston, Tony Mitchell, Lochgelly, Wullie Mitchell, Plymouth, Steven Mitsy, Coatbridge, Steven Mitsy, Coatbridge, Janice Moan, E/K, John Paul Moan, East Kilbride, William Moan, Glasgow, Michelle Moane, Glasgow, Nikki Moane, Glasgow, Norrie Moane, Cumbernauld, Michelle Moans, Glasgow, John Mochan, Hamilton, Lynnette Mochan, Co Durham, Steve Mochan, Clydebank, Toni Mochan, Co Durham, Aidan Moffat, Teeside, Allan Moffat, Yoker, Glasgow, Carole Moffat, Easglescliffe, Teeside, Carole Moffat, Teeside, James Moffat, Glasgow, Roy Moffat, Stockton-on-Tees, Ryan Moffat, Eaglescliffe(Xdumfries), Ryan Moffat, Easglescliffe, Teeside, Ryan Moffat, Teeside, Scot Moffat, Prestonpans, R Mohammed, Ayrshire, Jordan Mohan, Bothwell, Keith Moir, Millerston, Matt Moir, Kilbarchan, Pamela Mollahan, Novato, California, Usa, Annemarie Molloy, Greenock, Eddie Molloy, Germany, Gerry Molloy, Glasgow, James Molloy, Louth, Jim Molloy, Greenock, Joe Molloy, Glasgow, John Molloy, Staffordshire, Jordan Molloy, Pollockshields, Julie Molloy, Greenock, Kerri Molloy, Greenock, Laura Molloy, Cardonald, Mairi Molloy, Cardonald, Paul Molloy, Glasgow, Susan Molloy, Glasgow, Tracey Molloy, Greenock,   James Molloy Jnr, Lincolnshire, James Molloy Snr, Lincolnshire, Brian Monaghan, Cambuslang, Craig

226

Monaghan, Livingston, Harry Monaghan, High Wycombe, Ian Monaghan, Easterhouse, Glasgow, Joe Monaghan, Livingston, Joe Monaghan, Livingston, John Monaghan, , Kate Monaghan, Cambuslang, Leah Monaghan, Garrowhill, Glasgow, Mary Monaghan, City Centre, Megan Monaghan, Clarkston, Glasgow, Shaun Monaghan, Ayrshire, Sinead Monaghan, Clarkston, Stephen Monaghan, Clarkston, Susan Monaghan, Clarkston, Cassie Monaghans, Ayrshire, Joe Monaghans, Ayrshire, Carden Monahan, Irvine, Lorna Moncrieff, Rutherglen, Ally Monk, Isle of Benbecula. John Monk, Mount Florida, Glasgow, Monty Monk, Isle of Benbecula, Willy John Monk, Isle of Benbecula, Davie Monroe, Johnstone, Ian Monstro, East Kilbride, Amon Montague, Ashford, John Montague, Ashford, Montanna, Livingston, John Monteith, Sandyhills, Amanda Montgomery, Dumbarton, Andrew Montgomery, Glasgow, Elaine Moodiesburn, Ian Moodiesburn, Glasgow, Paul Moodiesburn, Toddy Moodiesburn, Alec Moody, East Kilbride, Alex Moody, East Kilbride, Mark Moohan, Prestonpans, Christine Moon, Motherwell, William Patrick Moon, Alex Mooney, Glasgow, Andrew Mooney, Motherwell, Chris Mooney, Glasgow, Danny Mooney, Ballycastle Co.Antrim, Frankie Mooney, Wishaw, Lanarkshire, Gary Mooney, Castlemilk, Gerry Mooney, Coventry, Isa Mooney, Glasgow, John Mooney, Bellshill, Lanarkshire, John Mooney, Motherwell, Kevin Mooney, Ballycastle, Eire, Kieran Mooney, Parkhouse,Glasgow, Kim Mooney, Wishaw, Lanarkshire, Martin Mooney, Motherwell, Michael Mooney, Airdrie, Patrick Mooney, Edinburgh, Paul Mooney, Crookston, Paul Mooney, Crookston/Kp, Peter Mooney, Hamilton, Peter Mooney, Wishaw, Lanarkshire, Shug Mooney, West London, Stephen Mooney, Castlemilk, Stephen Mooney, Motherwell, Steven Mooney, Glasgow, Andrew Moore, Castle Douglas, Andrew Moore, Dunbar, East Lothian, Brian Moore, Kirkintilloch, Gary Moore, Dunbar, East Lothian, James Moore, Bridgeton Glasgow, Jane Moore, Shotts, Jermery Moore, Johnstone, John Moore, Cumbernauld, Paddy Moore, Ashby, Leics, Paul Moore, Washington, USA, Robert (Bobby) Moore, London, Shug Moore, Barrhead, Shuggie Moore, Barrhead, Stephen Moore, Renfrew, Paul Mora, Drongan, Anthony Moran, , Barry Moran, Glasgow, Brian Moran, Kingspark, Daniel Moran, Isle of Jura, David Moran, Coatbridge, David Moran, Coatbridge, David Moran, , Edna Moran, Harthill, Gary Moran, Isle of Jura, Jim Moran, Portsmouth, Joe Moran, Kensington, London, John Moran, Ballachulish, Joseph Moran, London, Laura Moran, Cumbernauld, Michael Moran, Cumbernauld, Michael Moran, Renfrew, Noel Moran, Derry, Patricia Moran, Glasgow, Paul Moran, Ormiston, Rita Moran, Swinton, Simon Moran, Isle of Jura, Tony Moran, Deans, Livingston, Liam Morcombe, Whitburn, Niki Morcombe, Whitburn, Owen Lennon Morcombe, Whitburn, Ryan Morcombe, Whitburn, Wullie Morcombe, Whitburn, Gordon More, Shetland, Jenson More, Grangemouth, John More, Grangemouth, Stuart More, Grangemouth, John Moreland, Scotstoun, Glasgow, Peter Moreland, Airdrie, Lauren Morell, Balornock, Alan Morgan, Kingseat, Fife, Andrea Morgan, Glasgow, Ashley Morgan, Southsea, Barry Morgan, Larbert, Brenda Morgan, Coatbridge, Catherine Morgan, Renfrew, Cheryl Morgan, Summerston, Colin Morgan, Leslie Fife, Conor Morgan, Summerston, Gerard Morgan, Greenock, Josie Morgan, Airdrie, Kailey Morgan, Southsea, Kevin Morgan, Greenock, Kim Morgan, Glasgow, Lisa Morgan, Dunfermline, Paul Morgan, Glasgow, Robert Morgan, Southsea, Sharon Morgan, Summerston, Stephen Morgan, Muirhead, Willie Morgan, Maryhill, Willie Morgan, Summerston, David Moriarty, Renfrew, Gary Lubo Morisson, Blantyre, Jackie Mornian, Dunfermline, John Mornian, Dunfermline, Stephen Morning, Kilbarchan, Patrick Moroney, Portumna, County Galway, Brendan Morran, Old Kilpatrick, Fritz Morrice, Banffshire, Cari Morrin, Glasgow, Charli Morrin, Glasgow, Charli (Juicy) Morrin, South West Glasgow, Will Morrin, London, Allan Morris, Harthill, Arthur Morris, Renfrew, Craig Morris, Striling, Jane Marie Morris, Chapelhall, Kenny Morris, Glenrothes, Fife, Kris Morris, Coatbridge, Michael Morris, Glasgow, Paul Morris, Airdrie, Sally Morris, Glasgow, Sally Morris, Glasgow, Thomas Morris, Chapelhall, Kenny Morris Jnr, Glenrothes, Kenny Morris Snr, Glenrothes, AJ Morrison, Isle of Benbecula, Alan Morrison, Isle of Benbecula, Alan Morrison, South Uist,

Alan Morrison, South Uist, Biz Morrison, Auldearn, Biz Morrison, Auldearn, Cameron Morrison, Charles Morrison, Coatbridge, Charlot Ann Morrison, South Uist, Chris Morrison, Newarthill, Ciaran Morrison, Coatbridge, George Morrison, London, George Morrison, London, George Morrison, Turiff, Aberdeenshire, Jack Morrison, Cardiff, Jackie Morrison, West London, James Morrison, Saltcoats Ayrshire, Joseph Morrison, Glasgow, Katline Morrison, Cockburnspath, Kevin Morrison, Clydebank, Liam Morrison, Glasgow, Maria Morrison, Coatbridge, Martin Morrison, Glasgow, Nicola Morrison, Coatbridge, Patricia Morrison, Glasgow, Patrick Morrison, Glasgow, Reid Morrison, West London, Richard Morrison, Turiff, Aberdeenshire, Robert Morrison, Glasgow, Ronny Morrison, Skarry Morrison, Stornoway, Stacey Morrison, Glasgow, Steven Morrison, Glasgow, Tammy Morrison, Irvine, Terry Morrison, Bishopbriggs, Tommy Morrison, Old Kilpatrick, Bernie Morrocco, Preston Athletic, Ebony Morrow, Uddingston, Iona Maria Morrow, Sheffield, James Morrow, Sheffield, Sally Morrow, Glasgow, Alicia Mortimer, East Kilbride, Jim Mortimer, Knightswood, Abbie Morton, Abbingdon, Betty Morton, Tullibody, Betty Morton, Tullibody, Craig Morton, Knightswood, Danielle Morton, Burnside, Dominic Morton, Burnside, Iain Morton, Clydebank, Joanne Morton, Abbingdon, John Morton, Knightswood, Kristopher Morton, Burnside, Rebecca Morton, Abbingdon, Trudy Morton, Liverpool, Bertie Moss, Falkirk, Alex Mosson, Cumbernauld, Con Moston, Manchester, Craig Moston, Manchester, Ernie Moston, Manchester, John Moston, Manchester, Mick Moston, Manchester, David Moultrie, Moodiesburn, Paul Mowat, Witney, Oxon, Ron Mowat, Witney, Oxon, Ian Mowatt, Wester Hailes, John Mowen, Lynwood, Malcolm Moye, Wallsend, Chris Moyes, Tranent, Phil Moylan, Liverpool, Steven Moynes, Poole, Gary Mroz, Galston, Ayrshire, Ms Bannigan, Glasgow, Ms Boyle, Glasgow, Ms Brown, Glasgow, Ms Finlason, Cupar, Ms Haider, Glasgow, Ms Hawk, Coatbridge, Ms McLaughlin, Dundee, Ms McVay, Glasgow, Andreas Muhlberg, Stockholm, Alison Muir, Glasgow, Andy Muir, Garrowhill, Brian Muir, Tollcross, Glasgow, Charlotte Muir, Glasgow, Chris Muir, Greenock, Christopher Muir, Blantyre, Christopher Muir, Glasgow, David Muir, Kings Park, Eleanor Muir, Paisley, Frank Muir, Bearsden, Gary Muir, Glasgow, Gerard Muir, Bearsden, Hugh Muir, Paisley, James Muir, Priesthill, James Muir, Rutherglen, Jennifer Muir, Glasgow, Joe Muir, Bearsden, John Muir, Bannockburn, Stirling, Natalie Muir, Pollok, Natalie Muir, Priesthill, Peter Muir, Greenfield, Glasgow, Robert Muir, Priesthill, Robert Muir, Priesthill, Steven Muir, Rutherglen, Suzanne Muir, Rutherglen, Therese Muir, Priesthill, Therese Muir, Priesthill, Andrew Muirhead, Erskine, Bill Muirhead, Kuwait, Jim Muirhead, Polbeth, Ann Mulcacky, West Lothian, Daniel Mulcahy, East Kilbride, Daniel Mulcahy, East Kilbride, Joe Mulcahy, Ralston, Joe Mulcahy, Ralston, Kevin Mulcahy, Paisley, Kevin Mulcahy, Paisley, Sharon Mulcahy, East Kilbride, Sharon Mulcahy, East Kilbride, Blain Muldoon, Bogner Regis, Christopher Muldoon, Bogner Regis, John Muldoon, Parkhead, Linda Muldoon, Parkhead, Slim Jim Muldoon, Bogner Regis, Muldoon, Wishaw, Gary Mulgrew, Linthouse, Norrie Mulgrew, Govan, Caroline Mulhall, Rutherglen, Terry Mulhern, Worcester, Steven Mulheron, Lanarkshire, Anne Peterina Mulholand 33, Low Craig Ends Kilsyth, Alison Mulholland, Linlithgow, Alison Mulholland, Linlithgow, Arthur Mulholland, Coatbridge, Christopher Mulholland, Falkirk, Gerard Mulholland, Brussels, John Mulholland, Glasgow, John Mulholland, Linlithgow, John Mulholland, Linlithgow, John Mulholland, Port Glasgow, Mark Mulholland, Linlithgow, Mark Mulholland, Linlithgow, Michael Mulholland, Glasgow, Pauline Mulholland, Chippenham, Ripa Mulholland, Coatbridge, Stevie Mulholland, Halfway, Cambuslang, Thomas Mulholland, Falkirk, Kyle James Mulholland 10, St Margarets Polmont Falkirk, James Scott Mulholland 33, Low Craig Ends Kilsyth, William Robert Mulholland 37, St Margarets Polmont Falkirk, Lorna Mary Mulholland 39, St Margarets Polmont Falkirk, Ryan Mulholland 7, Low Craig Ends Kilsyth, Ann Mullan, Bridgetown, Barry Mullan, Glasgow, Barry Mullan, Riddrie, Declan Mullan, Isle Of Man, Frank Mullan, Glasgow, Jason Mullan, Wishaw, Laura Mullan, Glasgow, Mark Mullan, Stirling, Paddy Mullan, Falls Road, Peter Mullan, Cumbernauld, Robert Mullan, Glasgow,

Stuart Mullan, Greenock, Vicky Mullan, Wishaw, Jim Mullan(jnr), Wishaw, Mark Mullane, Cowie Stirling, Marty Mullaney, Ralston, Paisley, Pat Mullaney, Ralston, Paisley, Robert Mullarkey, Lanarkshire, Adam Mullen, Paisley, Arthur Mullen, Cork, Ireland, Christopher Mullen, Scotstoun, Claire Mullen, Falkirk, Clare Mullen, Greenock, Craig Mullen, Bishopbriggs, Danny Mullen, Rosyth, Danny Mullen, Rosyth, David Mullen, Hamilton, Debbie And Benny Mullen, Locharbriggs Dumfries, Edith Mullen, Greenock, Francie Mullen, Greenock, Francis Mullen, Glasgow, Henry Mullen, Dumbarton, Jacqui Mullen, Clydebank, Jason Mullen, Newmains, Jason Mullen, Wishaw, Jason Mullen, Wishaw, Joe Mullen, Blairdardie, John Mullen, Bellshill, Glasgow, John Mullen, Birmingham, John Mullen, Govan,Glasgow, John Mullen, Maryhill, Josh Mullen, Mossend, Karren Mullen, Parkhall, Matthew Mullen, Glasgow, Michael Mullen, Bellshill, Patrick Mullen, Gorbals, Patrick Mullen, Gorbals, Paul Mullen, Blairdardie, Peter Mullen, Glasgow, Peter Mullen, Lenzie, Robert Mullen, Duntocher, Robert Mullen, Duntocher, Stephen Mullen, Baillieston Glasgow, Stevie Mullen, Baillieston Glasgow, Stevie Mullen, Glasgow, Stuart Mullen, Greenock, Jamie Mullen Snr, Wishaw, Joshua Mullenger, Colchester, William Muller, Edinburgh, Megan Mullholland, Glasgow, Paul Mullholland, Coatbridge, Daniel Mulligan, Nottingham, Erin Mulligan, Nottingham, Jordan Mulligan, Nottingham, Joseph Mulligan, Nottingham, Kathleen Mulligan, Barlanark, Luke Mulligan, Nottingham, Michael Mulligan, Barlanark, Niamh Mulligan, Nottingham, Owen Mulligan, Glasgow, William Mulligan, Nottingham, David Mullin, Govan, Derek Mullin, Glasgow, Donna Mullin, Tollcross, Donna Mullin, Tollcross, Gerard Mullin, Renton, John Paul Mullin, Govan, Lee Mullin, Glasgow, Margaret Mullin, Glasgow, Nancy Mullin, Susan Mullin, Glasgow, T Mullin, Cambuslang, Gerard Mullon, Glasgow, Paul Mulrainey, Shettleston, Kerry Mulraney, Knightswood, Glasgow, Derek Mulrine, Mount Florida, Paul Mulvaney, Donegal, Joe Mulvenna, Dumbarton, Joe Mulvenna, Dumbarton, Jim Mulvey, Dundee, Jim Mulvey, Kilmarnock, Karen Mulvey, Shaftesbury, Kathleen Mulvey, Glasgow, Tommy Mulvey, Whinall, Airdrie, Gerry Mungha, Kilmarnock, Greg Mungin, Port Glasgow, Stephen Munn, Glasgow, Alastair Munro, Peterborough, Barry Munro, Greenock, David Munro, Ballieston, Dennis Munro, Inverness, Ian Munro, Newmains, Jamie Munro, St Ninians, Leo Munro, St Ninians, Rory Munro, Inverness, Ian Munroe, Wishaw, Isa Murchie, Gorbals, Isa Murchie, Gorbals, Elaine Murdie, Cowcaddens, Alan Murdoch, Glasgow, Fraser Murdoch, Glasgow, John Murdoch, Glasgow, Louise Murdoch, Craigneuk, Wishaw, Teresa Murdoch, Glasgow, William Murdoch, Barlanark, David Murdock, Rosshire, Edward Murdock, Glasgow, Frank Murdock, Glasgow, Ian Murdock, Glasgow, James Murdock, Glasgow, Matthew Murdock, Roshire, Stephen Murdock, Rosshire, Hugh Murhy, Ayr, Matt Murney, Linwood, Matthew Murney, Linwood, Michael Murney, Linwood, David Murnin, Glasgow, Alan Murphy, Erskine, Allan Murphy, Blantyre, Andrew (Weebob) Murphy, Coatbridge, Angela Murphy, Port Glasgow, Ben Murphy, Ballingry, Fife, Billy Murphy, Townhead, Brady Murphy, Plymouth, Brian Murphy, Mosspark, Christopher Murphy, Eaglesham, Claire Murphy, Glasgow, Conor Murphy, Carluke, Craig Murphy, Glasgow, Danny Murphy, Cambuslang, Deborah Murphy, Glasgow, Edward Murphy, Rochdale, Elaine Murphy, Cambusnethan, Elaine Murphy, Canada, Frank Murphy, Chicago, USA, Frank Murphy, Hamilton, George Murphy, Toryglen, Gerry Murphy, Aylesbury, Bucks, Gerry Murphy, Canada, Gerry Murphy, Dumbarton, Gerry Murphy, Glasgow, Gerry Murphy, Motherwell, Gerry Murphy, Pollok, Glasgow, Gillian Murphy, Fife, James Murphy, Glasgow, James Murphy, Mosspark!, Jane Murphy, Hamilton, Jimmy Murphy, Rosyth, Joe Murphy, Kilmarnock, John Paul Murphy, Newmains, Johnscot Murphy, Glasgow, Joseph Murphy, Carluke, June Murphy, Motherwell, Justin Murphy, Rocksburn, Kevin Murphy, Dumbarton, Kevin Murphy, Dumbarton, Kevin Murphy, Nottingham, Kieran Murphy, Co.Kildare, Ireland, Kirsty Murphy, Mosspark, Liam Murphy, Plymouth, Lynn Murphy, Glasgow, Matthew Murphy, Fife, May Murphy, Hamilton, May Murphy, Hamilton, Melissa Murphy, Motherwell, Michael Murphy, Coatbridge, Michael Murphy, Prestonpans, Mick Murphy, Wolverhampton, Neil

Murphy, Glasgow, Neil Murphy, Hamilton, Owen Murphy, Port Glasgow, Pamela Murphy, Easter Queenslie, Patrick Murphy, Eaglesham, Paul Murphy, Glasgow, Paula (Plug) Murphy, Coatbridge, Rab Murphy, St Ninians, Scott Murphy, Bellshill, Scott Murphy, Hamilton, Sharon Murphy, Wishaw, Stephen Murphy, Dumbarton, Stephen Murphy, Rosyth, Tom Murphy, Portugal, Tony Murphy, Blackburn.West Lothian., Victor Murphy, Knighswood, William Murphy(Billy), Bellsbank, Dalmellington, Ayrshire, John Murphy(Mepp), Newcastle-Upon-Tyne, Aaron Murray, Prestonpans, Aidan Murray, Clydebank, Alan David Murray, Erskine, Allan Murray, Erskine, Anne Marie Murray, Hamilton, Anthony Murray, Clydebank, Barry Murray, Toryglen, Brenda Murray, Prestonpans, Brian Murray, Cleland, Cammy Murray, Fife, Christopher Murray, Wishaw, Colette Murray, Cleland, Connor Murray, Glasgow, Craig Murray, Hamilton, Craig Murray, Motherwell, Daniel Murray, Cumbernauld, Derek Murray, Denny, Dexy Murray, Aviemore, Dominick Murray, Kirkintilloch, Donald Murray, Possil, Donny Murray, Bearsden, Donny Murray, Linwood, Frank Murray, Castlemilk, Glasgow, Franny Murray, Govanhill, George Murray, Fortrose, Ger Murray, Barrhead, Gerard Murray, Bangor, Gerard Murray, Castlemilk, Graeme Murray, Aberdeen, Helen Murray, Blackburn, James Murray, Tenerife, Janice Murray, West Dunbartonshire, Jeannie Murray, Greenock, Jim Murray, Cleland, Motherwell, Joe Murray, Baillieston, Joe Murray, Baillieston, John Murray, Craigbank, John Murray, Glasgow, John Murray, Hamilton, Karen Murray, Fortrose, Kathleen Murray, Old Kilpatrick, Kenny Murray, Kyle, Kevin Murray, Aberdeen, Kevin Murray, Australia, Kevin Murray, Cleland , Motherwell, Kieran Murray, Muirend, Lee Murray, Barnstaple, Leon Murray, Boghall, Louise Murray, Larkhall, Lynne Murray, Brechin, Angus, Martin Murray, Gourock/Costa Del Sol, Megan Murray, Cleland , Motherwell, Michael Murray, Hamilton, Mick Murray, Glasgow, Nathan Murray, Cleland, Nicholas Murray, Linwood, Paul Murray, Darnley, Paul Murray, Linwood, Paul Murray, Linwood, Richard Murray, Glasgow, Rickey Murray, Cumbernauld, Ryan Murray, Glasgow, Scott Murray, Baillieston, Sean Murray, Glasgow, Sonny Murray, Airdrie, Stephen Murray, Cleland, Motherwell, Stephen Murray, Falkirk, Stephen Murray, Hamilton, Steven Murray, Cumbernauld, Stuart Murray, Paisley, Thomas Murray, Larbert, Tony Murray, Clydebank, Tracy Murray, Motherwell, Vincent Murray, Larkhall, Wullie Murray, Pollok, David Murray, Black, Stornoway, Paul "Ickie" Murry, Grangemouth, Benny Murtagh, Wishaw, Kevin Murty, Drumchapel, Glasgow, Kevin Murty, West Haven, Connecticut, Demi Mutch, Edinburgh, Leigh-Anne Mutch, Edinburgh, Stevie Myatt, Preston Athletic, Ryan Myles, Bellshill, Stuart Myles, Denny,

Bob Nairn, Dave Nairn, Jim Nairn, Lee Nairn, David Naismith, Glasgow. David Naismith, Glasgow, Laurence Naismith, Glasgow, Steven Naismith, Glasgow, Psycho Nanda, Isle of South Uist, Bobby Napier, Bathgate, John Napier, Paisley, Kevin Napier, Belfast, Peter Naughton, Newmains, Grant Naysmith, Paisley, Ryan Naysmith, Kelty, Fife, Justin Neagle, Stanwell, Colin 'Nana' Neale, Ibrox, Angela Nearish, Glasgow, Gerry Neary, Dennistoun, Liam Neary, Blantyre, Liam Neary, Blantyre, Jack Neave, Dundee, Andy Nee, Hamilton, Andy Nee, Hamilton, Mairi-Claire Nee, Hamilton, Paul Neenan, Forfar, Ashleigh Neil, Hamilton, Derek Neil, Barmuir Tarbolton, Gordon Neil, Port Seton, Graham Neil, Larkhall, Grant Neil, Glasgow, Kenny Neil, Switzerland, Mark Neil, Shawlands, Mark Neil, Shawlands, Gordon Neil Jnr, Port Seton, Danny Neill, Alexandria, Andy Neilson, Mossend, Billy Neilson, Inverness, Jim Neilson, Maryhill, Fiona Neish, Rhondda South Wales, Gerry Neish, Crosshouse, Joe Neish, Crosshouse, Albert Nelson, Stirling, Alex Nelson, Cambuslang, Brogan Nelson, Newmains, Chris Nelson, Cawdor, Colin Nelson, Salisbury, Colin Nelson, , David Nelson, Glasgow, David Nelson, Mid Lothian, Dean Nelson, Garrowhill, Dessy Nelson, Newmains, Douglas Nelson, Ayr, Gary Nelson, Glasgow, Gavin Nelson, Cambuslang, Hugh Nelson, Glasgow, J Nelson, Livingstone, James Nelson, Glasgow, James Nelson, New Lanark, Jordan Nelson, Garrowhill, Karne Nelson, Newmains, Kathleen Nelson, Glasgow, Paul Nelson, New Lanark, Paul Nelson, Peterson Park, Rob

Nelson, North Ferriby, E Yorks, Robert Nelson, London, Ryan Nelson, Newmains, Sharon Nelson, Garrowhill, Stephen Nelson, Hamilton, Steven Nelson, Glasgow, Yvonne Nelson, Cambuslang, Nelson, Glasgow, Lorraine Ness, Perth, Michelle Ness, Perth, Tony Nevan, Glasgow, Chris New, Auchinleck, Gary New, Stevenston, Brian Newlands, Stirling, David Newlands, Croftfoot Glasgow, David Newlands, Croftfoot Glasgow, Hannah Newlands, Bridge of Weir, Dadeo Newton, Glasgow, Dadeo Newton, Glasgow, Mik Newton, Glasgow, Patsy Newton, Glasgow, David Nibloe, Stranraer, Jamie Nichol, Hamilton , David Nicholson, Helensburgh, June Nicholson, Pollokshaws, Laura Nicholson, Pollokshaws, Neil Nicholson, Pollokshaws, Lee Nickson, Neath, South Wales, Alex Nicol, , Billy Nicol, Ewan Nicol, At Home Called Celtic View In West Suss, Mark Nicol, Linlithgow, Mark Nicol, Linlithgow, Stephen Nicol, Tullibody, John Nicolas, Airdrie, Angie Nicoll, Edinburgh, Keith Nicoll, Edinburgh, Leah Nicoll, Edinburgh, Scott Nicoll, London, Sinead Nicoll, Edinburgh, Colin Nicolson, Falkirk, Rab Nicolson, Methilhill, Fife, Hannah Nightingale, Bedworth, Warwickshire, Hannah Nightingale, Bedworth, Warwickshire, Margaret Nightingale, Bedford, Warwickshire, Margaret Nightingale, Bedworth, Warwickshire, Robbie Nimmo, Glasgow, Robbie Nimmo, , Cameron Nisbet, Gulberwick, Shetland, Colin Nisbet, Scotland, David Nisbet, Hamilton, Lynn Nisbet, Bellshill, Murray Nisbet, Wishaw, Stuart Nisbet, Gulberwick, Shetland, Tony Nisbett, Brackley Northamptonshire, Tony Nisbett, Brackley, Northants, Karen Nish, Dumfries, Gerry Niven, East Kilbride, Mark Niven, Stenhouse, Edinburgh, Jonathen Nixon, Grangemouth, Louie Nixon, Glasgow, Aisling Nolan, Dublin, Brian Nolan, Glasgow, Brian Nolan, Glasgow, Des Nolan, Cleland, Margaret Nolan, Glasgow, Ms. Chelle Nolan, Leith, Peter Nolan, Buckingham, Reece Nolan, Wishaw, Sean Nolan, Wishaw, Sonia Nolan, Ireland, Stevie Nolan, Ardoyne, Belfast, Tomo Nolan, Ireland, Gary Noon, Castlemilk, Joe Noon, Glasgow, John Noon, Castlemilk, Kath Noon, Glasgow, Angela Noonan, Milton, Brendan Noone, Glasgow, Gergus Noone, Corby, Northants, Saira Noorani, Crouch End, London, Norman Norey, Glasgow, Rob Norman, Corby, Rob Norman, Corby, Northants, Dylan Norris, Alloa, Ethan Norris, Alloa, Peter Norton, Wishaw, Gerald Norval, Glasgow, Walter Norval, Glasgow, Irene Nugent, Springburn, Glasgow, James Nutent, Glasgow, Finbar Nyhan, Co Cork, Sean Nyhan, Co Cork.

Hugh O Brien, Castlemilk. James O Connor, , Patricia O Connor, Glasgow, Rod O' Hanlon, Dublin, Allan O`Hare, Herford, Germany, Dean O`Hare, Herford, Germany, Elaine Oakley, Fife, Rossina O'Bert, , Kieran O'Brian, Garthamlock, Aiden O'Brien, Allan O'Brien, Port Glasgow, Chloe O'Brien, Port Glasgow, Denis O'Brien, Yeading, Des O'Brien, Airdrie, Des O'Brien, Airdrie, Des O'Brien, Airdrie, Dot O'Brien, Germiston, Elaine O'Brien, Norwich, Gerry O'Brien, Viewpark, Gerry O'Brien, Viewpark, Kerry O'Brien, Norwich, Louise O'brien, Govanhill, Margo O'Brien, Cramlington, Martyn O'brien, Scotstoun, Mary O'Brien, Viewpark, Mhari O'Brien, Royston, Michael O'Brien, Port Glasgow, Moira O'Brien, Scotstoun, Pat O'Brien, Kirkaldy, Paul O'Brien, Scotstoun, Peter O'Brien, Auckland, New Zealand, Rachel O'Brien, Port Glasgow, Sean O'Brien, Port Glasgow, Stacey O'Brien, Glasgow, Stephanie O'Brien, Viewpark, Steve O'Brien, Cramlington, Stevie O'Brien, Viewpark, Stevie O'Brien, Viewpark, Stuart O'Brien, Coal Island, Ireland, William O'Brien, Bathgate, William O'Brien, Mid Calder, William O'brien, Mid Calder, William O'Brien, West Lothian, William O'Brien (Snr), Whitburn, William O'Brien Jnr, Mid Calder, Gerry O'Brien snr, Viewpark, Molly O'Callaghan, Morecambe, Pat O'Connell, Athy, Co Kildare, Philip O'Conner, Merthyr Tydfil, Michael O'Connoll, Stirling, Laura Oconnor, Largs, Lesa O'Connor, 15A Hole House Road Largs Ayrshire, Dennis O'Connor, Lochgoil, Dorothy O'Connor, , Gerald O'Connor, New Jersey, USA, Grant O'Connor, Newtongrange, Holly O'connor, Dalkeith, John O'Connor, Wishaw, Kevin O'connor, Dalkeith, Kevin O'Connor, Lochgoil, Lainey O'Connor, Woodburn Dalkeith, Laura O'Connor, Largs, Lauren O'connor, Dalkeith, Louise O'Connor, Athy, Co Kildare, Michael O'Connor, New Jersey, USA, Mick O'Connor, Glasgow, Mick & Catherine O'Connor, High Street, Dalkeith, Patrick O'Connor,

Greece, Paul O'Connor, Greenock, Peter O'Connor, Glasgow, PJ O'Connor, Athy, Co Kildare, Roy O'Connor, Glasgow, Steven O'Connor, Irvine, Ashley Od, Greenock, Chell Od, Greenock, Paul Odens, Bathgate, Raymond O'Donaghue, Coatbridge, Joseph O'Donnaghue, Clyde, Gary O'Donnall, Glasgow, Gary O'Donnall, Glasgow, Kevin O'Donnall, Glasgow, Paul O'Donnall, Carrickfergus, Jameela O'Donnel, Govanhill, Shannon O'Donnel, Govanhill, Alan O'Donnell, Rutherglen, Angie O'Donnell, Salisbury, Annmarie O'Donnell, Clydebank, Barbara O'Donnell, Govan Hill, Glasgow, Bobby O'Donnell, Stenhousemuir, Brian O'Donnell, Drumchapel, Brian O'Donnell, Glasgow, Burt O'Donnell, London, Carol O'Donnell, Newton Mearns, Glasgow, Catherine O'Donnell, Cumbernauld, Charly O'Donnell, Clydebank, Chris O'Donnell, Newton Mearns, Glasgow, Christina O'Donnell, Perth, Christine O'Donnell, Calton, Glasgow, David O'Donnell, Dunfermline, David O'Donnell, Greenock, Eamonn O'Donnell, Dundee, Gerry O'Donnell, East Kilbride, Hugh O'Donnell, Canada, Ian O'Donnell, Lanark, J O'Donnell, Rutherglen, Jackie O'Donnell, Govanhill, Jade O'Donnell, Crieff, Jamie.V. O'Donnell, Balloch Eastfield, Joanne O'Donnell, Clydebank, Joe O'Donnell, Clydebank, John O'Donnell, Clydebank, John O'Donnell, Clydebank, John O'Donnell, Croy, John O'Donnell, Glasgow, John O'Donnell, Springburn, John O'donnell, Wishaw, John F O'Donnell, Perth, John Fitzgerald O'Donnell, Perth, Kerry O'Donnell, Clydebank, Kevin O'Donnell, Falkirk, Kevin O'Donnell, Govan, Kevin O'Donnell, Stanford, Essex, Kiera O'Donnell, Crieff, Kieran O'Donnell, Glasgow, Lesley O'Donnell, East Kilbride, Liam O'Donnell, Crieff, Louise O'Donnell, East Kilbride, Maggie O'Donnell, Glasgow, Manus O'donnell, Paisley, Maria O'Donnell, East Kilbride, Marion O'Donnell, Salisbury, Mark O'Donnell, Armadale, Martin O'Donnell, Glasgow, Mauler O'Donnell, Stenhousemuir, Michael O'Donnell, Glasgow, Michael O'Donnell, Stenhousemuir, Michael O'Donnell, Tollcross, Mike O'Donnell, Grangemouth, Neil 'Nod ' O'Donnell, Balloch, Paul O'Donnell, Paisley, Pod O'Donnell, Salisbury, Robert O'Donnell, Fullertonpark, Tollcross, Ryan O'Donnell, East Kilbride, Ryan O'Donnell, Stenhousemuir, Ryan O'donnell, Wishaw, Sean O'Donnell, Clydebank, Sean O'Donnell, Salisbury, Sheila O'Donnell, Stirling, Stephen O'Donnell, Stenhousemuir, Susan O'Donnell, Greenock, Susie O'Donnell, Stanford, Essex, Theresa O'Donnell, Stenhousemuir, Tom O'Donnell, London, Tracy O'donnell, Wishaw, Vince O'Donnell, Morecambe, Will O'Donnell, Springburn, Michael O'Donnell Jnr, Newton Mearns, Glasgow, James O'Donnell Snr, Motherwell, Michael O'Donnell Snr, Newton Mearns, Glasgow, Barry O'Donovan, London, Frank O'Dowda, Denny, Kevin O'Dowda, Denny, Mary O'Dowda, Denny, Colin Ogilvie, Paisley, Duncan Ogilvie, Walsall, West Midlands, Eric O'Gorman, Stepps, Tony O'Grady, , Andrew O'Hagan, Port Glasgow, Andrew O'Hagan, Port Glasgow, Dylan O'Hagan, Coatbridge, John O'Hagan, Coatbridge, Liam O'Hagan, Paisley, Renfrewshire, Mark O'Hagan, Coatbridge, Richie O'Hagan, Port Glasgow, David O'Hagen, Port Glasgow, Brenda O'Hanlon, Stockport, Dagan O'Hanlon, Dalmurie, Donna O'Hanlon, Clydebank, James O'Hanlon, Denny, Joe O'Hanlon, Dalmuir, Karena O'Hanlon, Denny, Kevin O'Hanlon, Denny, Shannon O'Hanlon, Dalmurie, Mick OHara, Possilpark, Glasgow, Angie O'Hara O'Hara, Drumchapel, Benny O'Hara, Glasgow, Betty O'Hara, Glasgow, Billy O'Hara, Tranent, Brendan O'Hara, Seville, Brian O'Hara, Stenhousemuir, Caitlin O'Hara, East Kilbride, Caitlin O'Hara, East Kilbride, Catressa O'Hara, East Kilbride, Connor O'Hara, Glasgow, Daniel O'Hara, Glasgow, David O'Hara, Crete, David O'Hara, Plakias, Crete, Diarmid O'Hara, Seville, Dominic O'Hara, Seville, Heather O'hara, Bathgate, Joe O'Hara, Glasgow, Kelly O'Hara, Tranent, Kevin O'Hara, Bathgate, Lisa O'Hara, Glasgow, Margaret O'hara, Bathgate, Martin O'Hara, East Kilbride, Peter O'Hara, Inverness, Shug O'Hara, Drumchapel, Stephen O'Hara, Milton, Glasgow, Tam O'Hara, Bathgate, Terry O'Hara, Bathgate, Andy O'Hare, Luton, Brian O'Hare, Bannockburn, Colin O'Hare, Shotts, Colin O'Hare, Shotts, Danielle O'Hare, Shotts, David O'Hare, Birmingham, Eileen O'Hare, Wishaw, Jackie O'Hare, Shotts, Jackie O'Hare, , Jamie O'Hare, Glasgow, Jim O'Hare, Wishaw, Kathryn O'Hare, Wishaw, Kirsty O'Hare, Birmingham, Martin O'Hare, East

Kilbride, Paul O'Hare, Glasgow, Peter O'Hare, Carntyne, Glasgow, Peter O'Hare, Glasgow, Peter O'Hare, Luton, Shaun O'Hare, Fallin, Stirling, Steve O'Hare, Fintree, Dundee, Tam O'Hare, Birmingham, Victor O'Hare, Bishopbriggs, Kevin O'Hear, Bornemouth, Norah Okane, Wishaw, Neil O'Keefe, Riddrie, Glasgow, Tommy O'Keefe, Kilburn, David Old, Cumbernauld, Craig O'Leary, Cotridge, Karen O'Leary, Coatbridge, Sean O'Leary, Coatbridge, Michael Oliver, Falkirk, Gavin O'Malley, Silverton, Dumbarton, Sinead O'Malley, Linwood, Jim O'Mara, Leicester, Michael O'Mellon, Croy, David Omozik, Glasgow, Karen Omozik, Glasgow, Kenny O'Neil, Coatbridge, Rab O'Neil, Brent Bravo, John O'Neil, Drongan, Ayrshire, Patrick & Ryan O'Neil, Dunfermline, Susan Cat O'Neil, Stewarton, Chris O'Neil, Stewarton, Susan O'Neil, Stewarton, Andrew O'Neill, East Kilbride, Angela O'Neill, Glasgow, Barry O'Neill, Cumbernauld, Billy O'Neill, Easterhouse, Glasgow, Brian O'Neill, Govan, Brian O'Neill, Greenock, Brian O'Neill, Upper Paradise, Caitlin O'Neill, Glasgow, Chris O'Neill, Paisley, Christopher O'Neill, Queensland Austrialia, Daniel O'Neill, Glasgow, Danielle O'Neill, Newarthill, David O'Neill, Castlemilk, David O'Neill, Helensburgh, Declan O'Neill, Glasgow, Edward O'Neill, Johnston/Glasgow, Gerald O'Neill, Greenock, Gerard O'neill, Glasgow, Hugh O'Neill, Hugh O'Neill, , James O'Neill, Easterhouse, Glasgow, James O'Neill, Kilmarnock, John O'Neill, Hamilton, John O'Neill, Perth, Katie O'Neill, Glasgow, Kerry O'Neill, King's Park, Glasgow, Kevin O'Neill, Coatbridge, Kevin O'Neill, Cumbernauld, Kieran O'Neill, Moodiesburn, Lea O'Neill, Glasgow, Mark O'Neill, Renfrew, Mark O'Neill, Saltcoats, Martin O'Neill, Stepps, Neil O'Neill, Kirkintilloch, Padraig O'Neill, Ballymena, Padraig O'Neill, Ballymena, Patrick O'Neill, Norwick, Norfolk, Patrick O'Neill, Queensland Australia, Paul O'Neill, London, Paul O'Neill, Renfrew, Paul O'Neill, Renfrew, Paul O'Neill, Wyndford, Pauline O'Neill, Paisley, Rab O'Neill, Greenock, Raymond O'Neill, Uddingston, Richard O'Neill, Stepps, Richard O'Neill, Stepps, Roddi O'Neill, Glasgow, Shannon O'Neill, Glasgow, Shaun O'Neill, Glasgow, Sonya O'neill, Glasgow, Stephen O'Neill, Moodiesburn, Thomas O'neill, Keighley, Tony O'Neill, Glasgow, Vinny O'neill, M'bro Bowls Celtic Supporteres Club, William O'Neill, Kilmarnock, Yvonne O'Neill, Glasgow, Vincent O'Neill Jnr, M'bro Bowls Celtic Supporters Club, Jason Only, Cambuslang, Bernadette Ontario, Canada, Daniel O'Donnell, Motherwell, Jim O'Donnell, Paisley, Shane O'Donnell, Gilmerton, Edinburgh, Shaun O'Hagan, Port Glasgow, Mark O'Hara, Birkenshaw, Jim O'Mara, Canon, Coalville, Brian O'Neill, Motherwell, Raymond O'Neill, Uddingston, Raymond O'Neill, Uddingston, Francis O'Rourke, Motherwell, Pat O'Rourke, Motherwell, Rose O'Quinn, Croy, Giuseppe Orabona, Largs, Andrew O'Raw, Glasgow, David Oraw, Glasgow, Joe O'Raw, Holytown, John O'Raw, Bonnybridge, Clare O'Rawe, Ballymena, Graham Ord, Isle of Islay, George Orden, Wishaw, Maria Ore, Gourock, Alex O'Reilly, Baillieston, Amy O'Reilly, Renfrew, Andy O'Reilly, Baillieston, Andy O'Reilly, Baillieston, Glasgow, Brian O'Reilly, Airdrie, Danny O'Reilly, London, Paul O'Reilly, East Kilbride, Terry O'Reilly, Dunfermline, Tony O'Reilly, London, Brett [Shuggie] Orman, Ipswich, Kev Orman, Ipswich, Michael Ormonde, Waterford, Ireland, Wilson O'Rouke, Ayrshire, Elaine Orourke, Castlemilk, Gerry O'Rourke, Whitburn, West Lothian, Linda O'Rourke, Whitburn, West Lothian, Louise Orourke, Whitburn, West Lothian, Pamela Orourke, Whitburn West Lothian, Pat Orourke, Dungannon, Courtney O'Rourke, Glasgow, David O'Rourke, Chapelhall, Diana O'Rourke, , Kerry O'Rourke, Castlemilk, Kerry Marie O'Rourke, Newarthill, Michael O'Rourke, Cardonald, Sharlene O'rourke, Hamilton, O'Rourke, Cardonald, Brendan Orr, Sydney, Australia, Donny Orr, Gourock, Graham Orr, Cumbernauld, Grimmy Orr, Abronhill, Ishbel Orr, Cumbernauld, James Orr, Hamilton, Kenny Orr, Paisley Loyal, Nicola Anne Orr, Abronhill, Stevie Orr, Barrhead Glasgow, Michael Orsi, Head of Muir, Carly Orwin, Bradford, West Yorkshire, Mark Orwin, Dunfermline, Michael Osbaldstone, East Kilbride, Scott Osbaldstone, East Kilbride, Emily Osborne, Port Glasgow, Hugh Osborne, Sandyhills, Mark Osborne, Sandyhills, Mhairi Osborne, Port Glasgow, Toni Osborne, Port Glasgow, Brian O'Shea, Glasgow, James O'Shea, Scole, Mike O'Shea, Dundee, Donal O'Suileabhain,

Southampton, Gary Oswald, Broxburn, Paul Ovens, Milton Of Campsie, Tony Ovens, Kings Park, Tricia Ovens, Kings Park, Peter O'Viel, Glasgow, Julie Owen, Dundee, Kirsten Owen, Alloa, Kirstyne Owen, Sauchie, Paul Owen, Dundee, Alun Owens, Stoneyburn, Andy Owens, Bellshill, Brendan Owens, Sallins, Co Kildare, Daniel Joseph Owens, Cumbernauld, Edward Owens, Glasgow, George Owens, Bellshill, Jim Owens, Tallagh, Dublin, Jimmy Owens, Bathgate, Katrina Owens, Bellshill, Kevin Owens, Coatbridge, Patrick Owens, Glasgow, Tommy Owens, Oban, William Owens, Hamilton, Ali Ozmus, Inverness,

Claire P, Kilsyth. Scottie P, Bankside, Falkirk, Jamie Pace, Glasgow, Mick Pace, Glasgow, Alan Pacitti, Falkirk, Christine Padden, Saltcoats, Sheina Mcfadyen Palfreman, Springburn, Glasgow G21 1Sf, John Pallan, Falkirk, John-Paul Pallar, Cardiff, Andy Palmer, Bearsden, Cheryl Palmer, , Peter Palmer, Pendas Fields, Rab Palmer, Windygates Gen, Christine Palmeri, Rochester, New York, Jason Palmeri, Rochester, New York, Liam Palmeri, Rochester, New York, Ryan Palmeri, Rochester, New York, Vic Palmeri, Rochester, New York, Ian Palshaw, , Martin Pant, Liverpool, Ross Pant, Liverpool, Baby Paris, Inverness, Alex Park, Glasgow, Andy Park, Bonhill, Cathryn Park, Wirral, Christopher Park, Springburn, Derek Park, Cumbernauld, Emma Park, Springburn, Stuart Park, Glasgow, Tos Park, Moodiesburn, Billy Parker, Dundonald, Ayrshire, Brett Parker, Boghall, Charlie Parker, London, Chris Parker, London, Davie Parker, East Kilbride, Ian Parker, Bathgate, James Parker, Turriff, Jean Parker, Canada, Nicola Parker, Bathgate, Willie Nosey Parker, Rockingham Western Australia, Shawn Parkes, Easterhouse, Charlie Parkinson, Bellshill, Jenny Parr, Paisley, Steven Robert Parson, Renfrew, Jilly Partick, Glasgow, Sean Partner, Kilmarnock, Stuart Parvesson, Renfrew, Andrew Pascall, Linlithgow, Alfie Pasty, Bishopbriggs, Big Pat, Wishaw, Graham Pate, Glasgow, Archiebald Paterson, Glasgow, Billy Paterson, Southnitshill, Declan Paterson, Craigshill, Diane Paterson, Lennoxtown Glasgow, George and Ina Paterson, Calton, Glasgow, Graeme Paterson, Clydebank, Graeme Paterson, Clydebank, Hugh Paterson, Croy, James Paterson, Croy, Jim Paterson, Kennoway, Joe Paterson, Gallowgate, Glasgow, Joe,Liz,Charlene And Joseph Paterson, Gallowgate, Glasgow, John Paterson, Newmilns, Ayrshire, Katrina Paterson, High Valleyfield, Keith Paterson, Craigshill, Kevin Paterson, Rothesay, Kieron Paterson, Bishopbriggs, Laura Paterson, Glasgow, Leigh Paterson, Castlemilk, Lynn Paterson, Glasgow, Michael Paterson, Kincardine, Robert Paterson, Coatdyke, Ronnie Paterson, Bishopbriggs, Sandy Paterson, Baillieston, Scott Paterson, Castlemilk, Stewart Paterson, Peterhead, Trish Paterson, Ruchill, Winnie Paterson, Carntyne, Wullie, Audrey,Kris,Liam Paterson, Moodiesburn, Agnes Paton, Glasgow, David Paton, Lochinver, Sutherland, Mike Paton, Dunfermline, Ronnie Paton, Cumnock, Scott Paton, Hamilton, Dale Patrick, Coyne, Glasgow, Donny Patrick, Bishopbriggs, Glasgow, James Patrick, Hossack, Edinburgh, John Patrick, Cambuslang, Martin Patrick, Perth, Pourreau Patrick, Bayonne (France), Robert Lynass Patrick, Glasgow, Thomas Patrick, Stanton, Port Glasgow, Colin Patterson, Pollok, James Patterson, Musselburgh, Jimmy Patterson, Glasgow, John Patterson, Glasgow, Sean Patterson, West Kilbride, Steven Patterson, Glasgow, Stewart Patterson, Aridre, Stuart Patterson, West Kilbride, Mick Pattinson, Cleator Moor, Jamie Lee Patton, Glasgow, Joe Patton, Dunblane, Kierian Patton, Dunblane, Pat Patton, Johnstone, Suzanne Patton, Dunblane, Dale Pattrick, Coyne, Glasgow, Christopher Paul, Lenzie, Jacqui Paul, Fife, James Paul, Bonhill, Martin Paul, Peebles, Sean Paul, Fae, Glenmavis, Airdrie, Frank Paxton, Northwood, Middlesex, Rab Paxton, Lochgelly, Stephen Paxton, Garrowhill, Gary Payne, Port Glasgow, Mark Payne, Port Glasgow, Joseph Payton, Roslin, Steven Payton, , John Peacock, Dalkeith, William Peacock, Port, Glasgow, John Pearce, Wishaw, Brian Pearson, Glasgow, Geroge Pearson, Linwood, Jim Pearson, Knightswood, Tracey Anne Pearson, Knightswood, Robert Pearson JR, Coatbridge, Graeme Peden, Rosneath, Stewart Robert Peden, Rosneath, Marco Pellegrini, Cardonald, Joyce Pellicci, Alloa, Symon Pellicci,

Alloa, Amy Penman, Broxsburn, Chelsea Penman, Broxburn, Chris Penman, New Stevenson, Jason Penman, Harthill, John Penman, Broxburn, John Penman, Glasgow, Kenneth Penman, Broxsburn, Pat Penman, Ontario Canada, Sharon Penman, Glasgow, David Pentland, Newmains, Terry Periconn, Glasgow, Aaron Perratt, Oxgangs, Nicky Perratt, Oxgangs, Adam Perrie, Alva, Amy Perrie, Alva, Ann Marie Perrie, London, Seonagh Perrie, Alva, William Perrie, Sussex, Elaine Perry, Blairdardie, Sean Perry, Belfast, Alan Persaud, Hackney, London, Michael Pesill, Birmingham, Ross Petal, , Evelyn Petale, Denny, Rachel Petale, Denny, Roddy Petale, Denny, Shannon Petale, Denny, Stephen Peteranna, South Uist, Mark Peters, Ayrshire, Sandra Petree, Dundee, Ross Petrol, Helensburgh, Franco Petrucci, Glasgow, Alan Pettigrew, Port Glasgow, Roger Pheely, Bellshill, Deirdre Phelan, Ireland, Joan Philbin, John Philbin, East Kilbride, Michael Philbin, Fleetwood, Janice Philip, Clydebank, Alan Philliben, Cowie, Robert Philliben, StNinians, Brian Phillips, Falkirk, John Phillips, Kilmarnock, Mark Phillips, Dorset, Ray Phillips, Arbroath, David Phin, East Kilbride, Tony Phinn, Calton, Alison Pickersgill, Annan, Joe Pickett, Kirkintilloch, Tweetie Pie, Aberdeen, Joe Piedie, Winey, Ben Piercy, Cheltenham, Lio Pierotti, Renfrew, Julie Pignatelli, Barrhead, Joe Pilkington, Luton, Andrew Pillans, Castlemilk, Davie Pillans, Castlemilk, Kieran Pillans, Castlemilk, Fiona Ping, Darvel, David Pippin, Glasgow, Billy Pitt, Dunmore, Seaneen Pleimeann, North Belfast, Tomas Pleimeann, North Belfast, Merry Plough Bhoys, Essex, Margaret Plunkett, Glasgow, Billy Pole, Glasgow, Alan Pollard, Blantyre, Stevie Polley, Tillicoultry, John Paul Pollock, Wishaw, Kevin Pollock, Kilwinning, Tracy Pollock, Lanarkshire, John Polockus, Glasgow, Ronald Pols, Lincolnshire, Michael Ponsonby, Glasgow, Michael Ponsonby Jnr, Castlemilk, Michael Ponsonby Snr, Castlemilk, Alan Popowicz, London, Ashley Popowicz, Middlesex, William Porange, Perth, Western Australia, Brian Porteous, Coatbridge, David Porteous, Basra, Iraq, Kevin Porteous, Hameln, Germany, Ryan Porteous, Coatbridge, Sabine Porteous, Hameln, Germany, Stephen Porteous, Hameln, Germany, Billy Porter, Port Glasgow, Chloe Porter, Airdrie, Chloe Porter, Airdrie, Christopher Porter, Glasgow, Christopher Porter, Glasgow, Erin Porter, Airdrie, Erin Porter, Airdrie, Mary Porter, Airdrie, Mary Porter, Airdrie, Paul Porter, Airdrie, McLelland Possi, Fife, Davie Possil, , Kevin Pott, Gasgow, Billy Potter, Cardonald, John Potter, Castlemilk, John Potter, Livingston, Kevin Potter, Castlemilk, Glasgow, Logan Potter, Livingston, John Potter Jnr., Castlemilk, John Potter Sn, Castlemilk, Glasgow, Mark Poutney, Bellshill,Ally Pow, Peebles, Graeme Powell, Shettleston, Martin Powell, Clydebank, Brian Power, Bradley, Junior Power, Halifax, Kevin Power, Dublin, Paul Power, Birkenshaw, Uddingston, Paul Power, Uddingston, Kevin Prasiey, Coatbridge. Craig Pratt, Kirkcaldy, Agnes Preece, Barrhead, Andy Preece, Livingston, Bert Preece, Barrhead, Natalie Preece, Cambuslang, Susan Preece, Livingston, Craig Prentice, East Kilbride, Derek Prentice, Knightswood, Gemma Prentice, Croftfoot, Jason Prentice, Croftfoot, Johnnie Prentice, Balornock, Kevin Prentice, Larkhall, Lynn Prentice, Lanark, Morry Prentice, Larkhall, Robert Prentice, Croftfoot, Shaun Prentice, Garngad, Mark Prenty, Stephen Prenty, John Prete, Tony Prete, Cumbernauld, Amanda Price, Mossblown, Christopher Price, Paisley, Eammon Price, Leighlinbridge, Harry Price, Coatbridge, Henrietta Price, Ayrshire, John Price, Denny, John Price, Denny, Natalie Price, Mossblown, Pat Price, Leighlinbridge, Jamie Proctor, Renfrew, Stuart Proctor, California, Proctor, Renfrew, Ian Proud, Kettering, Jimmy Pryce, Centurion Edinburgh, Old Barns Pub, Barras, Gerry Puczynski, Greenock, Brian Puddey, Wishaw, Tonu Pugh, Cardonald, Andy Pullar, Bishopbriggs, Megan Pullar, Walsall, Julie Pullen, Lochee, Julie Pullen, Lochee, Ann Pulser, Airdrie, Richard Dean Purden, Oxgangs, Edinburgh, James Purdie, Drumclog, Kilmarnock, Shirley Purdon, Kirkintilloch, Shirley Purdon, Kirkintilloch, Walter Purdon, Kirkintilloch, Walter Purdon, Kirkintilloch, Steven Purdy, Buckley, Harvey Purewall, Bearsden, Sam Purvaze, Glasgow, Jimmy (The Hill) Purves, Dartford, Kent, Cliff Purvis, Loanhead, John Gilmartin & Les Purvis, Edinburgh, Tam Purvis, Boness, Aaron Pyott.

Danny Queen, Carfin, Jim Queen, Shettleston, Kevin Queen, Hamilton, Lorna Queen, Falkirk, Martin Queen, Falkirk, Sam Queen, Falkirk, Sarah Queen, Falkirk, John Queen Jnr, Hamilton, Ben Queenan, Gallowgate, Christopher Queenan, Gallowgate, Billy Quentin, Mossend, Bellshill, Catherine Querage, Dumfries, Stephen Quigg, Greenock, Barry Quigley, Mount Florida, Brian Quigley, Glasgow, Dennis Quigley, Maryhill, Glasgow, Derek Quigley, Garrowhill, Glasgow, Dominc Quigley, Glasgow, Gerry Quigley, Glasgow, Gerry Quigley, Greenock, Gerry Quigley, Mount Florida, Graeme Quigley, Glasgow, Joe Quigley, Glasgow, John Quigley, South Queensferry, John Quigley, Toronto, Laurie Quigley, Dover, Paul Quigley, Motherwell, Susan Quigley, Clarkston, Eddy Quillan, East Kilbride, Gerry Quin, Bishopbriggs, Aidan Quinn, Glasgow, Andrew Quinn, Chryston, Glasgow, Anne Quinn, Coatbridge, Anne-Marie Quinn, Airdrie, Anne-Marie Quinn, Airdrie, Annie Quinn, Govanhill, Glasgow, Ann-Marie Quinn, Airdrie, Anthony Quinn, Glasgow, Anthony Quinn, Irvine, Bob Quinn, Dykebar, Paisley, Brian Quinn, Belfast, Brian Quinn, Bishopbriggs, Glasgow, Brian Quinn, Livingston, Cara Quinn, Glasgow, Christopher Quinn, East Kilbride, Christopher Quinn, Glasgow, Claire Quinn, Glasgow, David Quinn, East Kilbride, Dennis Quinn, Glasgow, Eddie Quinn, Condorrat, Francis Quinn, Kennet Village, Frank Quinn, Glasgow, Frank Quinn, Glasgow, Gary Quinn, Belfast, Gary Quinn, Glasgow, Gary Quinn, Glasgow, Gary Quinn, Glasgow, Gerry Quinn, East Kilbride, Gerry Quinn, Knightswood, Glasgow, Gillian Quinn, , Haley Quinn, Glasgow, Helen Quinn, Cumbernauld, Henrik Quinn, Paisley, Jack Quinn, Barrhead, Jack Quinn, , Jacqueline Quinn, East Kilbride, James Campbell Quinn, Channel Islands, Janette Quinn, Irvine, Janice Quinn, Irvine, Joe Quinn, Paisley, John Quinn, Ardrossan, John Quinn, Coatbridge, Joseph Alexander Quinn, Channel Islands, Joseph Alexander Quinn, Channel Islands, Kaitlin Quinn, , Karen Quinn, Viewpark, Kevin Quinn, Gorebridge, Kevin Quinn, Gorebridge, Midlothian, Kris Quinn, Irvine, Marc Quinn, Denny, Martin Quinn, Glasgow, Michael Quinn, Irvine, Moira Quinn, Penicuik, Neal Quinn, Dundee, Nicky Quinn, Bournemouth, Pamela Quinn, Glasgow, Pat Quinn, Irvine, Patrick Quinn, Belfast, Patrick Quinn, Hogganfield, Paul Quinn, Belfast, Phil Quinn, Balornock, Glasgow, Rebecca Quinn, Edinburgh, Robert Quinn, Denny, Ryan Quinn, Glasgow, Ryan Quinn, Glasgow, Ryan Quinn, Glasgow, Ryan Quinn, Glasgow, Shaun Quinn, Saltcoats, Stephanie Quinn, Cumbernauld, Stephen Quinn, Barrhead, Stephen Quinn, Cumbernauld, Stephen Quinn, Kilsyth, Stevie Quinn, Stevie Quinn, Barrhead Glasgow, Stevie Quinn, Belfast, Stuart Quinn, Chryston, Glasgow, Susan Quinn, Duntocher, Terry Quinn, Dundonald, Ayrshire, Thomas Quinn, Glasgow, Thomas Quinn, Johnstone,

Big Rab, Bedworth. Gerard Radka, Bathgate, Robert Radley, Bonnybridge, Angela Rae, Kirkintilloch, Angela Rae, Kirkintilloch, Billy Bob Rae, Greenock, Danny Rae, Paisley, J. Rae, Lynwood, Jimmy Rae, Portsoy, John Rae, Motherwell, Kyle Rae, Portsoy, Liam Rae, Kirkintilloch, Liam Rae, Kirkintilloch, Neil Rae, Portsoy, Mark Raeside, Blantyre, Monica Raeside, Blantyre, John Raffertty, Canon, Coalville, Alan Rafferty, Kinning Park, Glasgow, Angela Rafferty, Coatbridge, Betty Rafferty, Calton, Glasgow, Edward Rafferty, Glasgow, James Rafferty, Hamilton, John Rafferty, Leicester, Kieron Rafferty, Hawick, Paul Rafferty, Coatbridge, Rebecca Rafferty, Glasgow, Richard Rafferty, Motherwell, Stephen Rafferty, Kirkshaws, Coatbridge, Shaheed Rafique, Glasgow, Davie Raige, Greenock, Brian Rainey, Alexandria, Brian Rainey, Alexandria, Brian Rainey, Alexandria, Dunbartonshire, Brian Rainey, Bonhill, Alexandria, Chris Rainey, Alexandria, Derek Rainey, Shawlands, James Rainey, Rugby Warwickshire England, Marie Rainey, Rugby Warwickshire, Steven Rainey, Alexandria, Steven Rainey, Alexandria, Dunbartonshire, Steve Raisey, Manchester, Graeme Ralph, Ayr, Tony Ralph, Glasgow, Nicola Ralston, Uddingston, Scott Ralston, Newton Mearns, Glasgow, Joanna Ralston and Chris, Uddingston, Stephanie Ralston and Willie, Motherwell, Dan Ramage, Gordon, Ian S Ramage, Gordon, Jane Ramage, Gordon, Lesley Ramage, Paisley, Linda Ramage, Bishopbriggs, Louise Ramage, Bishopbriggs, Mary

Ramage, Bishopbriggs, Chris Ramsay, Port Glasgow, Ian Ramsay, Mount Florida, Glasgow, Janie Ramsay, St Ninians, Jim Ramsay, Port Glasgow, Karen Ramsay, Carradale, Argyll, Louise Ramsay, Markinch, Fife, Lyndsay Ramsay, St Ninians, Paul Ramsay, Port Glasgow, Des Ramsey, Coatbridge, Fiona Ramsey, Stirling, Mark Ramsey, Old Kilpatrick, Kevin Rankan, Alloa, James K Rankie, Pitlochry, Charlie Rankin, Edinburgh, Helen Rankin, Renfrew, Marco Rankin, Coatbridge, Paul Rankin, Airdrie, Paul Rankine, Ashby, Leics, Clare Rattray, London, Connor Rattray, Glenrothes, Louis Rattray, Wishaw, Tyler Rattray, Glenrothes, Sharon Ray, Alloa, Tamara Rayment, Glasgow, Antonio Rea, Newmains, Drew Rea, Belfast, Louis Rea, Niagara Falls, Canada, Charlie Read, Grimsby, Gordon Read, Falkirk, Jim Read, Grimsby, Paul Read, Grimsby, Sarah Read, Grimsby, Stephen Walker & Melissa Readman, East Kilbride, Joe Ready, Balornock, Glasgow, Sandra Ready, Balornock, Glasgow, Paul Reardon, Wishaw, The Late Willie Reavey Snr, Glasgow, Marco Rebecchi, Greenock, Declan Reburn, Glasgow, Declan Reburn, Kings Park, Tony Redmond, Basingstoke, England, Matthew Rees, Alness, Rosshire, Alan Reeve, Port Glasgow, Barrington Reeves, Coatbridge, C Reeves, , Declan Reeves, Cambuslang, Kenny Reeves, Cambuslang, Ann Reford, Port Glasgow, Claire Regan, Merrylee, Dominic Regan, Giffnock, John Regan, Giffnock, Kevin Regan, Bailleston, Marie Regan, Giffnock, Steven Regan, Bailleston, Tommy Regan, Gourock, John Regan Jnr, Giffnock, Eddie Reic, Wishaw, Caitlin Reid, Edinburgh, Collette Reid, Motherwell, Debbie Reid, Edinburgh, Deck Reid, Brechin, Desmond Reid, Puerto De La Cruz, Tenerife, Desmond Reid, Puerto De La Cruz, Tenerife, Div Reid, Newhaven, Doreen Reid, Bank Nock, Eileen Reid, Harthill, Erin Reid, Edinburgh, Garry Reid, Fife, Ian Reid, Leicester, Jamie Reid, Waterside, John Reid, Kyleakin, John Reid, Toronto, Canada, Jonathon Reid, Cumbernauld, K Reid, Edinburgh, Kelly Reid, Castlemilk, Ken Reid, Williamwood, Kenny Reid, Clackmannanshire, Kenny Reid, Clackmannanshire, Kia Reid, Castlemilk, Laurence Reid, Glasgow, Lee Ann Reid, Harthill, Lindsey Reid, Ayrshire, Lisa Reid, Renfrew, Liz Reid, Edinburgh, Lynsey Reid, Crookston, Glasgow, Margaret Reid, Aberdeen, Michael Reid, Crieff, Michael Reid, , Paul Reid, Motherwell, Paul Reid, Paisley, Paul Reid, Toronto Canada, Peter Reid, Edinburgh, Roddy Reid, Edinburgh, Ryan Reid, Bridge of Don, Sean Reid, Edinburgh, Shawn Reid, Irvine, Steven Reid, Isle Of Skye, Steven Reid, Isle Of Skye, Stuart Reid, Edinburgh, Stuart Kevin Reid, Edinburgh, Tam Reid, Barrhead, Tracey Reid, Edinburgh, Vicky Reid, Dingwall, William Reid, Girvan, William Reid, Glasgow, William Reid, Toronto Canada, Gary Reilley, Glasgow, Alastair Reilly, Linwood, Ann-Marie Reilly, Brian Reilly, Bangor, Brian Reilly, Bristol, Brian Reilly, Gourock, Brian L Reilly, Maryhill, Glasgow, Cairen Reilly, , Catherine-Jane Reilly, Sydney - Australia, Conor Reilly, Dundee, Courtney Reilly, Clydebank, Danny Reilly, Renfrew, Darrin Reilly, Linwood, Eamonn Reilly, Kirkwood, Elizabeth Reilly, Glasgow, Elizabeth Reilly, Glasgow, Eric Reilly, Glasgow, George Reilly, Frome, George Reilly, , Gerard Reilly, Carnbroe, Henry Reilly, Cumbernauld, James Reilly, Coatbridge, James Reilly, Glasgow, Jim Reilly, Pather, Jimmy Reilly, Motherwell, John Reilly, Coatbridge, John Reilly, Cowcaddens, John & Liz Reilly, Woodburn,Dalkeith, Jonathon Reilly, Bathgate, Jordan Reilly, Linwood, Joseph Reilly, Glasgow, Julie Reilly, Austrailia, Kathleen Reilly, Glasgow, Kenny Reilly, Glasgow, Kerrie Reilly, Linwood, Kieran Reilly, Huelva, Spain, Kieran Reilly, Springboig, Lewis Reilly, Motherwell, Liam Reilly, Carnbroe, M. Reilly, Bellshill, Margaret Reilly, , Marie Reilly, Springboig, Mark Reilly, Livingston, Martin Reilly, Glasgow, Mary Reilly, Glasgow, Mary Reilly, Motherwell, Maureen Reilly, Bellshill, Michael Reilly, Glasgow, Michael Reilly, Glasgow, Michael Reilly, Port Glasgow, Michael Reilly, Springboig, Michelle Reilly, Forfar, Molly Reilly, Dundee, Nicola Reilly, Australia, Nigel Reilly, Glasgow, Paige Reilly, Barrhead, Pat Reilly, Carnbroe, Paul Reilly, Belfast, Paul Reilly, Clydebank, Paul Reilly, Wishaw, Peter Reilly, Johnstone, Peter Reilly, Kilcreggan, nr Helensburgh, Peter Reilly, Linwood, Peter Reilly, Rosneath, Peter Reilly, Rosneath, Philip Reilly, Boston, USA, Ryan Reilly, Airdrie, Sammy Reilly, Tollcross, Sean Reilly, Motherwell, Shannon Reilly, Barrhead, Shaun Reilly, Barrhead, Shaun Reilly, Glasgow, Stephen Reilly, Stephen Reilly, Coatbridge, Stephen

Reilly, Coatbridge, Stevie Reilly, Gilmerton, Edinburgh, Terry Reilly, Lambhill, Glasgow, Thomas Reilly, London, Tom Reilly, Bathgate, Veronica Reilly, Livingston, Reilly, Gourock, Peter Reilly Snr, Linwood, Scott Reilly`, Barrhead, John Reily, Glasgow, Jim Y Reilly, Austrailia, Emma Rendall, Irvine, David Rennan, Pearthshire, Paul Rennan, Motherwell, Brian Rennie, Dunfermline, Craig Rennie, Penrith, Cumbria, Daniel Rennie, Craigend, Darin Rennie, Craigend, Dean Rennie, Craigend, Gary Rennie, , Jackie Rennie, Craigend, John Rennie, Standburn Falkirk, John Rennie, Standburn. Falkirk, Mick Rennie, Chapelhall, Paul Rennie, Fauldhouse, West Lothain, Peter Rennie, Pollockshields, Allison Renwick, Bargeddie, Gregor Renwick, Lochfoot, Jan Renwick, Lochfoot, Kacey Renwick, Edinburgh, Michelle Renwick, Edinburgh, Mike Renwick, Lochfoot, Simon Renwick, Edinburgh, Mike Renwick Lochfoot, , Jamie Restrick, Lytham, Lancs, Tenrag Retnuh, , Derek Revie, Renfrew, Elaine Revie, Sandyhills , Glasgow, Aidan Reynolds, West Lothian, Alison Reynolds, Coatbridge, Bobby Reynolds, West Lothian, Connor Reynolds, Muirhouse, David Reynolds, Armadale, West Lothian, David Reynolds, Lochore, Fife, George T Reynolds, Baillieston, John Reynolds, Motherwell, Jordan Reynolds, Hamilton, Kevin Reynolds, Bishopbriggs, Lisa Reynolds, Motherwell, Mark Reynolds, Kirkliston, Nichola Reynolds, Coatbridge, Stacy Reynolds, Lochore, Fife, Stephen, Gayle, Jonathan, Sarah Reynolds, Coalsnaughton, Stevie Reynolds, Jersey, Eric Rhodes, Perth, Dougie Riach, Inverness, Lydia Riach, Inverness, Aidan Riano, New York, Usa, Brian Riano, New York, Usa, Darcy Riano, New York, Usa, Dylan Riano, New York, Usa, Eileen Riano, New York, Usa, Gavin Riano, New York, Usa, Brendan Rice, Milngavie, Donny Rice, Milngavie, Kieran Rice, Newry, Meg Rice, Milngavie, Micha Rice, Milngavie, Michaela Rice, Milngavie, Sean Rice, Toronto, Canada, Brian&Carrie Richards, Luncarty,Perth, Emma Richards, C-Hill, Mark Richards, Perth, Sheila Richards, Perth, Aiden Richardson, Irvine, Andrew Richardson, Brixham, Devon, Bob Richardson, Glasgow, Brian Richardson, Peterborough, Calvin & Kyle Richardson, Castlemilk,Glasgow, Charles Richardson, Pollokshields,Glasgow, Connor Richardson, Newmarket,Suffolk, Cortney Richardson, East Sussex, Courteney Richardson, , Darren Richardson, Seville,Spain, Ina Richardson, Newmarket,Suffolk, Jim Richardson, Raploch, John Richardson, Cambuslang, Liz Richardson, Raploch, Stirling, Lorraine Richardson, Overtown, Mark Richardson, East Sussex, Mary Richardson, Cambuslang, Megan Richardson, Cambuslang, Nicola Richardson, Port Glasgow, Peter Richardson, Newmarket,Suffolk, Tam Richardson, Fort William, Tony Richardson, Carnbroe, Coatbridge, Marcus Richford, Castlemilk, Stu Richford, Castlemilk, Alan Richie, , Charlie Richmond, Cheltenham, Jackie Richmond, Kilmaurs, Ayrshire, Lesley Richmond, Govan, Steven Richmond, Kilmaurs, Ayrshire, Stevie Richmond, Kilmaurs, Ayrshire, Martin Rickaby, Canon, Coalville, Martin Rickaby, Leicester, Alan Riddell, Glasgow, Craig Riddell, Paisley, Deborah Riddell, Glasgow, Norrie Riddell, Barrhead, Lee Riddex, Ardrossan, Paul Riddex, Ardrossan, Roy Riddex, Ardrossan, Roy Riddex, Glenrothes, Archie Riddle, Bonnybridge, Alison & Chelsea Riddrie, , Henry Ridge, Glasgow, Peter Ried, Falkirk, Karis Riggins, Barrowfield, Glasgow, Amie Riley, Cowie, Charlie Riley, East Kilbride, Chris Riley, Cambuslang, Hugh Riley, Cowie, Jonathan Riley, Bathgate, Michael Riley, Glasgow, Peter Riley, Couden, Bishopauckland., Shannon Riley, Cowie, Sharon Riley, Cowie, Shug Riley, Cowie, Stephen Riley, Shotts, Tony Riley, Bathgate, Jordan Rind, , Bosshog Riordan, Tallaght, Dublin, Alan Ritchie, Bangor, Alisdair Ritchie, Beauly, Andy Ritchie, Castlemilk], Cameron Ritchie, Portpatrick, Chris Ritchie, Dundee, Craig Ritchie, Dundee, Craig Ritchie, Stirling, Gary Ritchie, West Wemyss, Greg Ritchie, Linlithgow, Greg Ritchie, Linlithgow, Heather Ritchie, Cork, Kenneth Ritchie, Paul Ritchie, Castlemilk, Sean Ritchie, Cork, Stephen Ritchie, Ballingry, Steven Ritchie, 'D' Shift, St Fergus, Charles Roach, Paisley, Michael Roache, Townhead, Coatbridge, Ann Roan, Glasgow, Ann Roan, Glasgow, Sarah Roan, Glasgow, Sarah Roan, Glasgow, Gary Robb, Camelon, Martin Robb, Dundee, Martin Robb, Dundee, Gary Roberts, Fife, Mark Roberts, Fife, Mick Roberts, , William Roberts, Girvan, Ayrshire, William Roberts, Johnstone, Jay Roberts, Peckham, South London, Alan Robertson, Kinlochleven, Alan Robertson, South

Africa, Aldwyn Robertson, Stirling, Amanda Robertson, Milton, Andrew Robertson, Clarkston, Andrew Robertson, East Kilbride, Andrew Robertson, Glasgow, Anthony Robertson, Plains, Ashleigh Robertson, Kilmarnock, Bernie Robertson, Port Glasgow, Billy Robertson, Viewpark Uddingston, Cathrine Robertson, Stirling, Chelsea Robertson, Glenrothes, Cheryl Robertson, Bonhill, Claire Robertson, Bannockburn, Corinne Robertson, Glasgow, Craig Robertson, Bannockburn, Craig Robertson, Campbeltown (The Wee Toon), Craig Robertson, Govan, Glasgow, David Robertson, Glenrothes, David Robertson, Stirling, Eleanor Robertson, Plains, Emma Robertson, Kilmarnock, Graham Robertson, Livingston, Hannah Robertson, Plains, Ian Robertson, Dundee, Ian Robertson, Dundee, James Robertson, Croy, James Robertson, South Queensferry, Jim Robertson, Kilmarnock, John Robertson, Elgin, John Robertson, Geelong, Australia, John Robertson, Maryhill, Glasgow, Leon Robertson, Channel Islands, Lorna Robertson, Bannockburn, Louise Robertson, Aberdeen, Louise Robertson, Stenhousemuir, Mary Robertson, Bo'ness, Paul Robertson, Kingspark, Peter Robertson, Croy, Robert Robertson, Stirling, Sandra Robertson, Cumbernauld, Sandy Robertson, A. R., Services, Sandy Robertson, Bannockburn, Scott Robertson, Carrick Knowe, Edinburgh, Scott Robertson, Stenhousemuir, Steven Robertson, Glasgow, Stevie Robertson, Ardrossan, Stuart Robertson, Innerleithen, Stuart Robertson, Stevenston, Stuart Robertson, Strathaven, Tony Robertson, St Ninians, William Robertson, Maryhill, Glasgow, Willie Robertson, Kilsyth, Alan Robertson Jnr, Kinlochleven, Rab Robertson Jnr, Livingston, Rab Robertson Snr, Livingston, Mark Robetson, Rutherglen, Glasgow, Andrew Robinson, Johnstone, Isabelle Robinson, Oldham, John Robinson, Barrhead, John Robinson, , Kate Robinson, Stirling, Michael Robinson, Bathgate, Michael Robinson, Oldham, Michael Robinson, , Nuggy Robinson, San Diego, California., Richard Robinson, Dumbarton, Willie Robinson, Struan, Robinson, Oldham, Keni Robson, Glasgow, Erl Rocket, The Brig Pub, Alan Rodan, Glasgow, Angela Rodden, Kilbirnie, Barry Rodden, Summerston, Glasgow, Brian Rodden, Giffnock, Glasgow, Derek Rodden, Kilbirnie, Hannah Rodden, Maryhill, Glasgow, Lewis Rodden, Summerston, Glasgow, Martyn Rodden, Giffnock, Glasgow, Morag Rodden, Giffnock, Glasgow, Patrick Rodden, Maryhill, Glasgow, Paul Rodden, Summerston, Glasgow, Daniel Roddie, Paisley, James Roddie, Paisley, James Roddie, Paisley, John Roddie, Paisley, Alex Rodger, Nitshill, Glasgow, Alex Rodger, Priesthill, Glasgow, Colin Rodger, Glasgow, Dave Rodger, Cumbernauld, Rab Rodger, Methil, Alan Rodgers, Glasgow, Barrie Rodgers, Whitburn, Eddie Rodgers, Canada, Gavin Rodgers, Cookstown, Gerald Rodgers, Cookstown, Gerry Rodgers, Cookstown, Holly Rodgers, Kilmarnock, John Rodgers, Port Glasgow, John (Weejay) Rodgers, Port Glasgow, Josh Rodgers, Kilmarnock, Sharon Rodgers, Coatbridge, Stephen Rodgers, Whitburn, Wendy Rodgers, Motherwell, Carol Roe, Ayr, Paul Roe, Glasgow, Jimmy Rogan, Darnley, Glasgow, Paul Rogers, Chryston, Fiona Rogerson, Carnforth, John Rogerson, Falkirk, Liz Rogerson, Falkirk, Derek Rolink, Airdrie, Sharon Rolink, Airdrie, Jordan Ronald, Bellshill, Jordan Ronald, , Allan Ronney, Irvine, Gail Ronney, Irvine, Jim Ronney, Irvine, Squadron Leader Rooke, Partick, Aidan Rooney, Glasgow, Alan Rooney, Airdrie, Alex Rooney, Kirkintilloch, Brian Rooney, Kirkintilloch, Catherine Rooney, Elderslie, Christoper Rooney, Kirkintilloch, Clar Rooney, Bothwell, Daniel Rooney, Arden, Daniel Rooney, Glasgow, Frank Rooney, Arden, Frank Rooney, Ibrox, Gill Rooney, Arden, Glasgow, Hugh Rooney, London, Hugh Rooney, Somewhere In London, Irene Rooney, Lanarkshire, James Rooney, Kirkintilloch, Jamie Rooney, Easterhouse, Jennifer Rooney, Watford, Hertfordshire, Kathy Rooney, Abingdon, Kevin Rooney, Carluke, Kiernan Rooney, Arden, Lorraine Rooney, Kirkintilloch, Margo Rooney, Glasgow, Paul Rooney, Abingdon, Paul Rooney, Cambuslang, Peter Rooney, Glasgow, Peter Rooney, Howood, Samantha Rooney, Ibrox, Susan Rooney, Glasgow, Tracy Rooney, Easterhouse, Spoon Roonster, Belfast, Craig Rorison, Kilmarnock, Harry Jnr Rorke, Dundee, Harry Rorke Jnr, Dundee, Joe Rorrison, Port Glasgow, Kevin Rorrison, Port Glasgow, Mick Rorrison, Port Glasgow, Chris Rose, Newcastle, Josie Rose, London, Peter Rose, Cumbernauld, Andrew Ross, Alloa, Claire

Louise Ross, , Danny Ross, London, Dave C. Ross, Colchester, Essex, David Ross, Portree, Isle of Skye, Euan Ross, Denny, Frank Ross, Leith, Edinburgh, Ian Ross, Jeff Ross, Fife, John-Paul Ross, Sauchie, Kenny Ross, Maryburgh, Liam Ross, Alloa, Linda Ross, Maryburgh, Malky Ross, Livingston, Marc Ross, Kilmarnock, Margaret Ross, Trinity, Edinburgh, Mark Ross, Motherwell, Michael Ross, High Valley Field, Fife, Nathan Ross, Gairloch, Ross-shire, Nathan Ross, Gairloch Ross-Shire, Owen Ross, Gairloch Ross-Shire, R Ross, Maryburgh, Ranald Ross, Maryburgh, Rev. Richard Ross, Scourie, Rhona Ross, Gairloch, Ross-Shire, Steve Ross, Forres, Morayshire, Stuart Ross, Beauly, Wayne (Bobo) Ross, Ross-shire, Xander Ross, Livingston, West Lothian, Aldo Rossi, Paisley, Andy Rossi, Ayr, Steven Rougvie, Kirkcaldy, Don Rousen, Johnstone, Nicholas Roviezzo, Glenrothes, David Rowan, Forth, Fiona Rowan, Forth, Leigh Rowan, Lochee, Dundee, Roisin Rowan, Forth, Sean Rowan, Forth, Mark Rowe, Ayr, Colette Rowell, York, Liam Rowell, York, Claire Rowen, Glasgow, Kelly-Ann Rowen, Glasgow, Alan Roy, Inverness, Aldo Roy, , Barry Roy, Coatbridge, David Roy, Uddingston, Fiona Roy, Tillicoultry, Fiona Roy, Tullibody, Marlyn Roy, Tullibody, Robert Roy, Biggar, Tony Roy, , Dom Ruane, Dumbarton, Anna Rubertazzi, Ayr, Marina Rubertazzi, Ayr, Nick Rubertazzi, Ayr, Chris Ruchazie, Glasgow, Craigie Bhoy Ruchazie, , Paddy Ruddy, Renfrew, Martin Rudzinski, Glasgow, Monk Rugeley, Staffs, Paddy Rugeley, Staffs, Scott B. Rugeley, Staffs, Steven Rule, Cambusbarron, Alan Rundell, Birmingham, Shaun Rundell, Balloch, Evan Rush, Irvine, James Rush, Irvine, Lisa Rush, Cumbernauld, Stephen Rush, Kilbarchan, Joe Rushforth, Stirling, Alan Russell, Dundee, Alan Russell, Fife, Angie Russell, Dundee, Anthony Russell, Faifley, Chip Russell, Dunfermline, Craig Russell, Pollokshaws, Lee Russell, Lumphinnans, Lynsey Russell, West End, Glasgow, Mags Russell, Stenhouse, Edinburgh, Marianne Russell, Drumchapel, Michael Russell, Lumphinnans, Mike Russell, Stenhouse, Edinburgh, Pauline Russell, London, Shannon Russell, Shettleston, Vikki Russell, Garrowhill, Glasgow, Derek Rutherford, Fife, Gerry Rutherford, Dumfries, Ian Rutherford, Largs, Paul Rutherford, Dumfries, Stengo Rutherglen, , Derek Ryan, Blackburn(England), Donna Ryan, Glasgow, John Ryan, Bearsden, Glasgow, John Ryan, Reading, Kelly Ryan, Denny, Michael Francis Ryan, Barrhead, Paul Ryan, Bearsden, Glasgow, Scott Ryan, Guernsey, Scott Ryan, Guernsey, Todd Ryan, North Carolina, USA, Jan Rybacki, Penilee, Christer Ryderfelt, Stockholm, Michael Ryderfelt, Stockholm, Susan Ryles, Winchburgh, West Lothian, Tommy Rynolds, Shotts.

Joseph Sabatelli, Glasgow. Tom Sabatelli, Cumbernauld, Anhtony Sadler, Castlemilk, Craig Sadler, Edinburgh, Mags Sadler, Edinburgh, Ross, Anthony Sadler, Tormusk, Glasgow, Tam Sadler, Edinburgh, Jane Safeway, , Frank Sallie, New Zealand, Maggie Salsburgh, , Marco R Sambucci, Liverpool, Pat Sammers, Sleaford, Satan Sammy, Pollok, Aidan Samson, Hamilton, Alan Samson, Letham, Angus, Alex Samson, Hamilton, David Samson, Forfar, Gary Samson, Dundee, Lisa Samson, Hamilton, Hugh Sanaghan, Blantyre, Hugh Sanaghan, Blantyre, Dennis Sandeman, Dundee, Dennis Sandeman, Dundee, G Sanders, Glasgow, James Sanders, Glasgow, K. Sanders, Glasgow, Lorraine Sanders, Glasgow, Lorraine Sanders, Glasgow, Neil Sanders, Clowne, Paul Sanders, Erskine, Gerry Sanderson, East Kilbride, Robert Sands, Belfast, Ireland, Robert Sands, The Brig Bar, Sanjeey Sanghera, Giffnock, Piero Sanguigni, Isle of Sky, Jerry Sanning, Glasgow, Charles Sassmut, , Sophie Sauchie, , Andrew Savage, Bodrum, Turkey, Jamie Savage, Glasgow, John Savage, Bodrum, Turkey, Lynne Savage, Bodrum, Turkey, Davy Sawden, Dumfries, Martin Scahill, Crosshill, Glasgow, Jamie Scally, Castlemilk, Glasgow, Jim Scambler, Anniesland, Jim Scandler, Glasgow, Brian Scanlan, Knightswood, Mark Scanlin, Hamilton, Terry Scanlon, StAndrews, Graham Scarff, Dublin, Leanne Schiavone, Kirkintilloch, Paul Schiavone, Stoneyburn, Darryl Scholey, Chapeltown, Sheffield, Bruno Schultz, Falkirk, Paul Schultz, Falkirk, Andre Scotland, Tillicoultry, Chevon Scotland, Tillicoultry, Alan Scott, Ulsan, Korea, Ashley Scott, Germiston, Glasgow, Ashley Scott, Glasgow, Billy Scott, Coatbridge, Craig Scott, Dublin, Craig Scott, Greenock, Darren Scott, Cowdenbeath, Darren Scott, Cowdenbeath, Daryl

Scott, Glenfarg, David Scott, Jedburgh, David Bowie Scott, Pollok, Eddie Scott, Germiston, Glasgow, Frank Scott, , Garath Scott, Kelso, Gary Scott, Troon, Ayrshire, Gary Scott, Gerry Scott, Hogganfield, Gordon Scott, Cowdenbeath, Hamilton Scott, Musselburgh, Jackie Scott, Sunderland, Janet Scott, Cowdenbeath, Jeanette Scott, Denmark, Jim Scott, Bellshill, Jim Scott, Croy, Jim Scott, Glenfarg, John Scott, Clarkston, John Scott, Sheffield, June Scott, Glenfarg, Kerry Scott, Clarkston, Lauren Scott, Clarkston, Lee Scott, Denny, Liz Scott, Glasgow, Margaret Scott, Clarkston, Mark Scott, Saltire Court, Edinburgh, Martin Scott, Kilmarnock, Michael Scott, Barrhead, Peter Scott, Glenfarg, Richard Scott, Cowdenbeath, Robert Scott, Coatbridge, Sandy Scott, Temple Bar, Norwich, Sean Scott, Croftfoot, Shannon Scott, Germiston, Glasgow, Sonny Scott, Provanmill, Glasgow, Steven Scott, Irvine, Stevie Scott, Arbroath, Gordon Scott Jnr, Cowdenbeath, Ken Scriven, Dundee, Brian Scullen, Bangor, John Scullen, Bangor, Gary `El Skud` Scullion, Torrevieja, Spain, Philip Scullion, , Robbie Scullion, Craigavon, Robert Scullion, Inverness, Shug Scullion, Coatbridge, Tony Scullion, Ballycastle Co.Antrim, Martin Sean, Glasgow, Grant Seenan, Cumbernauld, Derick Seery, , Stuart Seggie, Greenock, Alan Sellstrom, Falkirk, Angela Semple, Bishopbriggs, Brendan Semple, Glasgow, Frank Semple, Glasgow, John Semple, Bishopbriggs, Paul Semple, Bishopbriggs, Mary Serevena, Luton, Beds, Michael Serevena, Luton, Beds, Steven Sewell, Glasgow, Frank Sexton, Croftfoot, Angela Shade, Uphall, Steve Shadlow, Luton, Stephen Shah, Yoker, Glasgow, Derek Shaker, Fuengirola, Derek Shaker, Fuengirola, Phil Shalley, Ontario Canada, Jackie Shand, Summerston, Jackie Shand, , Karen S Shanks, Falkirk, Marc Shanks, Bo'ness, Paul Shanks, Cumbernauld, Steven Shanks, Airdrie, Liam Shanley, Glasgow, Michael Shanley, Drumchapel, William Shanley, Glasgow, Alex Shannon, Baillieston, Alex Shannon, Easterhouse, Danny Shannon, Coventry, David Shannon, Cathkin, Glasgow, Gerald Shannon, Newarthill, Joe Shannon, Cathcart, Glasgow, Judy Shannon, Cathcart, Glasgow, Kevin Shannon, Paisley, Kirsty Shannon, Dennistoun, Glasgow, Kirsty Shannon, Dennistoun, Glasgow, Margaret Shannon, Baillieston, Martin Shannon, Baillieston, Mary Shannon, Dennistoun, Glasgow, Mary Shannon, Easterhouse, Michael Shannon, Easterhouse, Morgan Shannon, Knightswood, Peter Shannon, Knightswood, Tam Shannon, Dennistoun, Glasgow, Thomas Shannon, Dennistoun, Glasgow, Thomas Shannon, Dennistoun, Glasgow, Andrew Sharkey, Lanarkshire, Darren Sharkey, Glasgow, P .J .Sharkey, Glasgow, P. J. Sharky, Mullaghduff, Ron Sharp, Port, Glasgow, Steven Sharp, Alloa, Steven Sharp, John Paul Sharpe, Springburn Glasgow, Brendan Shaw, Stepps, Bryan Shaw, Linwood, Callum Shaw, Balliston, Charlie Shaw, Cambusbarron, David Shaw, Glasgow, Derek Shaw, Stirling, Elaine Shaw, Easterhouse, Glasgow, Erin Shaw, Coatbridge, Henry Shaw, London, Jason Shaw, Penicuik, Joe Shaw, Glasgow, John Shaw, Glasgow, Kenny Shaw, Blantyre, Matthew Shaw, Stirling, Nicole Shaw, Yoker, Glasgow, Paul Shaw, Glasgow, Paula Shaw, Airdrie, David Shea, Erskine, David Shea, , Al Shearer, Rutherglen, David Shearer, Cumbernauld, David Shearer, Glenburn, Paisley, David Shearer, Scotstoun, Glasgow, Iain Shearer, Cumbernauld, Paul Shearer, Hamilton, Ritchie Shearer, Ruchill Glasgow, Christopher Shearin, Pollok, Glasgow, Joe Shearin, Pollok, Glasgow, Stevie Shearon, Cadder, Scott Shedden, Ruchill, Clare Sheerins, Ayrshire, Sean Sheerins, Ayrshire, Debbie Sheffield, Lenzie, East Dunbartonshire, Irene Sheffield, Lenzie, East Dunbartonshire, John Sheffield, Lenzie, East Dunbartonshire., Karen Sheffield, Lenzie, East Dunbartonshire., Adam Sheilds, Hamilton, Anthony Sheilds, Glasgow, Jamie Sheilds, Greenock, Adam Sheils, Hamilton, Amanda Shelids, Glasgow, Stuart Shepard, Kilsyth, Douglas Shepburn, Shettleston, Bill Shepherd, Fife, Janet Shepherd, East Kilbride, Sammy Shepherd, Glasgow, Tommy Shepherd, Glasgow, Gary Sheppard, Clarkston, Emma Sheridan, Dumbarton, Joe Sheridan, Crookston, Joseph Sheridan, Crookston, Michael Sheridan, Paisley, Allan Sherod, Glasgow, Mary Sherriff, Cowenbeath, Jennifer Sherring, Bathgate, Gavin Sherry, West Lothian, Heather Sherry, West Lothian, Bobby Sherville, Dunoon, Hugh Shevlin, Cambuslang, James Shevlin, Cambuslang, Pat Shevlin, Motherwell, Pat Shevlin, Motherwell, Pat Shevlin, Scotland, Sara Shevlin,

Banknock, Elaine Shewan, Inverness, Karen Shewan, Inverness, Kevin Shewan, Inverness, Liam Shewan, Inverness, Mike Shewan, Inverness, Nicole Shewan, Inverness, Andrew Shields, Glasgow, Barry Shields, Greenock, Marieche Shields, Wishaw, Mike Shields, Carrick Knowe Edinburgh, Liam Shine, Palmers Green, Daniel Shipman, Edinburgh, Stewart Shirley, Port Glasgow, Owen Shoeness, Blackburn, Andy Short, Faifley, Brad Short, Glenrothes, Jade Short, Glenrothes, John Short, Glasgow, John Short, Glasgow, Murray Short, Glenrothes, Nicki Short, Glasgow, Nicky Short, Glasgow, Nicole Short, Glenrothes, Thomas Short, Glenrothes, Thomas Short, Glenrothes, Barry Shovelin, Drumchapel, Glasgow, Jim Shovelin, Drumchapel, Glasgow, Margaret Shovelin, Drumchapel, Glasgow, Big Shug, Methilhaven Depot, Craig Tim Sibbald, Magdalene, Edinburgh, John Sieyes, Garrowhill, Glasgow, Barry Sigerson, Glasgow, Linda Sigerson, , Michael Sigerson, John Silvestro, Parkhead, Glasgow, Chris Sim, Lerwick, Shetland, Fraser Sim, Bexleyheath, Lindsay Sim, Bexleyheath, Laura Sim, Bexleyheath, Barry Simeon, Newtyle, Don Simeon, Newtyle, Liz Simeon, Newtyle, Christopher Simm, Glasgow, Robert Simmonds, Clydebank, Alan Simpson, Wick, Andrew Simpson, Donegal, Andrew J Simpson, St Ninians, Andy Simpson, Buckie, Anne Simpson, Glasgow, Barry Simpson, Lhanbryde, Big Phil Simpson, Tilburg Nederlands, Bob Simpson, Aberdeen, Bobby Simpson, Boness, Catherine Simpson, Penilee, Charlie Simpson, Stirling, David Simpson, Glasgow, David Simpson, Kirkcaldy, Donna Simpson, Easterhose, Donna Simpson, Easterhouse, Iain Simpson, Possilpark, Lorraine Simpson, St Ninians, Margaret Simpson, Paisley, Michelle Simpson, Penilee, Patrick Simpson, Donegal, Ross Simpson, Clarkston Glasgow, Roy Simpson, Wolverhampton, Shaun Simpson, Lhanbryde, Stuart Simpson, Boness, Stuart Simpson, Carronshore, Falkirk, Stuart Simpson, Carronshore, Falkirk, Camron Sinclair, Lanark, Harry Sinclair, Glasgow, James Sinclair, Glasgow, Jim Sinclair, Balornock, Jodie Sinclair, Barnanark, John Sinclair, Wembley, John Paul Patrick Sinclair, Santa Barbara, California, Liam Sinclair, Glasgow, Mark Sinclair, Baillieston, Paul Sinclair, Baillieston, Robbie Sinclair, Paisley, William Sinclair, Glasgow, James Sindley, Airdrie, Alex Sinnet, Bathgate, Chris Sinnet, Bathgate, Francis Sinnet, Bathgate, Alan Sirling, Glasgow, Gerry Skeith, Old Kilpatrick, Sean Skelly, Erskine, Simon Skelly, Ruchill, Glasgow, Stephen Skelly, Ruchill, Glasgow, Stephen Skelly Jnr, Ruchill, Glasgow, Kevin Skey, Rutherglen, Sean Skey, Rutherglen, Andrew Skinner, Dornoch, Hilda Skivington, Livingston, West Lothian, Michael Slack, Glasgow, Melissa Slane, Anderston, Shannon Slatem, Beith, Billy Slater, Glasgow, Gorbals, Liam Slattery, Bargeddie, Liam Slattery, Coatbridge, Robbie Slaven, Sandyhills, Glasgow, Andy Slavin, Elderslie, Frank Slavin, Wishaw, George Sleet, Inverness, C Slevin, High Blantyre, Deborah Slevin, Bournemouth, John Slevin, Clydebank, Sinead Slevin, Clydebank, Steven Slevin, High Blantyre, Eric Slivinski, Halfway, Charlene Sloan, Motherwell, David Sloan, Newmains, Dean Sloan, Motherwell, John Sloan, Motherwell, Mark Sloan, Galston, Ayrshire, Martin Sloan, West Belfast, Paul Sloan, Newmains, Pauline Sloan, Motherwell, Steven Sloan, Kennoway, Karen Sloane, Hamilton, Anne Slowey, Coatbridge, Antony Slowey, Hamilton, Dominic Slowey, Yoker, Frances Slowey, Yoker, Guy Slowey, Yoker, Jim Slowey, , John Slowey, Yoker, Paul Slowey, Larkhall, Thos. Slowey, Coatbridge, Tosh Slowey, Coatbridge, Danielle Sludden, Corby, Northants, Danny Sludden, Corby, Northants, Eddie Sludden, Corby, Northants, Jaynie Sludden, Corby, Northants, John Sludden, Corby, Northants, John Patrick Sludden, Corby, Northants, Pat Sludden, Corby, Northants, Pat Sludden, Sauchie, Shannon Sludden, Corby, Northants, Ted Sludden, Corby, Northants, Billy Small, Greenock, Scott Small, Glasgow, Scott Small, Pollock, Shaun Small, Greenock, Steven Small, Elderslie, Billy Small Jnr, Greenock, Billy Small Snr, Greenock, Chris Smart, Edinburgh, Jamie Smart, Leeds, Nick Smart, Edinburgh, Aidan Smith, Sydney, Australia, Andrew Smith, Dundee, Andy Smith, Glasgow, Andy Smith, Glasgow, Andy Smith, Sandyhills,Glasgow, Anne Marie Smith, Elgin, Antony Smith, East Kilbride, Audrey Smith, Dundee, Audrey Smith, Dundee, Becca Smith, Hillhead, Bernadette Smith, Linwood, Billy Smith, Glasgow, Brendan Smith, Hamilton, Brian Smith, Airdrie, Brian Smith,

Glasgow, Brian Smith, Rutherglen, Glasgow, Caitlin Smith, Possil, Callum Smith, Possil, Calvin Smith, Buckie, Carrie-Anne Smith, Edinburgh, Catherine Smith, Paisley, Charles Smith, Crookston, Cheryl Smith, Glasgow, Conner Smith, Glasgow, Craig Smith, Dennistoun, Daniel Smith, Newarthill, David Smith, Bishopton, David Smith, Elgin, David Smith, Kent, David Smith, Shepherds Bush, London, David Smith, St. Andrews, Davy Smith, Prestwick, Dawn Smith, Kirkintilloch, Dennis Smith, Cardiff, Erik Smith, Cumbernauld, Erik Smith, Cumbernauld, Fiona Smith, Kirkby, Frank Smith, Wishaw,Lanarkshire, Frankie Smith, Dundee, Frankie Smith, Dundee, Gary Smith, Dalbeattie, Gary Smith, Glasgow, Gavin Smith, Bishopbriggs, Gemma Smith, Glasgow, George Smith, Irvine, George Smith, Stoneyburn, West Lothian, Geraldine Smith, Barrhead, Gerry Smith, Wishaw, Graham Smith, Glasgow, Graham Smith, St Ninians, Hollie Smith, Grantown-on-Spey, Ian Smith, Barrhead, Ian Smith, East Kilbride, Ian Smith, Glasgow, Ian Smith, Northampton, Ian Smith, Northampton, Jacqueline Smith, Glasgow, James Smith, Duntocher, Jamesie Smith, Uddingston, Jamie Smith, Glasgow, Jessie Smith, Glasgow, Jim Smith, Glasgow, Jimmy Smith, Dundee, Jimmy Smith, Dundee, Jimmy Smith, East Kilbride, Jodie Smith, Hawick, Joe Smith, Linlithgow, Joe Smith, Linlithgow, John Smith, Chichester, John Smith, Cumbernauld, John Smith, Hamilton, John Smith, Newarthill, John Smith, Wishaw, John D. Smith, Renfrew, John T. Smith, Bonhill, Jordan Smith, Springboig, Jordan Paul Smith, Bothwell, Joseph Smith, Glasgow, Josie Smith, Cardenden, Karen Smith, Wishaw, Kevin Smith, Barrhead, Kevin Smith, Glasgow, Kevin Smith, Kilwinning, Kevin Smith, Netherlee, Glasgow, Kevin Smith, Newtongrange, Kevin Smith, Rutherglen, Glasgow, Lee Smith, West Lothian, Lenny Smith, Drunchapel, Letitia Smith, Uddingston, Lex Smith, Borrhead, Liam Smith, Hawick, Lindsey Smith, Glasgow, Margaret Smith, Kirkintilloch, Margaret Smith, Newtongrange, Margaret Smith, Overtown, Mark Smith, Bishopbriggs, Mark Smith, Glasgow, Mark Smith, Kilcreggan, nr Helensburgh, Mark Smith, Killcreggan, Marnee Smith, Newport, Wales, Matthew Smith, Glasgow, Matthew Smith, West Lothian, Michael Smith, Carfin, Michael Smith, Clydebank, Michael Smith, Glasgow, Michael Smith, Irvine, Michelle Smith, Anglesey, North Wales, Mick Smith, Courthill, Glasgow, Mick Smith, Johnstone, Mike "Maestro" Smith, Cumbernauld, Moira Smith, Rutherglen, Glasgow, Morris Smith, Edinburgh, Nathan Smith, Springboig, Glasgow, Nathan Smith, Wishaw, Nicola Smith, Blantyre, Nicola Smith, Irvine, Ayrshire, P Smith, Portsmouth, Patrick Smith, Shettleston, Paul Smith, Haddington, Peter Smith, Airdrie, Peter Smith, Chichester, Peter Smith, Kelvindale, Glasgow, Phil Smith, Glasgow, Rab Smith, Pollock, Raymond J Smith, Watford, Hertfordshire, Rebecca Smith, Staffordshire, Robert Smith, Glasgow, Robert Smith, Kirkintilloch, Robert Smith, Prestwick, Robert Smith, Burn Bank, Rory Smith, Wishaw, Sandy Smith, Arbroath, Saskia Smith, Springboig, Glasgow, Sean Smith, Hamilton, Sean Smith, Wishaw,Lanarkshire, Shaun F Smith, Renfrew, Siobhon Smith, Glasgow, Stephanie Smith, Greenock, Steven Smith, Airdrie, Steven Smith, Glasgow, Steven Smith, Motherwell, Susan Smith, Glasgow, Susan Smith, Motherwell, Tam Smith, Motherwell, Terry Smith, Newtongrange, Thomas Smith, Ruchill, Tony Smith, Pollok , Tracey Smith, Glasgow, Wullie Smith, Easterhouse, Brian Smith [Smiddy], Florida Usa, Mick Smith Jr, Johnstone, Edward Smyth, , John Smyth, Glasgow, Keiron Smyth, Glasgow, Michael Smyth, Bothwell, Paul Smyth, Bothwell, Paul Smyth, Croftfoot, Glasgow, Richard Smyth, Glasgow, Michael Smyth(Snr), Uddingston, Karen Snaddon, , Andrew Sneddon, Edinburgh, Andrew Sneddon, Stirling, David Sneddon, Kilmarnock, Jim Sneddon, Wishaw, John Sneddon, Wishaw, Mark Sneddon, East Kilbride, Mark Gerard Sneddon, East Kilbride, Nicole Sneddon, Scotland, Ryan Sneddon, Kilmarnock, Tommy Sneddon, Livingston, Mark Snell, Glasgow, Norma Snockers, Edinburgh, Norma Snockers, Edinburgh, Kellyanne Soden, Glenmavis, Airdrie, Alan Somerville, Armadale, Michael Somerville, Stenhousemuir, Michael Somerville, Stenhousemuir, Jannette Sommerville, Wishaw, Nicole Sommerville, Wishaw, Glenn Sore, Emsworth, Hampshire, Tricia Sore, Emsworth, Hampshire, Johnny Sorensen, Linlithgow, Greame Souness, Edinburgh, Abby Soutar, Gartcosh, Angela Soutar, Gartcosh, Dago Soutar,

Perth, Liz Soutar, Perth, Robert Soutar, Gartcosh, Soapy Soutar, Corby, Ally Souter, Wishaw, Iain Southall, London, Iain Southall, London, Iain Southall, London, Iain Southall, London, William Speirs, Paisley, Aiden Spence, Glasgow, Brian Spence, Kinlochleven, Charlie Spence, Glasgow, Eddie Spence, East Kilbride, Marcus Spence, Kinlochleven, Michael Spence, Glasgow, Pamela Spence, Glasgow, Ronnie Spence, Glasgow, James Spencer, Canada, James Spencer, Leeds, Margo Spencer, Coatbridge, James Spiers, Brightons, Thomas John Spiers, Sydney, Australia, Arthur Spittal, Durham Celtic Club, Whitby, Ontario, Adam Spotheringham, Cumbernauld, Boo Springwell, Blantyre, Moira Springwell, Blantyre, Graeme Sproat, Arrochar, Graeme Sproul, Craigmalloch, Hannah Sproul, Craigmalloch, Abigail Squire, Blackpool, Carl Squire, Blackpool, George St John, Bracknell, Liz Stacey, Mayfield, Paul Stackpool, Store Club Staff, Musselburgh, Daniel Stafford, Ayr, Erine Stafford, Ayr, Gary Stafford, Burnside, Lauren Stafford, Ayr, Natalie Stafford, Ayr, Alice Stakim, Ayr, Charlie Stakim, Lancing, Derek Stakim, Lancing, Jo Stakim, Lancing, Liam Stakim, Ayrshire, Liz Stakim, Ayr, Michael Stakim, Ayr, Lynn Stalker, Aberdeen, Stewart Stanfield, Kincardine, Padraig Stanley, Glasgow, Annemarie Stanton, Johnstone, Iain Stanton, Winsford, Martin Stanton, Johnstone, Amanda Stark, Twechar, Brian Stark, Dundee, Chris Stark, Brisbane, David Stark, Brisbane, Fiona Stark, Sandyhills, Glasgow, Michael Stark, Sandyhills, Glasgow, Paul Stark, Glasgow, Robert Stark, Sandyhills, Glasgow, Tommy Stark, Johnstone, Joe Starr, Luton, Eddie Staunton, Merrylee, Glasgow, Gary Stead, Falkirk, Ray Stead, Falkirk, Shaun Steadman, Bathgate, David Steel, Stirling, Mick and Scott Steel, Winsford, Cheshire, Chris Steele, E.London, David Steele, Stirling, Jimmy and Kenny Steele, Arbroath, Liz Steele, Glasgow, Martin Steele, Glasgow, Tim Steele, Barrow in Furness, John Stein, Hamilton, Richard Steinbach, Dunfermline, Colin Stephen, Glasgow, James Stephen, Croftfoot, Glasgow, Jane Stephen, Croftfoot, Glasgow, Keith Stepps, Alan Sterling, Glasgow, Deborah Stevely, Duntocher, Ian Steven, Aberdeenshire, Kirsty Stevens, Winchmore Hill, London, Andrew Stevenson, Grangemouth, Angela Stevenson, Kirkintilloch, Bob Stevenson, Neilston, Brenda Stevenson, Alloa, Brian Stevenson, Banbury, Oxon, Brian Stevenson, Motherwell, Carol Ann Stevenson, Uddingston, Darren Stevenson, Isle of Skye, Helen Stevenson, Renfrew, Jim Stevenson, Renfrew, John Stevenson, Campbeltown, John Stevenson, Glasgow, Kelly Stevenson, Grangemouth, Lara Stevenson, Portobello, Liam Stevenson, Grangemouth, Philip Stevenson, Glasgow, Phyllis Stevenson, Glasgow, Richard Stevenson, Thurso, Sharon Stevenson, Glasgow, Thomas Stevenson, Grangemouth, William Stevenson, Cumbernauld, Big Stevo, Livingston, Angela Steward, Doncaster, Adam Stewart, Rutherglen, Alan Stewart, Easterhouse, Allison H. Stewart, East Kilbride, Amanda Stewart, Bridgetown, Barry Stewart, Edinburgh, Billy 'Bhoy' Stewart, Lochgelly, Brandon Stewart, Plymouth, Bruce Stewart, Chris Stewart, Gunnet Ct Muirhouse, Claire Stewart, Glasgow, Craig Stewart, Glasgow, Daniel Stewart, Crieff, David Stewart, Larkhall, David Stewart, Musselburgh, David Stewart, Springsburn, Dylan Stewart, Crieff, Fiona Stewart, Drumchapel, Glasgow, Fred Stewart, Renfrew, Gillian Stewart, Glasgow, Ian Stewart, Paisley, Irene Stewart, Glasgow, Joedan Stewart, Faside Wallyford, John Stewart, Glasgow, John Stewart, Rutherglen, John G. Stewart, West Belfast, Katline Stewart, Glasgow, Lee Stewart, Plymouth, Lisa Stewart, Renfrew, Louise-Clair Stewart, Carfin, Mark Stewart, Edinburgh, Martin Stewart, Crieff, Michelle Stewart, Aberdeen, Nora Stewart, Glasgow, Panda Stewart, South Gyle, Paul Stewart, Glasgow, Rab Stewart, Glasgow, Rab Stewart, Surrey, S Stewart, Bridgetown, Stephen Stewart, Dublin, Ireland, Stephen Stewart, Fernhill, Steven Stewart, Cupar, Fife, Tim Stewart, Aberdeen, Wendy Stewart, Ayrshire, Grant Stigg, Leven, D Stirling, Bridgwater, Daniel Stirling, Larkhall, Danni Stirling, Carntyne, James Stirling, Bellshill, Jimmy Stirling, Carntyne, John Stirling, Carntyne, Martin Stirling, Coatbridge, Patricia Stirling, Carntyne, Terry Stirling, Rossshire, Beverley Stirling and girls, Bellshill, Andrew Stirrup, Manchester, James Stirrup, Manchester, Robbie Stirrup, Glasgow, Robert Stirrup, Glasgow, Elayne Stoddart, Cumbernauld, Liz Stoddart, Cumbernauld, Paul Stoddart, Cumbernauld, Corin Stone, Alloa, David J. Stone, Alloa, David W. Stone, Alloa,

Garry Stone, Alloa, Michael Stone, Belfast, Stanley Stone, Cumbernauld, Steve Stones, Doncaster, Aiden Storer, Erskine, Betty Storer, Drumchapel, Glasgow, Michael Storer, Chessington, Jackie Storey, Glasgow, Euan Storrie, Troon, Gemma Storrie, Scotstoun, Jack Storrie, Troon, Jacqueline Storrie, Glasgow, Joe Storrie, Scotstoun, Paul Storrie, Troon, Laura Strachan, Motherwell, Lee Strachan, Arbroath, Lee Strachan, Arbroath, Lynn Janetta Strachan, East Kilbride, Paul W. M. Strachan, Stockholm,Sweden, Adam Strain, Arden, Barry Strain, Drumchapel, James Strain, Govanhill, John Strain, Germiston, Johnny Strain, Scotstoun, Kerry Strain, Scotstoun, Glasgow, Vincent Strain, Scotstoun, Glasgow, John Straiton, Leith, Darren Strang, Shotts, Martin Strange, Glasgow, Carol Strathearn, Paisley, Colin Strickland, Ayr, David Strickland, Ayr, Debbie Strickland, Govan, Scott Strickland, Ayr, Claire Strife, Kent, Robert Strock, Uddingston, Andrew Stronach, Huntley, Aberdeenshire, Gavin Stronach, Keith, Banffshire, Mark Strugess, Grangemouth, Ann Struthers, Paisley, John (Jonah) Struthers, Milton, Glasgow, Andrew Strutton, Glasgow, Bob Stuart, Aberdeen, Brian Stuart, Coldstream, Charlie Stuart, Lossiemouth, Daryl Stuart, Aberdeen, David Stuart, Inverness, Gary Stuart, Hampshire, Ian Stuart, Airth, John Stuart, Liverpool, Kevin Stuart, Hampshire, Wendy Stuart, Girvan, Barry Sullivan, Summerston, Glasgow, Christopher Sullivan, Summerston, Glasgow, Gary Sullivan, Leith, Edinburgh, Rab Sullivan, Bellshill, Stephen Sullivan, Summerston, Glasgow, John Sullivan (Sully), Coatbridge, Gary Summers, Edinburgh, Joe Summers, Glasgow, Pat Summers, Sleaford, Paul Summers, Glasgow, Paul Summers, Vancouver, Gerry Summner, Rugby, David Support, Glasgow, James Surgeon, Musselburgh, John Surgeon, Glasgow, Barry Sutherland, Glasgow, Brian Sutherland, Camelon, David Sutherland, Glasgow, Edward Sutherland, Glasgow, Joseph Sutherland, Glasgow, Kevin Sutherland, Edinburgh, Lauren Sutherland, Linthouse, Glasgow, Margaret Sutherland, Dingwall, Mark Sutherland, Croy, Ross Sutherland, Renton, Sandy Sutherland, Harrogate, Scott Sutherland, East Kilbride, Vicky Sutherland, Emsworth, Hampshire, Gary Suttie, Gallogate, Roberta Suttie, Ardrossan, Andy Swan, Colchester, Essex, Cloe Swan, Greenock, David Swan, Perth, Lee Swan, Perth, Liam Swandle, Motherwell, Lanarkshire, Scott Swandle, Abingdon, Oxford, James Swandle Jnr, Abingdon, Oxford, Andy Swanson, Leeds, Adrian Swanston, Peebles, Auld Gerry (Auld Grumpy) Sweeney, Pinebank, Livingston, Benny Sweeney, Letterkenny, Co Donegal, Brendan Sweeney, Glasgow, Brian Sweeney, Glasgow, Denis Sweeney, Leicester, Denise Sweeney, Glasgow, Dennis Sweeney, Glasgow, Dennis Sweeney, Whitburn, Donna Sweeney, Airdrie, Eddie Sweeney, Oldbury, West Midlands, Eddie Sweeney, Renfrew, Frankie Sweeney, Glasgow, Gary Sweeney, Ayr, Gordon Sweeney, Glasgow, Grace Sweeney, Renfrew, Graeme Sweeney, London, James Sweeney, Leicester, Jason Sweeney, Glasgow, Jim Sweeney, Renfrew, John Sweeney, Airdrie, Kevin Sweeney, Glasgow, Kieran Sweeney, Chaser, Liam Sweeney, Glasgow, Martin Sweeney, Sydney, Aust, Mary Sweeney, Renfrew, Michael Sweeney, Isle Of Mull, N. Sweeney, Isle of Mull, Paul Sweeney, Bournemouth, Paul Sweeney, Milton, Dumbarton, Paul Sweeney, Moss Park, Rachel Sweeney, Edinburgh, Robert Sweeney, Cadder, Ronan Sweeney, Whitburn, Ronan Patrick Sweeney, Whitburn, Scott Sweeney, Australia, Shaun Sweeney, Edinburgh, Teresa Sweeney, Edinburgh, Todd Sweeney, Edinburgh, Tom Sweeney, Glasgow, Tony Sweeney, Edinburgh, Linda Sweeny, Livingston, Michael Patrick Sweeny, Livingston, West Lothian, Nicola Sweeny, Livingston, West Lothian, Steven Cooper Sweeny, Livingston, West Lothian, David Sweeten, Shettleston, Glasgow, Gordon Swift, Denny, Stephen Swift, Co. Fermanagh, Michael Swindon, Newton Mearns, Pauline Sykes, Kirkintilloch, Sharn Sykes, Airdrie, Derek Symon, Stirling, Scott Szaranek, Amsterdam (Originally Leslie,Fife), Tam Szultka, Dumfries.

Baz T, Dunfermline, Fife. Ciaran Taggart, Belfast, Garry Taggart, Glasgow, Jamie Taggart, Paisley, Kirsty Taggart, Paisley, Paul Taggart, Balornock, Shirley Taggart, Gallowgate, Alison Tait, Dumbarton, Annalisa Tait, Hamilton, Billy Tait, Cumnock, Ayrshire, Brian Tait, Woodburn, Elizabeth Tait, Dumbarton, John Tait, Rugby, Warwickshire, Stacey Tait,

Woodburn, Stephen Tait, Cambuslang, Tommy Tait, Ayr, John Tam, Uddingston, Henry Tannock, Livingston, Amy Tarrant, Luton, Fiona Tarrant, Luton, Sean Tarrant, Luton, Alan Taylor, Mount Vernon, Glasgow, Alasdair Taylor, London, Ali Taylor, Aberdeen, Blair Taylor, Mount Vernon, Glasgow, Brian Taylor, Blackpool, Brian Taylor, Wishaw, Bryan Taylor, Leeds, Chris Taylor, Nottingham Uni, Connor Taylor, Carfin, Craig Taylor, Duddingston, David Taylor, Coatbridge, Derek Taylor, Braco, Perthshire, Derek Taylor, Invergordon, Derek Taylor, Knotty Green, Buckinghamshire, Freddie Taylor, MacMerry, Gary Taylor, Harpenden, Gary Taylor, Harpenden, Gavin Taylor, Cumbernauld, Geoff Taylor, Newlands, Geoff "County" Taylor, Shawlands, Jamie Taylor, Rutherglen, Jim Taylor, Garrowhill, Glasgow, Jim Taylor, Rutherglen, Jimmy Taylor, Campbeltown, Jimmy Taylor, Rutherglen, Larry Taylor, Duntocher, Clydebank, Mark Taylor, Glasgow, Mark Taylor, Glasgow, Mary Taylor, Barlanark, Glasgow, Mary Taylor, Glasgow, Michael Taylor, Drumchapel, Robbie Taylor, Fife, Sandy Taylor, Buckie, Sean Taylor, Bellshill, Stacey Teresa Taylor, Newarthill, Stevie Taylor, Kennishead, Tony Taylor, Glasgow, Tony Taylor, Angela Te Haara, New Zealand, Gillian Tear, Glasgow, Kevin Teirney, Bailiston, Audrey Telfer, Glasgow, Stephen Telford, Carlisle, Connor Templeton, Stevenston, David Templeton, Cumbernauld, Robert Temporal, Port Glasgow, Hugh Tenbry, Erskine, Malcolm Tennyson, Luton, Stuart Tennyson, Luton, Catriona Thacker, Kilsyth, Kevin Thacker, Kilsyth, Margaret Thain, Dundee, Adrien The Temple Bar, Norwich, Gordon The Temple Bar, Norwich, Mick The Temple Bar, Norwich, Sandy The Temple Bar, Norwich, Seamus The Temple Bar, Norwich, Marie Therese, Motherwell, Anjay Thet, Budhill Square, Glasgow, Chris Thom, Falkirk, Jenny Thom, Inverness, Joe Thom, Bathgate, Claire Thomas, Old Kilpatrick, Claire Thomas, Old Kilpatrick, Davy Thomas, Leven, Delia Thomas, Old Kilpatrick, Delia Thomas, Witney, Kev Thomas, Shotts, Margaret Ann Thomas, Shotts, Arthur Thompson, Renfrew, Bernadette Thompson, Toronto Canada, David Thompson, Glasgow, Dolly Thompson, Glasgow, Gary Thompson, Paisley, Irene Thompson, Cambuslang, Jennette Thompson, Daventry, Jim Thompson, Dunfermline, Linda Thompson, Glasgow, Louise Thompson, Kilwinning, Mark Thompson, Dundee, Mark Thompson, Glasgow, Mark Thompson, Inverness, Mark Thompson, Livingston, Mary Thompson, Greenock, Mary Thompson, Greenock, Megan Thompson, Irvine, Natalie Thompson, Holytown, Nicola Thompson, Glasgow, Paul Thompson, Bedford, Paul Thompson, Bedford, Paul Thompson, Cambuslang, Paul Thompson, Glasgow, Rachael Thompson, Holytown, Sarah Thompson, Kilwinning, Sharon Thompson, Irvine, Steven Thompson, Prestonpans, Stevie Thompson, Patrick, Glasgow, Stuart Thompson, Milngavie, William Thompson, Stirling, Alex Thomson, Erskine, Andrew Thomson, Cirencester, Angeline Thomson, Stirling, Bob Thomson, Nairn, Bobby Thomson, Aberdeen, Brian Thomson, Fenwick, Carol Thomson, Holytown, Charlie Thomson, Kilwinning, Christopher Thomson, Queen's Park, Glasgow, Daryll Thomson, Donald Thomson, Mulben, Dougie Thomson, Maybole, Douglas Thomson, East Kilbride, Ed Thomson, Edinburgh, Eddie Thomson, Coatbridge, Emma Thomson, Buckie, Gary Thomson, Glasgow, Grant Thomson, Baillieston, Ian Thomson, Springburn, Glasgow, Jim Thomson, Battlefield, Joe Thomson, Methilhill, John Thomson, Queen's Park, Glasgow, JoJo Thomson, Uddingston, Keith Thomson, Mayfield, Kevin Thomson, Blantyre, Mark Thomson, Gorbals, Norman Thomson, Inverness, Scott Thomson, Cambuslang Glasgow, Scott Thomson, Springburn,Glasgow, Stephen Thomson, Jersey, Stephen Thomson, Springhill, Tracy Thomson, Coatbridge, Walter Thomson, Methil, Yvonne Thomson, Knightswood Glasgow, Andy Thorburn, Mossblown, Mark Thorburn, Maryhill, Christopher Thornbury, Coatbridge, Garry Thornton, West Lothian, Robert Thornton, Dunoon, Garry Threlfall, Glasgow, Thomas Threwal, Yoker, David Tierney, Clydebank, Dumbartonshire, James Tierney, Stirling, Jamie Tierney, Stirling, Jim Tierney, Motherwell, Joe Tierney, Stirling, John Tierney, Blantyre, Margaret Tierney, Motherwell, Paul Tierney, Bathgate, Peter & Teresa Tierney, Motherwell, Tommy Tierney, Aberdeen, C&B Tiffney CFC, Perth, Ashleigh Timmins, Scotstoun, Glasgow, Barbara Timmins, Scotstoun, Glasgow, Brian

246

Timmins, Fauldhouse, Kieran Timmins, Scotstoun, Glasgow, Linsday Timms, Glasgow, Lorna Timms, Glasgow, Tommy Timms, Bo'ness, Andrew Timoney, Bailliston, Brian Timoney, Inverness, Brian John Timoney, Inverness, Clare Timoney, Tollcross, Joe Timoney, Rutherglen, Lynzie Timoney, Inverness, Michael Timoney, Mr Timoney, Rutherglen, Hamish Tindall, Dundee, Jake Tindall, London, Charlie Tinney, Glasgow, Big Tippy, Bellshill, Hayley Tjon-Aloi, Mississauga, Ontario, Canada, Marcus Tjon-Aloi, Toronto Canada, Brian Toal, Newry, Chris Toal, Coatbridge, Christopher Toal, Coatbridge, Daniel Toal, Glasgow, Danny Toal, Kingspark, Diane Toal, Bonnybridge, Erin Jane Toal, Coatbridge, Jacqueline Toal, Coatbridge, Jim Toal, Coatbridge, Joseph Toal, N. Ireland, Pat Toal, Glasgow, Patrick Toal, Coatbridge, Ryan Toal, Coatbridge, Aidan Michael Toall, Barmulloch, Glasgow, Amanda Toall, Barmulloch, Glasgow, Mathew Toall, Barmulloch, Glasgow, Colin S. Tobin, Airdrie, Lynn Tobin, Airdrie, Tommy Tobin, East Kilbride, Jacqui Tochel, Tannochside, Kevin Tocher, Aberdeen, Stuart Tocher, Aberdeen, Alan Todd, Kirkintilloch, Colette Todd, Glasgow, Connor Todd, Portsmouth, England, Erin Ashling Todd, Croftfoot Glasgow, Frankie Todd, Glasgow, James Todd, Bannockburn, John Todd, Boc Carfin, John Todd, Glasgow, Liam Todd, Croftfoot Glasgow, Paul Todd, Paisley, Ron Todd, London, Shay Todd, Croftfoot Glasgow, Stuart Todd, Kirkintilloch, Susan Todd, Belfast, Tommy Todd, Carntyne, Tommy Todd, Kirkintilloch, Willie Todd, Glasgow, Gerry Togneri, Stirling, Michele Togneri, Motherwell, Adrian Tolan, Renfrew, Anne Tolan, Renfrew, Bernadette Tolan, Renfrew, Kevin Tolan, Renfrew, Mark Tolan, Glasgow, Steven Tolan, Port Glasgow, Joe Tolland, Glasgow, John Tolland, Hamilton, Mark Tolland, Uddingston, Mark Tolland, Uddingston, William Tollins, Grangemouth, Frank Tolmie, Southampton Hampshire, James And Cobbie Tolmie, Southampton Hampshire, Ian Tom, Hall Brookes, Daniel Tomescu, Edinburgh, Benny Tominey, Blackpool, John Tominey, Tollcross, Pamela Tominey, Motherwell, Rab Tominey, Tollcross, Robert Tominey Jnr, Carmyle, Tom Tomminey, Glasgow, Alan Tomson, Linwood, Alan Toner, Kilsyth, Catherine Toner, Dalmuir, Clair Toner, Dalmuir, Eddie And Shug Toner, Wee Mans Bar, Gallowgate, Kellie Toner, Sandyhills, Kieran Toner, Livingston, Marion Toner, Dalmuir, Steven Toner, Canada, Willy Tones, Grangemouth, Alex Tonner, Blackpool, Johnnie Tonner, Marylebone, Kieran Tonner, Whitburn, Pete Tonner, London, Stephen Tonner, Whitburn, William Toohill, Renfrew, Chloe Torley, Cambuslang, Colin Torley, Prestonpans, Connor Torley, Cambuslang, David Torley, Cambuslang, Eddie Torley, Prestonpans, Frank Torley, Cambuslang, James Torley, Prestonpans, Jay Torley, Prestonpans, Jayne Torley, Cambuslang, Katie Torley, Cambuslang, Mark Torley, Cambuslang, Michelle Torley, Cambuslang, Kevin Tosh, Perth, Tom Toshack, Cambridgeshire, David Tossnie, Balornock, Stephen Tossnie, Balornock, Graham Totton, Clydebank, Mick Toulose, Perth, Western Australia, Joe Toward, Scots DG, John Towler, Newcastle Upon Tyne, Allan Townsley, Renfrew, Carrie Townsley, Bellshill, Matt Townsley, Bellshill, Robert Townsley, Renfrew, Stephen Townsley, Saltcoats, Tommy Townsley, Saltcoats, Joe Toy, Lanark, Scott Toye, Ayr, Scott Toye, Ayr, Tony Toye, Ayr, Fiona Tracey, Greenfield, Fiona Tracey, Greenfield, Frank Tracey, St Catharines, Canada, Frank Jr Tracey, St Catharines, Canada, Grant Tracey, Glasgow, Jordan Tracey, Greenfield, Jordan Tracey, Greenfield, Kirsty Tracey, Greenfield, Natalie Tracey, Greenfield, Tony Tracey, Greenfield, Eleanor Trainer, Bishopbriggs, Lynn Trainer, Port Glasgow, Maureen Trainer, Hamilton, Michael Trainer, Bishopbriggs, Paul Trainer, Dublin, Julie Trainner, Port Glasgow, Barry Trainor, South Armagh, Rory Trainor, South Armagh, Cecil Tranier, Glasgow, Richard Tranter, Didcot, Oxfordshire, David Travers, Neilston, Emma Travers, Kettering, James Travers, Neilston, John Travers, Kettering, Mike Travers, Kettering, Thomas Travers Jnr, Shettleston, Brian Traynor, East Kilbride, Brian Traynor, Kirkton, Dundee, Cara Traynor, Clydebank, Charlotte Traynor, Clydebank, Chrissy Traynor, Stirling, Debbie Traynor, Glasgow, Eddy Traynor, Duntocher, Eddy Traynor, Duntocher, Gordon Traynor, Kirkton, Dundee, Helen Traynor, Glasgow, Ian Traynor, London, Jacqueline Traynor, Florida, Jacqui Traynor, watching in Florida, James Joseph

Traynor, Clydebank, Jim Traynor, East Kilbride, John Traynor, Barrhead, Mark Traynor, Glasgow, Matthew Traynor, Michael Traynor, Garrowhill, Glasgow, Paul Traynor, Glasgow, Paul Traynor, Peter Traynor, Glasgow, Ronnie Traynor, Clydebank, Sara Traynor, John Trewern, Coatbridge, Iain Trotter, Dumfries, James Trotter, Glasgow, Kevin Trotter, Cambusbarron, Kiela Trotter, Glasgow, Walter Trotter, Cambusbarron, Neil Troup, Aberdeen, Jim Troy, Glasgow, Elinor Truss, Greenock, Paul Truss, Greenock, Alex Truten, Kirkintilloch, Brian Tugman, Bathgate, Carrie-Anne Tugman, Bathgate, Jamie Tugman, Bathgate, Michael Tugman, Bathgate, Stephanie Tugman, Bathgate, Stephen Tugman, Bathgate, Brian Tugnell, Bathgate, Charlie Tully, Bankside, Falkirk, Brendan Tumlity, Ardrossan, Kieran Tumlity, Ardrossan, Steven Tuohy, Bonnyrigg, Andy Turnbull, Peterhead, James Turnbull, Thornliebank, Marion Turnbull, Greenfield, Midge Turnbull, Hawick, Sarah Turnbull, Livingston, James Turner, Johnstone, Janice Turner, St Austell, Cornwall, Jason Turner, Dalgety Bay, Jim Turner, Newquay, Cornwall, Kirstin Turner, Glasgow, Paul Turner, Berwick-upon-Tweed, Stephen Turner, Stevenson, Ayrshire, Thomas Tutty, Linwood, Gerard Tweddie, Falkirk, Frank Tweed, Greenock, Amanda Tweedie, Grangemouth, Janis Tweedie, Grangemouth, John Tweedie, Grangemouth, Kevin Tweedie, Grangemouth, Mark Tweedie, Grangemouth, Mort Tweedie, Galashiels, Janice Tweedy, Grangemouth, John Tweedy, Grangemouth, Gary Twigg, Glasgow, Lisa Tyrrell, Barrhead, Paul Tyson, Stirling.

Fraser Unett, Glasgow. Steven Unett, Glasgow, Steven Unett, Glasgow, Angus Unker, Glasgow, William Urban, Gorebridge, Stevie Urbaniak, Inverkeithing, John Urie, Dalmellington, Ayreshire, Maryanne Urie, Dalmellington, Ayreshire, Sarah Urie, Dalmellington, Ayreshire, Aiden Urquhart, Fraserburgh, Billy Urquhart, Drumnadrochit, Graeme Urquhart, Clydebank, Ian Urquhart, Jordanhill, Glasgow, Kevin Urquhart, Fraserburgh, Nicola Urquhart, Fraserburgh, Pamela Urquhart, Fraserburgh, Stevie Urquhart, Springburn, Glasgow, Gary Urquhart, East Kilbride, Wilma Urquhart, East Kilbride, Stefano Usai, East Kilbride.

Graham Vale, Wishaw. Paul Valentini, Hamilton, David Vallance, Castlemilk, Alan Vandermotten, Yoker, Glasgow, Alan Michael Vandermotten, Yoker, Glasgow, Alicia Vandermotten, Yoker, Glasgow, Amy Vandermotten, Yoker,Glasgow, Bethan Vandermotten, Yoker, Glasgow, Craig Varney, East Wemyss, Fife, Liam Varney, East Wemyss, Fife, Tam Varney, East Wemyss, Tommy Varney, East Wemyss, Fife, Bill Vasil, Norwalk, Connecticut, USA, Ruan Vata, Yokohama,Japan, Rudi Vata, Yokohama,Japan, Bernadette Vaughan, Glasgow, Jimmy Vaughan, Brent Bravo, Malky Vaughne, Inverkeithing, Mary Vedy, Gorbals, Amanda Veegan, Wishaw, Pat Veldon, Torquay, Rossie Velez, Roberts House Glasgow, Luke Ventisei, Carnwardric, Glasgow, Matthew Ventisei, Carnwadric, Matthew Ventisei, Carnwadric, Glasgow, John Vermout, Baillieston, Carla Vernel, Balornock, Enrique Mont Vicente, Renfrew, Anthony Vincent Price, Brightons, Jonathan Viney, Edinburgh, Gary Vinney, Ayr, Stephen Viveycare, Bellshill.

Gary Waddell, Kirkintilloch. Ian Waddell, Dennistoun, Sacha Waddell, Glasgow, William Wade, Islington, London, Maggie Waldonald, Glasgow, Darren Waldron, Motherwell, Andy Wales, Cumbernauld, Andy Wales, Los Angeles, Jim Wales, Stevenson, John Wales, Katie Wales, Los Angeles, Andrew Walker, Livingston, Angela Walker, Barnsley, Anthony Walker, Coatbridge, Arthur Walker, Newmains, Brian Walker, Cambuslang, Brian Walker, Neilston, Cassie Walker, Dalmuir, Clydebank, Chloe Walker, Denny, David Walker, Holytown, David Walker, Tollcross, Glasgow, Eddie Walker, Neilston, Eric Walker, Ayrshire, Gary Walker, Stepps, George Walker, Newmains, Graham Walker, Denny, Heather Walker, Ayrshire, Jack Walker, Paisley, John Walker, Clydebank, Kenny Walker, Brighton, Louise Walker, Dundee, Natalie Walker, Denny, Robert Walker, Glasgow & Nederlands, Robert Walker, Netherlands,

Ryan Walker, Johnstone, Stuart Walker, Dalmuir, Clydebank, Wendy Walker, Neilston, Willow Walker, Dalmuir, Clydebank, Ian Walkinshaw, Glenrothes, Neil Walkinshaw, Glenrothes, Alan Wallace, Inverness, Alan Wallace, Kilmarnock, Alec Wallace, Summerston, Glasgow, Andrew Wallace, Larbert, Arlene Wallace, Bellshill, Christopher Wallace, Glasgow, David Wallace, Glasgow, Dylan Wallace, Drumchapel, Frankie Wallace, Scarborough, Jamie Wallace, Summerston, Glasgow, Josh Wallace, Rutherglen, Kayleigh Wallace, Arbroath, Lorraine Wallace, Rutherglen, Morgan Wallace, Arbroath, Robert Wallace, Kilwinning, Ross Wallace, Inverness, Ruby Wallace, Glasgow, Tam Wallace, Rutherglen, Thomas Wallace, Glasgow, Chris Wallis, Rutherglen, Joe Walls, Glasgow, Kenny Walmsley, Pollok, Babs Walsh, Renfrew, Charlie Walsh, Belfast, Christopher Walsh, Thornliebank, Glasgow, Dianne Walsh, Glasgow, Evelyn Walsh, Bo'ness, Gerry Walsh, Gerry Walsh, Giffnock, Glasgow, Heather Walsh, Glasgow, James Walsh, Newstevenston, John Walsh, Bellshill, Marie Walsh, Glasgow, Martin Walsh, Tallaght, Dublin, Michael Walsh, Glasgow, Michael Walsh, Thornliebank,Glasgow, Mick Walsh, Croy, Mike Walsh, Bo'ness, Nathan Walsh, Bo'ness, Nikitta Walsh, Bo'ness, Paul Walsh, Bo'ness, Ryan Walsh, New Stevenston, Sasha Walsh, Bo'ness, Sean Walsh, Croftfoot, Sharon Walsh, Kilwinning, Sophie Walsh, Thornliebank, Glasgow, Steven Walsh, Fenwick, Suzanne Walsh, Shortroods, Paisley, Thomas Walsh, Carmyle, Tommy Walsh, Bo'ness, Tony Walsh, Carmyle, Tahiti, Peter Walsh Snr, Glasgow, Mick Walsh (Jnr), Croy, C Walters, Glasgow, Gillian Walters, Glasgow, Kevin Waltingham, Dundee, Danielle Walton, Musselburgh, Kevin Walton, Dundee, Barry Ward, Dundee, Barry Ward, Dundee, Barry Ward, Dundee, Calven Ward, Leeds, Clare Ward, Newarthill, Colin Ward, Motherwell, Eddie Ward, Belfast, George Ward, Baillieston, Hannah Ward, Newarthill, Harry Ward, Parkhead, James Ward, Glasgow, James Ward, Inverness, Jason Ward, Clackmannan, Karen Ward, Glasgow, Kevin Ward, Clydebank, Linda Ward, Baillieston, Linda Ward, Burnbank, Louise Ward, Newarthill, Marc Ward, Croftfoot, Margaret Ward, Hamilton, Pat Ward, Linlithgow, Pat Ward, Linlithgow, Patrick Ward, Glasgow, Rachael Ward, Baillieston, Rachel Ward, Newarthill, Richard Ward, Glasgow, Richard Ward, Paisley, Richard Ward, Ross Ward, Burnbank, Sean Ward, Tillicoultry, Stephen Ward, Newarthill, Valerie Ward, Cambuslang, William Ward, Glasgow, Richard Ward Jnr, Glasgow, Jordan Warder, Glasgow, Leigh Jaye Wardlaw, Mount Florida, Craig Wares, Thurso, Paul Wares, Thurso, Cathy Waribbon, Glasgow, John Waring, Haydock, St. Helens, Louise Wark, Paisley, Mikey Warlow, East Kilbride, Leigh Warren, Glasgow, Tommy Warren, Milton, Glasgow, Una Warren, Blackburn,West Lothian, Carolann Warrender, Aberdeen, James Warrender, Aberdeen, Binky, Lisa, Lauren Warwick, Annan, Keir Wason, Finnieston, Glasgow, Willie Wassell, Calton, Glasgow, Pauline Waters, Corby, Sammy Waters, Fife, Samuel Waters, Corby, Samuel Waters, Stephen Waters, Corby, Andy Watson, Luton, Caitlyn Watson, Ballingry, Fife, Craig Watson, Barrowfield, Craig Watson, East Kilbride, Craig Watson, Glasgow, Darren Watson, Castlemilk, Darren Watson, Forfar, David Watson, Rotterdam, Derek Watson, Springburn, Iain Watson, Inverness, Ian Watson, Inverness, Jackie Watson, Fife, James Watson, Carnbroe, Coatbridge, Jamie Watson, Ballingry, Fife, Jamie Watson, Springburn, Jim Watson, Pollokshields, Jimmy Watson, Methill, Lee Watson, London, Mark Watson, Luton, Mark Watson, Milton, Glasgow, Micky Watson, Glasgow, Paul Watson, London, Paul Watson, New York, Rab Watson, Stirling, Scott Watson, Ballingry, Fife, Steven Watson, Sydney, Australia, Watson, Glasgow, David Watson (Ymca), Ibrox, David Watt, Glasgow, Jim Watt, Glasgow, Lorna Watt, Coatbridge, Russell Watt, Port Glasgow, Stephen Watt, Dunfermline, Fife, Steven Watt, Dunfermline, Thomas Watt, Glasgow, William Watt, London (Formerly Glasgow), Wullie Watt, London, Reegan Watt, Kelly Greenock, Kieran Watton, County Derry, NI, Lynne Waugh, Renfrew, Stevie Waugh, Glasgow, John Weatley, Bromley, William Weaving, Banknock, Frank Webster, Angus, Frank Webster, Coupar, Angus, Stephen Webster Jnr, Port Glasgow, Alan Weir, Plean, Alison Weir, Cowie, Andrew Weir, Drumoyne, Andrew Weir, Paisley, Bethany Weir, Sanquhar, Bob Weir, Paisley, Calum Weir, Tighnabruaich, Colin Weir, Cambusbarron,

David Weir, Cowie, Elaine Weir, Cumnock, Ellen Weir, Easterhouse, Gary Weir, Paisley, Graeme Weir, Dundee, Heather Weir, Sanquhar, Ian Weir, Cumnock, Lee Weir, Garrowhill, Glasgow, Liam Weir, Sanquhar, Margaret Weir, Glasgow, Nicky Weir, Garrowhill, Glasgow, Patrick Weir, Johnstone, Paul Weir, Nottingham, Sean Weir, Sanquhar, Wally Weir, Paisley, Verity Welch, London, Andy Weldon, Paisley, Paul Weldon, Uddingston, Alan Welsh, Falkirk, Andrew Welsh, Glasgow, Colette Welsh, Cowie, Colette Welsh, Cowie, David Welsh, Greenock, David Welsh, London, Dylan Welsh, Kirkintilloch, Fergus Welsh, Glasgow, Frank Welsh, Glasgow, Helen Welsh, Cambusbarron, Jeanette Welsh, Cowie, John Welsh, Cambusbarron, John Welsh, Erskine, John Welsh, Glasgow, Karen Welsh, Dumfries, Laddel Welsh, Greenock, Lee Welsh, Glasgow, Nelly Welsh, Greenock, Nelly Welsh, Greenock, Nick Welsh, Glasgow, Nicky Welsh, Cowie, Nicky Welsh, Cowie, Pat Welsh, Glasgow, Scott Welsh, Dumfries, Stephen Welsh, Kirkintilloch, Steven Welsh, Glasgow, Susan Welsh, Hamilton, Tam Welsh, Cowie, Thomas Welsh, Cowie, Michael Wert, Billy West, Castlemilk, Liz Westcliff, Dumbarton, May Westfield, Cumbernauld, James Wharrie, Bellshill, Caroline Wharton, Carlisle, Richard Wharton, Carlisle, Henry Wheat, Royston, Charlene & Hayley Wheeler, Glasgow, Bernadette Whelan, Coatbridge, Gavin Majella Whelan, J. Whelan, Leyland, Martin Whelan, Motherwell, Thomas Whelan, Motherwell, Lesley Wheldon, Hull, Brian White, Clydebank, Denise White, Easterhouse, Gary White, Bearsden, James White, Bearsden, Jimmy White, Leslie, Fife, John White, Bathgate, John White, Clydebank, John White, Cumbernauld, John White, Easterhouse, Jonathan White, Ayr, Keiran White, Medway, Lynsey White, Falkirk, Maggie White, Medway, Margaret White, Glasgow, Ryan White, Clydebank, Stephen White, Rowville, Vic, Australia, Steven White, Partick, Glasgow, Thomas White, Easterhouse, Sharon Whitecross, Dalkeith, Robert Whiteford, St Hellier, Jersey, Chris Whitehead, Glasgow, Fred Whitehead, Glasgow, Gail Whitehead, Edinburgh, Pat Whitehill, Tommy Whitehill, George Whitelaw, Glasgow, Scotland, Kenny Whitelaw, Newton Mearns, Molly Whitelaw, Newton Mearns, Richie Whitelaw, Cadiz, Spain, Allan Whiteside, Corkerhill, Harry Whitley, Garngad, Leigh Whittaker, Coventry, Nicola Whitton, Coatbridge, S. Whitworth, Montrose, Steven Whitworth, Montrose, Michael Whoriskey, Glasgow, Andy Whyte, Bexleyheath, Shaun Whyte, Port Seton, Teresa Whyte, Pollok , Steve Wicks, Bournemouth, Walter Wier, Glasgow, Jordan Wiggins, Ayr, Paul Wiggins, Ayr, Paul Wiggins, Ayr, Paul Wiggy, Alexandria, Big Wilf, Kirkintilloch, Kay, Wilf, David & John Bain, Hungry Hill, Thurso, Shazza Wilkes, Leicester, Jack Wilkie, Larbert, John Wilkie, Dundee, Kevin Wilkie, Garrowhill, Glasgow, Liam Wilkie, Larbert, Megan Wilkie, Larbert, Paul Wilkie, Garrowhill, Paul Wilkie, Garrowhill, Glasgow, Stuart Wilkie, Fife, James Wilkins, Livingston, Jonathan Wilkins, Livingston, West Lothian, James Will, Glenrothes, Leroy William, Benbecula, Daniel Williams, Gallowgate, Eddie Williams, Wishaw, Frank Williams, Wantage, Franny Williams, Port Glasgow, Jade Williams, Busby, Jennifer Williams, Sidcup, Kent, John Williams, Glasgow, John Williams, Glasgow, Joseph Williams, Wishaw, Kimberly Williams, Southsea, Larsson Williams, Oban, Leroy Williams, Benbecula, Louise Williams, Oban, Margaret Williams, Oban, Matt Williams, Plymouth, Pat Williams, Kilmarnock, Sandra Williams, Port Glasgow, Steven Williams, Glasgow, Tom Williams, Glasgow, Tony Williams, Burnely, Aidan Williams (4), Glasgow, James Williams (7), Glasgow, Chloe Williamson, Glasgow, Emma Williamson, Glasgow, James C. Williamson, Hawick, Jason Williamson, Edinburgh, John Williamson, Bonhill, Keith D.N. Williamson, Hawick, Paul Williamson, Glasgow, William Williamson, Kirkintilloch, Stuart Wills, Kirkintilloch, Ryan Wilsn, Alexandria, A. Wilson, Glasgow, Alan Wilson, Gourock, Alex Wilson, Coltness, Wishaw, Alex Wilson, Stirling, Andrew Wilson, East Kilbride, Andrew Wilson, Uddingston, Angela Wilson, Kingspark, Glasgow, Audrey Wilson, Midlothian, Barry Wilson, Lockerbie, Big John Wilson, Uddingston, Brian Wilson, Glasgow, Brian Wilson, Glossop, Brogan Wilson, Glasgow, Bruce Wilson, South Africa, Craig Wilson, Renfrew, Daniel Wilson, Corby, David Wilson, Beith, David Wilson, Eyemouth, Douglas Wilson, Tillicoultry, Elaine Wilson,

Tillicoultry, Emma Wilson, Cambusnethan Wishaw, Euan Wilson, Saltcoats, George Wilson, Dumfries, George Wilson, Dumfries, George Wilson, Westerton, Gordon Wilson, Blackburn, West-Lothian, Graham Wilson, Cleland, Hugh Wilson, Glasgow, Iain (leroy) Wilson, Perthshire, Jackie Wilson, Possilpark, James Wilson, Govan, Jim Wilson, Bishopbriggs, John Wilson, Glasgow, John Wilson, Perthshire, K. Wilson, Troon, Karl Wilson, Staffs, Kate Wilson, Lenzie, Kenny Wilson, Alexandria, Kenny Wilson, Alexandria, Kirsteen Wilson, Dalmuir, Clydebank, Leroy Wilson, Perthshire, Mark Joseph Wilson, Robroyston, Michael Wilson, Beith, Patrick Wilson, Troon, Paul Anthony Wilson, Simshill, Glasgow, Peter Wilson, Simshill, Glasgow, Rab Wilson, Dumfries, Rab Wilson, Midlothian, Rab Wilson, Robert Wilson, Paisley, Robert Wilson, Saltire Court, Edinburgh, Scott Wilson, Chapelhall, Shaun Wilson, Pollok, Stuart Wilson, Glasgow, Sye Wilson, Forfar, Thomas Wilson, Dennistoun, Thomas Wilson, Drumchapel, Glasgow, Tracey Wilson, Govan, Val Wilson, Glasgow, Valerie Wilson, Auchterarder, Robert Wilson Jnr, Glasgow, Andy Wiltshire, Bathgate, Alan Windram, Eyemouth, John Windram, Eyemouth, Sam Windsor, Glasgow, Ivan Winning, Springburn, Glasgow, Ivan Winning, Springburn, Scott Winning, Larkhall, William Winning, Springburn, Glasgow, Natasha Winterbottom, Pollok, Glasgow, Callum Winters, Houston, Carol Winters, Fernhill, Jim Winters, Fernhill, Kenneth Winters, Houston, Paul Winters, Glasgow, Tam Winters, Cumbernauld, Tommy Winters, Cumbernauld, John Winton, Moodiesburn, Nicola Winton, Moodiesburn, Sandra Winton, Moodiesburn, Stacey Winton, Moodiesburn, Brenda Wisdom, Invergordon, Tamara Wisdom, Invergordon, David Wisom, Eyemouth, Rowley Wolverhampton, Billy Wood, Kelso, Carolann Wood, Rutherglen, Caroline Wood, Dublin, Chilli Wood, Bannockburn, Edward Wood, Bathgate, Edward Wood, Glasgow, George Wood, Tillicoultry, Morag Wood, West Lothian, Pauline Wood, Tillicoultry, Peter Wood, Yoker, Raymond Wood, Hamilton, Rodger Wood, Ruchill, Sandra Wood, Dunbarton, Stephen Wood, Bathgate, Steven Wood, Musselburgh, Vincent Wood, Bathgate, Rodger Wood Jnr, Ruchill, Royston Woodford, Brackley, Simon Woodford, Brackley, John Woodhouse, Ballycastle, Marcus Woodhouse, Swindon, Alister Woods, Kilmarknock, Ciaran Woods, Cleland ,Motherwell, Darren Woods, Tranent, David Woods, Glasgow, Eddie Woods, Old Kilpatrick, Gerry Woods, Dumbarton, Jim Woods, Joe Woods, Glasgow, John Woods, Irvine, Kenny Woods, Irvine, Kirstie Woods, Carfin, Nicola Woods, Tranent, Thomas Woods, Coatbridge, Tommy Woods, Cleland, Motherwell, Philip Woods Snr, Auchinleck, Christine Woodward, Keighley, Ian Woodward, Keighley, Thomas Woodward, Keighley, Andy & Tina Woolway, Kent, Michael Woolwith, Bellshill, George Word, Glasgow, Tom Workman, Morpeth, Northumberland, Richard Wrethman, Haldane,Balloch,Alexandria, Brian Wright, Dianne Wright, Edinburgh, George Wright, Harthill, Jim Wright, St Ninians, Jim Wright, Stirling, John Wright, Govan, Leslie Wright, South Queeneferry, Stevie Wright, Erskine, Ted Wright, Brent Bravo, Ted Wright, Greenock, William Wright, Clydebank, Anthony Wyber, Kilsyth, Paul Wyber, Amsterdam, Jamie Wylie, Balfron, Liam Wylie, Irvine, Pete Wylie, Balfron, William Wylie, Renfrew, Brian Wyllie, Saltcoats, Brian Wyllie, Saltcoats, Colin Wyllie, Mayfield, James Wyllie, Saltcoats, James Wyllie, Saltcoats, Lynn Wyllie, Bonhill, Reece Wyllie, Mayfield, Christine Wynne, Stepps, Christine Wynne, Stepps, Claire Wynne, Stepps, Claire Wynne, Stepps, David Wynne, Bathgate, Kevin Wynne, Stepps, Kevin Wynne, Stepps.

Rebecca Yagci, Blantyre, Glasgow, Yahya Yagci, Blantyre, Glasgow, Jim Yardley, Wishaw, Seraffin Yildiz, Livingston, Donna York, Toryglen, Margaret York, Slough, Andrew Young, Glasgow, Anne F. Young, Shawlands, Glasgow, Brian (Youngy) Young, Tullibody, Chris Young, Dean Park, David Young, Macclesfield, Donald Young, Aberhill, Donald Young, Dumfries, Donald Young, George Young, East Kilbride, Gillian Young, Bishopbriggs, Gillian Young, Hamilton, Jackie Young, Ayr, James Young, Airdrie, Jim Young, Uddingston, Joshua Young, Prestwick, Josie Young, Lenzie, Ken Young, Lilongwe, Malawi, Southern Africa, Linda Young, Newcastle, Martin Young, Uddingston, Matthew Young, Glasgow,

Nicola Young, Oban, Nicola Young, Tullibody, Paul Young, Deanpark Renfrew, Paul Young, Lochee, Pauline Young, Ayr, Pauline Young, Glasgow, Rachel Young, Paisley, Ricky Young, Des Moines Iowa, Ricky Young, Uddingston, Scott Young, Livingston, Stephen Young, Paisley, Thomas Young, Nottingham, Thomas Young, Nottingham, Totti Young, Nottingham, Toty Young, Nottingham, Kenny Young, Ayr, Grant Young (Tooty), Darvel, Ayrshire, John Young Jnr, Helensburgh.

Tommy Zoe, Glasgow. -

AND FINALLY .. for those who didn't provide their second names, or left it to the last minute ...

Robert Auld, Cambuslang, A G, Port Seton. Aaron, Aftab, Warrington, Aga, Campsie, Aggy, Aylesbury, Aidan, Maghera, Aishia, Warrington, Aitchie, Vancouver, Alex, Greenock, Alex, Greenock, Shamrock Supporters Club, Alex, Kirkintilloch, Alex, South Africa, Alison, Bannockburn, Ally & Ally B, Parkview, Glasgow, Amanda, Croftfoot, Amy, , Andi, Johnstone, Andrew, Aberdeen, Andy, Dunblane, Andy, Greenock, Ange, Drymen, Angela, Rutherglen, Angie, , Anne, Renfrew, Anne, , Annmarie, Glasgow, Ann-Marie, Glasgow, Ann-Marie, Motherwell, Arif, Warrington, Ashleigh, Airdrie, Ashly, Auchinleck, Auntie Rosie, Wellhouse, Aussie Bob, Santa Ponsa, Mallorca.

Babs, Greenock, Badger, Coatbridge, Badger, Motherwell, Baj, Castlehill, Dumbarton, Barry, Brighton, Barry, Gorebridge,Barry, Eon ,Cmac ,Neil, Pat, Joe, Danny, Jack,Dalmuir,Batsey, Greenock, Shamrock Supporters Club, Ben, Richmond, Kilmaurs, Benny Boy, Johnstone, Benny, Hazel, Ger And Suzanne, Dubliner Bar, Santa Ponsa Majorca, Bernie, Castlemilk, Biffa, Milton Keynes, Big Bim The Tim, Airdrie, Big Boab, Viewpark, Big Brucy Boy, Drumchapel, Big Curly, Wellhouse, Big Dermy, Easterhouse, Big Eck, Bankside, Falkirk, Big Ellis, Kilsyth, Big Fad, Port Glasgow, Big G, Maryhill, Big Grady, Linwood, Big Hovis, Newmains, Big Jenny, Port Glasgow, Big Kendo, Port Glasgow, Big Mitch, Denny, Big Rab, Maryhill, Glasgow, Big Stan & Barbara, Sheffield, Big Stew, Highlander Pub, Paderborn, Germany, Bigdauie, Castlemilk, Bilal, Warrington, Billy, Driffield, Billy, Glasgow, Billy, South Africa, Blooter, Wishaw, Boycie, East Kilbride, Brendan, Larbert, Brian, Fortwilliam, Seville, Brian, Greenock, Brian, Lennoxtown, Brolly, Castlemilk, Glasgow, Broxburn Celtic Supporters Club, Broxburn, Bruce, Glasgow.

Caddy, Westfield, Cal, Govanhill, Calshy, Newton Mearns, Calum, Garelochhead, Cameron, Lennoxtown, Camerons, Thurso, Carfin Celtic Supporters Club, , Caroline, Casey, Troon, Caskie Family, Pollock, Cat, Greenock, Cath, Macmerry, Catriona, Fortwilliam, Seville, Charlene, Stevenston, Charlotte, , Chatty, Castlehill, Dumbarton, Chatty Bhox, Castlehill, Dumbarton, Chelly, Greenock, Cherie, Castlemilk, Chips and Gravy, Livingston, Chloe, Alloa, Chloe, , Chris, Cambuslang, Christine, Dalmuir, Clair, Dunblane, Claire, Ayrshire, Claire, Blyth, Claire, Lumphinnans, Clarkolini, Milngavie, Colshy, Halfway, Conlan, Hamilton, Conny, Benalmadena, Conte Family, Baillieston, Courtney, Newmains, Craig, Garelochhead, Craig, Livingston, Crink, Orkney, Cusby, Airdrie.

Dale, Sandyhills, Dan B, Benalmadena, Daniel, Edinburgh, Daniel, Johnstone, Daniel, , Danielle, Glasgow, Danny, Benalmadena, Danny, Greenock, Danny, Greenock, Shamrock Supporters Club, Danny, Tilbury, Essex, Danny, Superman, Abbot, Garland & Aaron, Hamilton, Darryl, , Dave, Garelochhead, Dave, Paisley, Dave, , David, Coatbridge, Davie, Castlehill, Dumbarton, Davie, Rothesay, Isle of Bute, Davie,Margaret & Megan, South Queensferry, Deccy, Newmains, Declan, Cambuslang, Declan, Paisley, Deep End Tims, East Kilbride, Delbhoy, Stornoway, Demi, Largs., Derek, Dunfermline, Derek, Kilwinning,

Derek, Lumphinnans, Des, Coatbridge, Dez 'N' Stevie, Kingspark, Dino, , Dionne, Stevenston, Discoduce, Castlemilk, Dod, Greenock, Shamrock Supporters Club, Dodger, Govan, Dolphin C S C Partick X, Glasgow, Dom Murnin, Glasgow, Dom The Bom, Plains, Airdrie, Donna, Croftfoot, Donna, Cumbernauld, Dougie, , Duffy Family, Greenock, Dumbarton Harp, Duncan, Ayrshire, Dunk, Coatbridge, Dutchy, Livingston,

Eamonn, Coventry. Ebony, Eddie, Cambuslang, Eddie McCarroll, Blantyre, Eddy, Gourock, Eileen, Croftfoot, Eileen, Leicester, Eileen, Rothesay, Isle of Bute, Eilidh, Aberdeen, Emerald CSC, Belfast, Emma, Fife, Emma, Govan Hill, Glasgow, Emma, Kilwinning, Emma, Larbert, Eunice, Larbert,

Fairhill Green And White Brigade CSC, Hamilton, Festa, Castlemilk, Fiazia, Warrington, Finlay, Oban, Fitch Family, Provanmill, Glasgow, Fod, Glasgow, Foxy, Busby, Frances, Bellshill, Frank, Raploch, Frankie, Derry, Fraz, Dumfries, Elizabeth Fagan, London.

Gail, Slough, Gareth, Kilwinning, Gary, Eastleigh, Southampton, Gary, Edinburgh, Gary & Carla, The Botany, Maryhill, Gav, Springburn, Gav, , Ged, Edinburgh, Gemma, Coatbridge, Genna, George, Bannockburn, George, Benalmadena, George, Pollock, Dundee, George, Tilbury, Essex, Gerry, Greenock, Gerry, Sandyhills, Gerry, Glasgow Mail Centre CSC, Glasgow, Glenbar CSC, Gordon, Rothesay, Isle of Bute, Gows, Thurso.

Neil Hurman, London, H, Glasgow, Hannah, Gourock, Hannah, Greenock, Hanny-Boy, Easterhouse, Glasgow, Hanzo, Coatbridge, Harkie, Ayrshire, Harper, Airdrie, Harry & Chris, Motherwell, Harry-Bo, Hassan, Priesthill, Hewitt family, Glasgow, Hitchi, Greenock, Shamrock Supporters Club, Hoody, Ayr, Hoss, Falkirk, Hugh, Oldpark, Hutchies, Port Glasgow, Hynd, Kilbirnie.

Ian, Gourock, Icey, Glasgow, Inner Sanctum CSC, Garngad.

Jack, Falkirk, Jack, , Jackie, Glasgow, Jacqueline, Glasgow, Jacqui, Santa Ponsa, Mallorca, Jade, Glasgow, Jade, Kelty, Jaggy Man, Kirkintilloch, James, Livingston, James, , Jamesy, Campsie, Jamie, Renfrew, Jane, Largs., Janet, Fife, Jay, Alloa, Jeff, Castlehill, Dumbarton, Jenny, Ross-Shire, Jerry, London, Jim, Dalmuir, Jim, Fife, Jim, Kildonan, Jim, Uddingston, Jimba, Greenock, Shamrock Supporters Club, Jimmy, Ayr, Joanne, Busby, Joanne, Kirkintilloch, Jock, Alloa, Jock Stein C.S.C, Hamilton, "On Tour", Hamilton, Jocky, Newmains, Jocky, Portugal, Joe, Muirhead, Joe, Newton Mearns, Joe, , Joe Jnr, Cambuslang, Joe Snr, Cambuslang, John, Darlington, John, Glasgow, John, Glasgow, John, Hamilton, John, Kildonan, John, Larbert, John, London, John, Lumphinnans, John, Renfrew, John, Springburn, John, Stevenston, John, Uddingston, John, , John McCafferty, Canada, Jojie, Kirkintilloch, Jon, Slough, Jordan, Falkirk, Jordan, Hamilton, Josh, Lesmahagow, Joyce, , JP, Castlemilk, Jud, Boness.

Karen, Clydebank, Kasih, Warrington, Kate, Newmains, Kate, Wishaw, Kathie, , Kathy, Inverness, Katie, Auchinleck, Katie the Bog, , Kay, Thurso, Keiran, Dunblane, Kennady, Wishaw, Kenny, , Kerry, Ayr, Kev, Greenock, Shamrock Supporters Club, Kevin, Johnstone, Kevin, Port Glasgow, Kevin, Whitecrock, Kevin McCloskey, Motherwell, Kieran, Fife, Kirsty, Clydebank, Krink, Nottingham, Kris, Cumbernauld.

Lanie, Ayrshire, Lauren, Glasgow, Leanne, Newcastle, Leigh, Eastleigh, Southampton, Lewis, Bridgeton, Liana, Muirhead, Libby McGuire, Chapelhall, Linda, Lumphinnans, Linda, Lisa, Lumphinnans, Liz, Port Glasgow, Liz, Red Lion, Lofty, Knightswood, London Underground CSC, London, Lorraine, Greenock, Lorraine, Kirkintilloch, Lorraine, San

Antonio, Ibiza, Louis, Bellshill, Lucy, Greenock, Lyndsay, Cumbernauld, Lynsey.

Rosalind Mellon, Bishopbriggs, Maggie, Ayrshire, Manny, Glasgow, Margaret, Bridgeton, Margaret, Hillington, Margaret, Renfrew, Marie, Glasgow, Marie, Marine Celtic Bar, Bundoran, Ireland, Mark, Dunfermline, Mark, Liam, Cora, Deaglan, Tiarna, Poleglass Belfast, Martin, Brighton, Martin, London, Martin, Macmerry, Martin, Majorca, Martin, Rothesay, Isle of Bute, Martin & Alan, Tennents Bar, Glasgow, Martyn, Gourock, Martyn, Greenock, Mary, Bellshill, Mary, Gorebridge, Matt, Drumchapel, Maureen, Lennoxtown, Maureen, , Maureen, , Maxine, Coatbridge, Maxine, Newcastle, Maz, Glasgow, McKibbens Family, Livingston, McScruff, , Meg, Springburn, Megan, Glasgow, Megan, Mephy, Rutherglen, Merco, Govanhill, Michael, , Michael McCloskey, Jersey, Michelle, Newton Mearns, Mick, Benalmadena, Mick, Coatbridge, Mick, Drumchapel, Mick, , Mickey, Livingston, Midge and the Bhoys, Maple Penge, Mike Fraser, Inverness, Mitch, Campsie, Mitchell, Lennoxtown, Molly, Lumphinnans, Molly, , Mooney's Lad, , Morel, Muirhouse, Motherwell, Morris, Wishaw, Moscow, Greenock, Shamrock Supporters Club, Myra, Gourock.

Natalie, Maryhill, Nathan, Dunfermline, Nibs, Govan , Nick, London, Nicky, Kildonan, Nicky, Uddingston, Nicola, London, Nicole, Maghera, Nicole, Motherwell, Nicole, Raploch, Nicole, Rutherglen, Nikki, Govan Hill, Glasgow, Noodles, Barlanark, Nora, Govanhill, Nora, Oldpark, Northampton Shamrock CSC.

O'Hares, Shotts,Owen, Moira, Shaun, Maria & Lorena, Crookston.

Pam, Gorebridge, Pat, Blyth, Pat, Johnstone, Pat, Tilbury, Essex, Pate, Berwick, Patrick Four, Paul, Coatbridge, Paul, Gourock, Paul, Greenock, Paul, Greenock, Shamrock Supporters Club, Paul, Renfrew, Paul, Renfrew, Paul, Slough, Paul, , Peter, Glasgow, Peter, Philip, Priesthill, Piglet, Inverness, Poshco, Berwick, Prof, Leeds.

Rabbi, Wishaw, Rachel, Greenock, Ralph, Motherwell, Ramie, Benalmadena, Raymy, London, Regan, Armadale, Reggie, Rutherland, Reid, Largs., Rhona, Rothesay, Isle of Bute, Rita, Johnstone, Ritchy, Kilwinning, Robbie, Eastbourne, Rory, Paisley, Ross, Cumbernauld, Ross, Greenock, Shamrock Supporters Club, Roxy, Drumchapel, RPW, Tilburg, Ryan, Lumphinnans.

Brian Smith, Cumbernauld, Saints & Sinners, Bellshill, Samantha, Nottingham, Sameene, Glasgow, Sandy, Norwich, Scooby, Stirling, Seamus, Santa Ponsa, Mallorca, Sean, Coventry, Sean, Cramlington, Sean, Dunfermline, Sean, Johnstone, Sean, Kathleen & Kane, Govan, Shadlow Brothers, Luton, Shannon, Armadale, Sharon, Ayr, Sharon, Blyth, Sharon, South Africa, Sharon, Stevenston, Shaun, Renfrew, Shelly, Greenock, Sherry, Paisley, Simmyoke, Glasgow, Siobhan, Coatbridge, Skegg, Cumbernauld, Skegg, Bill And Wee John, Cumbernauld, Smiddy, Maryhill, Smudger, Duntocher.

Tam, Alloa, Tam, Cambuslang, Tam, Glasgow, Tam, Wishaw, Temple Bar Crew, Norwich, Terry, Greenock, The Baldy Man, The Cairn, The Blue Bell Inn, Harthill, Sheffield, The Breen Family, Blairgowrie, The Brittania Pub, Northampton, The Burns Tavern, Bellshill, The Cavendish 7-1 CSC, Nitshill, Glasgow, The Cotter Family, Croftfoot, Glasgow, The Crawford Family, Whiterock,Belfast, The Doherty Family, Dunfanaghy, Co Donegal, Ireland, The Duffy Family, East Kilbride, The Fusion Experience, Glasgow, The Heraty Bhoys & Mhum, Mt Vernon, Glasgow, The Kenny Richey Campaign, Cambuslang/Ohio, The Marine Celtic Bar, Bundoran, Ireland, The Morgel Family, Blyth, The O'Byrne Family, Gartcosh, The Red Rooster, Mull Of Kintyre, The Reilly Family, Coatbridge, The Rogers

Family, Edinburgh. The Three Amigos Jimmy Chris And Lee, Tivoli Snooker, Dundee.

Vicki, Ayrshire, Victoria Bar, Govanhill, Glasgow.

Denise West, Edinburgh, Wattie, Caroline, Rory, Katty & Snowy, Nottingham,Wee Bav Ya Dancer, Dumfries, Wee Button, Newmains, Wee Claire, Port Glasgow, Wee Dauie, Castlemilk, Wee Peachy, Maryhill, Glasgow, Wendy, Lumphinnans, Wilf, Thurso.

Yasin, Warrington, Yvonne, Clydebank, Yvonne, Livingston.

Zoko, Lochgelly.